# ANTHROPOCENE ENCOUNTERS: NEW DIRECTIONS IN GREEN POLITICAL THINKING

Coined barely two decades ago, the Anthropocene has become one of the most influential and controversial terms in environmental science and policy. Yet it remains an ambivalent and contested formulation, giving rise to a multitude of unexpected, and often uncomfortable, conversations. This book traces in detail a broad variety of such "Anthropocene encounters": in science, philosophy, and literary fiction. It asks what it means to "think green" at a time when nature no longer offers a stable backdrop to political analysis. Do familiar political categories and concepts, such as democracy, justice, power, and time, hold when confronted with a world radically transformed by humans? The book responds by inviting more radical political thought, plural forms of engagement, and extended ethical commitments, making it a fascinating and timely volume for graduate students and researchers working in earth system governance, environmental politics, and studies of the Anthropocene.

FRANK BIERMANN is Research Professor of Global Sustainability Governance with the Copernicus Institute of Sustainable Development, Utrecht University, the Netherlands. He is the founding chair of the Earth System Governance Project, a global transdisciplinary research network launched in 2009, and editor-in-chief of the new peer-reviewed journal *Earth System Governance*. In April 2018, he won a European Research Council Advanced Grant for a research program on the steering effects of the Sustainable Development Goals.

EVA LÖVBRAND is Associate Professor in Environmental Change at the Department of Thematic Studies and is also affiliated with the Centre for Climate Science and Policy Research, both at Linköping University, Sweden. Much of her work focuses on the ideas, knowledge claims, and expert practices that inform and legitimize global environmental politics and governance. Since 2015 she has been the co-convenor of the Earth System Governance Project's task force on the Anthropocene together with Frank Biermann.

The **Earth System Governance Project** was established in 2009 as a core project of the International Human Dimensions Programme on Global Environmental Change. Since then, the Project has evolved into the largest social science research network in the area of sustainability and governance. The Earth System Governance Project explores political solutions and novel, more effective governance mechanisms to cope with the current transitions in the socio-ecological systems of our planet. The normative context of this research is sustainable development; earth system governance is not only a question of institutional effectiveness, but also of political legitimacy and social justice.

The **Earth System Governance series** with Cambridge University Press publishes the main research findings and synthesis volumes from the Project's first ten years of operation.

## Series Editor

Frank Biermann, Utrecht University, the Netherlands

## Titles in print in this series

Biermann and Lövbrand (eds.), *Anthropocene Encounters: New Directions in Green Political Thinking*

# ANTHROPOCENE ENCOUNTERS

## New Directions in Green Political Thinking

*Edited by*
### FRANK BIERMANN
*Utrecht University, the Netherlands*

### EVA LÖVBRAND
*Linköping University, Sweden*

# CAMBRIDGE
## UNIVERSITY PRESS

University Printing House, Cambridge CB2 8BS, United Kingdom

One Liberty Plaza, 20th Floor, New York, NY 10006, USA

477 Williamstown Road, Port Melbourne, VIC 3207, Australia

314-321, 3rd Floor, Plot 3, Splendor Forum, Jasola District Centre, New Delhi - 110025, India

79 Anson Road, #06-04/06, Singapore 079906

Cambridge University Press is part of the University of Cambridge.

It furthers the University's mission by disseminating knowledge in the pursuit of education, learning and research at the highest international levels of excellence.

www.cambridge.org
Information on this title: www.cambridge.org/9781108481175
DOI: 10.1017/9781108646673

© Cambridge University Press 2019

This publication is in copyright. Subject to statutory exception and to the provisions of relevant collective licensing agreements, no reproduction of any part may take place without the written permission of Cambridge University Press.

First published 2019

*A catalogue record for this publication is available from the British Library*

ISBN 978-1-108-48117-5 Hardback
ISBN 978-1-108-74041-8 Paperback

Cambridge University Press has no responsibility for the persistence or accuracy of URLs for external or third-party internet websites referred to in this publication, and does not guarantee that any content on such websites is, or will remain, accurate or appropriate.

# Contents

| | |
|---|---|
| *List of Figures* | *page* vii |
| *List of Contributors* | viii |
| *Acknowledgments* | xiii |

1 Encountering the "Anthropocene": Setting the Scene    1
FRANK BIERMANN AND EVA LÖVBRAND

**Part I    The Conceptual Politics of the Anthropocene: Science, Philosophy, and Culture**    23

2 The "Anthropocene" in Global Change Science: Expertise, the Earth, and the Future of Humanity    25
NOEL CASTREE

3 The "Anthropocene" in Philosophy: The Neo-material Turn and the Question of Nature    50
MANUEL ARIAS-MALDONADO

4 The "Anthropocene" in Popular Culture: Narrating Human Agency, Force, and Our Place on Earth    67
ALEXANDRA NIKOLERIS, JOHANNES STRIPPLE, AND PAUL TENNGART

**Part II    Key Concepts and the Anthropocene: A Reconsideration**    85

5 Power, World Politics, and Thing-Systems in the Anthropocene    87
ANTHONY BURKE AND STEFANIE FISHEL

6 Time and Politics in the Anthropocene: Too Fast, Too Slow?    109
VICTOR GALAZ

7 Democracy in the Anthropocene: A New Scale    128
AYŞEM MERT

v

8  Global Justice and the Anthropocene: Reproducing
   a Development Story                                                150
   JEREMY BASKIN

**Part III   The Practices of Political Study in the Anthropocene**   169

9  The "Good Anthropocene" and Green Political Theory: Rethinking
   Environmentalism, Resisting Eco-modernism                          171
   ANNE FREMAUX AND JOHN BARRY

10 Coproducing Knowledge and Politics of the Anthropocene:
   The Case of the Future Earth Program                               191
   SILKE BECK

11 The Ethics of Political Research in the Anthropocene               212
   PAUL WAPNER

12 Epilogue: Continuity and Change in the Anthropocene                228
   JAMES MEADOWCROFT

*Index*                                                               243

# Figures

| | | |
|---|---|---|
| 2.1 | Humanity's proximity to planetary boundaries | page 34 |
| 2.2 | The principal meanings of the word "nature" in contemporary Anglo-European societies | 38 |
| 6.1 | Comparing temporal scales: "deep time" versus "political time" | 112 |
| 6.2 | Contrasting the temporal assumptions of a selection of disciplines in environmental social sciences and political science | 122 |
| 9.1 | A postmodernist-most-modernist mapping of the ecological field | 176 |
| 10.1 | The knowledge arena: sustainability science as a collective learning process | 203 |

# Contributors

**Manuel Arias-Maldonado** is an associate professor of Political Science at the University of Málaga, Spain. His research focuses on environmental political theory, with an emphasis on the relationship between sustainability and democracy, the concept of nature, and more lately, the Anthropocene. He has been a visiting scholar at the Institute of International Studies at Berkeley; the Rachel Carson Center in Munich; and the Department of Environmental Studies at New York University. His books include *Real Green. Sustainability after the End of Nature* (2012) and *Nature and Society. Socionatural Relations in the Anthropocene* (2015). He is coeditor, with Zev Trachtenberg, of *Rethinking the Environment for the Anthropocene. Political Theory and Socionatural Relations in the New Geological Epoch* (forthcoming).

**John Barry** is professor of Green Political Economy in the School of History, Anthropology, Philosophy, and Politics at Queens University Belfast, Ireland. His areas of research include green moral and political theory; green and heterodox political economy; the greening of citizenship; and civic republicanism. His books include *Environment and Social Theory* (2nd edition, 2007) and *Citizenship, Sustainability and Environmental Research* (2000). His latest book is *The Politics of Actually Existing Unsustainability: Human Flourishing in a Climate-Changed, Carbon-Constrained World* (2012). He is currently working on a book provisionally entitled *The Story of Unsustainable Growth: Understanding Economic Growth as Ideology, Myth and Religion and What Replaces It*.

**Jeremy Baskin** is a senior research fellow in the School of Government at the University of Melbourne, Australia. After extensive involvement in social activism in South Africa and a period working with the postapartheid government there, and then with private sector organizations globally, he was a latecomer to academia. He completed his PhD on *Solar Geoengineering, the Anthropocene and the End of*

*Nature* in 2017. His current research interests cover climate policy and emerging technologies, environmental justice, and Southern perspectives on science and development. He is currently working on a project looking at the rise in distrust of experts and expertise in contemporary democracies and its effect on policymaking.

**Silke Beck** is deputy chair at the Department of Environmental Politics, Helmholtz Centre for Environmental Research, Leipzig, Germany. Her research focuses on the relationship between expertise and decision-making in response to global environmental change.

**Frank Biermann** is a research professor of Global Sustainability Governance with the Copernicus Institute of Sustainable Development, Utrecht University, the Netherlands. He is the founding chair of the Earth System Governance Project, a global transdisciplinary research network launched in 2009, and editor-in-chief of the new peer-reviewed journal *Earth System Governance*. In April 2018, he won a European Research Council Advanced Grant, the highest personal award from European institutions, for a research program on the steering effects of the Sustainable Development Goals. His most recent books are *Earth System Governance: World Politics in the Anthropocene* (2014) and *Governing through Goals: Sustainable Development Goals as Governance Innovation* (coedited, 2017).

**Anthony Burke** is Professor of International and Political Studies at University of New South Wales, Canberra, Australia, and a senior fellow of the Earth System Governance Project. He is an author of the *Planet Politics* manifesto (2016) and has research interests in critical security studies, political theory, and global ecological change and governance. His recent books include *Uranium* (2017), *Ethics and Global Security: A Cosmopolitan Approach* (with Katrina Lee-Koo and Matt McDonald, 2014), and *Global Insecurity: Futures of Global Chaos and Governance* (edited with Rita Parker, 2017).

**Noel Castree** is a professor of Geography at the University of Manchester, United Kingdom, and a visiting professorial research fellow at the University of Wollongong, Australia. His research into the political economy of environmental change has been informed by Marxian and Polanyian approaches to capitalism. He has published widely, with a focus on the commodification of nature in general and neoliberal environmental policy in particular. His recent research focuses on global change research and the politics of knowledge creation, circulation, and consumption. He is author of the books *Nature: The Adventures of an Idea* (2005) and *Making Sense of Nature* (2014). He is managing editor of the journal *Progress in Human Geography* and a fellow of the British Academy of Social Science.

**Stefanie Fishel** is Lecturer in Politics at the University of the Sunshine Coast, Australia. Her research focuses on bodies and biomes and their metaphorical and material relationship to global politics. She is the author of *The Microbial State: Global Thriving and the Body Politic* (2018). Past publications include "Theorizing Violence in the Responsibility to Protect" in *Critical Studies on Security* (2013); "Microbes" in *Making Things International 1: Circuits and Motion* (2015); "Remembering Nukes: Collective Memories and Countering State History" in *Critical Military Studies* (2015); and "Planet Politics: A Manifesto from the End of IR" in *Millennium: Journal of International Studies* (2016).

**Anne Fremaux** has completed her doctoral thesis entitled "Towards a Critical Theory of the Anthropocene: A Post-Growth Green Republican Analysis" at Queens University Belfast, Ireland. Her publications include *La nécessité d'une écologie radicale. La pensée à l'épreuve des problèmes environnementaux* (2011) and *L' Ère du levant* (2016).

**Victor Galaz** is an associate professor of Political Science and deputy director at the Stockholm Resilience Centre, Stockholm University, Sweden. He is also a senior academy researcher and program director at the Royal Swedish Academy of Sciences and a senior fellow of the Earth System Governance Project. His research focuses on the governance challenges posed by complexity in the earth system, including "planetary boundaries" and notions about the Anthropocene, and the earth system governance challenges posed by rapid technological change. His publications include *Global Environmental Governance, Technology and Politics: The Anthropocene Gap* (2014) and the edited *Handbook on Global Challenges, Governance and Complexity* (forthcoming).

**Eva Lövbrand** is an associate professor at the Department of Thematic Studies: Environmental Change at Linköping University, Sweden. Her work revolves around the ideas, knowledge claims, and expert practices that inform environmental politics and governance. Climate change has served as her prime empirical example, but in recent years she has also explored how the Anthropocene is figured and narrated as a political problem. Her work has been extensively published in journals such as *Global Environmental Politics, Science, Technology and Human Values, Critical Policy Studies, Review of International Relations*, and *Global Environmental Change*. She is coeditor of the volumes *Environmental Politics and Deliberative Democracy: Exploring the Promise of New Modes of Governance* (2010) and *Research Handbook on Climate Governance* (2015).

**James Meadowcroft** holds a Canada Research Chair in Governance for Sustainable Development at Carleton University, Canada. He is a professor in both the Department of Political Science and the School of Public Policy and

Administration. His research is focused on the ways governments are adjusting their practices and policies to cope with problems of the environment and sustainable development. Meadowcroft has written widely on environmental politics and policy, democratic participation and deliberative democracy, sustainable development strategies, environmental limits, and socio-technical transitions. Recent work focuses on energy and the transition to a low carbon society, and includes publications on carbon capture and storage, smart grids, the development of Ontario's electricity system, green technology, and negative carbon emissions. He has recently coedited (with Daniel J. Fiorino) *Conceptual Innovation in Environmental Policy* (2017).

**Ayşem Mert** is Associate Senior Lecturer at the Department of Political Science, Stockholm University, Sweden, and adjunct faculty at the Vrije Universiteit Amsterdam, the Netherlands. She is also a research fellow with the Earth System Governance Project. Previously, she worked for the Centre for Global Cooperation Research (Duisburg, Germany), the Amsterdam Global Change Institute, and the Institute for Environmental Social Sciences and Geography at Freiburg University, Germany. Her research focuses on discourses of democracy and environment at transnational and global levels; political storytelling; and public–private cooperation and partnerships, using mixed and interpretive methods. She is the author of *Environmental Governance through Partnerships: A Discourse Theoretical Study*.

**Alexandra Nikoleris** is a postdoctoral researcher at the Department of Environmental and Energy Systems Studies at Lund University, Sweden. She specializes in the study of energy systems and the role of visions and imaginaries of sustainability transitions. She has published in *Research Policy, Climatic Change*, and *Carbon Management*, among other journals.

**Johannes Stripple** is an associate professor at the Department of Political Science, Lund University, Sweden. His research is concerned with the politics of climate change and its governance through a range of sites, from the United Nations and financial markets to the urban and the everyday. He has recently coedited *Governing the Climate: New Approaches to Rationality, Politics and Power* (Cambridge University Press, 2014) and *Towards a Cultural Politics of Climate Change: Devices, Desires and Dissent* (Cambridge University Press, 2016).

**Paul Tenngart** is an associate professor in Comparative Literature at the Centre for Literature and Languages, Lund University, Sweden. He has published four monographs on Swedish and French poetry, one book on literary theory, and articles on literary translation, proletarian fiction, and ecopoetry. He has also edited two volumes on politics and literature.

**Paul Wapner** is Professor of Global Environmental Politics in the School of International Service at American University, United States. His work focuses on environmental political thought. His most recent research examines the ethical dimensions of climate change and specifically "climate suffering" – the lived experience of those on the frontlines of climate intensification. He is the author of *Living through the End of Nature: The Future of American Environmentalism* and *Environmental Activism and World Civic Politics*, and coeditor of *Principled World Politics: The Challenge of Normative International Relations* (with Lester Ruiz), *Global Environmental Politics: From Person to Planet* (with Simon Nicholson), and *Reimagining Climate Change* (with Hilal Elver). Wapner is a lead faculty member of the Earth System Governance Project, serves on the boards of the Lama Foundation and RE-volv, and leads workshops for professors and activists on contemplative environmentalism.

# Acknowledgments

The "Anthropocene encounters" that this book reports on are the result of a long-standing collaboration of numerous scholars who jointly explored the manifold political trajectories of the Anthropocene; at times through in-person meetings at conferences and workshops and, more often, through intense correspondence. At the core of this collaboration stands the Anthropocene task force under the auspices of the global research alliance, the Earth System Governance Project. This task force was part of a larger research network on the conceptual foundations of earth system governance that was set up and led by James Meadowcroft, a long-standing member of the Lead Faculty of the Earth System Governance Project. We owe our gratitude, therefore, first and foremost to James – without his infectious enthusiasm, his unstoppable energy, and his intellectual stimulus, this project would probably not have taken off in the first place. We also thank him for his reflections on the other chapters that he reports in the concluding chapter of this book.

Thanks also to the many colleagues who have commented on previous drafts and initial outlines. First drafts of most chapters to this volume have been presented at numerous international and national conferences, workshops, and seminars. In particular, we thank participants at a lunch seminar during the 2015 Canberra Conference on Earth System Governance, and at roundtables and panels at the 2017 Lund Conference on Earth System Governance, for their valuable input and comments.

In addition, a large number of public research institutions, foundations, and think tanks have supported the research for this volume. In particular, we wish to thank the following institutions, agencies, and colleagues:

Frank Biermann has conducted research for this volume while based as a senior research fellow with the Institute for Advanced Sustainability Studies, Potsdam, Germany. He wishes to thank this institute – in particular its director, Ortwin Renn – for the very warm welcome and excellent research environment that the institute could offer. Eva Lövbrand's contributions to this volume are the result of fruitful collaboration with colleagues within the two research programs: "Mistra

Geopolitics: Sustainable Development in a Changing Geopolitical Era" and "The Seedbox: An Environmental Humanities Collaboratory," funded by the Swedish Foundation for Strategic Environmental Research (Mistra) and the Swedish Research Council Formas. Noel Castree would like to acknowledge audiences at the universities of Melbourne, Oslo, and Wollongong, who commented constructively on spoken versions of his chapter. Anne Fremaux wishes to thank the organizers and participants of a workshop from the European Consortium for Political Research in April 2016 on "Environmental Political Theory in the Anthropocene" (with special thanks to Luigi Pellizzoni for bringing Adorno and critical theory into the debate). Victor Galaz's research for this project has been supported by the Mistra foundation, Sweden, through a core grant to the Stockholm Resilience Centre, a cross-faculty research center at Stockholm University; through grants from the Futura Foundation; and through the Global Economic Dynamics and the Biosphere Programme at the Royal Swedish Academy of Sciences. Galaz is further grateful to all colleagues participating in the T-Lab "The Biosphere Code" in Stockholm in 2015 (especially Fredrik Moberg) for helping him to develop some of his ideas about algorithmic governance. Paul Wapner would like to thank the National Endowment of the Humanities (United States) for financial support and Jessie Mehrhoff for valuable research assistance.

Special thanks to Henok Debessai of Linköping University, who did a marvelous job in the final editorial stages of this project. We are also very grateful to Tom Peek of Utrecht University, who did a fantastic job in compiling the index data for this book while serving as assistant manager of the 2018 Utrecht Conference on Earth System Governance at the same time. At Cambridge University Press, we are especially grateful to Emma Kiddle, commissioning editor for Earth, Environmental and Planetary Science, who shared our enthusiasm for this topic and smoothly guided our manuscript through the review process while starting a harvesting series for the Earth System Governance Project with Cambridge University Press at the same time, along with a new separate series of shorter books, the Cambridge Elements in Earth System Governance. Many thanks also to the reviewers who helped improve our manuscript with invaluable advice and critique.

The book is, in the end, just a snapshot on the state of debate on the Anthropocene and its manifold implications – including for the field of green political thinking. Undoubtedly, the debate will continue, and more research and reflection is urgently needed. Our network will hence continue. The Earth System Governance Project is currently in the process of reinventing itself, after ten years of operation, and developing a new strategic science and implementation plan for the 2019–2028 period. We are confident that reflections on the Anthropocene and its implications for green political thinking will remain a key topic for debate also in the new phase of earth system governance research, and we hope that the contributions to this volume will help to drive the debate further.

# 1

# Encountering the "Anthropocene": Setting the Scene

FRANK BIERMANN AND EVA LÖVBRAND

There are few concepts that have made such a rapid career as the "Anthropocene." Coined barely two decades ago by Paul J. Crutzen and Eugene Stoermer (2000), the Anthropocene has become one of the most influential, most cited, but also most controversial terms in environmental policy, theory, and practice. In global change research, where the concept was invented, the Anthropocene encapsulates the unprecedented changes to the earth's biosphere following the industrial revolution and the past sixty years of economic activity, consumption, and resource use (Steffen et al. 2004; Brondizio et al. 2016). In contrast to the past 12,000 years of relative climate stability – known to geologists as the Holocene – the Anthropocene symbolizes the profound and accelerating human transformations of the earth's climate and environment. Demonstrated changes in atmospheric composition, stratospheric ozone, the climate system, water and nitrogen cycles, marine ecosystems, land systems, tropical forests, and terrestrial biosphere are all taken as indications that modern civilization is altering the functioning of the earth system at a rapid speed (Steffen et al. 2011 and 2016). In the Anthropocene, we are told, humans are no longer spectators of a natural drama to which we have to adapt. The fundamental and irreversible human imprint on natural systems and processes has turned us into a geological agent and master of a world increasingly of our own making (Dalby 2014).

Despite the rapid elevation and uptake of the Anthropocene in scientific discourse, however, it remains an ambivalent and contested formulation that has given rise to a multitude of unexpected, and often uncomfortable, meetings and conversations. In geology, scholars are debating the stratigraphic evidence of the proposed "geology of mankind" (Lewis and Maslin 2015; Waters et al. 2016), with an international working group of the Subcommission on Quaternary Stratigraphy exploring whether the human signature in the earth's strata is significant enough to formalize the Anthropocene as a "material time-rock unit" within the geological time scale (Zalasiewicz et al. 2017). In the social sciences, scholars have engaged in parallel debates over "the Anthropos" that propels this new social geology. Rather than accepting the scientific staging of the Anthropocene as the unintended outcome of a unified humanity – a planetary "We" – social theorists have highlighted the unequal geographies, political-economic relations, insecurities, and bodily labors that underpin the current era in planetary history (Malm and Hornborg 2014; Lövbrand et al. 2015; Moore 2016; Harrington and Shearing 2017). Across the humanities, philosophers have drawn upon the Anthropocene to further rethink the Western division between natural and human history (Chakrabarty 2009) and to imagine new ways of becoming "human" in connection with earth and its multiple ecologies (Gibson et al. 2015; Haraway 2016; Clark and Yusoff 2017). At a time when human societies are "irrevocably folded into the Earth's systems" (Dibley 2012: 143), the Anthropocene has become an urgent call to vitalize traditional concepts of ethics, care, and virtue (Rose et al. 2012).

How, then, can students of environmental politics contribute to these multiple and often contested Anthropocene encounters? Can we just carry on with politics as usual in view of the profound and possibly irreversible transformations of the earth's climate, oceans, terrestrial systems, and species? Or does the Anthropocene proposition prompt a reconsideration of the assumptions and practices upon which our scholarship rests? These questions are important motivations for this book. We note that the Anthropocene disrupts concepts central to the study of environmental politics, such as nature, environment, power, democracy, and justice. The rapid unmaking of nonhuman life-forms raises uncomfortable questions about the possibility of wild nature untainted by humans, the capacity of technology to fix the damage done, and the ability of our political institutions to govern the environments we make and give voice to those who suffer from the environments we destroy. Some have argued that our scholarship needs a new language and novel analytical categories to grapple with the world that we are continually remaking. Familiar concepts such as *nature* and *environment*, which have long served as building blocks for elaborated arguments, theories, discourses, and ideologies (Meadowcroft and Fiorini 2017: 3), now fail to capture the scale and complexity of earth system transformations (Biermann 2014; Galaz 2014) and the "social nature" that is turning upon us (Burke et al. 2016).

In this volume we take this challenge seriously by examining how established political categories and assumptions in green political thinking hold in view of the Anthropocene formulation. We refer to *green political thinking* neither as an ideological position (Dobson 1990) nor as a coherent theoretical project (Barry 1999). Instead, we ask what it means to "think green" at a time when nature no longer functions as a stable backdrop for political analysis or as a given source of moral instruction (Wapner 2013; Trachtenberg 2015). Our volume is not the first to address the politics of the Anthropocene. Numerous publications have invited us to explore what this new epoch in planetary history means for political thinking and practice (e.g., Dalby 2009; Biermann 2014; Galaz 2014; Arias-Maldonado 2015; Purdy 2015; Nicholson and Jinnah 2016; Harrington and Shearing 2017; Hickmann et al. 2018; Arias-Maldonado and Trachtenberg forthcoming). In this expanding scholarship, disagreement prevails over the political potency and usefulness of the Anthropocene concept as such. While some welcome this new term as an invitation to rethink conventional philosophical and political categories (Wapner 2013; Clark and Yusoff 2017), others insist that it encapsulates everything that is wrong about contemporary environmentalism and planetary eco-managerialism (Lepori 2015; Luke 2015).

This book does not take sides in this debate, but pursues a different aim: to examine how the Anthropocene formulation has been encountered by environmental politics scholarship over the past fifteen years, and the various analytical struggles and confrontations that it has given rise to. Here, the word "encounter" does not only connote an unexpected meeting, but also combines elements of discovery, exchange, struggle, and even conflict (Walters 2012: 5). The core argument of the volume is that the Anthropocene has left profound traces in multiple political terrains and provoked unexpected, and often critical, conversations about some of the most pressing issues of our time. Where these conversations will lead us is too early to tell. The politics of the Anthropocene remain emergent, ambiguous, complex, and risky. It is at this uncomfortable juncture, however, filled with troubling contradictions, that we expect green political thinking to develop and thrive in the years to come.

### Has Nature Really Ended? The Anthropocene in Science, Philosophy, and Literary Fiction

The Anthropocene is a term that has brought with it grand debates about what it means to inhabit a planet radically transformed by human activity. For many, it marks an existential moment for modern civilization and its promise of human emancipation from the shackles of nature (Dibley 2012; Tsing 2015; Hamilton 2017). Zalasiewicz et al. (2010: 2231) stage the Anthropocene as a new phase in planetary history when natural and human forces are so intertwined that the fate of one determines the fate of the other. It is a dangerous era, we are told, when humanity is undermining the planetary life-support systems upon which we depend (Steffen et al. 2004; Rockström et al. 2009). The proposition that our social, economic, and political processes now are woven into, and coevolve with, some of the great forces of nature is at once ambitious and ambiguous (Hamilton et al. 2015). On the one hand, it suggests that humans have turned into earth-shaping agents with the power to "heat the planet and to cool it right down, to eliminate species and to engineer entirely new ones, to resculpt the terrestrial surface and to determine its biology" (Vince 2014: 6). On the other hand, it radically unsettles the epistemological and ontological ground upon which this human world-making project rests and invites humility in face of our dependence upon earth and its multiple ecological systems (Baskin 2015; Tsing 2015).

In this volume, several chapters engage with the challenging claim that wild and untainted "nature" is coming undone. In a time when late modern society is altering the biosphere and its environments at a rapid speed, many seem to agree that the grand separation between nature and society, inherited from the Enlightenment era, no longer holds. The entangled relationship between human and nonhuman worlds is fostering novel understandings of nature, humanity, and the earth.

## *The Anthropocene and the Earth System Sciences*

The functioning of the earth is changing, and we as humans are the change-makers. This is the radical finding from the global change research community that paved the way for the formulation of the Anthropocene at the turn of the millennium. In an edited volume from 2004, leading representatives of the International Geosphere-Biosphere Programme conclude that "profound transformation of Earth's environment is now apparent, owing not to the great forces of nature or to extraterrestrial sources but to the numbers and activities of people" (Steffen et al. 2004: 2). In Chapter 2, Noel Castree illustrates how this grand claim is linked to developments within the earth system sciences during the past thirty years. The chapter lays out in great detail how this "science of integration" has affected ecological thinking and resulted in a radical reinterpretation of the relationship between humanity and nature. The "earth system," comprised of the tightly linked atmosphere, hydrosphere, biosphere, and lithosphere, is today no longer understood as external to human societies. The magnitude, spatial scale, and speed of human-induced change to the earth's biogeochemical processes and cycles have collapsed the modern distinction between nature and culture. This is what makes the Anthropocene proposition such an arresting one, suggests Castree. Nothing, it seems, is immune to human influence any more. Humans have entered the "engine room" of the earth system and are now drivers of the "planetary machinery" (Schellnhuber 1997; Steffen et al. 2004).

This recognition has profound ontological implications. Within the earth system sciences, Castree finds that the conception of nature as external – a totality beyond the realm of human influence – is increasingly outdated. Nature is a thing of the past, a trait of the Holocene against which "epochal change" is evaluated. In geology, efforts to assemble and assess geological signals in sediments of human changes to the earth system are still ongoing, and it is too early to tell whether these signals (e.g., novel minerals and materials, geochemical signals reflecting industrial development, changing atmospheric composition) will persist throughout geologically significant time intervals (Zalasiewicz et al. 2017). Even so, notes Castree, geologists have now achieved sufficient scientific momentum that the possibility of the Holocene's end is considered a realistic one. Enter the Anthropocene – a post-natural world where humans have a dominant earth-shaping influence.

What should social scientists do with this daunting prospect brought to us by our scientific peers? Castree predicts that existing ideas about political actors, subjects, and institutions will be challenged in the years to come. The colossal ontological implications of nature's ending reset the compass for any attempt to understand "the political." However, he also cautions against a passive acceptance of the epochal claims of earth system science and insists that social scientists demystify the scientific facts that underpin the Anthropocene. Time has certainly come to "geologize" political thought and hereby engage more thoroughly with the material dynamics of our changing earth (Clark and Gunaratnam 2017). However, such engagement also requires that we "politicize" the unfolding social geology that results from our encounters with the Anthropocene.

## *The Material Philosophy of the Anthropocene*

The proposition that nature has morphed into human environment has brought the environmental sciences and humanities together in interesting and unexpected ways. In Chapter 3, Manuel Arias-Maldonado explores at length the intersections and tensions between Anthropocene science and new materialist philosophy. While these bodies of scholarship share an interest in the Anthropocene, their entry points to this new geological era differ rather dramatically. Firmly grounded in the Enlightenment tradition, earth system science approaches global change as a mounting empirical demonstration of the damage done to the earth and its complex life-support systems. When Crutzen and Stoermer announced the "geology of mankind" in 2000, they could draw upon century-long scientific observations of human alterations to the global environment (Crutzen and Stoermer 2000). New materialist scholars, for their part, are also interested in the very materiality of our changing environment. However, embracing key insights from poststructuralism and social constructivism, they bring with them a view of the material world in which modern dualisms such as body/mind or nature/culture are transcended and part of a relational and ever-changing flux. Old passive nature, as described by the mechanistic tradition, is here replaced by lively and vibrant matter in constant transformation (Bennett 2010).

This view, notes Arias-Maldonado, drives new materialism to the controversial claim that agency is distributed across a vast range of entities and processes. In contrast to earth system science – which often is accused of cultivating the exceptional human powers that have brought about the Anthropocene in the first place (Baskin 2015) – new materialist philosophy ascribes generative powers and inventive capacities to a whole "political ecology of things" beyond human control (e.g., wind, rain, nonhuman species, technological artifacts) (Bennett 2010; Burke and Fishel, Chapter 5). By challenging the human subject as the center of all things, work in this field seeks to foster greater humility and responsibility towards the earth and its multiple life forms (Gibson et al. 2015). The Anthropocene is thus not the culmination of modern civilization or human rationality but a sign of our limited powers and inevitable embeddedness in the web of life.

While new materialists hereby depart from the anthropocentrism that informs Anthropocene science, Arias-Maldonado notes that both traditions converge in a hybrid ontology of nature-cultures (Arias-Maldonado 2015). In the Anthropocene, a neat separation between natural and human history is no longer possible or desirable. In place of this Cartesian dualism, a hybrid world is unfolding, where social and ecological processes are deeply entangled and interconnected. When earth system scientists and new materialists speak of "the end of nature," claims Arias-Maldonado, it is this hybrid ontology that they have in mind (Arias-Maldonado 2015). Despite the grandeur of the statement, it is a simple idea: nature can no longer be defined by its independence from human beings and society. This is an important ontological claim that challenges the social constructivist scholarship that has influenced environmental thinking in recent decades. It is not the cultural construction of nature but the ultimate materiality of it that signifies the Anthropocene, suggests Arias-Maldonado (Arias-Maldonado 2015). He thus foresees that a material version of constructivism will shape our thinking of environmental politics in the years to come. Such a tradition directs attention to the force of things/matter (e.g., animals, plants, minerals) in political life and opens up new possibilities for imagining the relationship between scientific and political practices (see Burke and Fishel, Chapter 5). At a time when nature and society are deeply entwined, a post-natural understanding of environmental politics and nature conservation is unfolding.

### *Anthropocene Traces in Literary Fiction*

Contemporary stories of planetary transformation do not only circulate within the environmental sciences. In Chapter 4, Alexandra Nikoleris, Johannes Stripple, and Paul Tenngart encounter the Anthropocene through modern literary fiction. By engaging with the expanding field of climate fiction ("cli-fi"), they suggest, we can better explore what led us to the Anthropocene, what it means to be here, and where we should go next. Fiction has the power to narrate everything that can go wrong, claim Nikoleris, Stripple, and Tenngart. Fiction can take effects to their extremes, whether it is an earth without insects or a spaceship on its path to certain death. By following particular persons in particular contexts, literature lets us experience the global implications of the Anthropocene through a situated specificity that is often not our own.

Following the eco-critical tradition in literature and cultural studies (Glotfelty and Fromm 1996), this chapter makes use of literary protagonists as inspirational examples to give planetary visions of global environmental change a "sense of place" and "an ethics of proximity" (Heise 2008). Through Robinson's *Science in the Capital*, for instance, Nikoleris, Stripple, and Tenngart give us a glimpse of how we may transcend an excessively "rational" modern society and enter into a world where spiritual and emotional connectivity guides our actions. The reader learns that doing something about climate change could be the starting point for a better society and new forms of humanity. The story tells us that no matter how well humans try to plan the evolution of socio-ecological relations, it is not desirable to be in total control. Rather than perfect planning, we need to rethink our relationship with the earth and its inhabitants, not as stewards but as cohabitants.

Many of the novels analyzed in this chapter reject both the idea of humans being outside nature and the notion that humans and nature are so intertwined that they are inseparable. Nature proceeds, prods back, reacts in unforeseen ways to what humans do, claim Nikoleris, Stripple, and Tenngart, showing that while humans might now be a geological force, it is far from being the only one. Several of the characters that we get to know in this chapter imagine and embrace a "zoopolis" that can sustain close interrelationships between humans and animals, new forms of connectivity, different social arrangements, and new forms of being political in a hybrid world. The political effects of this expanded Anthropocene imagination are, of course, difficult to trace. Narrating global environmental change through the lives of fictional individuals does not bring us closer to any direct political responses. As illustrated in this chapter, eco-critical accounts of the Anthropocene can, however, participate in the search for stories and images of an environmentalism that links global patterns of connectivity to local places, ecologies, and cultural practices (Heise 2008).

## Anthropocene Politics: Revisiting Familiar Categories and Concepts

Many scholars have presented the Anthropocene as a turning point or rupture in the history of earth, life, and humans that demands we set accustomed understandings aside and develop original political thinking (Bonneuil and Fressoz 2015;

Hamilton 2017). In the second section of this volume, several authors respond to this invitation by revisiting established political concepts in view of their encounters with the Anthropocene. These chapters demonstrate that the hybridity, complexity, and nonlinearity of contemporary socio-ecological relations bring profound challenges to established conceptions of power (as conceived in International Relations) (Burke and Fishel, Chapter 5); political time (Galaz, Chapter 6); democracy (Mert, Chapter 7); and the eternal quest for global justice (Baskin, Chapter 8). While political theory may have been late in responding to the fundamental ontological reorientation postulated by the Anthropocene (Hamilton et al. 2015), these chapters demonstrate that green political scholars certainly have taken up the challenge.

## *Thing-Power in World Politics*

In Anthropocene discussions, environmental change and globalization merge into one (Dalby 2009). The flows across boundaries of people, goods, fuel, and pollution create new forms and degrees of interdependence among formally sovereign countries, extending to areas beyond national jurisdiction, such as the high seas and Antarctica (Biermann 2014). As local actions become linked to social, economic, and political processes on transnational or even global scales, we also see growing problems of displacement, distancing, and disconnection between decision-makers and "environments," between perpetrators and victims, between consumers and producers (Christoff and Eckersley 2013: 11). New configurations of power are one major consequence, which stand at the center of Burke and Fishel's contribution (Chapter 5).

In a world where social and ecological systems are increasingly entangled, traditional conceptualizations of power are radically outdated, claim Burke and Fishel. The essentially and often purely anthropocentric theorization of power in world politics makes it almost impossible to see power as something that operates systemically, structurally, anonymously, and accidentally; as something that can bring about unintended effects and consequences; and as something that can also account for the impacts of nonhuman agency. In the Anthropocene, they argue, eventually nonanthropocentric power will resist anthropocentric power in its complexity, its nonintentionality, and its heterogeneity. Yet, a novel focus on the power of nonhuman agents, argue Burke and Fishel, leads also to profound consequences for political practice, and eventually for political ethics. A new focus on what they call "thing-system power" requires us to go beyond traditional bargaining among state governments and their diplomatic representatives. Instead, activism, resistance, and subversion are becoming equally important, as well as novel ways of representing nonhuman agents (animals, ecosystems, and so forth) in what Burke and Fishel envision as "cross-national and ecosystem-centered deliberative democracy" (however this might concretely evolve in global political institutions and agreements).

Given their broad and far-reaching vision, Burke and Fishel remain inherently skeptical of the chances of reform within the context of existing intergovernmental treaties, agreements, and institutions, which grant – in their view – still too much freedom to states to control and exploit the ecosystems within their jurisdictions. A new theory of power, claim Burke and Fishel, is hence needed – along with a new practice of politics that becomes much more radical, subversive, and resistant than what most current organizations in civil society and social movements are known for. Burke and Fishel's vision can hence be seen as a radical interpretation of the consequence of our encounters with the Anthropocene – even though the concrete implications of this radical critique remain to be elaborated in future research.

## *Reconsidering Political Time*

The Anthropocene creates novel interdependencies not only across space, but also across time. The notion of historic responsibility, central to the politics of climate change, has since the 1990s created ties of responsibility between present generations and the activities of their ancestors. The history of fossil fuel burning in Europe has, argue many developing countries, resulted in a climate debt that industrialized countries now should repay by extra mitigation efforts. As demonstrated in Victor Galaz's contribution to this book (Chapter 6), the Anthropocene also links current people with future generations over many centuries. Sea-level rise, for example, is expected within a time-range of a hundred years and more, necessitating planning horizons that exceed the lifetime of present generations. This "deep-time" horizon of the Anthropocene gives the democratic legitimacy of environmental policies an intergenerational dimension. What rights and responsibilities do present generations – and their representatives in parliament – owe to their unborn successors? Contemporary debates on climate engineering offer a case in point; that is, purposeful modifications of the earth system by means of, for instance, aerosol injections into the atmosphere (which would block parts of the sun's light and hence cool the planet), massive planting of fast-growing trees or crops to increase uptake of atmospheric carbon dioxide (combined with later sequestration and storage of the carbon), or direct capture of carbon from the air through massive deployment of air capturing devices. Whatever the merit of such technologies – none of which is yet sufficiently understood – all would only be employed at scale in the second half of this century, and they would need to be functional for many decades afterwards. In other words, the current discourse on climate engineering is nothing less than a debate on the type of large-scale technologies that the next generations, inevitably, would need to employ in order to keep the climatic conditions sufficiently stable. This linking of past and future generations within current political decisions is one of the key characteristics of the Anthropocene condition. Current political systems – as well as the field of political science – are poorly equipped to deal with these novel challenges of politics in "deep time."

Victor Galaz (Chapter 6) adds another, equally fascinating element of the role of time in the Anthropocene: "ultra-speed." More and more of the key processes of modern societies are taken over by powerful computers, which operate at the speed of split seconds. Major transactions in global markets occur in just tiny fractions of a second, following complex algorithms that become every day more influential in shaping our lives. Warfare is computerized and follows reaction times of fractions of seconds. Major infrastructures in heavily urbanized spaces are equally functioning according to the algorithms of "ultra-speed." Again, political systems and political scientists still have to grapple with the new condition of "ultra-speed" decisions, which might be equally challenging to the "deep-time" context in which the Anthropocene places human societies and politics.

## *New Scalar Challenges for Democracy*

The Anthropocene also poses novel and profound questions for democracy. This concerns, for one, democracy at the national level and the key functions of the state (Eckersley 2004). Novel complexities and uncertainties may grant a more prominent role to experts and technocrats, reducing the influence of citizens. The deep-time character of problems requires new types of democratic legitimacy for actions that affect future generations. Increasing needs of adaptation to earth system transformations could support authoritarian discourses, and the increasing reliance on private governance raises new questions about the democratic legitimacy and accountability of such new steering mechanisms. Not the least, the global character of the Anthropocene, with all its resulting interdependencies, erodes the steering capacities of governments. This has raised the question of whether the United Nations, built in its core around notions of sovereign equality of states and intergovernmental diplomacy, is still the appropriate model of global governance in the twenty-first century, in particular with a view to the Anthropocene challenges. Reform proposals abound, from the introduction of weighted majority voting to the establishment of a world parliamentarian assembly, or a global forum of civil society as a second chamber next to the United Nations General Assembly, or a global deliberative assembly (Biermann 2014, chapter 5).

This new reality is the starting point of Ayşem Mert's contribution in Chapter 7. The Anthropocene implies that new polities are emerging across the world which cannot be captured by traditional democratic procedures and norms. These emergent polities present a challenge to the contemporary democratic imaginary, particularly because they involve future generations and nonhuman agents. To address the questions of the Anthropocene, we need to rethink democratic dynamics and institutions, claims Mert. The measures with which the question of democracy has been addressed at the global level thus far have been largely based on the democratic principles of the nineteenth and twentieth centuries. Mert proposes, instead, to understand the Anthropocene as a new scale in democratic theory. The ideals and foundations of democracy were once before rearranged when the scale of the nation-state required a new and different democratic imaginary than that of the Greek city-states. The debates during the French and American Revolutions were similar to those of our time: What is the right scale and method for decision-making in view of a new and larger *demos*? Rather than democratizing existing modes of global governance, Mert invites us to imagine a whole new "post-natural" democracy that can adequately address governance at the planetary scale.

### *Challenging the Western Development Story*

Finally, politics in the Anthropocene has to operate in a global situation of large inequalities in resources and entitlements. In a world where the richest 20 percent of humanity account for 76.6 percent of total private consumption, while the poorest 20 percent consume just 1.5 percent (World Bank 2008: 4), global environmental change is deeply tied to global landscapes of inequality. While wealthy people who contribute most to environmental degradation see their advantages multiply, they are seldom asked to take responsibility for the impacts on distant people and places. How is this profound disconnect between those who make decisions that generate environmental risks and those who suffer the consequences reflected in mainstream writings on the Anthropocene?

In Chapter 8, Jeremy Baskin responds to this question by tracing some of the most important texts in the scientific Anthropocene discourse, from the original accounts by Paul Crutzen through to the more recent work on the "Great Acceleration" and the professional *Welcome to the Anthropocene* video that was produced in 2012 to inform the United Nations Conference on Sustainable Development in Rio de Janeiro. Baskin finds that scientific advocates of the Anthropocene pay little attention to politics or power relations (also Biermann et al. 2016). Most texts in this field ignore, or evade, the profound inequalities within human societies that mark the Anthropocene, for instance by ascribing responsibility to (anonymous) processes such as the "industrial revolution" or "globalization," yet without naming the political, social, and economic inequalities that resulted from such processes and the political agency that stood behind them.

Baskin also sees a common trend in Anthropocene discourse towards technical and managerial responses to the impacts of global change, as opposed to a more fundamental discussion of political, social, or economic reform. In the end, argues Baskin, key documents in the Anthropocene discourse remain linked to a traditional development narrative that makes possible the adoption of "Promethean proposals" such as solar radiation management. Radical alternatives, such as "degrowth" thinking, however, are less represented in the mainstream Anthropocene texts that Baskin analyzes. Instead, argues Baskin, what is needed now is to see "development" as part of the problem rather than of the solution. He hence concludes with an emphatic call for alternatives-to-development thinking, for degrowth approaches, and for the convergence towards a more equal world – reflecting here similar conclusions in this book by Burke and Fishel (Chapter 5), Fremaux and Barry (Chapter 9), Wapner (Chapter 11), and others.

## The Ethics of Political Research in a New Era: Radicalizing and Pluralizing Modes of Engagement

Over a decade ago, Will Steffen and colleagues (2004) proposed that the challenges of a rapidly changing earth demand entirely new forms of scientific knowledge creation. In order to understand the dynamics of the planetary life support system *as a whole*, environmental scientists need to put the pieces together in innovative and incisive ways and invite the social sciences to new forms of interdisciplinary collaboration and knowledge integration (Steffen et al. 2004). Their call became part of what today is known as "earth system science" – "the integrative meta-science of the whole planet as a unified, complex, evolving system beyond the sum of its parts" (Hamilton 2016: 94). More than a decade later, policy relevance has surfaced as an increasingly important mandate for environmental research. In order to effectively respond to the mounting environmental challenges of our times, scholars are today invited to codesign solutions with societal stakeholders and thereby begin the transition to global sustainability (Future Earth 2013: 10).

How should green political scholars respond to these calls for coordinated and solutions-oriented Anthropocene research? Do the epistemological foundations of our scholarship still hold in a time of intensified global environmental change, or does our entry into a post-natural era prompt a rethinking of established practices of political research and ethics? These questions have been intensely debated in recent years and are addressed in several chapters of this volume. Some contributors insist that political scholars should maintain critical distance from the scientific assumptions of the Anthropocene and instead direct analytical energy to their political origins and effects (Castree, Chapter 2; Baskin, Chapter 8). Others call for a deeper political and ethical sensibility towards the complex social geology of the

Anthropocene (Wapner, Chapter 11). To paraphrase Clark and Gunaratnam (2017: 148), can we really "politicize the Anthropocene" without also opening "the political" to climate, geology, and earth system change?

In this volume, most authors seem to agree that the study of politics cannot simply carry on when confronted with the daunting prospects of a world radically transformed by humans. At a time when nature no longer offers a stable background to political analysis, new scholarly investments, responsibilities, and, indeed, possibilities await us. The Anthropocene requires, in short, a radical revision of our scientific undertakings.

### *Radicalizing Green Political Thinking*

First, the Anthropocene proposition gives new energy to long-standing tensions between radical and more reformist wings of environmentalism. Sustainable development, which after the 1992 Rio Summit became the beacon and promise of global environmental politics, is today increasingly challenged for its failure to deliver structural transformation of industrial capitalism and the consumer culture that drives global environmental change (Blühdorn 2015). One decade ago, Jacob Park and colleagues declared this Rio model of environmentalism dead (Park et al. 2008). To many environmentalists, the eco-modern promise of sustainable development through technological innovation and market expansion has become a source of major disappointment, and a legitimizing strategy of economic globalization rather than environmental protection (Dauvergne 2017). Enter the Anthropocene.

In Chapter 9, Anne Fremaux and John Barry approach the Anthropocene as a reason to radicalize green political thinking and hereby reinstate the critical edge of environmentalism. To that end, they caution against an uncritical acceptance of nature's ending. New materialist constructivists have, they claim, offered eco-modernist champions of "the good Anthropocene" (Asafu-Adjaye et al. 2015) a new rationale for the technical domination of nature that has characterized the late modern era. By referring to the nonhuman world as "socio-nature" or "techno-nature," it is possible to justify a continued capitalization of nature as a "natural" fact. Recent proposals to govern climate change through large-scale geoengineering typify such anthropocentric hubris and point to the dangers of technological responses to global environmental concerns.

To Fremaux and Barry, nature can never be merely a social product. Nor is it a simple raw material that passively awaits human inventiveness and ingenuity. Nature must instead be approached as a complex system that reacts in surprising and unpredictable ways to human intervention and disturbance. The great challenge that lies ahead, claim Fremaux and Barry, is therefore not the further humanization of the planet but rather, the introduction of restraint and precaution in our political responses to environmental change. What needs to be managed and controlled is not the earth and its various biophysical entities and processes, but humanity's relationship to the earth. This clear focus on human self-governance brings green politics and ethics "back in" to Anthropocene conversations.

In order to counter the dangers of a planet radically transformed by humanity, Fremaux and Barry search for an environmentalism that is guided by precaution and respect for the nonhuman world. Such environmentalism challenges the excesses of capitalism and consumerism, and invites green political scholars to actively engage in democratic contestation and debate around alternative visions of the good (green) society. In contrast to the exhausted paradigm of sustainable growth and innovation, Fremaux and Barry welcome a new generation of green political thinking that fosters the utopian and critical impulses of environmentalism. At a time when the scale and speed of environmental transformations are accelerating in unprecedented ways, the Anthropocene should be used to revitalize the critical and normative features of green political theorizing and hereby articulate radical alternatives to the profit-oriented development, corporate-run solutions, and consumer-led responsibility of eco-modern society (Dauvergne 2017: 151).

### *Pluralizing Modes of Engagement*

The profound challenges of the Anthropocene have in recent years affected how environmental research is conceived and practiced across a diversity of disciplines. Some would even suggest that the Anthropocene has brought about a scientific revolution and fostered entirely new ways of thinking about and studying the earth (Hamilton 2016). In Chapter 10, Silke Beck traces how this paradigm shift is interpreted and received, especially by scholars involved in the global research platform "Future Earth: Research for Global Sustainability." This ten-year initiative was developed by a confederation of national research agencies to redirect the integrated study of the earth system towards global solutions. In particular, Beck interrogates what Future Earth's mandate to "coproduce" knowledge with societal stakeholders means for social science.

Beck finds that coproduction has become an epistemic instrument that promises to intensify the impacts of environmental research by making Anthropocene findings "usable" and "actionable." To many, this solution-oriented turn of global environmental research represents a major shift, a reorientation from autonomous, curiosity-driven basic research to applied research designed to facilitate society's transition towards sustainability. This shift has many critics. Beck reports from heated debates where scientists have voiced concern that their freedom, autonomy, and creativity are at stake. Social scientists have, in turn, pointed to the political risks and implications of a solutions-oriented research agenda. If informed by too narrow an understanding of global environmental problems, coproduced science will inevitably restrict the types of policies and institutions that can be imagined in response. Optimistic ideas that more and better coproduction will automatically achieve better outcomes may thus fail and, paradoxically, lead to their opposite (Lövbrand et al. 2015).

Rather than seeking to direct science towards predefined solutions, Beck concludes that we must let knowledge creation free in an Anthropocene era. The outcomes and impacts of knowledge production are always open-ended, unpredictable, and uncertain. Such uncertainty may seem risky when confronted with the mounting challenges of a world transformed by human activity. However, unpredictable knowledge can also create transformative breakthroughs that change social ways of thinking and acting, claims Beck. Green political scholars who seek to constructively engage in such transformative processes can no longer find comfort in their ivory towers. Effective analyses of green political futures require an active engagement with contemporary sociopolitical developments. This does not, of course, imply that scholars of environmental politics should passively accept the contemporary quest for usable and actionable research. In order to turn the Anthropocene into a critical political event, it is important, claims Beck, to safeguard an analytical space where it is possible to revisit and debate the cultural and social assumptions that inform how we collectively make sense of and respond to a changing environment. To Beck, this means pluralizing the modes of engagement and the reflexively engaged roles available to the social sciences in the continued study of nature's and society's entanglement.

### *Extending Ethical Responsibilities*

If we take seriously the proposition that humans have deflected the earth from its geological path, the Anthropocene is more than a political event. It is also an ethical condition that introduces new responsibilities to scholars of environmental politics (Hamilton et al. 2015). In Chapter 11, Paul Wapner reflects upon this new scholarly condition in view of the global inequalities and planetary injustices following global environmental change. The Anthropocene is not ethically neutral, claims Wapner. It extends contemporary injustices into the future, when societies may need to deal with mass migration from coastal plains following sea level rise, threats to food security, and possibly entirely novel political debates on climate engineering. "Climate suffering" might increase the pressures that already exist for the poorest, with 800 million people today lacking sufficient food. This condition of inequality, injustice, and suffering cannot leave political science and the political scientist untouched.

Wapner suggests two kinds of adjustment to this new ethical condition. First, he calls upon political scholars to embrace normative work and a critical stance in their research. In the shadow of the Anthropocene, Wapner argues, value-neutrality appears as a luxury. In essence, human transformations of the earth challenge the basic assumption of modern science: the idea that scientific research and personal values must be kept apart, separated by strong "firewalls" of university-based training, the structure of funding programs, journal acceptance policies, and tenure track commissions that value scientific "excellence" but not personal conviction. This separation, claims Wapner, must change. Time has come for researchers to embrace their normative commitments and let them direct, guide, and discipline scholarship. Of course, Wapner is quick to add that ethically informed scholarship does not mean "jettisoning methodological rigor, turning scholarship into moral exhortation, or relaxing the standards of honest inquiry ... It simply entails infusing one's scholarly aims with ethical momentum and deploying tools of research in the service of understanding and building a more humane Anthropocene." In Wapner's words, political scholarship was never completely free from normative sensibilities but always looked down on them as impediments to quality work. The Anthropocene calls for looking up at them.

In addition, Wapner argues, political scholars need to expand their object of analysis by considering the more-than-human dimension of life that includes other animals, plants, microbes, minerals, and general ecological features of the earth. This, again, is one of the consequences of the Anthropocene: even though "humanity" has become the defining species in this conceptual innovation, the Anthropocene does not imply complete domination. To Wapner, the Anthropocene represents an age when humans and nature are conjoining forces that move towards a coevolutionary future. Nonhuman agency is still pervasive, and invites us to consider and take responsibility for an entire assemblage of living and nonliving things.

## Conclusion

Nothing is more powerful than an idea whose time has come, once wrote Victor Hugo. The proposition that we have entered into a geological era of humanity's own making is, indeed, such an idea that contains many of the questions, provocations, and passions that have inspired green political thinking over the past decades. In this book, we ask ourselves how significant our encounters with the Anthropocene are for the study of environmental politics. Does the Anthropocene formulation present a rupture in our thinking about nature, humanity, and the earth; a true turning point that prompts a rethinking of green political thought and practice? Or are contemporary Anthropocene debates a continuation of a long-standing and still unfolding research agenda? The chapters included in this volume do not offer any firm answers to these questions. The manifold Anthropocene encounters made here suggest that the "geology of mankind" remains an ambivalent and emergent idea with multiple interpretations and political trajectories. As noted by Dibley (2012: 144), the very concept contains an "element of indecision." The Anthropocene is a discourse that speaks of both human mastery and retreat, of ecological collapse and restoration, of political crisis and possibility. While this ambivalence remains a central trait of contemporary Anthropocene debates, we find at least three reasons why these debates should engage scholars of environmental politics in the years to come.

Firstly, it is clear from the chapters included in this volume that the Anthropocene formulation has introduced *a new sense of urgency* to our scholarly pursuits. If we take seriously the proposition that the earth is being radically transformed by human activity, the Anthropocene is not about politics as usual (Burke and Fishel, Chapter 5). Instead, it prompts thorough scrutiny of contemporary political practices, norms, and institutions, and their ability to respond to the profound environmental challenges of our times. Take climate change as an example: a world comparable to the one we live in today is only feasible, we are told, if global mean warming is limited to less than 2 – if not 1.5 – degrees above preindustrial levels. Climate modelers have demonstrated that this goal requires that we reach negative emissions by the second half of this century – that is, that we then remove more carbon dioxide from the atmosphere than is released through fossil fuel burning and land use change. In order to meet this ambitious climate target, carbon dioxide removal programs are now being explored at unprecedented (global) scale. Vast areas of agricultural land would need to be used for crops that sequester carbon from the atmosphere – only to be stored away for centuries. These dire prospects signal that climate change is more than ever a matter of *earthly politics*. Nature is being reassembled at the largest possible scale, and political thinking has to come to terms with the geopolitical implications (Biermann 2014; Dalby 2016; Burke and Fishel, Chapter 5).

Secondly, the Anthropocene leaves us with *a novel type of unease* – about humanity's role in the world, about the kinds of environments we create, about the deep inequalities in causation and suffering, and about the planetary eco-managerialism that may follow. The elevation of "the human" into a geological agent with the capacity to determine the future of the planet is challenging and troubling at once. It signals that modernity's emancipatory quest now has reached a point where the possibility of any pristine, simple nature is irretrievably gone (Castree, Chapter 2). Through technological advancement, the spread of hyper-consumerism, and carbon-intensive forms of economic globality, the species-life of humans is now so entangled with the earth's biogeochemical cycles that life is no longer simply biological (Dibley 2012: 147). "Nature is us," as proclaimed by Crutzen and Schwägerl (2011). Many chapters in this volume challenge this grandiose claim and point to the risks of overemphasizing human agency and control. The Anthropocene is indeed a discourse inescapably entangled in notions of reason and liberty inherited from the Enlightenment era, and the managerial and eco-colonial impulse is therefore close at hand. As noted by Last (2017: 163), speculative geoengineering proposals such as cooling down our planet through solar radiation management draw upon and reinforce stereotypes of "imperialist man" as the engineer of his own destiny. In an effort to take control of the unfolding ecological crisis, this new geological agent is now granting himself an epoch-given right (or duty) to govern the planet for the benefit of humanity as a whole (Baskin 2015: 14; Fremaux and Barry, Chapter 9).

As the Anthropocene becomes a field of technological intervention, the questions for green political scholars are mounting. Who will take responsibility for the worlds that we make, and those that we destroy, in our efforts to govern contemporary socio-ecological relations? How do we make sure that ongoing and future transformations of the planet do not create, or reinforce, global landscapes of inequality and injustice? Does salvation lie with a cosmopolitan epistemic community, with multilaterally negotiated treaties, and the products and services provided by environmental markets? Can liberal environmental institutions and established practices of political representation foster inclusive debates about the future of the earth? Questions of this sort resonate with a long-standing and thriving green political scholarship and are thus far from new. However, as demonstrated by the chapters in this book, the Anthropocene adds new temporal and scalar dimensions to these questions and invites environmental scholars to critically interrogate the politics of a world transformed by humans.

Thirdly, the Anthropocene therefore also calls for *new ethical commitments* and novel ways of engaging with the objects of our study – nature (if it still exists), the environments we create, and our many socio-ecological relations, from local to global levels. As economy, ecology, and politics unite with growing intensity, complex patterns of environmental risks may reinforce unequal relations of political and economic power (Purdy 2015: 46). As outlined by Wapner (Chapter 11), the Anthropocene is not ethically neutral, but rife with social and ecological injustices. The age of humans should more accurately be termed the age of some humans. Any effort to understand the political dynamics of the Anthropocene will therefore require careful consideration of what is at stake, for whom, and where. While this new era in planetary history is closely tied to a Western development tale of human liberation and progress (Baskin, Chapter 8), it is also a sobering lesson in humility (Eckersley 2017). The complex interdependencies that characterize this new era in planetary history are now inspiring scholars to transcend the idea that the nonhuman world is devoid of meaning, value, and agency, and to cultivate new imaginaries of community, recognition, representation, and answerability (Gibson et al. 2015; Eckersley 2017; Burke and Fishel, Chapter 5). This expanded notion of environmental ethics and democracy is taking shape at a time when nature no longer works as a natural reference point for our scholarly pursuits, or as a given source of moral and political instruction (Wapner 2013). Instead, a post-natural version of environmentalism is unfolding, in which the very meaning of nature is open for debate.

It is too early to tell where this new generation of green political thinking will end up. As demonstrated in this book, the Anthropocene is an uncertain and risky proposition that calls many of our taken-for-granted assumptions, categories, and concepts into question. The vocabulary, ethics, and aesthetics of this hybrid era lack the stability and reassurance offered by more familiar narratives such as sustainable development or ecological modernization. While the ambivalence of the Anthropocene may frustrate scholars concerned with the mounting environmental challenges of our times, it can also be seen as an invitation to revisit and vitalize concepts central to green political thinking – nature, politics, power, democracy, justice, liberalism. The chapters included in this volume take important steps in that direction. The Anthropocene encounters made here draw upon a long tradition of green philosophy, ethics, and political theory. However, as old ideas are refashioned in response to changing ecological circumstances, novel tensions, contradictions, and disagreements come to the fore. To engage with the many ambiguities of the Anthropocene is challenging. It demands that political scholars take seriously scientific claims about nature's ending, but also critically interrogate their epistemological, political, and ethical foundations and implications. To some, this may appear as a dangerous distraction. However, as demonstrated by the chapters in this book, encountering the Anthropocene can also be an analytical possibility that may push green political thinking in unexpected and productive directions.

## References

Arias-Maldonado, Manuel. 2015. *Environment and Society: Socionatural Relations in the Anthropocene*. Cham: Springer.

Arias-Maldonado, Manuel, and Zev Trachtenberg, eds. Forthcoming. *Rethinking the Environment for the Anthropocene. Political Theory and Socionatural Relations in the New Geological Age*. London and New York: Routledge.

Asafu-Adjaye, John, Linus Blomqvist, Edwart Brand, et al. 2015. An Ecomodernist Manifesto. www.ecomodernism.org.

Barry, John. 1999. *Rethinking Green Politics*. London, Thousand Oaks and New Delhi: Sage Publications.

Baskin, Jeremy. 2015. Paradigm Dressed as Epoch: The Ideology of the Anthropocene. *Environmental Values* 24: 9–29.

Bennett, Jane. 2010. *Vibrant Matter: A Political Ecology of Things*. Durham: Duke University Press.
Biermann, Frank. 2014. *Earth System Governance: World Politics in the Anthropocene*. Cambridge, MA: MIT Press.
Biermann, Frank, Xuemei Bai, Ninad Bondre, et al. 2016. Down to Earth: Contextualizing the Anthropocene. *Global Environmental Change: Human and Policy Dimensions* 39: 341–350.
Blühdorn, Ingolfur. 2015. A Much Needed Renewal of Environmentalism? Eco-Politics in the Anthropocene. In *The Anthropocene and the Global Environmental Crisis. Rethinking Modernity in a New Epoch*, edited by Hamilton, Clive, Christophe Bonneuil and François Gemenne, 156–167. London and New York: Routledge.
Bonneuil, Christophe, and Jean-Baptiste Fressoz. 2015. *The Shock of the Anthropocene*. London and New York: Verso.
Brondizio, Eduardo S., Karen O'Brien, and Xuemei Bai. 2016. Re-conceptualizing the Anthropocene: A Call for Collaboration. *Global Environmental Change* 39: 318–327.
Burke, Anthony, Stefanie Fishel, Audra Mitchell, Simon Dalby, and Daniel Levine. 2016. Planet Politics: A Manifesto from the End of IR [International Relations]. *Millennium: Journal of International Studies* 44 (3): 499–523.
Chakrabarty, Dipesh. 2009. The Climate of History: Four Theses. *Critical Inquiry* 35 (2): 197–222.
Christoff, Peter, and Robyn Eckersley. 2013. *Globalization and the Environment*. Lanham, Boulder and New York; Rowman and Littlefield Publishers.
Clark, Nigel, and Yasmin Gunaratnam. 2017. Earthing the Anthropos? *European Journal of Social Theory* 20 (1): 1–18.
Clark, Nigel, and Kathryn Yusoff. 2017. Geosocial Formations and the Anthropocene. *Theory, Culture and Society* 34 (2–3): 3–23.
Crutzen, Paul, and Christian Schwägerl. 2011. Living in the Anthropocene: Towards a New Global Ethos. *Yale Environment 360*. http://e360.yale.edu/feature/living_in_the_an thropocene_toward_a_new_global_ethos/2363
Crutzen, Paul, and Eugene Stoermer, 2000. The "Anthropocene." *Global Change Newsletter* 41: 17–18.
Dalby, Simon. 2009. *Security and the Anthropocene*. Cambridge and Malden: Polity Press.
Dalby, Simon. 2014. Rethinking Geopolitics: Climate Security in the Anthropocene. *Global Policy* 5 (1): 1–9.
Dalby, Simon. 2016. Framing the Anthropocene: The Good, the Bad and the Ugly. *The Anthropocene Review* 3(1): 33–51.
Dauvergne, Peter. 2017. *Environmentalism of the Rich*. Cambridge MA and London: MIT Press.
Dibley, Ben. 2012. The Shape of Things to Come: Seven Theses on the Anthropocene and Attachment. *Australian Humanities Review* 52: 139–153.
Dobson, Andrew. 1990. *Green Political Thought*. London and New York: Routledge.
Eckersley, Robyn. 2004. *The Green State: Rethinking Democracy and Sovereignty*. Cambridge, MA: MIT Press.
Eckersley, Robyn. 2017. Geopolitan Democracy in the Anthropocene. *Political Studies* 65 (4): 983–999.
Future Earth. 2013. Future Earth *Initial Science Report*. Paris: International Council of Science.
Galaz, Victor. 2014. *Global Environmental Governance, Technology and Politics. The Anthropocene Gap*. Cheltenham: Edward Elgar Publishing.

Gibson, Katherine, Deborah Bird Rose, and Ruth Fincher, eds. 2015. *Manifesto for Living in the Anthropocene*. Brooklyn, NY: Punctum Books.

Glotfelty, Cheryll, and Harlond Fromm, eds. 1996. *The Ecocriticism Reader: Literary Studies in an Age of Environmental Crisis*. Athens: University of Georgia Press.

Hamilton, Clive. 2016. The Anthropocene as Rupture. *The Anthropocene Review* 3 (2): 93–106.

Hamilton, Clive. 2017. *Defiant Earth. The Faith of Humans in the Anthropocene*. Cambridge and Malden: Polity Press.

Hamilton, Clive, Christophe Bonneuil and François Gemenne, eds. 2015. *The Anthropocene and the Global Environmental Crisis*. London: Routledge.

Haraway, Donna J. 2016. *Staying with the Trouble. Making Kin in the Chthulucene*. Durham and London: Duke University Press.

Harrington, Cameron, and Clifford Shearing. 2017. *Security in the Anthropocene. Reflections on Safety and Care*. Bielefeld: Transcript Verlag.

Heise, Ursula K. 2008. *Sense of Place and Sense of Planet. The Environmental Imagination of the Global*. Oxford and New York: Oxford University Press.

Hickmann, Thomas, Lena Partzsch, Philipp Pattberg, and Sabine Weiland, eds. 2018. *The Anthropocene Debate and Political Science*. London and New York: Routledge.

Last, Angela. 2017. We Are the World? Anthropocene Cultural Production between Geopoetics and Geopolitics. *Theory, Culture and Society* 34 (2–3): 147–168.

Lepori, Matthew. 2015. There is No Anthropocene: Climate Change, Species-Talk, and Political Economy. *Telos* 172: 103–124.

Lewis, Simon, and Mark Maslin. 2015. Defining the Anthropocene. *Nature* 519: 171–180.

Lövbrand, Eva, Silke Beck, Jason Chilvers, et al. 2015. Who Speaks for the Future of Earth? How Critical Social Science Can Extend the Conversation on the Anthropocene. *Global Environmental Change* 32: 211–218.

Luke, Timothy. 2015. On the Politics of the Anthropocene. *Telos* 172: 139–162.

Malm, Andreas, and Alf Hornborg. 2014. The Geology of Mankind? A Critique of the Anthropocene Narrative. *The Anthropocene Review* 1 (1): 62–69.

Meadowcroft, James, and Daniel J. Fiorino, eds. 2017. *Conceptual Innovation in Environmental Policy*. Cambridge MA and London: The MIT Press.

Moore, Jason W., ed. 2016. *Anthropocene or Capitalocene? Nature, History, and the Crisis of Capitalism*. Oakland, CA: PM Press.

Nicholson, Simon, and Sikina Jinnah, eds. 2016. *New Earth Politics: Essays from the Anthropocene*. Cambridge MA and London: The MIT Press.

Park, Jacob, Ken Conca, and Mattias Finger, eds. 2008. *The Crisis of Global Environmental Governance. Towards a New Political Economy of Sustainability*. London and New York. Routledge.

Purdy, Jedediah. 2015. *After Nature. A Politics for the Anthropocene*. Cambridge MA and London: Harvard University Press.

Rockström, Johan, Will Steffen, Kevin J. Noone, et al. 2009. A Safe Operating Space for Humanity. *Nature* 461: 472–475.

Rose, Deborah Bird, Thom van Dooren, Matthew Chrulew, et al. 2012. Thinking through the Environment, Unsettling the Humanities. *Environmental Humanities* 1: 1–5.

Schellnhuber, Hans J. 1999. "Earth System" Analysis and the Second Copernican Revolution. Nature 402: C19–C23.

Steffen, Will, R. A. Sanderson, P. D. Tyson, et al. 2004. *Global Change and the Earth System*. Berlin: Springer.

Steffen, Will, Åsa Persson, Lisa Deutsch, et al. 2011. The Anthropocene: From Global Change to Planetary Stewardship. *Ambio* 40 (7): 739–761.

Steffen, Will, Reinhold Leinfelder, Jan Zalasiewicz, et al. 2016. Stratigraphic and Earth System Approaches to Defining the Anthropocene. *Earth's Future* 4 (8): 324–345.

Trachtenberg, Zev. 2015. The Anthropocene, Ethics and the Nature of Nature. *Telos* 172: 38–58.

Tsing, Anna. 2015. The Mushroom at the End of the World. On the Possibility of Life in Capitalist Ruins. Princeton: Princeton University Press.

Vince, Gaia. 2014. *Adventures in the Anthropocene. A Journey to the Heart of the Planet We Made*. London: Chatto and Windus.

Walters, William. 2012. *Governmentality: Critical Encounters*. London and New York: Routledge.

Wapner, Paul. 2013. *Living through the End of Nature. The Future of American Environmentalism*. Cambridge MA and London: The MIT Press.

Waters, Colin N., Jan Zalasiewicz, Colin Summerhayes, et al. 2016. The Anthropocene Is Functionally and Stratigraphically Distinct from the Holocene. *Science* 351 (6269): 137.

World Bank. 2008. *World Development Indicators 2008*. Washington, DC: International Bank for Reconstruction and Development/The World Bank.

Zalasiewicz, Jan, Mark Williams, Will Steffen, and Paul Crutzen. 2010. The New World of the Anthropocene. *Environmental Science and Technology* 44: 2228–2231.

Zalasiewicz, Jan, Will Steffen, Reinhold Leinfelder, et al. 2017. Petrifying Earth Process: The Stratigraphic Imprint of Key Earth System Parameters in the Anthropocene. *Theory, Culture and Society* 34 (2–3): 83–104.

# Part I

The Conceptual Politics of the Anthropocene: Science, Philosophy, and Culture

# 2

# The "Anthropocene" in Global Change Science: Expertise, the Earth, and the Future of Humanity

NOEL CASTREE

The Anthropocene is currently a *buzzword*. The neologism now circulates far and wide – and not only in academia, from whence (to little initial fanfare) it originated nineteen years ago (Crutzen and Stoermer 2000). Soon it might become a *keyword*: that is, one of those terms that are absolutely central to the way we understand ourselves and the world in which we live. Its rapid rise to prominence since about 2010 is due to three things.

First, it signifies a striking and unprecedented development in the relationship between people and planet. For the first time, there is strong evidence to suggest that humans are changing the nature of *all* of the earth's constituent spheres. It turns out that anthropogenic climate change, one of the defining problems of our time, is but one element of a much larger story. Second, the evidence for the Anthropocene's onset has been presented by international groups of geoscientists. Though the cultural authority of science is not what it was twenty or thirty years ago, it remains sufficiently high that when numerous credentialized experts speak with one voice, people tend to listen (even if not everyone believes the messages being conveyed). Third, the credibility of these experts' epochal claims has been enhanced by over three decades of prior research, media reporting, and political action relating to large-scale anthropogenic environmental changes – not only atmospheric warming, but also ozone layer thinning, ice sheet melting, deforestation, and overfishing (among others). These well-documented and widely publicized changes mean that when various geoscientists now declare the end of the Holocene – the 11,700-year period during which *Homo sapiens* have flourished – only a relative minority simply scoff in disbelief.

This chapter has two aims, one exegetical and the other evaluative. First, I detail the scientific origins and content of the "Anthropocene hypothesis." I do so because the wider social credibility of the Anthropocene concept – today and in the future – rests almost entirely on the perceived quality of the underpinning science. Yet few people outside science have the time or inclination to read the scientific literature, while digests of the research are frequently partial and journalistic (see Biermann and Lövbrand, Chapter 1). Anthropocene science has two arms, one stratigraphic and the other not.[1] What unites them, as we will see, is the claim that "planetary nature" is no longer natural (or, at least, is significantly less so than heretofore). Disagreements exist about the onset date, and precise magnitude of, this denaturalization of the earth. Nonetheless, the scientists involved place an analytical premium on revealing humanity's capacity to instigate more than incremental planetary change.

Though a number of summaries of the science now exist (e.g., Steffen et al. 2016), few, if any, approach it through the underpinning concept of nature and its epistemic framing.[2] More common is the practice of using the science to explore the ethical and management issues of life in a post-natural world (e.g., Maris 2015; Arias-Maldonado, Chapter 3). Yet, the mounting evidence for planetary change makes little sense without a set of prior assumptions about what is natural – in both a historical and an ontological sense – and what is artificial or modified. These assumptions, just as much as the scientific evidence that suggests their "material reality," deserve to be understood and scrutinized. The social efficacy of the assumptions will be central to determining whether "the Anthropocene" becomes, in future, a keyword animating the discourses of politics, business, and civil society. The assumptions have a particular relevance to environmental theory and politics because "nature" remains such a foundational concept for both. That is precisely why this book has been conceived and published.

I am an environmental social scientist with long-standing interests in geoscience and in how what we by convention call nature is represented in modern societies.[3] I write as neither an uncritical believer in, nor a skeptic about, the science. I show how and why geoscientists in various disciplines have been speaking for the earth in the particular ways they have in recent years. As I will explain, the "onset" of the Anthropocene is not simply a scientific question: the science is inevitably freighted with extrascientific *baggage* rather than simply having extrascientific *implications*

---

[1] "Anthropocene science" is my term (though I discovered after writing this chapter that Christophe Bonneuil (2015) uses it too), while the term "global change science" is more conventional: it refers to any scientific attempt to understand the dynamics of global environmental change – primarily its biophysical elements, but also the "human drivers." It covers both stratigraphy and earth system science, more about which to follow. In this chapter, when I use the term "geoscience," I am referring to any and all areas of earth surface science (e.g., geomorphology) as they pertain to the study of humanly caused global change. While not all geoscientists study anthropogenic planetary change, a significant minority do just this.

[2] Though some have written about nature in the Anthropocene – Wapner (2014; see also chapter 11) and Hettinger (2014) are prime examples – few, if any, do so by examining how nature is referenced within Anthropocene science publications. An exception is the paper by Jeremy Baskin (2015) about what he calls "the ideology of the Anthropocene."

[3] See, for instance, Castree (2014 and 2015a, b, and c). I am in good company: over the last two decades, Soper (1995), Cronon (1996), and Hull (2006) are among a number of authors who have written and edited insightful books about nature as both an idea and a realm of processes and entities independent of human conceptions, perceptions, and actions.

after the proverbial fact. This speaks to my second aim: to give readers the tools necessary to be neither passive recipients of geoscientific claims nor overzealous critics doubtful about these claims' robustness. Even if we were to query the science (on evidential or ontological grounds), we might still have very good reasons to take very seriously the normative implications of what people are currently doing to the planet. Likewise, even if we accept the assumptions, findings, and predictions of the science, its implications can only be understood in extrascientific contexts without which science loses all meaning and purpose. Either way, I will argue, a set of arguments about "nature" are in play that are irreducible to their scientific components yet which would lack public credibility without being advanced by geoscientists in the first instance.

The formal study of political reasoning, political institutions, public debate, and political decision-making is one of the many contexts in which geoscientific claims about the earth assume wider significance. Such study can help to shape the wider "Anthropo(s)cene" (Castree 2015a): that is, the plethora of discourses (and linked policy proposals along with technical interventions) about people–planet relationships inspired by the science of the Anthropocene. More specifically, it can help societies navigate between the now familiar – and paralyzing – alternatives of a "scientized politics" and a "politicized science." But that is only possible if we develop a reflexive relationship to Anthropocene science. This chapter seeks to foster such a relationship among its readers on the basis of a clear understanding of the science's cognitive *and* normative content.

## Anthropocene Science

### *A Speculative Proposition: Can Humans Change Planetary History?*

The Anthropocene means "the age of humans." It is an arresting word because it uses a suffix normally employed in nomenclature designed to describe extremely large-scale biophysical changes – ones that, in the earth's 4.5-billion-year history, have not involved humans at all. In the discipline of geology, technical terms such as Miocene and Pleistocene delineate specific phases of planetary change and stability caused by "endogenous" and "exogenous" natural forces. The asteroid impact believed to have caused the extinction of the dinosaurs is one such force. Consequently, when the Dutch chemist and Nobel Laureate Paul Crutzen objected to continued use of the term "the Holocene" – at an International Geosphere-Biosphere Programme meeting in February 2000 – he was being deliberately subversive and provocative. His subsequent short articles in the program's *Global Change Newsletter* (Crutzen and Stoermer 2000) and in *Nature* (Crutzen 2002) helped to disseminate the proposition that humans were significantly altering not only the atmosphere but also – simultaneously – the cryosphere, lithosphere, hydrosphere, and biosphere.

Crutzen himself lacked the expertise to test his own (very grand) proposition. But he was vice-chair of the International Geosphere-Biosphere Programme, an international global change research program established in 1986. By 2000, the program had brought geoscientists across the disciplines – and nations – together over a period of years to work on a set of novel integrative research projects. The projects were innovative because the program's aim was uniquely ambitious. As its first executive director put it in the inaugural *Global Change Newsletter*:

The IGBP [International Geosphere-Biosphere Programme] objectives are to describe and understand the interactive physical, chemical, and biological processes that regulate the total Earth system, the unique environment that it provides for life, the changes that are occurring in this system, and the manner in which they are influenced by human action.

*(Roswell 1989: 2)*

In other words, the program was designed to produce new knowledge of the contemporary earth as a complex, integrated entity, with humans regarded as a significant component. Given this, Crutzen's neologism can be seen, with hindsight, as both a result of the program's first decade of scientific endeavor and an incitement for program participants to put empirical flesh on the conceptual bones of his epochal claim. In 2002, the International Geosphere-Biosphere Programme joined the three other international programs investigating global change – namely, the World Climate Research Programme, the International Human Dimensions Programme on Global Environmental Change, and Diversitas – in a so-called Earth System Science Partnership designed to produce greater integration between research projects on planetwide changes.[4]

In the years immediately after the term "the Anthropocene" was coined, leading scholars of the International Geosphere-Biosphere Programme provided a preliminary response to the question "Is the Holocene ending?" It took the form of a large synthesis published as a book in 2004 by American-Australian climate scientist Will Steffen and others, entitled *Global Change and the Earth System*. This 311-page volume linked evidence of environmental stability and change across all the earth's subsystems to the concept of a "natural" and "anthropogenically" altered earth system. As the book progressed, it contrasted a "human-

---

[4] The World Climate Research Programme was created in 1980. It was followed by the International Human Dimensions Programme on Global Environmental Change (1990, relaunched in 1996) and Diversitas (launched in 1991 and focusing on global biodiversity and biogeography). The Earth System Science Partnership emerged from an open science conference in Amsterdam in 2001 where scientists in all four programs came together. The latter two, with the International Geosphere-Biosphere Programme, have been folded into the new Future Earth research program, which is in its early stages (see for more detail Beck, chapter 10), even though it takes forward a set of existing projects from the three previous programs as well as introducing some new ones.

dominated planet" with a "nature-dominated" one. In an often-cited passage, the authors concluded that

Human changes to the Earth System are multiple, complex, interacting, often exponential in rate and globally significant in magnitude. They affect every Earth System component—land, coastal zone, atmosphere and oceans ... Today, humankind has begun to match and even exceed some of the great forces of nature ... [T]he Earth System is now in a no analogue situation, best referred to as a new era in geological history, the Anthropocene.

*(Steffen et al. 2004: 81)*

*Global Change and the Earth System* was among the first attempts to offer a holistic conceptual *and* empirical understanding of the planet as a single system in which humans are shown to be a key global (as opposed to local or regional) influence. It was, in other words, an early example of what is today known as earth system science.[5]

So much for the scientific backstory. Over the last ten years, two intersecting areas of science have sought to ascertain the "reality" of the Holocene's end. One emerged out of the International Geosphere-Biosphere Programme, and more broadly earth system science; the other from geology. Both fields of science have benefited enormously from the improved quality and quantity of earth surface data now available and the large improvements in computational modeling of earth surface dynamics (past, present, and predicted). Let us consider each in turn.

## *Testing the Proposition: Stratigraphic Research into a Holocene–Anthropocene Boundary*

The Anthropocene concept refers to recent and ongoing changes to the earth's outer layer. In the context of the planet's 4.5-billion-year history, these changes are occurring in the blink of a proverbial eye. Yet, it is arguably no surprise that a number of geologists – whose concern is normally with "deep time" – have become key scholars in Anthropocene science since around 2005. I say this for two reasons. First, Crutzen's use of the suffix "cene" in 2000, and its subsequent circulation in International Geosphere-Biosphere Programme

---

[5] For some, earth system science is synonymous with "global change science" or else describes research informed by complex system thinking applied at a planetary scale. However, others take a less strict view, presenting earth system science (ESS) as any research into global environmental change that is pursued in a scientific fashion (Mooney et al. 2014). In this chapter I take the latter view, not least because not all members of the Anthropocene Working Group – to be discussed later – see themselves as earth system scientists. However, in a more strict sense ESS first flourished in the early 2000s. When Steffen et al.'s book was published, and during the years immediately after, a raft of texts appeared that sought to depict the earth's outer layer as an integrated, complex system. Some were by continental European authors, others by North American ones. See Butz (2004), Clark et al. (2004), Ehlers et al. (2006), Hergarten (2002), Kump et al. (2004), and Neugebauer and Simmer (2003). Over a decade on, a leading former International Geosphere-Biosphere Programme scientist, Kevin Noone, noted that "Earth system science has gone from being an oddball notion to becoming recognized as a paradigm necessary for us to make progress on the 'wicked problems' facing society today" (Liss et al., 2015: 10). For a full history of ESS in the strict sense of the term, see the PhD thesis published by O. Uhrqvist (2014).

networks, spoke directly to geologists' preoccupation with qualitative shifts in the earth's normally slow evolution. Second, though rapid in geological terms, the scale, scope, and magnitude of human-induced changes to the earth's constituent spheres may now be akin to a "great force of nature" (to use a term favored by Crutzen, Steffen, and other researchers from the International Geosphere-Biosphere Programme in many of their publications). In other words, though geologists normally study natural endogenous and exogenous drivers of planetary change, contemporary *Homo sapiens* might legitimately be considered a "geological actor" (as per *Global Change and the Earth System* and subsequent publications in this vein).

By 2005, the "Anthropocene" concept had been noticed by a British geologist at Leicester University, Jan Zalasiewicz. At that time, he was chair of the Stratigraphy Commission of the Geological Society in London. He proposed to the other twenty commission members that the Anthropocene proposition should and could be tested using formal geological criteria for the identification of an epoch. The result was a coauthored article that appeared in *GSA Today*, the house periodical of the Geological Society of America (Zalasiewicz et al. 2008). Entitled "Are we now living in the Anthropocene?", it detailed the measures necessary to establish whether and when the Holocene had ended. To quote from it at some length,

Earth has endured changes sufficient to leave a global stratigraphic signature distinct from that of the Holocene or previous Pleistocene inter-glacial phases, encompassing novel biotic, sedimentary, and geochemical change. These changes, though likely only in their initial phases, are sufficiently distinct and robustly established for suggestions of a Holocene-Anthropocene boundary in the recent historical past to be geologically reasonable. The boundary may either be defined through a Global Stratigraphic Section and Point ("golden spike") location or by adopting a numerical date.

*(Zalasiewicz et al. 2008: 4)*

As a result of this paper and subsequent discussions among the academic networks of commission members, a subcommission of the International Commission on Stratigraphy – which is ultimately responsible for identifying geological epochs – established an Anthropocene Working Group in 2009. It appointed as chair Zalasiewicz, who was a member of the subcommission at that time. Since its formation, group members have worked tirelessly to assemble and assess evidence for possible stratigraphic markers of the Anthropocene's onset. In the context of geology as a discipline, their inquiries have been highly unusual for one obvious reason: most previous shifts in earth history have produced an enduring signal in rock layers, whereas human impacts on earth are so geologically recent that a globally synchronous signal likely to endure beyond this (or the next) century may not exist. Accordingly, not all group members are geologists or, more

specifically, stratigraphers (the membership can be found here: http://quaternary
.stratigraphy.org/workinggroups/anthropocene).

The group has broken new ground in trying to study a potential geological epoch that is still in formation: it is engaged in "real-time geology," as it were. Only in thousands of years' time might future geologists (if there are any) confirm that any markers the Anthropocene Working Group identifies as important today are, in fact, geologically significant: the markers are currently non-lithified. In 2015 and 2016, the group recommended that the period immediately after 1945 be considered the potential "base" of the Anthropocene (Zalasiewicz et al. 2015; Waters et al. 2016). During that period, it argues, there is clear evidence of new planetwide anthropogenic changes, such as the deposition of artificial radionuclides from testing weapons of mass destruction. This evidence, the group claims, indicates an alteration to the earth system when compared with Holocene norms.

At the time of writing, the group has not made a formal submission to the Subcommission on Quaternary Stratigraphy. If and when it does, the subcommission will assess the case and may reject it. If it accepts the plausibility of the case, it will make a positive recommendation to the International Commission on Stratigraphy, whose many members could decide to either endorse or reject the case for the Anthropocene. Currently, the prospects for endorsement look slim for several reasons. One is that the current chair of the International Commission on Stratigraphy, Stan Finney, has recently gone on record to question whether "the Anthropocene" can be a legitimate scientific concern for geologists (Finney and Edwards 2016). Another reason is that some senior Quaternary scientists have also doubted the wisdom of seeking to formalize the Anthropocene as a geological epoch (e.g., Gibbard and Walker 2013). The Anthropocene may be an idea before its geological time. In geographer Jamie Lorimer's (2017: 5) felicitous words, "the ICS [International Commission on Stratigraphy] will be asked to pronounce with unaccustomed speed on a new epoch whose evidentiary base is alien to the epistemic conventions of stratigraphy." Even so, the Anthropocene Working Group has now achieved sufficient scientific momentum and prominence that the possibility of the Holocene's end is considered by some geologists to be a realistic one. As Jeremy Baskin (2015: 10) notes, "The conceptual horse has bolted and the 'Anthropocene' is being widely adopted" in Quaternary stratigraphy.

### *A New Earth System State?*

Parallel to – and, as we shall see, sometimes as part of – the stratigraphic science pursued by the Anthropocene Working Group, several earth system scientists associated with the International Geosphere-Biosphere Programme and the Earth System Science Partnership have also concluded that the Anthropocene is a scientifically credible concept. However, because they are not bound by the rigors of stratigraphy – with its exacting criteria for identifying a Global Stratotype Section and Point and a Global Standard Stratigraphic Age – these scientists have been more free to venture claims about qualitative changes to the earth system.

Since 2010, these claims have been expressed in a series of published articles about two phenomena: the so-called "Great Acceleration" and so-called "planetary boundaries." In almost all cases, the Australian National University climate scientist Will Steffen has been a key author: he was the director of the International Geosphere-Biosphere Programme from 1998 to 2004 and lead author of *Global Change and the Earth System*. In their publications, Steffen and others use a battery of data about observed changes to both what they call "the human enterprise" and the earth's component subsystems. The objective has been to "formalize" the Anthropocene in a sense akin to how the Neolithic and the Bronze Age have become recognized terms in archaeology and beyond. As scientists who are building the ship of earth system science as they sail, they are not beholden to their predecessors in the way the Anthropocene Working Group's inquiries are beholden to the strictures of the International Commission on Stratigraphy.

A recent paper in *The Anthropocene Review* illustrates the way scientists from the International Geosphere-Biosphere Programme have tried to demonstrate earth system change "beyond the range of variability of the Holocene and driven by human activities" (Steffen et al. 2015a: 81). Using a wide variety of secondary data, the authors demonstrate a Great Acceleration after 1950 in terms of the size and rate of change to both "the human enterprise" and earth surface phenomena. Twelve indicators are used for the two interlinked "systems" (the human and the biophysical) – for instance, population growth and tropical forest clearance. These indicators are compared, where possible, with data for the Holocene period. The conclusion is that "only beyond the mid-20$^{th}$ century [is] ... there clear evidence of fundamental shifts in the state and functioning of the Earth System" (Steffen et al. 2015a: 86). This, the authors argue, means that by virtue of their activities, contemporary humans must now be seen *as part of* the earth system, not an "external force" that merely "perturbs" it.

Another example of earth system scientists proclaiming the Holocene's imminent eclipse is a 2015 paper on "planetary boundaries" (Steffen et al. 2015b). The concept was first coined in 2009 by Johan Rockström and colleagues, who used it to identify key global environment components constitutive of the earth system. Represented in a now familiar diagram (Figure 2.1), these planetary boundaries pertained to climate, ocean acidity, chemical balances, atmospheric aerosols, biodiversity, land use types, freshwater, nitrogen and phosphorus cycles, and stratospheric ozone density. For seven boundaries, Rockström and colleagues specified a quantitative boundary, the crossing of which might take the system beyond Holocene norms (for the remaining two, they were unable, in 2009, to quantify the boundary).

Together, the nine boundaries comprise what Rockström and colleagues called "a safe operating space for humanity" (2009: 472). Modern humans, they argued, have already transgressed several of these. Recognizing that "[d]etermining a safe distance involves normative judgements of how societies choose to deal with risk and uncertainty," they nonetheless commended their "new approach to defining biophysical preconditions for human development" (Rockström et al. 2009: 472 and 474). The more recent paper by Steffen and colleagues (2015b) highlights two especially critical boundaries, the transgression of which may be amplified through the seven others and thus take the earth system into a new post-Holocene state. Where "the Great Acceleration" paper, discussed earlier, details human activities, the planetary boundaries paper of Steffen and colleagues focuses solely on earth surface change using – again – secondary data in the context of expert judgements about how tolerant of change earth subsystems are likely to be.

To date, and unlike the response of some geologists to the Anthropocene Working Group's endeavors, the Anthropocene claims of Steffen, Rockström, and other earth system scientists have not been met with sharp criticism in the wider sciences of the physical environment. In large part, we might surmise, this is because these researchers do not have to conform to preestablished criteria for what can evidence "epochal change." Instead, they get to both create and apply evidential standards as to what counts as a phase shift in the earth system.

## *Stratigraphy Meets Earth System Science*

Despite their slightly different emphases, what unites these various analyses is a set of earth system ideas used to interpret factual information about planetary change. These include the concepts of "earth system states" (or regimes), subsystems and complexity, force and response, negative and positive feedbacks, stability and transition, natural and human forces, and – reflecting wider developments in systems thinking since the 1970s – tipping points. With supporting evidence, these concepts are used to show that humans are now driving the earth system in a new direction without entirely being able to control the metaphorical vehicle.

It is, perhaps, no surprise that scientists from the International Geosphere-Biosphere Programme such as Steffen have both informed the stratigraphic science summarized in the previous subsection and also drawn on it. As noted before, the unique remit of the Anthropocene Working Group has meant that its membership extends outside geology. Given their prominence within the International Geosphere-Biosphere Programme, both Steffen and Crutzen engaged with Jan Zalasiewicz early on, once

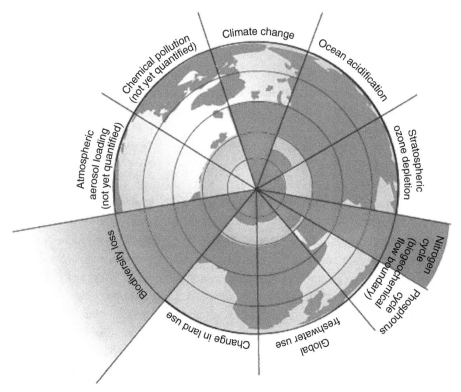

Figure 2.1 Humanity's proximity to planetary boundaries (reproduced with permission from Rockström et al. 2009, design by Azote Images/Stockholm Resilience Centre).

the Anthropocene Working Group was proposed in 2008. They came together in a short 2010 article on the Anthropocene (Zalasiewicz et al. 2010), in a special issue of the *Philosophical Transactions of the Royal Society* A (vol. 369, issue 1938, 2011), and – that same year – in a major article in the journal *Ambio* (Steffen et al. 2011). Since then they have collaborated routinely, not least because Steffen, Crutzen, and another former lead player of the International Geosphere-Biosphere Programme – James Syvitski – are all members of the Anthropocene Working Group.

One result in the string of publications authored by this group is that the term "the earth system" is used frequently when describing stratigraphic questions. Meanwhile, earth surface data assembled and evaluated by the Anthropocene Working Group has been used by Steffen and other earth system scientists in their recent papers on the Great Acceleration and planetary boundaries. A new article in the journal *Earth's Future* by the key scholars (Steffen et al. 2016) formally examines the character of, and relationship between, the two approaches to planetary change.

## The "Nature" of Earth System Change

As we have seen, the aim of Anthropocene science, in its several forms, is to determine the magnitude and rate of anthropogenic change to the earth system. The overriding reason why the science has received so much recent attention outside scientific circles is because it takes seriously something scarcely thought possible even twenty years ago: namely, that *Homo sapiens* can now alter nature not only in a laboratory or on a farm or even at an ecosystem level but at *a planetary scale and irreversibly so*. As Crutzen and Christian Schwagerl put it, in a much-quoted statement, "It is no longer us against 'Nature'. Instead, it's we who decide what nature is and what it will be" (2011: np). When environmentalist Bill McKibben (1989) lamented "the end of nature" thirty years ago, some felt he was overstating the case. But today, with geoscientists in the vanguard, the profundity of this "fact" explains why a book like this one has been published.

Because they are well aware of the momentous extrascientific implications of their research, many Anthropocene scientists have become preoccupied with establishing the "correct" onset date of the Anthropocene. For my purposes, this is interesting not so much for the scientific questions at stake as for what it reveals about the underlying ontological assumptions in play. By rehearsing one part of the "timing debate," I will now make those assumptions manifest. As we shall see, this affects how nonscientists should judge the significance of Anthropocene science.

### *What Is in a Date?*

A recent exchange in the pages of *The Anthropocene Review* reveals some very sharp scientific disagreements about when the Holocene (may have) ended. It involves the Australian economist, philosopher, and environmentalist Clive Hamilton – speaking for earth system science – and the British geographers Simon Lewis and Mark Maslin – writing with an eye on the requirements of the International Commission on Stratigraphy. The exchange was sparked by Maslin and Lewis's major paper published in *Nature*, entitled "Defining the Anthropocene" (2015). In the article, they consider the several possible onset dates of the Anthropocene proposed by the Anthropocene Working Group, earth system scientists, and others such as the historical climatologist Bill Ruddiman (who has talked of an "early Anthropocene" beginning in the early Middle Ages or before; e.g., Ruddiman 2013). In the piece, Lewis and Maslin carefully sift the evidence and conclude that only 1610 and 1964 could – according to Global Stratotype Section and Point criteria – count as inception dates. In the first of these two years, global carbon dioxide levels dropped significantly because of revegetation of the New World (linked with European colonialism and the trans-

Atlantic transfer of diseases). In the second, a peak global radionuclide signal was left by successive nuclear bomb detonations.

In his commentary "Getting the Anthropocene so wrong," Hamilton (2015) criticizes both scientists. For him, they mistake global signs of the human impact on earth for anthropogenic changes to the earth system. Though the latter were not at all evident in 1610, Hamilton argues, they were already occurring by 1964. Like various Anthropocene Working Group members (including Steffen and Crutzen), Hamilton dates the onset of the Anthropocene to 1945. In his view, Lewis and Maslin are blissfully unaware of the earth system concept and – as their 1610 date suggestion indicates to him – confuse *anthropogenic environmental change* with *humanly induced planetary change*. For Hamilton, the mere existence of a "global signal" is not at all the same as an anthropogenic global *impact*. In their response, Maslin and Lewis (2015) deny any ignorance of earth system thinking and point out that stratigraphic boundaries are usually markers of systemic change, not merely "disturbances" within system boundaries.

What is at stake in this dating dispute, beyond "interpreting the evidence correctly"? For the disputants, the answer is: a scientifically grounded capacity to identify which humans (when and where) are responsible for planetary change, with all this implies for how such change might be mitigated and managed (see Baskin, Chapter 8). For instance, choosing 1610 does not only reveal the global effects of early overseas trade and settlement, but implies – as Ruddiman's research does – that if humans were *already* global actors hundreds of years ago, then contemporary humans must be orders of magnitude *more* transformative of the earth system. By contrast, Hamilton regards selecting a pre-1945 date as not only scientifically wrong but politically problematic. For him, it is a "deflationary move" (Hamilton and Grinevald 2015: 60) in two senses: not only does it "gradualize" anthropogenic impacts on earth ("we've been doing this for centuries so present impacts are more of the same, just cumulatively bigger"); it also severely underplays "the suddenness, severity, duration and irreversibility" (Hamilton and Grinevald 2015: 66–67) of the biophysical changes occurring since 1945. In Hamilton's view, then, embracing the earth system approach directs us not to the last few hundred years – which has seen the passing of numerous forms of human society – but to the last few decades, when a small number of advanced capitalist societies have unwittingly altered planetary evolution.

I will not seek to adjudicate between the various scientists involved in the dating dispute.[6] The key point is this: claims like Hamilton's, vouchsafed by earth system

---

[6] Indeed, I will argue that the dating dispute is not only a "scientific question" and thus does not admit of a definitive scientific answer – this is because a set of assumptions about "significant change" are in play in any attempt to determine when the Anthropocene began, and these assumptions reflect social appraisals of how *much* change "matters."

science, rest on a set of judgements about when "unnatural history" begins which themselves rest upon beliefs about the nature of nature. It is to those beliefs that we now turn, since, without them, evidence of "planetary change" would quite literally be meaningless. Environmental change per se is not always considered a change to "nature," or if it is, then not always to the same degree or extent; yet the Anthropocene concept posits the emergence of a *post-natural globe* either in degree or in kind.

## What Counts as "System Change"? When Does an Earth Epoch End?

The history of the earth is a history of perpetual change: the geological record tells us as much. At a planetary scale, nature – left to its own devices – has evolved the most intricate and complex processes and phenomena (including *Homo sapiens* as a species). If, as is clear from the two branches of Anthropocene science, the Anthropocene is understood to mark the end of earth's *natural* history, then what, exactly, has ended, and why does it matter? How much change is considered enough to make global nature into something qualitatively new or at least generative of novel societal impacts?

"Nature" has been a keyword in European societies and their former colonies for over two centuries (Williams 1976). In a semantic sense it is, we might say, a quintessentially *ontological* word: its many meanings tend to denote things believed to be real, regardless of human perceptions, opinions, or beliefs. It seems that "nature" has four principal meanings, all of which are quite venerable and familiar to people in Anglo-European societies (Castree 2014 – see Figure 2.2). These meanings frequently attach to "collateral words," such as biology, matter, "race," environment, and genes. First, "nature" denotes the *nonhuman world*, especially those parts untouched or barely affected by humans ("the natural environment"). Second, it signifies the *entire physical world*, including humans as biological entities and products of evolutionary history. Third, it means the *essential quality or defining property of something* (e.g., it is natural for birds to fly, fish to swim, and people to walk on two legs). This third meaning crosscuts the first two, bringing human and nonhuman nature into a single categorical space. Finally, it refers to the *power or force governing some or all living things* (such as gravity, the conservation of energy, the instructions contained in human DNA, or the Coriolis effect). As shorthand, we can (respectively) call these meanings "external nature," "universal nature," "intrinsic nature," and "superordinate nature" (see Figure 2.2). Their differences notwithstanding, a common semantic denominator is that nature is defined by the absence of human agency or by what remains (or endures) once human agents have altered natural processes and phenomena. In Jacques Pollini's (2013: 26, emphasis added) apt words, "Nature ... is

| NATURE | | | |
|---|---|---|---|
| The nonhuman world of living and inanimate phenomena, be they "pristine" or modified. | The physical world in its entirety, including human beings as both products of natural history and as biological organisms. | The defining features or distinguishing quality of living and inanimate phenomena, including human beings. | The power, force or organising principle animating living phenomena and operating in or on inanimate phenomena. |
| "EXTERNAL NATURE" | "UNIVERSAL NATURE" | "INTRINSIC NATURE" | "SUPERORDINATE NATURE" |

Figure 2.2 The principal meanings of the word nature in contemporary Anglo-European societies (reproduced from Castree 2014).

considered as a world out there . . . that is not the outcome of human activities. *It's non-social by definition*." Since the European Enlightenment, of course, science has been perceived as the window through which to view the true nature of nature. Today, many still consider it the epistemological means whereby nature's ontological actualities can be made manifest, from the molecular to the cosmic scale.

In this context, it seems clear that Anthropocene scientists interpret evidence of earth surface change as pointing to a new human–nature hybrid in all four senses. This follows from the encompassing character of the earth system concept and from the rigors of stratigraphic dating. It is what makes the Anthropocene proposition such an arresting one: nothing, it seems, is immune to human influence any more. The Holocene baseline is taken as a "natural" reference point against which to compare "epochal change." It is taken as the most recent period in earth history where natural processes, causes, effects, and feedbacks have together governed the character of the planet's constituent subsystems. Today, the earth system is seen to be (i) no longer external to human societies, (ii) universally affected by those societies (since no part of the system is now immune to influence), and (iii) moving towards a new operating state (thus losing many of the "intrinsic" properties characteristic of the last 11,700 years), and (iv) in that new state, its superordinate forces are being redirected by human actions, possibly crossing thresholds in the centuries immediately ahead. This means that, at the planetary scale, a new biophysical actor that is not "natural" – or not natural in the same sense as ocean currents and carbon cycles are – is now *a component of* the earth system rather than subsumed by it. In other words, the society–nature dualism – whose local transgression is so familiar to us (think of genetically modified organisms or artificial wetlands) – is now compromised "all the way out and up." This implies that a new hybrid world is coming into being (Arias-Maldonado, Chapter 3). Less dramatically, Anthropocene science tells us that, at the very least, the zone marked "nature" is rapidly shrinking at *all* spatiotemporal scales. In this more moderate view, a powerful and lively nature endures but is having to adapt to escalating human impacts.

Of course, the scientists in question do not systematically distinguish the four meanings of nature in their various observations about earth past, earth present, and possible earth futures. This is because, as noted, the quintet is contained within the concept of the (pre-humanly altered) earth system, while specific meanings are manifest when Anthropocene scientists use the words nature, environment, earth, planet, and so on in their published papers. The "end of global nature" is thus reported in the research literature without recourse to mentioning each dimension of nature separately. Some quick examples will have to suffice to illustrate this. Steffen and colleagues (2016: 324) recently suggested that "the Earth may be approaching a third fundamental stage of evolution because of a wide range of human pressures." A year earlier, Steffen and colleagues (2015) asserted that "there is clear evidence for fundamental shifts in . . . the Earth System . . . driven by human activity and not by natural variability" (2015a: 13). Finally, in one of several recent papers, the Anthropocene Working Group concludes that "human changes [to earth] . . . are so extensive that it is reasonable to suggest that the biosphere has made one of the greatest transitions in the history of life" (Williams et al. 2016: 49). In all three cases, the status of nature as external, as a totality beyond the realm of human influence, as possessed of intrinsic qualities, and as a superordinate power is clearly called into question by the force of human intervention.

All this implies a new ontological monism, albeit one characterized by complexity and differentiation, not simplicity or harmony. The momentous nature of this insight into a "new reality" – what Valenti Rull (2016) calls "the humanized Earth System" – animates the dating dispute recounted above. Likewise, the Anthropocene Working Group recommendation is an attempt to "officially" demonstrate to nonscientists that the new "unnatural" epoch has begun. Meanwhile, the planetary boundaries concept, with its notion of a "safe operating space" for humanity, is an attempt to quantify how far towards "points of no return" the earth system is currently being pushed compared with the last 11,700 years.

In all cases, ontological claims about *qualitative change* are posited. These claims are presented in a realist mode as representing objectively occurring alterations: "the *concept* of nature is now outdated because, *in reality*, nature is increasingly a thing of the past – at all points of the compass!" The changes will be ongoing, and possibly both large and abrupt if boundaries are transgressed and tipping points are overshot. No wonder Anthropocene science is so attention grabbing for those outside science, like most readers of this volume. It raises very large questions about human agency and human responsibility, as well as about the autonomy, agency, and value of the nonhuman (see Arias-Maldonado, Chapter 3; Baskin, Chapter 8; Wapner, Chapter 11). It also raises organizational, technical, distributional, and temporal questions about whether, and how, societies can cope with, and consciously influence, future global environmental change. The questions are begged, because science retains considerable legitimacy as a "truth-seeking" enterprise perceived to be freer from bias and error than most other human endeavors.

## Post-natural "Realities": How Should Green Theory and Politics Respond to the Anthropocene?

I have summarized Anthropocene science and shown how it pivots on historical and ontological claims about the end of nature. In this final section of the chapter, I consider how nonscientists might want to respond to the science and its significant implications for present-day humanity.

To speak for the earth in its totality is an extraordinary act of epistemological representation. In the early twenty-first century, it comes with a huge burden of responsibility: "speaking out" about the state of the planet is not something many geoscientists are accustomed to, since it involves normative judgements about risk and harm. Anthropocene scientists, as we have seen, are adducing as much evidence as they can to make visible earth system changes that are utterly imperceptible to the naked eye or to most people "on the ground." To adapt Karl Marx's famous saying, "The earth system cannot represent itself: it must be represented!" Anthropocene scientists are representing in good faith: there is no reason to believe otherwise, even though some geoscientists worry that the science is led too much by barely concealed political values (see, for instance, Finney and Edwards 2016). The scientists observe, they measure, they compare past and present, and they make plausible predictions about earth system futures. They are metaphorical canaries alerting the rest of us to changes that, in their view, are worthy of very serious attention – be we academic researchers, political decision-makers, business executives, religious leaders, or ordinary citizens. Should we trust Anthropocene scientists, wait for more of a scientific consensus, or take an altogether different stance? Specifically, what should "people like us" – that is, social scientists and humanists – do with the insights provided by Anthropocene science?

### *The Anthropocene in Social Science and Humanities Scholarship*

In recent years, a small but increasingly visible group of social scientists and humanists (including myself; e.g., Castree 2017a and b) have paid close attention to the implications of Anthropocene science for people. We can learn some useful things by attending to the manner of their responses – though I do not have the space here to offer more than a brief sketch. Note that I do not consider the research of the relative minority of practitioners who actively collaborate with geoscientists in interdisciplinary global change research (e.g., within the various Future Earth projects; see Beck, Chapter 10).

A number of commentators in the "people disciplines" have sought to rethink their philosophical, analytical, and methodological "common sense" by virtue of the "force" of scientific insight. Dipesh Chakrabarty is perhaps the best-known example of this. He traces the implications of the science for his own field of professional endeavor. Chakrabarty (2009: 200) "assumes the science to be right in its broad outlines" and proceeds to argue that academic history will and should experience irrevocable change when the "environmental crisis" is fully acknowledged by practitioners. For instance, one of his four Anthropocene-inspired theses is that it is increasingly implausible to bracket out biophysical phenomena in the stories historians tell about humankind. The history of people and planet are now coterminous. Relatedly, Tim Clark's book *Ecocriticism on the Edge* (2015) explores the impacts on disciplinary norms of Anthropocene science. Ecocriticism involves interpreting creative works (e.g., novels) that call into question or valorize certain human perceptions and uses of the nonhuman world (see also Nikoleris, Stripple, and Tenngart, Chapter 5). Clark argues that the Holocene's eclipse disrupts the normative reference points of the field. This is because ecocritics can no longer presume that what appears environmentally progressive at one spatiotemporal scale will not have regressive impacts at other scales – such are the complex, ramified teleconnections of an earth system undergoing anthropogenic forcing.

In contrast to the likes of Chakrabarty and Clark, who attend to the "geologization of social thought" (Clark and Gunaratnam 2016: 1), others have used the existing resources of social science and the humanities to reflect critically on how Anthropocene science presents so-called "human dimensions." For instance, Marxist environmental historian Jason Moore (2015) unpacks the "human enterprise" category widely used in the literature from earth system science and the International Geosphere-Biosphere Programme. He endeavors to "socialize the geological" (Moore 2015) by showing how capitalist societies – with their specific ensemble of class relations, technologies, valuation processes, and growth logics – have changed earth history, thereby offering a worked-up explanation for the so-called Great Acceleration. He is one of several critics to take issue with the generalized "anthropos" apparently signified by the Anthropocene concept (see also Baskin, Chapter 8). The sort of detailed explanation he offers is missing in Anthropocene science – though, as noted earlier in the discussion of the dating debate, Anthropocene scientists seem well aware of the different ways the "human enterprise" can be narrated. Relatedly, a thorough exploration of the normative implications of the science for humans is also missing in the scientific literature.

Accordingly, some moral and ethical philosophers are trying to fill the gaps (e.g., Alberts 2012), while others (e.g., Biermann 2014 and 2018) attend to the governance implications of a world of almost 200 nation-states undergoing biophysical change.

Finally, some social scientists and humanists have focused less on the "missing (or misrepresented) human dimensions" of the Anthropocene proposition and more on the science itself. This focus arises from over forty years of historical, cultural, and political-economic research into science as a "socially constituted" enterprise, much of it contained in the field of Science and Technology Studies. Two illustrative examples will have to suffice here. Writing in the journal *Environmental Humanities*, Eileen Crist (2013) sees the science behind the Anthropocene proposition as suffused with contestable value judgements that scientists are trying to naturalize (wittingly or otherwise). For instance, Steffen and colleagues (2011) have talked several times about the need for planetary stewardship, an "ought" that for them flows from the "fact" of humans' planetary impact. However, for Crist (2013: 133), they thereby "veer away from environmentalism's dark idiom of destruction, depredation, rape, loss, devastation . . . and so forth into [a] . . . tame vocabulary that humans are changing [the earth]." From Crist's overtly ecocentric perspective, this bespeaks a short-circuiting of the is–ought link so as to narrow normative reasoning and human response. For instance, several geoscientists, including Crutzen, have made the case for large-scale geoengineering technologies as an emergency response to a "runaway" Anthropocene.

Writing in a less politically pointed way than Crist, Ola Uhrqvist and Eva Lövbrand (2014: 342) explore the role of earth system science and the International Geosphere-Biosphere Programme in planetary "governmentality." Following Michel Foucault, they examine "how thought produces [a] . . . governed reality and thereby directs the ways we act upon it." They treat systems thinking as one way of "framing" reality, and trace the evolution in earth system science from thinking that invites integrated "earth system management" to more complex thinking that, today, points towards a more distributed, differentiated and less orchestrated human response to a possible regime shift in the earth system. For them, this shift comports with an "adaptive" approach to planetary management that moves beyond the "systems engineer" approach. Like Crist, therefore, they challenge the neutrality of the concepts and metaphors favored by some Anthropocene scientists. Unlike Crist, though, they do not pass judgement on the cognitive or normative adequacy of the "frame," simply noting its contingency and historicity.

In sum, to date, social scientists and humanists have engaged Anthropocene science in three ways. Yet, despite the apparent differences involved, it seems to me that the examples above have an important thing in common: namely, they all at some level accept the epochal claims of Anthropocene science and so endorse its fundamental insight. Even Crist, who is highly critical of the terminology used by Anthropocene scientists, does not demur to the essential claim that we are entering a new geological epoch. Likewise, in their recent attempt to showcase different "narratives" about the human causes and consequences of the Anthropocene, Bonneuil and Fressoz (2015: xi) leave the kernel of the science intact: "The Anthropocene label," they write, "is an essential tool for understanding what is happening to us." Only by accepting the geoscientists' claims emanating from stratigraphy and the earth system approach does the two authors' attempt to offer different causal and normative accounts have purpose and punch. The same is true of Hamilton and colleagues' (2015) *The Anthropocene and the Global Environmental Crisis*, which showcases social science and humanities responses to the Holocene's end. "The Anthropocene," the three editors declare, "forces us to reconsider it all" (Hamilton et al. 2015: 11).

## *The Anthropocene in Green Political Thinking and Practice*

In this light, and relating all this to the concerns of this book, how should those who analyze green political theory and environmental politics react to Anthropocene science? Is it advisable to follow the lead of Chakrabarty, Hamilton, and others? Are the fundamental categories organizing the study of contemporary politics to be rethought in light of Anthropocene science? Who, now, is a political actor, who (or what) has civil rights, and who (or what) deserves representation in the political sphere? It may seem necessary to rethink the political in light of these Anthropocene-induced questions. Not only do we social scientists and humanists lack the expertise to assess the *quality* of the science, but the stakes in *ignoring* the science are extremely high: after all, if the scientists are right, then Naomi Klein's (2014) judgement about climate change is amplified by orders of magnitude, since the Anthropocene will "change everything" within a century. Intelligent, innovative analysis and prescription about political values, political reason, and political institutions in our post-Holocene world are thus, in this context, essential to shaping our collective future in ways that are both just and feasible. It is the sort of work undertaken in this book by Manuel Arias-Maldonado (Chapter 3), Anne Fremaux and John Barry (Chapter 9), and Paul Wapner (Chapter 11), among others. Moreover, the sort of impulses contained in Jason Moore and Eileen Crist's work suggests there is plenty of room for intellectual maneuver relative to the insights Anthropocene science provides: as these authors demonstrate, and as many a philosopher has shown before them, a "fact" never determines either the reasons for its existing (the causal "back story") or its normative implications (the possible or desirable future responses to it by people). In this scenario, green analysts should press ahead vigorously with "Anthropocene scholarship, activism, and policy work," since the worst that could happen is a premature pronouncement of the Holocene's end, even as – short of a worldwide anti-capitalist revolution – its termination is surely only a matter of time.

A different option is to proceed more cautiously and await greater scientific consensus. Rather than treat the Anthropocene as a virtual "fact," more patience may be advisable. The International Commission on Stratigraphy may need ten years or more to receive and assess a formal submission from the Anthropocene Working Group. Meanwhile, earth system science might benefit from the sort of external validation that climate change science has received from scientists who are not climate experts – such as Richard Muller at the University of California, Berkeley.[7] As Oldfield and Steffen (2014) argue, this validation will have to reckon with the challenge of verifying knowledge about a hypercomplex open system that even the best computational models cannot properly simulate. Without more time to develop and to be scrutinized, both the stratigraphic and earth system branches of Anthropocene science may be subject to the sort of politically led skepticism that so damaged the public reception of climate science through the early 2000s. In this second scenario, green analysts would avoid accusations of uncritical reliance on scientific expertise and, by extension, of trying to "scientize" the green arguments and proposals they wish to advance for altogether other reasons (such as a love of the nonhuman world).

Though rather different, these two scenarios possess a shared characteristic: they would hold green analysts at a distance from Anthropocene science. In the first case, uncritical reliance on expertise prevails, while in the second scenario, critical practices within science are relied upon to eventually yield robust claims about socio-natural reality. Both differ from a third scenario, one that returns me to this chapter's focus on how "the end of nature" is a predicate for Anthropocene science. In this scenario, some green analysts would follow the lead of the likes of Crist, Uhrqvist, and Lövbrand but go somewhat further. As we saw above, these authors effectively place the core insight of Anthropocene science "off limits," focusing on the language and framing used to convey the insight. Despite their "social constructionist" sensibilities, these authors ultimately default to an old-fashioned realism wherein evidence, models, and expert judgement decide upon the fundamental "reality" of our post-natural globe. In my third scenario, by contrast, green analysts would attend to the *contestable social judgements made in the very heart of Anthropocene science*.

---

[7] Muller and team at Berkeley reanalyzed data used by climate experts to offer an independent assessment of the Intergovernmental Panel on Climate Change's claim that global warming is almost certainly the result of human influence. The so-called Berkeley Earth Surface Temperature Project concluded in 2012 and endorsed the conclusions of the Intergovernmental Panel on Climate Change.

As hinted at earlier in this chapter, some of these judgements pertain to what we call "nature" both historically and ontologically. One judgement is that there really is – or was – a realm of (global) "nature" separate from "society." Anthropologists, among others, have shown that this is a culturally specific belief that pretends that science is "the culture of no culture," able to give us an unmediated perspective on the real (Descola 2013). Another set of judgements pertains to when, exactly, nature is natural no more (or notably less so): at what point does a change to "nature" become qualitative change? What quality of change counts as epochal and worthy of attention? What anticipated *future* biophysical changes should scientists reasonably enjoin us to care about *today*? Here, Raymond Williams' (1980) famous observation about references to nature remains relevant. In his historical analysis of nature in Anglo-European social discourse, Williams showed that, in important respects, people are usually talking about themselves when they discuss rivers, rocks, or the climate. Even in the laboratories, computer models, and published papers of scientists, evidence of biophysical change makes little sense without a set of prior judgements about when quantitative additions or removals become qualitative alterations. These judgements turn "matters of fact" into "facts that matter." In Bruno Latour's (2004) terms, they subsequently become a "matter of concern" not because "reality" *forces* such concern upon us all equally but because a set of spokespeople for "the real" give some of us reasons to care. In both areas of Anthropocene science, it seems to me, the notion of a "new" earth system has value content at its core rather than being only a scientific notion with detachable value content (Ellis and Trachtenberg 2013: 123).

All this may sound perilously close to the sort of "strong social constructionism" that led to the so-called "science wars" in the United States during the 1990s, triggered by Alan Sokal's (1996) hoax in the journal *Social Text*.[8] It may also appear to make green analysts de facto Anthropocene skeptics by "de-objectifying" claims about a post-Holocene transition.[9] However, far from "relativizing" Anthropocene science, green analysts would here make explicit, and assess the merits of, the judgements made by scientists about when the earth is natural no more. These judgements cannot be secured by recourse to "objective truths," but they can be appraised in a reasoned way. This much has already become evident in the fields of conservation and restoration biology, where "objectively" existing "natural baselines" have proved elusive. This would contribute to a more mature understanding of what Anthropocene science – like all science – has to offer

---

[8] Sokal famously published a paper analyzing one area of esoteric science as if he were a knowledgeable sociologist of science – his analysis was, deliberately, nonsense, yet it still got published! Sokal then went on to reveal his true identity, and his hoax called into question the credibility of the "social constructionist" approach to science that was, by the 1990s, a growth area in social science.

[9] Clive Hamilton, for instance, as an environmentalist and spokesperson for earth system science, would doubtless be alarmed at any whiff of constructivism or relativism when it comes to Anthropocene science.

nonscientists in all walks of life. By highlighting the social dimensions of geoscience, in its stratigraphic or earth system forms, green analysts – in this third scenario – would help navigate between attempts to scientize politics (and policy) and attempts to politicize science for nonscientific reasons while refusing to properly debate those reasons. To borrow Roger Pielke's (2007) useful terminology, they would avoid the antinomies of "hurricane politics" (where an "is" gets used to justify one all-encompassing "ought") and "abortion politics" (where science becomes the servant of incommensurable ethico-political agendas, often producing gridlock). They would also offer those pursuing scenario one a stronger basis on which to trust Anthropocene science.[10]

To summarize, it is likely that green political thinking will undergo a fundamental rethink in light of the colossal ontological implications of Anthropocene science. In the years ahead, existing ideas about political actors, political subjects, political institutions, and so on will be challenged because "the Anthropocene" resets the compass for any attempt to understand "the political," be it in descriptive-explanatory or normative terms. For some, the challenge is even more important if some societal actors try – as they assuredly will – to depoliticize the Anthropocene by advocating "post-political" arrangements, such as a new expert-led global governance body designed to "manage" the earth system (Fremaux and Barry, Chapter 9). However, it will be important for political theorists to scrutinize Anthropocene science "all the way down" when vouchsafing their own arguments. That will require a confident, knowledgeable approach to the science that many green political theorists currently lack.

## Conclusion

This chapter has sought to instill a reflexive attitude towards Anthropocene science. Despite nearly forty years of scholarship in science and technology studies, the social science and humanities reaction to the science so far has, I have shown, been either uncritical or else critical within certain parameters that insulate the science from further scrutiny. By exploring three future scenarios for how green analysts might respond to the science, I have cautioned against leaving the Anthropocene proposition "to the experts" even as I have resisted arguing that the Holocene's proclaimed end is merely a "social construction" fabricated by a cadre of geoscientists. Value judgements about nature – about how much of it is gone, how much of it is left, which parts to protect, and which technologies to use to ensure a "good Anthropocene" – are not only anterior to Anthropocene science. Though such

---

[10] And here I make critical mention of the Breakthrough Institute's "ecomodernist manifesto" (2015), which seeks to "objectify" its fundamental premise of a "post-natural world." Go to: http://thebreakthrough.org/index.php/voices/michael-shellenberger-and-ted-nordhaus/an

anterior considerations matter – as current debates about the propriety of "geoengineering" demonstrate – they do not exhaust the value dimension of Anthropocene science. Green analysts, like others in the social sciences and humanities, can help demystify the stubborn myth of scientific "objectivity" and so foster a mature debate about what grounds scientific statements about "an earth in crisis." What is needed is constructively critical engagement with Anthropocene science (Lövbrand et al. 2015), not undue deference or mere indifference to its messages. Such engagement can help "coproduce" science and politics in ways consistent with democratic debate and choice (see Beck, Chapter 10).

## References

Alberts, Paul. 2012. Responsibility towards Life in the Early Anthropocene. *Angelaki* 164 (1): 5–17.
Baskin, Jeremy. 2015. Paradigm Dressed as Epoch. *Environmental Values* 24 (1): 9–29.
Biermann, Frank. 2014. *Earth System Governance: World Politics in the Anthropocene.* Cambridge, MA: MIT Press.
Biermann, Frank. 2018. Global Governance in the Anthropocene. In *Oxford Handbook of International Political Theory*, edited by Chris Brown and Robyn Eckersley, 467–478. Oxford: Oxford University Press.
Bonneuil, Christophe. 2015. The Geological Turn. In *The Anthropocene and the Environmental Crisis*, edited by Clive Hamilton, Christophe Bonneuil, and François Gemenne, 17–31. London: Routledge.
Bonneuil, Christophe, and Jean-Baptiste Fressoz. 2015. *The Shock of the Anthropocene.* London: Verso.
Butz, Stephan D. 2004. *Science of Earth Systems.* New York: Delmar Learning.
Castree, Noel. 2014. *Making Sense of Nature.* London and New York: Routledge.
Castree, Noel. 2015a. Changing the Anthropos(c)ene. *Dialogues in Human Geography* 5 (3): 301–316.
Castree, Noel. 2015b. Unfree Radicals: Geoscientists, the Anthropocene and Left Politics. *Antipode* 49 (S1): 52–74.
Castree, Noel. 2015c. Geography and Global Change Science: Relationships Absent, Necessary and Possible. *Geographical Research* 54 (1): 1–14.
Castree, Noel. 2017a. Global Change Science and the People Disciplines: Towards a New Dispensation. *South Atlantic Quarterly* 116 (1): 55–68.
Castree, Noel. 2017b. Speaking For the People Disciplines: Global Change Science and Its Human Dimensions. *Anthropocene Review* 4 (3): 160–182.
Chakrabarty, Dipesh. 2009. The Climate of History: Four Theses. *Critical Inquiry* 35: 197–222.
Clark, Nigel, and Yasmin Gunaratnam. 2016. Earthing the Anthropos? *European Journal of Social Theory* 20 (1): 1–18.
Clark, William C., Paul Crutzen, and Hans-Joachim Schellnhuber, eds. 2004. *Earth System Analysis for Sustainability.* Cambridge, MA: MIT Press.
Crist, Eileen. 2013. The Poverty of Our Nomenclature. *Environmental Humanities* 3: 129–147.
Cronon, William, ed. 1996. *Uncommon Ground: Rethinking the Human Place in Nature.* New York: W.W. Norton.
Crutzen, Paul. 2002. Geology of Mankind. *Nature* 415: 23.

Crutzen, Paul, and Christian Schwagerl. 2011. Living in the Anthropocene: Toward a New Global Ethos. *Environment 360*, 24th January. Accessed June 19, 2018. https://e360.yale.edu/features/living_in_the_anthropocene_toward_a_new_global_ethos.
Crutzen, Paul J., and Eugene F. Stoermer. 2000. The Anthropocene. *Global Change Newsletter* 41: 17–18.
Descola, Philippe. 2013. *The Ecology of Others*. Chicago: Prickly Paradigm Press.
Ehlers, Eckart, Carol Moss, and Tomas Krafft, eds. 2006. *Earth System Science in the Anthropocene: Emerging Issues and Problems*. Berlin: Springer.
Ellis, Mark, and Zav Trachtenberg. 2013. Which Anthropocene Is It to Be? *Earth's Future* 1 (2): 122–125.
Finney, Stan, and Lucy Edwards. 2016. The Anthropocene Epoch: Scientific Decision or Political Statement? *GSA Today* 26 (3–4): 4–10.
Gibbard, Phil, and Mike J. Walker. 2013. *The Term Anthropocene in the Context of Formal Geological Classification*. Geological Society, London: Special Publications, 395. London: GSL.
Hamilton, Clive. 2015. Getting the Anthropocene So Wrong. *The Anthropocene Review* 2 (2): 102–107.
Hamilton, Clive, and Jacques Grinevald. 2015. Was the Anthropocene Anticipated? *The Anthropocene Review* 2 (1): 59–72.
Hamilton, Clive, Christophe Bonneuil, and François Gemenne, eds. 2015. *The Anthropocene and the Global Environmental Crisis*. London: Routledge.
Hergarten, Stefan. 2002. *Self-Organized Criticality in Earth Systems*. Berlin: Springer.
Hettinger, Ned. 2014. Valuing Naturalness in the Anthropocene: Now More Than Ever. In *Keeping the Wild: Against the Domestication of Earth*, edited by Gerhard Wuerthner, Eilenn Crist, and Tim Butler, 174–179. Washington, DC: Island Press.
Hull, Bruce. 2006. *Infinite Nature*. Chicago: Chicago University Press.
Klein, Naomi. 2014. *This Changes Everything*. New York: Simon and Schuster.
Kump, Leo, James F. Kasting, Robert G. Crane, et al. 2004. *The Earth System*. New Jersey: Prentice Hall.
Latour, Bruno. 2004. *Politics of Nature*. Cambridge, MA: Harvard University Press.
Lewis, Simon, and Mark Maslin 2015. Defining the Anthropocene. *Nature* 519, 12 March: 171–80.
Liss, Peter, Thomas Rosswall, Chris Rapley, et al. 2015. Reflections on Earth System Science. *Global Change* 84: 8–13.
Lorimer, J. 2017. The Anthropo-scene: A Guide for the Perplexed. *Social Studies of Science* 47 (1): 117–142.
Lövbrand, Eva, Silke Beck, Jason Chilvers, et al. 2015. Who Speaks for the Future of the Earth? *Global Environmental Change* 32 (2): 211–218.
Maris, Virginie. 2015. Back to the Holocene. In *The Anthropocene and the Global Environmental Crisis*, edited by Clive Hamilton, Christophe Bonneuil, and François Gemenne, 123–133. London: Routledge.
Maslin, Mark, and Simon Lewis. 2015. Anthropocene: Earth System, Geological, Philosophical and Political Paradigm Shifts. *The Anthropocene Review* 2 (2): 108–116.
McKibben, Bill. 1989. *The End of Nature*. New York: Random House.
Mooney, Hal, Anantha Duraiappah, and Anne Larigauderie. 2015. Evolution of Natural and Social Science Interactions in Global Change Research Programs. *Proceedings of the National Academy of Sciences* 110 (S1): 3665–3672.
Moore, Jason. 2015. *Capitalism in the Web of Life*. London: Verso.
National Science and Technology Council. 2012. *The National Global Change Research Plan 2012–22*. Washington, DC: National Science and Technology Council.

Neugebauer, H. J., and C. Simmer. 2003. *Dynamics of Multiscale Earth Systems*. Berlin: Springer.
Oldfield, Frank, and Will Steffen. 2014. Anthropogenic Climate Change and the Future of Earth System Science. *Anthropocene Review* 1 (1): 70–75.
Pielke, Roger. 2007. *The Honest Broker*. Cambridge: Cambridge University Press.
Pollini, Jacques. 2013. Bruno Latour and the Ontological Dissolution of Nature. *Environmental Values* 22: 25–42.
Rockström, Johan, Will Steffen, Kevin J. Noone, et al. 2009. A Safe Operating Space for Humanity. *Nature* 461: 472–475.
Roswell, Thomas. 1989. Introduction. *Global Change Newsletter* May: 1–2.
Ruddiman, William. 2013. The Anthropocene. *Annual Review of Earth and Planetary Sciences* 41: 45–68.
Rull, Valenti. 2016. The Humanized Earth System. *The Holocene* 26 (9): 1513–1516.
Sokal, Alan. 1996. Transgressing the Boundaries: Towards a Transformative Hermeneutics of Quantum Gravity. Social Text 46/47: 217–252.
Soper, Kate. 1995. *What Is Nature?* Oxford: Blackwell.
Steffen, Will, R. A. Sanderson, P. D. Tyson, et al. 2004. *Global Change and the Earth System*. Berlin: Springer.
Steffen, Will, Åsa Persson, Lisa Deutsch, et al. 2011. The Anthropocene: From Global Change to Planetary Stewardship. *Ambio* 40: 739–61.
Steffen, Will, Wendy Broadgate, Lisa Deutsch, Owen Gaffney, and Cornelia Ludwig. 2015a. The Trajectory of the Anthropocene. *The Anthropocene Review* 2, 1: 81–98.
Steffen, Will, Katherine Richardson, Johan Rockström, et al. 2015b. Planetary Boundaries: Guiding Human Development on a Changing Planet, *Science* 347 (6223): 736.
Steffen, Will, Reinhold Leinfelder, Jan Zalasiewicz, et al. 2016. Stratigraphic and Earth System Approaches to Defining the Anthropocene. *Earth's Future* 4 (8): 324–345.
Uhrqvist, Ola. 2014. *Seeing and Knowing the Earth as a System*. Doctoral dissertation. University of Linköping, Sweden.
Uhrqvist, Ola, and Eva Lövbrand. 2014. Rendering Global Change Problematic: The Constitutive Effects of Earth System Research in the IGBP [International Geosphere-Biosphere Programme] and the IHDP [International Human Dimensions Programme on Global Environmental Change]. *Environmental Politics* 23 (2): 339–356.
Wapner, Paul. 2014. The Changing Nature of Nature: Environmental Politics in the Anthropocene. *Global Environmental Politics* 14 (4): 1–19.
Waters, Colin N., Jan Zalasiewicz, Colin Summerhayes, et al. 2016. The Anthropocene is Functionally and Stratigraphically Distinct from the Holocene. *Science* 351 (6269): aad2622.
Williams, Mark, Jan Zalasiewicz, Colin N. Waters, et al. 2016. The Anthropocene: A Conspicuous Stratigraphic Signal. *Earth's Future* 4: 34–53.
Williams, Raymond. 1976. *Keywords*. London: Fontana.
Williams, Raymond. 1980. Ideas of Nature. In *Problems of Materialism and Culture*, edited by Raymond Williams, 68–102. London: Verso.
Zalasiewicz, Jan, M. Williams, A. G. Smith, et al. 2008. Are We Now Living in the Anthropocene? *GSA Today* 18 (2): 4–8.
Zalasiewicz, Jan, Mark Williams, Will Steffen, and Paul Crutzen. 2010. The New World of the Anthropocene. *Environmental Science and Technology* 44 (7): 2228–2231.
Zalasiewicz, Jan, Colin N. Waters, Mark Williams, et al. 2015. When Did the Anthropocene Begin? A Mid-Twentieth Century Boundary is Stratigraphically Optimal. *Quaternary International*, 383: 196–203

# 3

# The "Anthropocene" in Philosophy: The Neo-material Turn and the Question of Nature

MANUEL ARIAS-MALDONADO

Contemporary social science seems to be addicted to "turns," both as markers of theoretical shifts and as tools of disruption of established categories. All kinds of such turns are thus vindicated on a constant basis, from the digital to the aesthetical. Of course, some turns are more convincing than others – or, at least, they succeed in attracting attention and thus become more convincing for that simple reason. Either way, turns seem to be the new normal as far as academic research is concerned: they boost the reflection on a given topic, provide legitimacy to the latter, and create new combinations and recombinations as the new viewpoint is duly applied to existing topics or traditions of thought. In this chapter, two such turns will be connected as a means to illuminate a wider issue; namely, the nature of nature. In other words, I study the way in which both nature's reality and the social understanding of nature have evolved in the last decade or so.

On the one hand, there is the Anthropocene; that is to say, the Anthropocene turn that is taking place as the concept is gaining more and more recognition in both the natural and the social sciences. The proposition that human beings are now a geological force in their own right, so that social and natural systems have become coupled, is supported by a great deal of scientific evidence (see Castree, Chapter 2). Although there are a good number of dissenters, the conversation is increasingly focused on the meaning and interpretation of the notion rather than on its plausibility. After all, the Anthropocene is both a *state* of socio-natural relations and an *epistemic* tool that invites us to see such relations from a new standpoint (Arias-Maldonado 2015). As Clive Hamilton and colleagues suggest, "In the Anthropocene, social, cultural and political orders are woven into and co-evolve with techno-natural orders of specific matter and energy flow at a global level, requiring new concepts and methods in the humanities" (Hamilton et al. 2015: 4). And this is the case whether or not geologists officially recognize the Anthropocene as a new geological time or epoch, since the evidence gathered by the different scientific disciplines that measure human impact on earth is enough to make the term the best possible depiction of the socio-natural entanglement. To some, in fact, the Anthropocene is mainly a cultural idea that creates new political and ethical possibilities (Purdy 2015: 16–17). This shows that the idea of the Anthropocene has gained already some autonomy from its scientific foundation, which will, however, remain relevant as the ultimate source of legitimacy for the former. If there had not been such a material process of human colonization, the Anthropocene turn would have never taken place.

In this regard, it can be said that the Anthropocene confirms that nature has morphed into human environment. Obviously, nature as a deep structure of causation – a raw material upon which all existence rests – remains in place. But that does not make the change less significant, especially in the light of the ever deeper human interventions in "deep nature," as Kate Soper (1995) named it. Genetic engineering and synthetic biology are two apt examples of a reinforced human ability. At a different level, climate change is an unintended consequence of the same process; that is, the human colonization of nature. These material transformations suggest that the Anthropocene turn revolves mainly around the hybridization of nature, as it becomes less and less autonomous with respect to human actions and social processes. To sustain a clear separation between these two realms is now more difficult than ever (Castree, Chapter 2). For Hamilton and colleagues, the Anthropocene should even be the foundation for a new way of seeing reality: "Grand shifts in philosophical understanding are always built on new ontologies, new understandings of the nature of being" (Hamilton et al. 2015: 8). The suggestion is twofold: the Anthropocene is in itself a new material reality, and it opens up the possibility of understanding nature – writ large – in a new fashion.

Enter the neo-material turn – sometimes also called "ontological" – that has taken place in the social sciences for some years now. Needless to say, materialism is not a novelty in the history of thought, but the original way in which it has been reformulated by a number of scholars and the variety of disciplines that it covers (from sociology to geography and philosophy, not to mention technology studies and anthropology) merits the special recognition that it has been granted – as a proper "turn," that is. Above all, new materialists have rejected the deterministic explanations of early materialism, embracing instead key insights from poststructuralists and constructivists (Fox and Alldred 2016: 6). Paradoxically, then, a materialist shift that can be largely explained as an answer to the exhaustion of the linguistic turn that had dominated the social sciences since the early 1970s is also an outcome of such a paradigm. Be that as it may, the neo-material turn has brought about a new view of the material world with quite an emphasis on techno-scientific advancements, based upon a rejection of traditional dualisms such as body/mind or nature/culture (Pellizzoni 2015: 72). The latter should thus not be seen as distinct realms, but as part of a continuum in which entities are relational and in constant flux. As we shall see, this has important implications for agency, as the capacity to produce the social world extends far beyond human actors to the nonhuman and even the inanimate.

As it happens, these two turns can be fruitfully connected, although the connection itself will not be exempt from complications. Yet a constructive dialogue between new materialism and the Anthropocene concerning the nature of nature – as well as socio-natural relations – is worth the effort, as they help to illuminate each other in unexpected ways. How does the Anthropocene relate to new materialism? In which ways can new materialism help us to understand, conceptualize, or deal with the Anthropocene? And what does this all mean for the old but contested question of nature? Does a materialistic approach even allow the view that nature has ended? And also, what does the Anthropocene say about new materialism? How should we see the claims of the former under the light of the latter? The remainder of this chapter will deal with these questions, while searching for new answers to the old interrogation about nature in the new circumstances the Anthropocene has brought about.

## New Materialism and the Anthropocene (I): Ontology

New materialists should be well suited to understanding classical environmental concerns. Diane Coole (2013) has argued that one of the most recognizable features of new materialist thinking is a renewed attention to material changes and processes that are currently under way – complex and volatile transformations that are congruent with the new materialist ontology. Environmentalism has always emphasized the material character of socio-natural relations, pointing to earth's limits and to the actual damage done to ecosystems and nonhuman species. Besides, human colonization of natural systems resulting in the Anthropocene may very well be regarded as one of those "material changes and processes" Coole refers to. After all, a key Anthropocene insight is precisely that human *action* throughout history has altered the *reality* of nature, so that the latter can hardly be conceived – except in an abstract way – as a universal and timeless essence. Attention must thus be paid to actual nature, to the nature that we can observe, that is engaged in multiple exchanges with human beings and societies, being transformed by them while in turn constraining or influencing them. As we are about to see, this reciprocal influence is also recognized by new materialism, albeit in a particular and ultimately flawed way.

What distinguishes the new materialist ontology, and how well does it explain the puzzles posed by the Anthropocene? Despite a number of differences among its advocates, a number of basic features can be singled out. Coole and Frost summarize the neo-materialist position in this way:

Our existence depends from one moment to the next on myriad micro-organisms and diverse higher species, on our own hazily understood bodily and cellular reactions and on pitiless cosmic motions, on the material artifacts and natural stuff that populate our environment, as well as on socioeconomic structures that produce and reproduce the conditions of our everyday lives. In light of this massive materiality, how could we be anything other than materialist?

*(Coole and Frost 2010: 1)*

Yet the "matter" so invoked is a process rather than a state: being is less important than becoming. That is so because the old passive matter described by the mechanist tradition is replaced by a lively and vibrant one that is always transforming itself. Such dynamic self-organization lacks a plan: as it is not teleologically prefigured, matter's emergence cannot be predicted. Nature is just one of its configurations, but the neo-materialist emphasis on matter's unpredictability suggests that its future cannot be predicted either, despite the long-standing attempt by natural scientists to find patterns and laws in the unfolding of natural systems. Moreover, the very idea of nature as a separated realm is rejected by neo-materialism as an anachronistic categorization. Phenomena are closely intertwined, and entities lack clear boundaries, all sharing the same ontology – a "flat one," as Bruno Latour (1993) puts it, that does not privilege entities or agencies, as they are constantly emerging in new configurations and assemblages across a horizontal plane. This matter, however, is multiple: those entities and structures are multidimensional and move with variable speeds. It should be noted that new materialism is informed by modern physics' description of the underlying structure of reality as a field of subatomic particles. All things, living and nonliving, are constituted by the same basic elements. Connolly (2013a) describes this ontological position as a "protean monism." Under the surface, outer differences collapse.

Crucially, this view drives new materialism to the claim that agency is distributed across a vast range of entities and processes. This is a key and controversial insight that reverberates strongly in the debate on the Anthropocene. It is opposed to a long-standing Western tradition shaped by anthropocentrism and humanism, where agency – the ability to produce changes in the world – has been primarily assigned to human beings. New materialism thinks otherwise, claiming that even categories such as agency, self-consciousness, or rationality are abstractions that hide a complex and manifold process of reciprocal influence between different agentic capacities. The latter are distributed across a vast range of beings and entities, both human and nonhuman. Agency, in short, is decoupled from humanity and is said to emerge in diverse situations and unexpected ways (Burke and Fishel, Chapter 5).

This is formulated by Bruno Latour in his well-known actor-network theory, where a distinction is made between human *actors* and nonhuman *actants*, both possessing agentic capacities. The novelty is that the latter are explicitly ascribed to nonhuman beings and even inanimate entities, that is, actants that have efficacy: they produce effects and affects, influence human actors by encouraging or blocking them, alter a given course of events, and so forth. On her part, Jane Bennett (2010) espouses a new vitalism – or enchanted materialism – that, dwelling on Latour's actants, develops a whole "political ecology of things" in which matter is vital and active rather than passive and hence submissive to human ends. In her view, the very idea of a dead matter calls for an active human manipulation and should be corrected by emphasizing the "interfolding network of humanity and nonhumanity" that produces culture, subjectivity, and the social world. Her main example is telling: that of an electrical power grid that must be included in the "agentic assemblage" that explains a blackout. The notion of the assemblage is often invoked: temporary and unpredictable associations of actors and actants that exhibit agentic capacities. In the words of Karen Barad, though, "there is less an assemblage of agents than there is an entangled state of agencies" due to the "inescapable entanglement of matters of being, knowing, and doing, of ontology, epistemology, and ethics" (Barad 2007: 23 and 3).

Ontology, it should be mentioned, is at stake. Neo-materialism ascribes generative powers and inventive capacities to materiality, thus proposing a new ontology that stresses immanence rather than transcendence. Matter being vital and agential, it cannot be conceived in a Cartesian way anymore, especially since even inorganic matter is taken as "alive." The distinctions between organic and inorganic, animate and inanimate, human and natural are ontologically inconsistent according to new materialists, so that,

if everything is material inasmuch as it is composed of physicochemical processes, nothing is reducible to such processes, at least as conventionally understood. For materiality is always something more than "mere" matter: an excess, force, vitality, relationality, or difference that renders matter active, self-creative, productive, unpredictable.
*(Coole and Frost 2010: 9)*

It is interesting to note that this view has not been completely absent from the environmental debate, as Biesecker and Hofmeister (2006 and 2009) show. Although they do not go so far as new materialists and in fact approach the subject from a different angle, they stress that nature is a dynamic entity that changes on its own and changes in contact with humanity. Nature *lives* and is in itself *productive*, forming a non-separable unity of productivity and re-productivity with humanity. And it comes as no surprise that Marx (2009) himself, an old materialist, talked of a socio-natural "metabolism." What new materialism suggests is that ontology must also be reconsidered along with the primacy of human agency. Yet this is a contestable idea.

## New Materialism and the Anthropocene (II): Agency

At first sight, new materialism can help us to explain the Anthropocene, because it offers a framework that emphasizes the vitality of matter and the transformative power of agentic assemblages that comprise both human actors and nonhuman actants. By pointing to the geological dimension of planetary change, the Anthropocene seems also to displace human agency, or at least dissolve it into a wider field of agentic assemblages, as climate change would show. In fact, climate change would in turn act as an actant that constrains human actions, producing new ecological circumstances to which some form of adaptation is demanded. Moreover, the Anthropocene would be far from a deliberate effect of human actions, thus demonstrating how alive and productive matter is. From this viewpoint, the Anthropocene itself involves a rematerialization of human societies, as the biophysical basis of their existence and its changing quality – as the favorable conditions provided by the Holocene give way to an unpredictable new geological age – make themselves present in a dramatic way.

As its very name suggests, however, the Anthropocene is at odds with new materialism. After all, it puts human beings at the center in an admittedly peculiar manner: they would have massively transformed the planet without being aware of the scale of such change. But that does not make human beings any the less protagonists, a prominent role that does not fit well with neo-materialist claims about the distributed quality of agency. This is the much-discussed core of the Anthropocene turn: the unexpected capacity of human beings to become, by displaying their transformative powers, a major geological force. In this regard, an obvious problem of the neo-materialist account is that – despite offering a new view of socio-natural relations – it blurs the distinction between humans, nonhumans, and things. Such emphasis in connection and agency does not say anything about why assemblages are produced in the first place, or whether any causality can be established (Fuller 2000; Kirsch and Mitchell 2004). Neo-materialism seems to fall into the trap of fetishism, in that it attributes intrinsic qualities to entities and categories that are "extrinsic," that is, defined (at least in part) socioculturally (Bakker and Bridge 2006: 14). If we think of the Anthropocene, is it the outcome of an indefinite number of agentic assemblages or rather, the effect of one prevalent agentic capacity, that of humans?

The latter seems more likely. Thus, a balance must be kept between the recognition of the unintentional agentic capacities of nonhuman actants, on the one hand, and the far more powerful human agency, both intentional and unintentional, on the other. As this vast, transformative agentic capacity has been exerted throughout history as part of the human attempt to adapt to nature – an aggressive adaptation that involves adapting nature to human ends – the Anthropocene has been produced: a massive colonization of nonhuman matter that now exhibits multiple signs of direct and indirect human intervention. If we just talk of agentic assemblages that coproduce reality, we are neglecting the fact that some agencies are more significant than others. This is also the case with nonhuman agencies, as some actants accumulate more powers than the rest. For instance, it has been claimed that the Anthropocene is the age of "hyperobjects" (Morton 2013), defined as things that are massively distributed in time and space relative to humans – the biosphere, the Florida Everglades, the climate – and involve profoundly different temporalities from the human ones. Regarding human powers, they are outstanding even when they are not intentional – as when the increase in population in a given territory impacts on biophysical systems without anybody having planned it. In fact, when human beings act unintentionally but produce effects on the world, they might be considered human actants rather than actors. In either case, they show an exceptional ability to transform, influence, and colonize nature. Be the underlying ontology as it may, this ability has left its mark on socio-natural history. And it is history that counts. Actually, evolutionary history sets another limit to the neo-materialist view, insofar as human ultrasociality (the fact that human beings cooperate more efficiently than other species thanks to language and culture as storage and transmission devices of useful information) can be singled out as a key explanation for the Anthropocene – an ultrasociality that gradually, but sometimes exponentially, increases human transformative powers (see Gowdy and Krall 2013).

However, human exceptionality is sometimes recognized by neo-materialists, albeit implicitly. Coole (2013: 460) has argued that "responsibility" should be considered as an agentic capacity, in order to underline that human beings are particularly responsible for the endangering of planetary systems and the massive extinction of nonhuman species. She is careful enough to point out that she does not refer to "moral agency." Yet if human beings can be particularly responsible, do they not act more decisively than nonhuman actants? Moreover, if they can be warned about the damage they produce, it is because they can be forced to restrain those powers or to channel them in a different direction. As William Connolly (2013b) has aptly argued, humans may not be the center of things, but they think more profoundly about their situation than other species and thus have a greater responsibility; surely an indication of agency, if there ever was one.

## New Materialism and the Anthropocene (III): Hybridity

A more promising convergence takes place between new materialism and the Anthropocene regarding the notion – and the reality – of hybridization. Although neo-materialist thinkers are not solely concerned with the hybridity of nature, the latter is encompassed within the hybrid quality of matter, so that a fruitful dialogue can be established between neo-materialist accounts of hybridization and the socio-natural entanglement as revealed – or confirmed – by the Anthropocene. After all, the latter is grounded on the premise that natural and social systems are now "coupled" (Liu et al. 2007). And although this coupling does not necessarily involve an actual hybridization, in the sense that something *new* is produced, there is no lack of examples – from climate change to species alteration, from anthropogenic biomes to newly found rock formations that mix plastic and natural components. Hybridization is arguably one of the key features of a post-natural understanding of nature – a view reinforced by the Anthropocene.

Neo-materialism sees hybridization as the effect of breaking down old dualisms, such as those separating subject and object or the natural and the artificial. If the world is made up of heterogeneous materialities that form transient and unpredictable assemblages with agentic capacities, reality itself cannot be but hybrid, as there are no clear or fixed boundaries inside it. The human being itself has been presented as a "cyborg," a mixture of organic and technological constituents (Haraway 1991). As for nature, its ontology is less significant than its history – one that assembles the natural, the artificial, the social, and the cultural in a way that can only produce a "quasi-object" that is both material and discursive. That is at least Bruno Latour's view (1993, 2004, and 2005), one for which "naturalness" does not exist anymore, nor did it ever really exist: it was a cultural representation based upon the denial of hybridity.

For Latour, Western societies have emerged through the interaction of two processes: one of purification (involving the separation of the human world from the world of things and the scientific study of the world of nature) and one of hybridization, as we are caught in networks of interactions and relations between more or less natural and more or less social phenomena. That is why the human social world has never been pure and we have never been modern: it was all a delusion. Therefore, supposedly "natural" objects are actually nature–culture objects that are produced by social practices. Haraway (2007) has also talked about "naturecultures" to conceptualize a similar phenomenon. On their part, Cudworth and Hobden (2011 and 2015) advocate a "complex ecologism" that assumes the coevolution and co-constitution of social and natural systems in dynamic configurations, developing relations of dependency and reciprocity within complex natural/social systems. In the same vein, Swyngedow (1999: 47) has pointed out how the process of hybridization has ontological priority over any natural essence, describing it as a process of production, of becoming, of perpetual transgression. Interestingly, though, he claims that historical materialism offers a better explanation of the former than neo-materialism, given the latter's propensity to blur any distinction between different agencies – thus downplaying the exceptional human powers that seem to have brought about the Anthropocene itself.

It could be argued that the process of hybridization commingles society and nature in a promiscuous, productive way, generating new forms that result from their reciprocal influence. In other words, this process allows for change in all parties as they relate to one another, while at the same time it produces a novelty that cannot be reduced to its component parts (Hinchliffe 2007: 51). It is in this respect that a relational view of materiality makes sense – one that shows that the competencies and capacities of things are not intrinsic, but derive from association (Bakker and Bridge 2006: 16). Therefore, neo-materialism seems to offer a more convincing ontology than traditional dualist positions, as it emphasizes entanglements and connections over divisions and hierarchies.

But how well does the Anthropocene fit with this view? If we take it to be a given state of socio-natural relations, what does it teach us about hybridity and hybridization? And what about nature itself? On a general level, of course, the Anthropocene *même* could be seen as a hybrid: the novelty created by the intermingling of social and natural systems, a socio-natural entanglement whose main driver has been the transformative powers of the human species in its quest for adaptive survival; an aggressive adaptation, however, that includes both intentional and unintentional alterations of pristine nature. Perhaps climate change is the most obvious example of such hybridity, as the climate system has been unintentionally altered by human activity. But the latter has also left its mark on the components of ecosystems, as biologist Erle C. Ellis has tried to show. He has introduced the notion of "anthropogenic biomes" in order to describe how the unit of ecological analysis (the biome) can no longer be understood as being purely "natural," as recent studies suggest that human-dominated ecosystems now cover more of earth's surface than "wild" ecosystems (Ellis and Ramankutty 2008; Ellis 2013). This has been produced by deliberate as much as by unintentional human activity – but human all the same – over the last centuries. Ellis has even cautioned that "natural" biomes have never been the norm, as human beings have been treading the earth for a very long time.

Similarly, Young (2014) has called for a "biogeography of the Anthropocene" that adapts to a new reality where hybridization is the new normal. This includes the developing of methods that allow the study of "novel species assemblages." It has also been argued that "speciation by hybridization" might become one of the key signatures of the Anthropocene, as human development boosts diversity in unexpected ways: new anthropogenic habitats contain some new species previously rare or absent, while the ensemble of new and old habitats, together with climate change, increases habitat, evolutionary origination accelerates, and hybridization brings formerly separated species into contact (Thomas 2013). At the same time, species invasions have become normalized, a process by which some generalist species – those accommodating best to human systems – take over large portions of the planet, pushing out the specialist species that developed in isolation. Zoologist Gordon Orians has a name for this: the "Homogocene" (Rosenzweig 2011). Finally, in what looks like a phenomenon tailored for neo-materialist observers, hybridization can also combine "natural" and "artificial" inorganic matter, as the rock formations found in a Hawaiian beach demonstrate: formed from melting plastic in fires lit by humans who were camping or fishing, they are cobbled together from plastic, volcanic rock, beach sand, seashells, and corals (Corcoran et al. 2014). Tellingly, they have been named "plastiglomerate" – a humble but significant assemblage that could very well serve as a symbol for the Anthropocene as a whole.

As Noel Castree (2014; see also his contribution to this volume, Chapter 2) has argued, some human geographers see the Anthropocene as an opportunity to rethink old Western categories that foster a false separation between human beings and the nonhuman world. Moreover, this has implications for conservation and ecosystem management, as a post-natural paradigm is emerging that is grounded on the hybrid character of current "nature" (see Lorimer and Driessens 2013; Marris 2013). Castree points out that many conservationists now accept that "natural biomes" are a myth – one that is grounded on a "purified" view of nature hardly tenable in the Anthropocene age. In truth, this purity view has long been challenged by cultural historians (Cronon 1996). Yet the angle from which the argument is put forward is new: not the cultural construction of nature but the ultimate materiality of it. This is interesting because, as we have seen, Latour's view of nature as a hybrid involves both matter and discourse, physical realities as much as narratives and figurations. Yet this is not the kind of hybrid that the Anthropocene produces, as the latter reinforces the material dimension of socio-natural relations without overlooking its cultural dimension. Ultimately, what is at stake here is the social construction of nature – or rather, the validity of such a position.

In part, neo-materialism is an attempt to go beyond the realist–constructivist debate, taking the side of a newly found reality in which the distinction between nature and culture collapses under the unanimity of matter. This turn has resonated in geography as well, where a materialist revolt took place against the emphasis on the social dimension of nature: resource and environmental geography have conceptualized nature in predominantly physical terms (Bakker and Bridge 2006: 8). Waste studies, for instance, have accentuated an engagement with materiality as transformation and process (Kirsch 2012: 438). Such an emphasis also possesses a normative side, as this re-ontologization of nature is seen to remind us of its *resistance* against human transformative efforts, a quality that the constructivist account may help to obscure (Fitzsimmons 1989). Yet this resistance is weaker than it used to be, as human efforts are now more fruitful in more and more realms. Be that as it may, though, these views confirm that constructivism must incorporate the physical dimension of the socio-natural relation in order to be credible. In other words, a material version of constructivism is to be developed: the recognition of the fact that any social construction of nature is first and foremost a material reconstruction of nature, a process which, of course, is conditioned in turn by cultural representations of nature. Through this process, nature is transformed into human environment, so that it can be said to be a hybrid in at least two senses: as the Latourian quasi-object, where matter and ideas merge, and as a product of the complex process of hybridization that results in new socio-natural forms.

Remarkably, the social construction of nature reaches more and more deeply into nature due to the increase of human manipulative abilities – as genetic engineering and synthetic biology attest. This means that our understanding of what it means to reconstruct nature must change, since it cannot be restricted anymore to "shallow" nature (Demeritt 2002: 776). In turn, this leads to the existential question: does nature still exist? To put it differently: is a reconstructed and hybridized nature, the nature of the Anthropocene, natural at all? The question is not trivial, as the prior reference to conservation strategies shows.

## Nature Questioned

At first glance, there is nothing new in the claim that nature has ended. For over two decades, this event has been announced repeatedly, either by sociologists interested in risk or by environmentalists resigned to accept a sad reality (McKibben 1990; Giddens 1991; Beck 1992). Despite the *grandeur* of the statement, it is a simple idea: nature can no longer be defined by its independence from human beings and society. Socio-natural relations currently exhibit a number of features that reinforce this entanglement: hybridization, transformation, and manipulation. It is not that nature is seen as dead matter in a mechanistic fashion; rather, the process by which human beings colonize the natural world has reached a quantitative degree that makes for a qualitative change. This is reflected in the social sciences, where simple "nature" has been replaced by concepts such as social nature, second nature, or hybrid nature (Pollini 2013: 30). An uncomplicated nature is not on offer anymore.

Yet natural beings and forms stay out there, as a living proof in the eyes of many environmentalists of the nonsensical character of this absurdly anthropocentric claim. Even climate change can be seen as a denial of this premature death, reminding human beings of their dependency on the living conditions provided by natural systems. Moreover, nature *cannot* end: we should not conflate the shallow nature that is manifest in nonhuman beings and wild landscapes with the set of causal powers and deep structures upon which our social activity ultimately depends. In this regard, Valerie Plumwood (2006: 135) speaks of "elements of independence" that demonstrate the indestructibility of nature. All in all, this quarrel has been taking place for a long time now.

However, the Anthropocene seems to reinforce the claim that nature has ended. As the evidence about the socio-natural intermingling stacks up, the pristine autonomy of nature seems harder to defend. The latter existed *before humans*, whereas we are writing now *after history* and thus *after nature*. Erle C. Ellis (2011: 1027) reaches the same conclusion: "From a philosophical point of view, nature is now human nature; there is no more wild nature to be found, just ecosystems in different states of human interaction, differing in wildness and humanness." What Ellis is suggesting is that we should forget about the supposed essence of nature and focus instead on the socio-natural interaction as it is. Again, history trumps ontology. And from this standpoint we can simultaneously acknowledge nature's "elements of independence" and a state of relations marked by the coupling of social and natural systems, the development of more and more human manipulative abilities, as well as a hybridization process accelerated under the unpredictable conditions provided by the Anthropocene. To talk about the end of nature in the Anthropocene, then, is to claim that natural processes can no longer be defined as independent of human influence (except in a very general sense), as well as to observe that natural forms and processes have been influenced by human beings to a very high degree. It makes no difference whether this colonization has been intentional or unintentional, and the same goes for the visibility or invisibility of such influence: a dog may bear no traces of human manipulation of the species, but that does not make it less true.

Interestingly, neo-materialism seems to travel in the opposite direction. But it does so by operating on a different level; namely, that of *matter*. As the latter *becomes* rather than *is*, it makes scant sense to talk about nature's "end." This is especially patent in the case of the new vitalism advanced by Jane Bennett (2010), for whom nature is less a passive object of human action than a dynamic entity that changes on its own as well as in contact with human actors, while constraining and influencing them as well. She goes on to argue that nature's definition should make room for this natural creativity, so that the very term "nature" describes a process of morphing, formation, and deformation – the outcome of the strange conjunctions of things in motion. Therefore, if a "creative not-quite-human force capable of producing the new" is recognized as the main source of change, nature simply cannot ever end – it is just *transformed*. That is why she describes a "vibrant matter."

However, the neo-materialist position is not incompatible with the claim that nature has ended and can, in fact, help to illuminate it. Leaving aside for a moment the theory of agency defended by neo-materialists, the key here lies in the distinction between *matter* and *nature*: as they are not necessarily the same thing, neo-materialism may very well serve as an additional foundation for a post-natural conception of nature in the Anthropocene. The reason is that matter lies *below* nature or is contained *within* it, but is not identical with it: nature would be a *phenomenon* of matter, which remains as the *noumenon* that often escapes our senses. At first sight, matter would seem to be tantamount to "deep nature," so that this further reconceptualization might appear as unnecessary. But it is something else: matter in the neo-materialist understanding encompasses both shallow and deep nature, as well as the world of things and artifacts, as they all are made of it and, at a subatomic level, there are no differences among them. Therefore, nature can be said to end without matter ending at all. To put it differently: nature's end is not the same thing as nature's death, as the former can take place without the latter also happening. Because even if nature ceases to be autonomous with respect to humanity, matter retains its autonomy as a vital force that underpins the visible world. This vitality is, however, captured by human beings for their own goals through a number of techniques, in such a way and to such degrees that the distinction between shallow and deep nature becomes increasingly untenable. As we saw earlier, human agentic capacities are prevalent over those of nonhuman actants – a hierarchy that neo-materialism fails to recognize, but without which it is hard to make any sense of the Anthropocene. There is a distributive agency, to be sure, but one where human actors possess more influence than others.

On the other hand, such enhanced capacities do not provide anything close to human "control" of nature, as environmentalists rightly point out. For them, it is another proof of the impossibility of nature's end. But that is not necessarily the case, since the end of nature can take place in the precise sense that has been explained above, while an increasingly self-reflective control of socio-natural relations gradually takes shape. This is not a perfect control, but an increased one that proves to be sufficient for realizing a number of human goals – among them the protection of species and ecosystems.

What emerges from this reconceptualization is actually a post-natural understanding of nature; that is, one that accepts that we are not dealing with old nature anymore but rather, with a transformed, hybridized, humanized one. A questioned nature thus leads to a new formulation of the question of nature.

## Ontology in the Anthropocene: Does It Matter?

So far, I have taken the Anthropocene as a valid scientific observation, which in turn is deduced from a number of measurable facts that can be compared with previous data, in order to make a statement about the current state of socio-natural relations. To accept the basic facts communicated by scientists, of course, is not compulsory: it is well known that science is not isolated from society, and thus, a perfectly neutral scientific knowledge does not seem feasible. That said, the impact of sustained human activity on the planet seems uncontroversial, and the Anthropocene provides a new framework for studying the socio-natural entanglement, as well as a new vantage point from which to make normative claims about it. Thus, I would distinguish between the acceptance of the Anthropocene as a scientific observation and the conversation about its causes, meanings, representations, narratives, and normative implications.

In this chapter, I have reflected upon the relationship between neo-materialist thinking and the Anthropocene. The former's emphasis on matter over nature, on becoming over being, on a distributed over a human-centered agency, poses an interesting challenge for environmental thinking, as it offers new answers for old questions concerning socio-natural relations and, ultimately, their long-term sustainability. But how can we translate this into normative language? And what are the implications for environmental policy practice? In sum, what would a post-natural agenda entail for both environmental thinking and policy practice?

To begin with, such normative translation is not easy; at least not in the case of neo-materialist claims concerning ontology and agency. If nature, as well as the distinction between the natural and the human, dissolves into *matter*, what is left? Which would the object of environmental thought then be? Therein lies the danger of hollowing out not just "nature," but even socio-natural relations themselves. In other words, to talk about matter is, despite the ontological verisimilitude of neo-materialist claims, normatively sterile. Besides, there is a limit to the explanatory capacity of this approach as far as socio-natural relations are concerned: the loss of biodiversity might be irrelevant on a molecular level, as matter is simply transformed, but the same cannot be said if we adopt an ecological or a moral viewpoint. As for agency, similar issues can be raised, since a distributional view of the former cannot fully explain human impacts on the environment. Furthermore, placing too much emphasis on nonhuman agency and suprahuman processes such as those of geology or deep time may give the impression that human action does not count for much, thus weakening the case for political involvement and sustainable policies.

On the other hand, the neo-materialist case for hybridity should prove more helpful as a contribution to devising a post-natural understanding of nature that is both non-reductionist and nuanced. Hybridity, as manifested in a spectacular fashion in the Anthropocene hypothesis, means that society and nature are irrevocably entangled. In that sense, nature does not exist anymore. But this claim is not to be taken literally. Instead, the natural should be seen as a matter of degrees, as hybrids have a composition and a history that allow us to establish their place in the nature–social continuum. This has undeniable implications for environmental policy and the environmental research agenda. As Adams (2016) has pointed out, new conservation strategies can thus be conceived wherein the idea of a pristine or untouched nature is discarded. At the same time, the complexity of this socio-natural entanglement demands explanation on a number of levels, ranging from the ecological to the technological and, of course, the technonatural. Future emphasis should not be placed on the entity called "nature," but rather, on socio-natural relations in all their complexity.

## Conclusion

Human beings have been asking themselves about the nature of nature for millennia. Now, this question looks more pressing than ever – as the coupling of social and natural systems brought about by the aggressive adaptation that is typical of the human species has reached such a degree that a new geological epoch has been announced. In the Anthropocene, it is not just ecosystems or species that become endangered, but rather, the whole planet. Human transformative powers go more and more deeply into natural forms, processes, and even causal structures. As a result, leaving the risk of unsustainability aside, nature seems to lose its autonomy with respect to human beings and social systems. The question thus arises as to whether nature is still nature – or whether its end can finally be proclaimed. This chapter has tried to shed light on this intricate question by crossing the Anthropocene literature with that of neo-materialism, as both epistemological turns can fruitfully engage in a dialogue about the different aspects of nature's nature: from ontology to reproduction, from agency to representation. Neo-materialism proves to be an interesting angle from which to observe nature in the Anthropocene: its emphasis on matter, its claim about distributive agencies, as well as its view on hybridity illuminate the current state of socio-natural relations and thus the wider interrogation about nature. It also exhibits some limitations, the most troublesome of all being the neglect of human agency as the main source of natural transformation. In this sense, it is the Anthropocene that serves as a correction for neo-materialism. At the same time, though, the distinction between matter and nature creates new possibilities for framing the controversial "end of nature." By doing this, neo-materialism indirectly contributes to the urgent task of formulating a post-natural understanding of nature for the Anthropocene age.

## References

Adams, William M. 2016. Geographies of Conservation I: De-extinction and Precision Conservation. *Progress in Human Geography*, published online 18 May.

Arias-Maldonado, Manuel. 2015. *Environment and Society: Socionatural Relations in the Anthropocene*. Heidelberg: Springer.

Bakker, Karen, and Gavin Bridge. 2006. Material Worlds? Resource Geographies and the "Matter of Nature". *Progress in Human Geography* 30 (1): 5–27.

Barad, Keith. 2007. *Meeting the Universe Halfway: Quantum Physics and the Entanglement of Matter and Meaning*. Durham: Duke University Press.
Beck, Ulrich. 1992. *Risk Society. Towards a New Modernity*. London: Sage.
Bennett, Jane. 2010. *Vibrant Matter: A Political Ecology of Things*. Durham: Duke University Press.
Biesecker, Adelheid and Sabine Hofmeister. 2006. *Die Neuerfindung des Ökonomischen. Ein (re)produktionstheoretischer Beitrag zur sozialökologischen Forschung*. Munich: Oekom.
Biesecker, Adelheid and Sabine Hofmeister. 2009. Starke Nachhaltigkeit fordert eine Ökonomie der (Re)Produktivität. In *Die Greifswalder Theorie starker Nachhaltigkeit*, edited by Tanja von Egan-Krieger, Julia Schultz, Philipp Pratap Thapa, and Lieske Voget, 1679–1692. Marburg: Metropolis-Verlag.
Castree, Noel. 2014. Geography and the Anthropocene II: Current Contributions. *Geography Compass* 8 (7): 450–463.
Connolly, William. 2013a. The "New Materialism" and the Fragility of Things. *Millennium: Journal of International Studies* 41: 399–412.
Connolly, William. 2013b. *The Fragility of Things: Self-Organizing Processes, Neoliberal Fantasies, and Democratic Activism*. Durham: Duke University Press.
Coole, Diane. 2013. Agentic Capacities and Capacious Historical Materialism: Thinking with New Materialisms in the Political Sciences. *Millennium: Journal of International Studies* 41 (3): 451–469.
Coole, Diane, and Samantha Frost. 2010. Introducing the New Materialisms. In *New Materialisms. Ontology, Agency, and Politics*, edited by Diane Coole and Samantha Frost, 1–43. Durham and London: Duke University Press.
Corcoran, P., C. Moore, and K. Jazvac. 2014. An Anthropogenic Marker Horizon in the Future Rock Record. *Geological Society of America Today*, 24 (6): 4–8.
Cronon, William, ed. 1996. *Uncommon Ground. Rethinking the Human Place in Nature*, New York: W. W. Norton and Company.
Cudworth, Erika, and Hobden, S. 2011. *Posthuman International Relations. Complexity, Ecologism, and Global Politics*. London: Zed Books.
Cudworth, Erika, and Hobden, S. 2015. Liberation for Straw Dogs? Old Materialism, New Materialism, and the Challenge of an Emancipatory Posthumanism. *Globalizations* 12 (1): 134–148.
Demeritt, D. 2002. What is the "Social Construction of Nature"? A Typology and Sympathetic Critique. *Progress in Human Geography* 26(6): 767–90.
Ellis, Erle C. 2011. Anthropogenic Transformation of the Terrestrial Biosphere. *Philosophical Transactions of the Royal Society A* 369: 1010–1035.
Ellis, Erle C. 2013. Anthropocene. In *Encyclopedia of Earth*, edited by J. Cutler. Washington, DC: Environmental Information Coalition, National Council for Science and the Environment.
Ellis, Erle C., and Navin Ramankutty. 2008. Putting People in the Map: Anthropogenic Biomes of the World. *Frontiers in Ecology and the Environment* 6 (8): 439–447.
Fitzsimmons, Margaret. 1989. The Matter of Nature. *Antipode* 21: 106–120.
Fox, Nick, and Pam Alldred. 2016. *Sociology and the New Materialism. Theory, Research, Action*. London: Sage.
Fuller, Steve. 2000: Why Science Studies has Never been Critical of Science: Some Recent Lessons on How to be a Helpful Nuisance and a Harmless Radical. *Philosophy of the Social Sciences* 30: 5–32.
Giddens, Anthony. 1991. *The Consequences of Modernity*. Cambridge: Polity.

Gowdy, John M. and Krall, Lisi. 2013. The Ultrasocial Origin of the Anthropocene. *Ecological Economics* 95: 137–147.
Hamilton, Clive, Christophe Bonneuil, and François Gemenne, eds. 2015. Thinking the Anthropocene. In *The Anthropocene and the Global Environmental Crisis. Rethinking Modernity in a New Epoch*, edited by Clive Hamilton, Christophe Bonneuil, and François Gemenne,1–13. Abingdon: Routledge.
Haraway, Donna. 1991. *Simians, Cyborgs, and Women: The Reinvention of Nature*. New York: Routledge.
Haraway, Donna. 2007. *When Species Meet*. Minneapolis: University of Minnesota Press.
Hinchliffe, Steven. 2007. *Geographies of Nature. Societies, Environments, Ecologies*. London: Sage.
Kirsch, Scott 2012. Cultural Geography I: Materialist Turns. *Progress in Human Geography* 37(3): 433–441.
Kirsch, Scott, and Don Mitchell. 2004. The Nature of Things: Dead Labor, Nonhuman Actors, and the Persistence of Marxism. *Antipode* 36: 687–705.
Latour, Bruno. 1993. *We Have Never Been Modern*. Cambridge, MA: Harvard University Press.
Latour, Bruno. 2004. *Politics of Nature. How to Bring the Sciences into Democracy*. Cambridge: Harvard University Press.
Latour, Bruno. 2005. *Reassembling the Social: An Introduction to Actor-Network Theory*. Oxford: Oxford University Press.
Liu, Jianguo, Thomas Dietz, Stephen R. Carpenter, et al. 2007. Complexity of Coupled Human and Natural Systems. *Science* 317: 1513.
Lorimer, Jamie, and Clemens Driessens. 2013. Wild Experiments in the Oostvaardersplassen: Rethinking Environmentalism in the Anthropocene. *Transactions of the Institute of British Geographers* 39(2): 169–181.
Marris, Emma. 2013. *Rambunctious Garden*. New York: Bloomsbury.
Marx, Karl. 2009. *Ökonomisch-philosophische Manuskripte*. Frankfurt: Suhrkamp.
McKibben, Bill. 1990. *The End of Nature*. New York: Anchor Books.
Morton, Tim. 2013. *Hyperobjects. Philosophy and Ecology after the End of the World*. Minneapolis and London: University of Minnesota Press.
Pellizzoni, Luigi. 2015. *Ontological Politics in a Disposable World. The New Mastery of Nature*. Surrey: Ashgate.
Plumwood, Valerie. 2006. The Concept of a Cultural Landscape: Nature, Culture and Agency in the Land. *Ethics and The Environment* 11(2): 115–150.
Pollini, Jacques. 2013. Bruno Latour and the Ontological Dissolution of Nature in the Social Sciences: A Critical Review. *Environmental Values* 22: 25–42.
Purdy, Jeremiah. 2015. *After Nature. A Politics for the Anthropocene*. Cambridge and London: Harvard University Press.
Rosenzweig, Michael L. 2011. The Four Questions: What Does the Introduction of Exotic Species Do to Diversity? *Evolutionary Ecology Research* 3: 361–367.
Soper, Kate. 1995. *What Is Nature?* Oxford: Blackwell.
Swyngedow, Eric. 1999. Modernity and Hybridity: Nature, Regeneracionismo, and the Production of the Spanish Waterscape, 1890–1930. *Annals of the Association of American Geographers* 89: 443–465.
Thomas, Chris. 2013. The Anthropocene Could Raise Biological Diversity. *Nature*, 502 (7): 3.
Young, Kenneth R. 2014. Biogeography of the Anthropocene: Novel Species Assemblages. *Progress in Physical Geography* 38(5): 664–673.

# 4

# The "Anthropocene" in Popular Culture: Narrating Human Agency, Force, and Our Place on Earth

ALEXANDRA NIKOLERIS, JOHANNES STRIPPLE, AND PAUL TENNGART

The catchphrase "welcome to the Anthropocene" has been everywhere, from the cover of *The Economist* (2011) to an editorial in the journal *Nature* (2015). We are told that we have entered into a new geological era fully dominated by human activity – "the Anthropocene" – which changes our relationship with the planet, and which comes with a new responsibility. Coined at the turn of the millennium to describe the state of the global environment (Crutzen and Stoermer 2000), the concept has since then taken root in scientific and popular discourse. While originally wedded to a dystopian narrative of human resource exploitation, planetary tipping points, and environmental urgency (Rockström et al. 2009), the Anthropocene is a traveling idea that has opened up new imaginative worlds as it entered interdisciplinary conversations within and beyond academia (Lorimer 2012; Gibson et al. 2015; Hamilton et al. 2015). However, the Anthropocene is not just a scientific discourse, but also a social and cultural one that is inspiring scholars, artists, film producers, and novelists to reconsider the links between nature and culture, economy and ecology, science and fiction. As the cultural engagements with the Anthropocene are increasing in number, so are the stories told about this new era in planetary history, and the place of humans in it.

In this chapter, we do not approach the proposed "geology of mankind" (Crutzen 2002) as a phenomenon that can be settled empirically. We explore it as a powerful idea, or imagination, taking multiple forms and trajectories as it travels across the worlds of science and popular culture. Following Yusoff and Gabrys, we understand imagination as "a way of seeing, sensing, thinking and dreaming the formation of knowledge, which creates the conditions for material interventions *in* and political sensibilities *of* the world" (Yusoff and Gabrys 2011: 516, italics in original). As such an imagination, the Anthropocene works as a cultural and political space where particular understandings of environmental problems, relations, places, and futures take form, stabilize, are contested, and are made anew.

Meadowcroft (2017) has shown how the idea of "the environment," as an independent object of interest and action, was established in the 1970s. Its paramount success as a concept relates to its possibility to scale. The environment "may relate to a chemical discharge to a local stream, the preservation of wilderness areas, the movement of air pollutants across continents, or global biodiversity loss" (Meadowcroft 2017: 87). Thus, the very idea of "the environment" has been key for articulating societal concern and structuring political debate. Contemporary environmental politics, with its ministries, agencies, budgets, approaches, forms of calculations, and concerns about value, is built on the foundation that "the environment" is a distinct domain (a totality of biophysical processes and phenomena, separated from humanity) to be governed through modern forms of authority. With the advent of the Anthropocene imagination, some of these assumptions are intact and some are destabilized (Arias-Maldonado, Chapter 3; Burke and Fishel, Chapter 5). Crucially, the Anthropocene imagination invites a wide set of questions about "the political" in relation to environmental politics. What it might mean to live and act in the Anthropocene is far from a settled discussion. When nature no longer exists apart from humanity, when the world we inhabit is one we have created, what then does it mean to, for example, "protect the environment"? Is there a move from "mastery" to "mutuality," as proposed by McKay?

On the one hand, we lose our special status as Master Species; on the other, we become members of deep time, along with trilobites and Ediacaran organisms. We gain the gift of de-familiarization, becoming other to ourselves, one expression of the ever-evolving planet. Inhabiting deep time imaginatively, we give up mastery and gain mutuality.

*(McKay 2008).*

Which forms of political community are conceivable? What kind of agency is possible, and what forms of power and resistance are envisaged?

To us, the study of what the Anthropocene imagination does to environmental politics can benefit from a closer engagement with popular culture. There are different ways of knowing the Anthropocene. As McKibben once phrased it, "We can register what is happening with satellites and scientific instruments, but can we register it in our imaginations, the most sensitive of all our devices?" (McKibben 2005). While scientific and cultural engagements with the Anthropocene differ in terms of the knowledge they seek to create, the agents involved, and the methods and practices through which they are undertaken, they all rely on forms of *narrative*: of telling compelling stories about the nature of the Anthropocene and the means by which it can be mitigated or lived through. Science and popular culture are hence different "ways of world making" (Goodman 1978): cultural engagements will let us travel to new worlds, to strive there alongside others, and then to return armed with that experience. One of the most important devices of literature is the use of fiction. Literary fiction invents worlds in which both fundamental conditions and detailed elements are made up in order to tell a story with symbolical significance.

And yet, while students of environmental politics have swiftly incorporated scientific narratives of the Anthropocene (Castree, Chapter 2), stories told from within the cultural realm have received much less attention. This is surprising, since the questions that result from the Anthropocene imagination do not resonate much with either stratigraphy or earth system science. Morton (2013) has coined the term "hyperobjects" to capture entities (e.g., climate change or species extinction) that are so massively distributed in time, space, and dimensionality that it is difficult to perceive and comprehend them. Hyperobjects are abstractions, but at the same time catastrophically real.

Throughout the ages, literature has framed humanity's defining issues. Our ability to identify with fictional stories changes how we perceive ourselves and act in the world. While we do not question the diagnosis made by either stratigraphy or earth system science about an emerging post-natural world, it is far from clear what that insight entails. In this chapter, we seek to illustrate how the study of politics in the Anthropocene could be usefully extended beyond the traditional territories of political science. As suggested by Johns-Putra (2016), literature, art, and film invite us to inhabit other worlds and live other lives. To achieve reader identification, the invented worlds need to be specific, describing and depicting particular persons, places, events, and moments. Literary narratives are therefore always situated in specific human, cultural, geographical, and temporal conditions, thereby making it possible for the reader to be emotionally engaged in the scenarios displayed.

Our chapter is composed of three parts. In the first section, we use contemporary works of "climate change fiction" to grasp how fiction narrates what it means to live through a climate-changed world in particular places. We tease out spatial and temporal dimensions of the new conditions of life in the Anthropocene, paying particular attention to how fiction can facilitate the exploration of "radical discontinuities" (Evans 2015) that marks the Anthropocene. In the second section, we approach the key idea of the Anthropocene imagination; namely, humanity as a geological force. Even though the Anthropocene is often presented as something new, and while some of the material effects of the Anthropocene are only beginning to be known, the Anthropocene imagination, the very idea that humans are capable of shaping the conditions of life on earth, has a long lineage in the world of fiction. We then show how a key set of works from three continents, published from the 1950s onwards, imagine this newly acquired power of humanity, and how these fictional texts help us to think through what it might mean to be human after the end of nature. In the last section, we pay attention to how recent scholarship on the Anthropocene has served to open up a wider discussion and invites us to reconsider foundational categories of modern environmental political thought (e.g., nature versus culture, human versus animal). We illustrate with a few examples of how fiction narrates "the political" in the Anthropocene.

## Living through a Climate-changed World

Without policing or paying too much attention to genre-boundaries, there is now a large volume of books that could be identified as "Anthropocene fiction" (Trexler 2015). Many of those works are set in a future world in which climate change has come to matter (Trexler and Johns-Putra 2011; Johns-Putra 2016; Kaplan 2016). While climate change is only one part of the Anthropocene problematique, it does epitomize its discourse, and it is an angle that ordinary people can relate to and understand. That being said, literature that provides insights into the invention of agriculture in Mesopotamia, the steam engine in early modern capitalist Britain, the spread of the atomic bomb, or plastic waste in the oceans, also tells key stories about some of the drivers that are seen as markers of the Anthropocene. In this section, however, we take a closer look at five literary works that narrate particular worlds in which climate change is set and made as something to act upon: Ian McEwan's *Solar*, Kim Stanley Robinson's trilogy *Science in the Capital*, Saci Lloyd's *The Carbon Diaries 2017*, Barbara Kingsolver's *Flight Behavior*, and Liz Jensen's *The Rapture*. These narratives are all written by established authors, distributed by well-known publishers, and set in the present or near future. The circulation of the novels has varied, illustrating how climate change has come to figure in different genres and among different audiences.

The novels bring various imaginations of a climate-changed world to life, but they also situate climate action among numerous human concerns and characteristics. While scientific narratives of climate change can work with global averages (400 parts per million atmospheric carbon dioxide concentration; maximum mean global temperature increase of less than 2 degrees Celsius), literary narratives have to provide much more geographical and historical specificity. A novel is always set in one place or a couple of distinct places. Temporally, a novel is predominantly set in one particular historical moment, but may also – and often does – include other moments in time and descriptions of long-term gradual developments. Literary specificities not only create particular geographical and historical optics through which the changing climate is viewed, but also allow complex accounts of radical discontinuities to be explored. When a novel includes two or more geographical or historical settings, complex relations between the climate, different locations, and different moments are captured. While the Anthropocene imagination is *spatially* configured as a set of layers (stratigraphy) on an integrated sphere (earth system science), and *temporally* configured as a transition from one era to another, fiction can explore different spatialities and temporalities. Fiction has the freedom and ability to narrate any thinkable world, and to make us imagine how it would be to live, act, feel, and think in that world.

Barbara Kingsolver's *Flight Behavior* tells the story of a stay-at-home wife in rural Feathertown, Tennessee, and her discovery of an enormous community of monarch butterflies, whose migration pattern has been disturbed by global warming. This discovery sets many things in motion: it has a great social effect in the small community and it also attracts national media, activists, and scientists to Feathertown. In the end, these changes prompt the protagonist to leave her husband and begin education elsewhere. The novel is geographically and temporarily concentrated: all the action takes place in a small, rural town over the period of a couple of months. Still, geographical dynamics are addressed through animal as well as human migration. The butterflies are not supposed to be in Feathertown but in Mexico, and their impact on the Tennessee forest corresponds to the impact of their absence in the Mexican mountains. Information about the latter reaches the protagonist through Mexican immigrants in Feathertown. Different locales affect each other, even if they are many miles apart. And the behavior of the monarchs would not be alarming without the knowledge of how the butterflies have migrated in the past. The changed pattern of migration is the sign of a fundamental historical shift. Through the visiting scientists, the novel's protagonist learns about the differences between the present and the past – and what these differences say about the future.

Liz Jensen's *The Rapture* is set in the UK in a not very distant future. A teenage girl, institutionalized after having murdered her mother, starts to have visions of future natural disasters due to climate change, predicting exact dates and locations. When these predictions, one by one, turn out to be correct, her therapist needs to take action, especially since the foreseen catastrophes keep getting worse and closer to home. The depiction of climate change in this thriller provides an interesting contrast to *Flight Behavior*. Whereas Kingsolver's novel shows distinct local effects of a changing climate, *The Rapture* pictures a rapid and drastic development of an increasingly disastrous global catastrophe. In Jensen's novel, climate change as such is at the very center of the narrative. The story starts in a state of general threat: the temperature is rising, and people are passively waiting for things to get worse. At the end of the narrative, the worst imaginable scenario unfolds. The gradual change from one state of affairs to another corresponds with a geographical change, as the disaster is getting closer and closer to Great Britain – until it eventually hits London.

Ian McEwan's *Solar* depicts the life of Nobel laureate Michael Beard and follows his encounters with climate change and renewable energy. Having been a passive (but skeptical) supporter of climate change mitigation, Beard becomes an advocate of large-scale investments in renewable energy technologies. This progression is told alongside Beard's obsession with his fifth wife, the death of his post-doc, and Beard becoming a father against his will. The story mainly takes place in London but includes a minor excursion to Svalbard and ends in New Mexico, where the artificial photosynthesis that Beard has developed is to be demonstrated. In this novel, the development over time is marked by sudden time jumps that show how, overall, progress is slow. It takes ten years from idea to first prototype of the technology that Beard has developed (after he has stolen the idea from his post-doc Aldous). In the meantime, not much has changed in society. Historical change is represented as almost insignificant when faced with the task of climate change mitigation. Geographically, London is the center of the story, representing home but also staleness, void of constructive action. The excursion to Svalbard gives climate change a global dimension. This is the only passage in the book where Beard feels a glimpse of camaraderie among the international crowd of artists, all of whom are deeply concerned with climate change. But the USA is where the action is. This is the land of opportunity and investment, where new ideas are tested and technology demonstrated.

Kim Stanley Robinson's trilogy, *Science in the Capital – Forty Signs of Rain, Fifty Degrees Below,* and *Sixty Days and Counting* – follows the personal development of Frank Vanderwal while he struggles to find ways of mitigating the effects and causes of rising temperatures. Frank, who is almost obsessed with scientific findings of global warming and climate change, experiences a growing frustration with the lack of political action. As his emotional and practical engagement with mitigating climate change grows, he also begins a personal exploration of his inner and outer "wilderness." In this story, radical discontinuities are explored not so much in relation to the climate as to human cognition. The rising awareness of climate change in the USA marks a definite shift in the country's political climate and the conditions for dealing with the increasingly acute issue of climate change. Historical change is thus fundamental to the plot. Furthermore, the protagonist's personal development is strongly aided by his encounter with refugees from Khembalung, an island that has become uninhabitable because of sea level rise. One of their spiritual leaders makes him see that "an excess of reason is itself a form of madness" (Robinson 2004: 268), a thought that is a revelation to Frank. He then starts to look for a science that is not only reasonable but also passionate; a science that not only searches for truth in this world, but actively engages with it.

Saci Lloyd's *The Carbon Diaries 2017* – a sequel to *The Carbon Diaries 2015* – is set in an unequal world moving towards collapse. Laura is a student in London, plays in a band, and lives through her teenage years with friends and boyfriends, and with an increasing frustration with a government that limits her freedom and stands in the way of social change. In the first book, the UK introduces a system of carbon dioxide rationing, and Laura's family are put under pressure not to overspend their allocation and also increasingly to adapt to climate change impacts (flooding) within a dysfunctional emergency system. In the sequel, the UK is still under carbon rationing and London is flooded, but the entire society is now not only dysfunctional but rapidly moving towards collapse due to scarce resources, economic crises, African drought, fights over water access, a delegitimized authoritarian government, and a brutal police crackdown on demonstrations. A ruling elite that becomes increasingly authoritarian controls the citizens and restricts basic liberal freedoms of speech and movement. As civil unrest takes hold, Laura's rock band stops performing in the UK. They set off in a van towards southern Europe to perform at a music festival, but end up in a refugee camp on the Italian border. Along the way, Laura experiences a collapsing world from different geographical and cultural perspectives. As it is a sequel to *Carbon Diaries 2015*, the rapid historical development between 2015 and 2017 is central to the novel. The reader is confronted with two separate temporal developments as well as the relationship between these periods, which is highly dramatic both personally and historically.

These narratives let us imagine five very different perspectives on climate change. Different kinds of effects are put into focus, and they are viewed and interpreted from different geographic, social, and cultural points of view. Taken together, this small selection of novels from the large corpus of contemporary climate fiction do not only show a variety of imaginable climate futures. They also illustrate the diversity of human reactions to the compelling idea of the Anthropocene.

## Humans as a Geological Force

Whether or not the Anthropocene will be accepted as a geological epoch, the fact that humans now interfere with planetary processes is hard to dispute. This interference is of a global character, and the effects are so great that they will leave a mark behind (Ellis and Trachtenberg 2013). These effects have become more and more prominent lately, especially as climate change has made it painfully obvious that we are actually having an impact on the planet itself, and not only on specific species or geographically limited spaces (Chakrabarty 2009; Steffen et al. 2011).

But even if the effects of the Anthropocene have only just now become impossible to ignore, the *idea* of humans being capable of affecting the very conditions of life on earth has been around for quite some time. As Crutzen (2002) notes, the idea of humans being on a par with other forces on earth was introduced in the scientific literature as early as 1873 by the Italian geologist Antonio Stoppani. This idea has also figured in a number of literary works since the Second World War, particularly during the 1960s and 1970s. An early example of a story in which humans have interfered with the physical processes of the earth is *The Burning World* by J. G. Ballard (1964). *The Burning World* is part of a series of four books on environmental disaster, and explores the effects of industrialization and capitalism on life on earth, focusing on drought as the precipitation cycle is disturbed by human activity. Other examples include *Make Room! Make Room!* by Harry Harrison (1966), *The End of the Dream* by Philip Wylie (1972), and *Children of Morrow* by Helen Mary Hoover (1973). The cause of environmental destruction in these books ranges from overpopulation to pollution by means of toxic substances that cause mutation and mass extinction. *Aniara* by Harry Martinson (1956), Philip K. Dick's *Do Androids Dream of Electric Sheep* (1968), *Nausicaä of the Valley of the Wind* by Hayao Miyazaki (1983), and *The Mars Trilogy* by Kim Stanley Robinson (1993, 1994, and 1997) are four other well-known works of literature from three continents that explicitly deal with human powers that can alter the conditions on earth.

From all these works, the epic poem *Aniara* (1956) by Swedish Nobel laureate Harry Martinson is perhaps the first piece of literature to really deal with the Anthropocene. It follows the destiny of 8,000 people aboard a spaceship lost in space shortly after falling out of its path towards Mars. The Earth's population is being evacuated to Mars and Venus because Earth has been poisoned by radio-activity and become inhabitable. Wood is a rare material, and few people have seen fire. As the population aboard the ship are headed for certain death, their time is divided between mourning the past and enjoying themselves – to ward off death. In Robinson's *Mars Trilogy,* humans are leaving Earth before it has been destroyed, primarily as a scientific exploration. But as environmental problems, a scarcity of resources, pollution, and overpopulation ravage Earth, Mars becomes the chance for a second start to create not only a human ecosystem but, most importantly, another, better society. Because life is not found on Mars and humans cannot live there, they have to recreate everything, from introducing new life-forms to altering the composition of the atmosphere. Mars also figures in Dick's *Do Androids Dream of Electric Sheep?* But while the planet represents hope and a new beginning in Martinson's and Robinson's narratives, it is to be understood as the last resort in this story. Life on Mars is lonely, but life on Earth is potentially lethal: "The morning air, spilling over with radioactive motes, gray and sun-beclouding, belched about him, haunting his nose; he sniffed involuntarily the taint of death" (Dick 1968: 5). As in *Aniara*, Earth has been devastated by radioactivity. Apart from humans, very few species still exist, and the ones that do are kept alive under direct human care. Miyazaki's *Nausicaä of the Valley of the Wind* instead plays out in the far future. Space travel is not mentioned in this story; instead, scientists have decided to create a new beginning on Earth itself. Practically everything on Earth is therefore genetically engineered, including human beings, to be able to withstand the high levels of pollution released in the past. Whole ecosystems with entirely new species have been created by humans to neutralize the poisons, so that life as it was can be recreated.

As these stories tease out the extremes of the Anthropocene in different ways, showing a totally human-controlled world or mourning a lost Earth, they open up the imagination on what it means to be a geological force, and what we should do with that power.

## The Power of Humans

Death is everywhere in the four literary works introduced in the last section. As a force, a law of nature if you will, death is still one that we cannot escape. While humans have always been able to take life, the human geological force of the Anthropocene can bring death to an entire planet, influencing the very conditions of life on Earth. When people aboard the spaceship *Aniara* hear of the destruction of Earth, it seems that not only life has been killed but that the whole planet and even the rocks cry out in agony. While this evokes the image of the planet Earth as our home – even before the Apollo missions' images were taken from space – the story also reminds us of the double character of globality. As we saw in the first section, global matters are only experienced through situated practices and viewpoints. So while people aboard *Aniara* mourn the Earth, their mother planet and common home, they do so by telling stories of their specific homes, of Dorisburg and Rind.

But the human force in the Anthropocene is not only global in the geographical sense, or in the sense that we are now interfering with "deep nature" (see Arias-Maldonado, Chapter 3). It also contains the observation that humans are interfering increasingly with planetary processes. Quantities are an inherent part of the scientific Anthropocene discourse. Especially, the number of human inhabitants on Earth (Crutzen 2002; Chakrabarty 2009) and the image of exponential growth in a number of factors such as gross domestic product, water use, paper consumption, and urban population (Steffen et al. 2011) have become defining images of the Anthropocene. This focus on quantities enhances the understanding of the Anthropocene as a side effect; these influences that human activity has on its surrounding environment are unintentional. However, the literary works remind us that human power is two-fold, both unintentional and intentional, as technology also provides the means to actively manage the ecosystems, the composition of the atmosphere, and the acidity of the ocean. All four stories contain both these aspects of human power. The backdrop is primarily the unintentional side effects of human activities that have destroyed or are about to destroy (life on) Earth, and the main story is about how to utilize technology to manage and preserve life conditions.

## What Does It Mean To Be Human in the Anthropocene?

> ... but wilderness too is a garden now. A kind of garden. That's what it means to be what we are.
>
> *(Blue Mars: 90)*

Nature, in the Anthropocene, no longer exists as an entity in its own right, it is claimed, but has become part of human society and culture (see Castree, Chapter 2). If this is true, what is it that could be claimed to be managed by humans? Literary works can take us beyond the point of the "bad Anthropocene," in which humans have a great, but often unintended, impact on nature, into a future in which humans, with the help of technology, are actively pursuing the workings of the planet they inhabit. This is done with the hope of creating a second chance (*Aniara, Nausicaä*, and *Mars Trilogy*) or just to endure and to be able to survive (*Do Androids Dream of Electric Sheep?*).

These are all stories which are played out *after* the Earth has already been more or less destroyed. In *Aniara*, this is demonstrated by the tales from Mars and Venus, particularly as the new harsher conditions are compared with the old Earth when animals and plants were plentiful and nature easy to enjoy. In *Do Androids Dream of Electric Sheep?* dreams of extinct animals and access to fresh fruits and vegetables are used as a contrast to the new times. The conditions on Mars in *Mars Trilogy* – that it is, in fact, uninhabitable without the help of technology – also create specific conditions for societal organization and revolt. Life on a managed planet is lived under harsher conditions, a reminder of the plentiful Earth that we once lived on. But also, as the characters of the stories find ways to enjoy the lives they do have, the story serves as a reminder of the possibility of sharing, instead of exploiting, showing that life can go on despite harsher conditions.

Our power therefore offers both salvation and threat, and it leaves us with the ultimate question: What does it mean to be human and be in control? In *Aniara*, it is even questioned whether or not we still *are* humans after we have destroyed the Earth.

In *Do Androids Dream of Electric Sheep?*, the difference between humans and machines is explored in a future in which most of Earth has been destroyed by radioactive dust after "World War Terminus." But while many animal species are now extinct, and large areas of land are but a radioactive desert, human civilization (and capitalism) is maintained, and new technology is being developed. This technology is used to enable endurable lives for humans both on Mars and on Earth. As humanoid robots (androids) are being developed to work for humans on Mars, they are getting harder and harder to distinguish from humans. The state of mind of humans is being controlled by a "mood organ," an apparatus they can set to their own liking or convenience. A new religion, Mercerism, is practiced as a collective sharing of pain and pleasure. This is done using a technological device that connects those who choose to participate in a struggle up a hill while someone is hurling rocks at them. In the end, the only difference between an android and a human is the latter's ability to feel empathy towards other sentient beings. This difference is upheld through the practicing of Mercerism and the tending of animals. As the lost species of the old world are revered – particularly insects, frogs, and birds – every human has to take care of a living animal. It used to be illegal not to; now, it is just deemed highly immoral if you do not. Because the book's protagonist is on a mission to kill (retire) six androids that escaped Mars after they killed their owners, he is faced with this blurred boundary between created and "natural" life, and questions the taken-for-granted assumption that the latter is worth more than the former.

In *Nausicaä of the Valley of the Wind*, the protagonist, Princess Nausicaä, is out on a quest to find out the secret of the huge poisonous forests spreading on the Earth's surface. When she finally finds out that they are in fact the result of human engineering to "purify" the Earth, to make it "clean" again, she revolts against the very ideas of stewardship and maintained stability. The story tells us that no matter how well humans can plan the evolution of nature-society, it is not desirable to be in total control. Rather than perfect planning, we need to rethink our relationship with the Earth and its inhabitants, not as stewards but as cohabitants, respecting not only what is considered "pure" nature but also that which is modified, engineered, the cyborgs if you will, which are also life. Thus, she rages against the supercomputer that has been built by the old-time scientists to plan the future of the Earth and steer it towards a path of sustainability.

Our bodies may have been artificially transformed, but our lives will always be our own! Life survives by the power of life. . . . To live is to change. The ohmu, the mold, the grasses and trees, we human beings . . . we will all go on changing. . . . But *you* cannot change. You have only the plan that was built into you.

(Nausicaä: *508*)

Similar thoughts are expressed by some of the new inhabitants on Mars in Robinson's *Mars Trilogy*. While they all agree that humans will always affect, and be affected by, its environment, this interaction should be played out with respect. Mars is not to be transformed beyond recognition, but only to let humans coinhabit it. In a heated debate on the planet's future, on what to value and what to do with the power that technology lends us humans, one of the characters gets the final word:

I think you value consciousness too high, and rock too little. We are not lords of the universe. We're one small part of it. We may be its consciousness, but being the consciousness of the universe does not mean turning it all into a mirror image of us. It means rather fitting into it as it is, and worshipping it with our attention.

(Red Mars: *179*)

In line with Eckersley's (2017) notion of the "uncertain Anthropocene," these characters reject both the idea of humans being outside nature and the notion that humans and nature are so intertwined that they are somehow inseparable – nature proceeds, prods back, reacts in unforeseen ways to what humans do, showing that while humans might now be a geological force, they are far from being the only one.

## Politics, Agency, and the Anthropocene Imagination

Meadowcroft's (2017) thorough work on the concept of "the environment" shows how it emerged and was established in the 1960s and 1970s. Inscribed in the idea of "the environment" is the separation of man and his environment, which includes natural and man-made elements. From the early 1970s, "the environment" became a policy sphere on its own; "once the environment was conceptualized as a *critically-important-but-vulnerable* entity, it made sense to take systematic action to protect that environment" (Meadowcroft 2017: 62). This came to be seen as an important responsibility for governments, both at home and abroad. Agency in relation to the environment came to be understood as the crafting of a domain of policy with officials, organizations, and budgets configured through certain administrative procedures, analytical approaches, and policy tools. Recent reformulations, such as "planetary boundaries" with their "safe operating space for humanity" (Rockström et al. 2009), reiterate "the environment" as that which surrounds us, a discourse on limits, and a domain to be governed. Hence, the "planetary boundaries" approach is rather well in line with the environmental politics of the 1970s. There is a renewed emphasis on supra-state forms of governing as discussions have evolved around how humanity could assume a new form of responsibility and stewardship for the planet we have created (Steffen et al. 2011).

Several conversations have concerned capitalism. If a capitalist mode of production is understood not only as an economic system but also as a specific way of organizing nature, then agency in the Anthropocene, or "capitalocene" (Moore 2016), must be about resisting state-led capitalism (Klein 2014; Malm 2015). While there are many works of science fiction set in a postcapitalist climate-changed world, Kim Stanley Robinson's work is perhaps the best known. In his recent book *2312*, capitalism only exists on Earth, while elsewhere in the solar system a community-based organization ("the Mondragon Accord") defines the basic parameters of the economy.

In Saci Lloyd's *The Carbon Diaries 2017*, the future world is seen and experienced from the perspective of a teenager, capturing how we feel about living with climate change and the growing frustration and radicalization that are spurred when governmental authorities lose legitimacy. As a response to an imagined collapse of liberal democracy, some scholars have initiated an analysis on what kind of democratic agency could address the challenges posed by the Anthropocene. Eckersley (2017) sketches the contours of a "geopolitan democracy." Purdy (2015: 268–269) notes that while no one knows such a democracy, we could identify some attitudes that would be necessary. These revolve around skepticism towards expert judgements based on unilateralism or cost–benefit analyses, a belief that democratic engagement is possible, and an appreciation of the variety of ways that could bring us closer to shared identities and solidarities with humans and the rest of the living world. In Robinson's *Science in the Capital*, the reader gets such a glimpse of the possible change we could make from an excessive "rational" approach to life to a more spiritual and emotional relationship to nature and our fellow humans. The reader learns that doing something about climate change could be the start of exploring better ways of organizing a society and better ways of being humans.

While the animal question – how best to think about and to live with animals – is often only partly engaged in political theory, it is the starting point for those who see "the need to decenter the human in discourses on the Anthropocene" (Human Animal Research Network Editorial Collective 2015: ix). Their book, *Animals in the Anthropocene: Critical Perspectives on Non-human Futures*, provides many cases for nonhuman agency and what it might mean to act and intervene in the Anthropocene. In their view, attempts to rethink the political in the Anthropocene must also involve a repositioning of the social. We need to imagine and embrace a "zoopolis" that can sustain close interrelationships between humans and animals, new forms of connectivity, different social arrangements, and new forms of being political within this new world (Human Animal Research Network Editorial Collective 2015: xix).

It seems clear that the Anthropocene imagination easily sparks a much wider discussion. As Scranton puts it, "how do we make meaningful decisions in the shadow of our inevitable end?" (Scranton 2015: 20). Drawing on the arguments spelled out by Chakrabarty (2009), Scranton sees the need to confront the end of the world as we know it, and asks us to learn how to die (Scranton 2015). As described in one of the previous sections, this is a call similar to the people on board the spaceship *Aniara*. But it is not just fictional writings that are apocalyptic; philosophy shares this as well, while trying to tease out what that condition implies for us. Raffnsøe embraces Žižek's sense that this is "the end times." The world as we have known it is coming to an end. We are "stepping over the threshold into a new and unknown space in which fundamental new conditions apply" (Raffnsøe 2016: 6). While we are stepping into a new and unknown space, it is defined by a new heightened sense of human responsibility and recognition of human dependence and precariousness (Raffnsøe 2016: xii). But one cannot deduce a detailed agenda for political action from the idea of the Anthropocene; "it is a way of seeing, not a manifesto" (2016: 193), which offers a different starting point than "sustainability" for understanding and dealing with the specific contradictions of the current ecological crises. For Davis, there is no "escape from the crises of the Holocene into a world made indefinitely sustainable" (Davis 2016: 194). Literary protagonists, like Nausicaä and the Reds in the *Mars Trilogy*, can serve as inspirational examples of how to live with such a starting point. Even the Flatlanders in Nathaniel Rich's *Odds against Tomorrow*, with their attempt to live self-sufficiently in New York after it has been flooded, show us how we can live differently in this new world. Some of these themes also figure in the dystopian *MaddAddam* trilogy by Margaret Atwood, which is set in a genetically engineered world exploring cultish forms of social organization in the face of pandemic disasters.

While Bonneuil and Fressoz (2016) also speak about surviving and living (and possibly thriving) in the Anthropocene, they argue that we need to make sense of what happened to us. Instead of a universal history of humanity distorting the earth system, we need to produce "multiple, debatable and polemical narratives rather than a single hegemonic narrative that is supposedly apolitical" (Bonneuil and Fressoz 2016: 289). They offer several different histories that allow us to grasp what led us to the Anthropocene: the military apparatuses, consumerist desires and infrastructures, gaps of income and wealth, financial interests of globalization, and techno-scientific apparatuses (Bonneuil and Fressoz 2016: 291). Thus, there seems to be a need to diversify the Anthropocene imagination, to tell more stories about how we got here and what it might mean to us in whatever "plural ecologies" we might be situated. While many scientific writings on agency in the Anthropocene narrate humankind as a totality, literary fiction is filled with diverse human agency. New narratives depicting, for example, human subjects who experience climate change and its political, cultural, social, and psychological implications capture the ambiguities, paradoxes, and uncertainties of human life. Whereas earth system scientists aim for an outside perspective of "Spaceship Earth," novels provide a fictitious world filtered through the mind of one particular fictitious person. A literary protagonist is always part of a specific context. When a climate-changed world is described through the eyes of the protagonist, the description is therefore filtered through his or her social and cultural position. In Liz Jensen's *The Rapture*, a changing climate is deeply embedded in psychological factors. The novel's display of beliefs includes religious fundamentalism, parapsychology, radical post-humanism, and science, thereby suggesting that in every given place and time, human beings will conceptualize the fate of the planet from strongly diverging perspectives. In Barbara Kingsolver's *Flight Behavior*, the issue of climate change is embedded in a depiction of different types of personal restrictions – geographic, economic, educational, and social. An awareness of climate change and a willingness to do something about it are hence conditioned not solely by differences in worldviews, as in *The Rapture*, but predominantly, and more fundamentally, by the strongly uneven distribution of personal opportunities. In the recent book *Molecular Red: Theory of the Anthropocene*, Makenzie Wark uses the science fiction author Kim Stanley Robinson's *Mars Trilogy* to visit a "meta-utopia," which is needed for a "critical and creative approach to the selection out of the past, into the future, of ways of life that know that only if our species-being endures can it be said to touch the real" (Wark 2015: xix).

## Conclusion

The strongest device of literature is fiction, which enables us to imagine the consequences of our actions and tease out the repercussions and alternatives we have. Fiction has the power to narrate everything that can go wrong, in settings that seem twisted and unreal, but with resonance in our daily lives. Fiction can take the effects to their extremes, whether it is an Earth without insects and few other living animals, filled with a haze of radioactive dust, a spaceship on its path to certain death, a future filled with huge insects and pollution-eating mold, or experiments with new social configurations and economic systems of exchange.

Fiction, this power to imagine the far-reaching implications of the Anthropocene, provides us with a space to explore politics in ways that need not be understood at first glance as "realistic." First of all, literature reminds us that the *idea* of an Anthropocene is not new. Such a world was imagined when few believed that humans could have such an extensive impact. Older stories of an Anthropocene can serve as both warnings and inspiration for political thought and action. They do so by engaging us emotionally with the conditions of the Anthropocene. By following particular persons in particular contexts, literature lets us experience the *global* essence of the Anthropocene through a situated specificity and its political implication through a context that is often not our own. As such, it is a great device to connect the abstract global circumstances to the local and mundane in everyday life. Novels situate and specify what it means to act in stratified societies, thus bringing in diverging personal opportunities and social positions, clashing and merging belief-systems, religion, and romantic love. And, perhaps most importantly, literature can help us understand what it means to be human in the Anthropocene, to live in this age and have this power that is able to alter the conditions of life. It can help us explore our agency, shed light on the capacities and responsibilities of humans, and question what we value and what our place in nature-society is.

# References

Ballard, James Graham. 1964. *The Burning World*. Berkeley Books.
Bonneuil, Christophe, and Jean-Baptiste Fressoz. 2016. *The Shock of the Anthropocene: The Earth, History and Us*. New York: Verso Books.
Chakrabarty, Dipesh. 2009. The Climate of History: Four Theses. *Critical Inquiry* 35 (2): 197–222.
Crutzen, Paul J. 2002. Geology of Mankind. *Nature* 415: 23.
Crutzen, P. J., and Stoermer, E. F. 2000. The "Anthropocene." *Global Change Newsletter* 41: 17.
Davis, Jeremy. 2016. *The Birth of the Anthropocene*. Oakland, CA: University of California Press.
Dick, Philip Kindred. 1968. *Do Androids Dream of Electric Sheep?* London: Weidenfeld and Nicolson.
Eckersley, Robyn. 2017. Geopolitan Democracy in the Anthropocene. *Political Studies* 65 (4): 983–999.
Ellis, Michael A. and Zev Trachtenberg. 2013. Which Anthropocene Is It to Be? Beyond Geology to a Moral and Public Discourse. *Earth's Future* 2: 122–125.
Evans, C.L. 2015. Climate Change Is So Dire We Need a New Kind of Science Fiction to Make Sense of It. *The Guardian*, August 20.
Gibson, Katherine, Deborah Bird Rose, and Ruth Fincher, eds. 2015. *Manifesto for Living in the Anthropocene*. Brooklyn, NY: Punctum Books.
Goodman, Nelson. 1978. *Ways of Worldmaking*. Hassocks, UK: Harvester Press.
Hamilton, Clive, Christophe Bonneuil, and François Gemenne, eds. 2015. *The Anthropocene and the Global Environmental Crisis*. London: Routledge.
Harrison, Harry. 1966. *Make Room! Make Room!* UK: Penguin.
Hoover, Helen Mary. 1973. *Children of Morrow*. New York: Four Winds Press.
Human Animal Research Network Collective. 2015. *Animals in the Anthropocene: Critical Perspectives on Non-human Futures*. Sydney: Sydney University Press.
Jensen, Liz. 2009. *The Rapture*. London: Bloomsbury.
Johns-Putra, Adeline. 2016. Climate Change in Literature and Literary Studies: From Cli-fi, Climate Change Theater and Ecopoetry to Ecocriticism and Climate Change Criticism. *WIREs Climate Change* 7: 266–282.
Kaplan, E. Ann. 2016. *Climate Trauma: Foreseeing the Future in Dystopian Film and Fiction*. New Brunswick, NJ: Rutgers University Press.
Kingsolver, Barbara. 2012. *Flight Behavior*. New York: Harper.
Klein, Naomi. 2014. *This Changes Everything*. New York: Simon and Schuster.
Lloyd, Saci. 2009. *The Carbon Diaries 2017*. London: Hodder Children's Books.
Lorimer, Jamie. 2012. Multinatural Geographies for the Anthropocene. *Progress in Human Geography* 36 (5): 593–612.
Malm, Andreas. 2015. The Anthropocene Myth. Blaming All of Humanity for Climate Change Lets Capitalism off the Hook. *Jacobin*, March 30.
Martinson, Harry. 1956/1963. *Aniara*. Stockholm: Albert Bonniers förlag.
McEwan, Ian. 2010. *Solar*. London: Jonathan Cape.
McKay, Don. 2008. Ediacaran and Anthropocene: Poetry as Reader of Deep Time. *Prairie Fire* 29 (4) Winter.
McKibben, Bill. 2005. What the Warming World Needs Now Is Art, Sweet Art. *GRIST*, April 22.

Meadowcroft, James. 2017. The Birth of the Environment and the Evolution of Environmental Governance. In *Conceptual Innovations in Environmental Policy*, edited by James Meadowcroft and Dan Fiorini, 53–76. Cambridge, MA: MIT Press.

Miyazaki, Hayao. 1983. *Kaze no Tani no Nausicaä (Nausicaä of the Valley of the Wind)*, first published by Tokuma Shoten Co., Ltd. Deluxe edition, first printing 2012. San Francisco: VIZ Media, LLC.

Moore, Jason W., ed. 2016. *Anthropocene or Capitalocene? Nature, History, and the Crisis of Capitalism*. Oakland, CA: PM Press.

Morton, Timothy. 2013. *Hyperobjects: Philosophy and Ecology after the End of the World*. Minneapolis, MN: University of Minnesota Press.

*Nature*. 2003. Welcome to the Anthropocene. Editorial. Nature 424: 709 (August 14, 2003).

Purdy, Jeremiah. 2015. *After Nature. A Politics for the Anthropocene*. Cambridge and London: Harvard University Press.

Raffnsøe, Sverre. 2016. *Philosophy of the Anthropocene: The Human Turn*. New York: Palgrave Macmillan.

Rich, Nathaniel. 2014. *Odds against Tomorrow*. New York: Picador.

Robinson, Kim Stanley. 1992. *Red Mars*. New York: Bantam.

Robinson, Kim Stanley. 1993. *Green Mars*. New York: Bantam.

Robinson, Kim Stanley. 1996. *Blue Mars*. New York: Bantam.

Robinson, Kim Stanley. 2004. *Forty Signs of Rain*. New York: Bantam Spectra.

Robinson, Kim Stanley. 2005. *Fifty Degrees Below*. New York: Bantam Spectra.

Robinson, Kim Stanley. 2007. *Sixty Days and Counting*. New York: Bantam Spectra.

Rockström, Johan, Will Steffen, Kevin J. Noone, et al. 2009. A Safe Operating Space for Humanity. *Nature* 461: 472–475.

Scranton, Roy. 2015. *Learning to Die in the Anthropocene: Reflections on the End of Civilization*. San Francisco: City Lights Publishers.

Steffen, Will, Åsa Persson, Lisa Deutsch, et al. 2011. The Anthropocene: From Global Change to Planetary Stewardship. *Ambio* 40 (7): 739–761

*The Economist*. 2011. Welcome to the Anthropocene. Accessed June 13, 2018. http://www.economist.com/node/18744401.

Trexler, Adam. 2015. *Anthropocene Fictions: The Novel in a Time of Climate Change*. Charlottesville: University of Virginia Press.

Trexler, Adam, and Adeline Johns-Putra. 2011. Climate Change in Literature and Literary Criticism. *WIREs Climate Change* 2: 185–200.

Wark, Mark. 2015. *Molecular Red: Theory for the Anthropocene*. New York: Verso Books.

Wylie, Philip. 1972. *The End of the Dream*. New York: Daw Books.

# Part II

Key Concepts and the Anthropocene:
A Reconsideration

# 5

# Power, World Politics, and Thing-Systems in the Anthropocene

ANTHONY BURKE AND STEFANIE FISHEL

Power is widely understood to have both constitutive and generative force in the political. Particular concepts of power – especially those organized around the idea of power politics and the figure of state sovereignty – have had a profound constitutive effect on the practice of (world) politics and in political theory (Bially Mattern 2008). They work to generate both knowledge about politics and actual institutional structures, effects, and modes of behavior. What they do not do, however, is capture the complex actuality of power relations in international society when we consider the relationship between humanity and planet Earth that can be called "global social nature" (Dalby 2009: 6). This term is central to our materialist understanding of the Anthropocene and is a key conceptual marker in our earlier publication, "Planet Politics: A Manifesto from the End of IR [International Relations]" (Burke et al. 2016). It expresses the complex causal interpenetration of political, social, industrial, and ecological processes and change, along with the constant "translation" (as Bruno Latour names it) between the human and the nonhuman, such that nowhere on earth does "nature" exist outside of human social impacts or human society exist separate from "nature." At the same time, ecosystems and nonhuman communities have their own rhythms, agencies, and purposes pursued without regard for human ends. What results is a global *social\nature* that turns back on human institutions and living arrangements in ever more unpredictable and violent forms.

Theories of power in International Relations do not capture this interplay between humans and nonhumans, but rather, fix an image of a static mode of relations, one that works to explain particular instantiations of power within state and human-centered systems while silencing and disallowing other understandings and realities. These static images reflect a larger commitment within International Relations to state-centric understandings of world order. Major political and International Relations theories believe themselves to have accounts of political and state power that are settled and steadfast, expressing universal and continuing truths about human behavior and contestation that should rarely, if ever, be revisited. This demonstrates the ideological function of power itself; it reflects its instantiation within how International Relations, as a discipline, would understand its subjects of study: their location and ability to exercise power in a space understood as "international politics."

In this chapter, we contend that the time has come to fundamentally revisit many of these founding tenets of power in the light of the Anthropocene, both in International Relations as a disciplinary field and in global politics as a set of institutions and regimes. We develop an alternative theory of power exercised in complex and distributed ways across "thing-systems" that ineluctably connect society and nature. We do not argue that traditional state-based notions of power have no continuing salience or value – at least within restricted, anthropocentric domains. We do, however, argue against restricting our ideas of power to the human and the social. It is no longer tenable to understand social life as ontologically separate from ecosystems or the biosphere, as if there were an actual category separation between the social and the environmental (Latour 1993; Castree and Braun 2001).

Therefore, this chapter focuses on how power in the Anthropocene does not merely express relations between people or governments, but functions across entangled domains of institutions, ecologies, and things that are connected to more than human intention and influence. As such, this chapter can be seen as a contribution to political theory, in both its classical and green guises, and to the broad research project of earth system governance, which has identified power as a key "cross-cutting theme" (Biermann et al. 2010: 289). In short, in the face of the profound planetary ecological crisis and the paradigmatic shift wrought by the concept of the Anthropocene, traditional concepts and practices of power in International Relations are inadequate and dangerous.

Two such concepts are International Relations' twin poles of "anarchy" and "hierarchy," which imagine world politics simultaneously as an eternally competitive and ungoverned space of estrangement, and as minimally ordered by structures of hegemony and alliance. Given their constitutive power, these concepts are doubly anachronistic in an epoch in which "social nature" is rebounding brutally on humanity with uncontrollable power, and dangerous because of the way they have, when translated into practices and institutions, deepened the appalling ecological crisis facing the earth. The exercise of power politics has worsened conflict, protected and exacerbated the extraction and burning of fossil fuels, and compromised and weakened global environmental governance. Yet the power thus exercised is increasingly spectral, as an anthropocentrically affected biosphere is turning back violently on states and humanity with a power that mainstream social science cannot yet properly conceptualize and states cannot control.

At the same time, the classical idea of sovereignty operative in power politics and embedded fundamentally in international law and global governance – which sees power located and contained in a bounded *body politic* that is at once subject to and constitutive of the state – must also be rethought. The state imagined as Leviathan – as a metaphoric figure of the great human – is the ultimate in anthropocentrism, utterly divorced from the air it might breathe, the cosmos from which it draws its atomic complexity, the living materiality of its territory, and the biosphere it depends upon for survival. This figure, like the image in the frontispiece of Hobbes' *Leviathan* towering over its sovereign territory, can only embody mastery over nature. Can a global order built on this figure truly grapple with the Anthropocene?

In this chapter, we assert a double interpretation of the Anthropocene: the traditional picture, drawn from earth system science, which portrays humanity as a geological force having an enormous collective power to alter the earth's fundamental systems (Castree, Chapter 2), and an alternative picture, inspired by "new materialist" or post-constructivist ontology, which portrays nonhuman systems, things, and ecologies having great power over, and apart from, humanity. In both pictures, human power is in fact much weaker and more attenuated than we may assume, because industrialized "geologic" humanity produces effects that are unintended and cannot be controlled, and because subsequent ecological changes will have an unpredictable force independent of human ends and intents. Our theory thus modifies and complicates the traditional Anthropocene narrative, given its emphasis on the human power over – and modification of – nature. We are influenced here by Rafi Youatt's argument, in his *Counting Species*, that nonhuman life forms should be considered equal participants in the practices of environmental biopower represented by the Global Biodiversity Census (Youatt 2015: loc. 996). We extend his intuition that nonhumans can be "sites of resistance to biopower" into the political theory of power itself.

Our double interpretation of the Anthropocene has similarities to Clive Hamilton's emphasis on both the enhanced vulnerability and the "super-agency" of the human in his *Defiant Earth*. While we echo his appeal for an enhanced sense of human responsibility for earth system repair, our analysis cuts against his call for a "new Anthropocentrism" and his disdain for post-humanism (Hamilton 2017). We do not believe that the emergence of some kind of superhuman agency – which is certainly evident but has been chaotic, multiple, and often anonymous – amounts to a new human *power*. Here, we are also challenging Manuel Arias-Maldonado's criticism, in Chapter 3 of this book, of the new materialism – which he suggests is fundamentally at odds with the Anthropocene narrative's emphasis on "one prevalent agentic capacity, that of humans." We do not deny the enormous effects of industrialized human agency in the Anthropocene, but neither do we accept that this makes humanity a privileged agent or conflate it with "power" as such, which must now be thought of as shared with nonhuman life and geo-biophysical processes. This also has important ethical implications: an argument for humanity's enhanced responsibility to mitigate its planetary impacts must be paired with a profound sense of humility for human dependence on and vulnerability to the earth's ecology. We thus echo Anne Fremaux and John Barry (Chapter 9) in their call for "gratitude, humility, respect, and restraint" as the most appropriate ethical response to the Anthropocene. To assert that nonhuman systems and forms of life have power is, in fact, to oppose eco-modernist views that proclaim "the end of nature."

As part of our ongoing effort to encourage a profound rethinking of the membership, architecture, and purposes of global politics in the Anthropocene, we aim in this chapter to formulate answers to two key questions: What happens to our understandings of power and agency when they are no longer possessed by states or humans as such? What might a power that expresses humanity's complex entanglement with the planet look like, one that expresses and gives form to a global politics exercised with and for the earth rather than over it? This is far more than a wishful or theoretical agenda. After the United Nations General Assembly's adoption of the *2030 Agenda for Sustainable Development*, which stated its determination "to protect the planet from degradation," international society collectively faces a challenge to do so out of the very ontological and institutional architecture that has presided over that degradation. To challenge and change such structures of power will also require fundamentally rethinking our idea of it.

## Anthropocentric Power in World Politics

The dominant prevailing notion and institutionalization of power in world politics has two key features. It is state-centric – exercised by and for states – and anthropocentric – exercised by and for humans. *By* and *for* are interlinked but distinct considerations, pointing to the ways in which the Anthropocene challenges our mainstream images of power both analytically – in terms of how we understand power to function and be comprised – and normatively, in terms of the objects and purposes for which power must be exercised.

Whom, or what, power is assumed to be *exercised by* generates an ontological account of the units and structure of the system and, by default, may also generate the rudiments of matching ethics: what power – in a moral rather than a strategic sense – is meant to be *for*; hence the dominant account in realist International Relations theory that the key units of the international system are states and that power is exercised by them; following this, some accounts argue that power should exclusively be exercised for individual states and their clients, and other accounts create room for power to also be exercised collectively for the common good of states. Whatever the many disagreements in this literature, there is a common assumption that states are the key actors and beneficiaries of the exercise of power. This is a particular, narrowed, image of the *Anthropos* that struggles vainly to imagine "humanity" as a moral or political entity and to which the biosphere as a moral *or* physical entity is almost entirely invisible (Bull 1977: 80–82).

The question of what and whom power is to be exercised *for* is properly an ethical one, going beyond the strategic aims of states to what the overarching purposes of international society, order, and global governance should be. The Anthropocene and the global ecological crisis bring this question of what international order should be *for* into profound relief. Here, we are interested in how underlying concepts of power will shape those answers.

The dominant understanding of power in International Relations originates with Hans Morgenthau, and his notion of politics as a struggle for power remains at the core of International Relations theory (Holsti 1964: 179). Morgenthau defines power as "man's control over the minds and actions of other men" and, at the international level, argues that all states must seek to maximize power; therefore, international politics "can be conceived of and analyzed as a struggle between independent units seeking to dominate others." He declares famously that "international politics is of necessity power politics" (Morgenthau 1978: 30–33). Power is not the same as violence but is always about conflict, competition, dominance, and influence among humans and their communities. It is also made up of "material" capacities (economic and military strength, land and resources, gross domestic product) that can be accumulated and measured.

In a crucial, ontologically powerful move, Morgenthau distinguishes *political* power from "man's power over nature ... or over the means of production and consumption," and insists that power rests on an idea of "politics *as an autonomous sphere of action and understanding* apart from other spheres, such as economics ... ethics, aesthetics and religion." "Nature" here is solely understood as something man has "power over" and that has little relation to, or implications for, politics, while the idea of the biosphere or earth system is inconceivable; it lies entirely outside the sensible (Morgenthau 1978: 27, 5; emphasis added). Alternatively, realist or geopolitical environmental security literature acknowledges the force of biophysical environments but remains state- and anthropocentric in its commitments, centering its concerns on scarcity and the role of resources in conflict and war (Homer-Dixon 1999; Klare 2002).

Morgenthau's radical division between politics and other spheres enacts the constitutional "modern divide between the natural world and the social world" that was the target of Bruno Latour in *We Have Never Been Modern*, a practice of "purification" that "creates two entirely different ontological zones: that of human beings on the one hand; that of nonhumans on the other." In this chapter, we instead pursue his strategy of "translation" that "creates mixtures between entirely new kinds of beings, hybrids of nature and culture" and would understand climate change, for example, by "link[ing] in one continuous chain the chemistry of the upper atmosphere, scientific and industrial strategies, the preoccupations of heads of state [and] the anxieties of ecologists" (Latour 1993: 11–13).

In her analysis of power in International Relations, Janice Bially Mattern traces how International Relations opened up but failed to resolve a debate between "four faces" of power. The first was the behavioral realist view, which saw power as a material entity that could be accumulated and was concerned with dominance and influence; the second, an institutionalist view concerned with how institutions silence dissent and enforce consensus; the third, a Gramscian view focused on structural (economic and social) power and ideology; and the fourth, a constructivist view that power "is not an exercise carried out by interested agents, but a discursive process through which agents and their interests are produced in the first place" (Bially Mattern 2008: 693–694).

One significant example of the fourth face was the collection *Power in Global Governance*, in which two leading constructivist thinkers (re)defined power as "the production, in and through social relations, of effects that shape the capacities of actors to determine their own circumstances and fate" (Barnett and Duvall 2005: 3). Bially Mattern argues that in the fourth face of power "world politics happen, not where specific types of actors behave in specific ways, but where social processes produce particular actors and behaviours as meaningful." She argues for a new debate that would be less concerned with trying to enforce a common-ground definition and more with promoting pluralistic dialogue that would leave underlying assumptions exposed (Bially Mattern 2008: 694). However critical, this call is also based on a systemic exclusion: power is solely social. Power is not something possessed and exercised by nonhuman animals and processes, which would have an independent force outside and upon the social. Her account of the fourth face is thus ironic. The Anthropocene is hidden and ignored by the discursive process through which (global) agents and their interests are currently produced. Where does world politics *not* happen?

But, even within this resistance to theorizing power beyond the human, we can see an opening for a broader understanding of thing-systems power. If world politics is seen as relational and social, then other actors, agents, or facilitators of power (especially nonhuman ones) could challenge the very social processes that silence certain kinds of actors and behaviors – which occurred because "actors" and "behaviors" have been viewed as solely exhibiting human self-consciousness and intention. If we shed an anthropocentric bias, we can see that nonhuman animals and organisms; gases, liquids, and viruses; forests, glaciers, and permafrost act and behave and have effects in ways that profoundly cross the barrier between "society" and "nature." A similarly glimpsed opening can be found in Kal Holsti's 1964 essay "The Concept of Power in the Study of International Relations." His essay focuses strongly on power as a process of interstate *influencing* and seeks to draw out complexities missing in previous realist writings; in this, it is resolutely anthropocentric. However, he concludes the essay's introduction by asking: "Should we not however define power in a way which best clarifies what we observe and what we need to know? A definition should suggest areas of enquiry and reality ..." (Holsti 1964: 180). In the Anthropocene, "what we need to know" – the relationship between enquiry and reality – exceeds the social. It demands that we become sensitive to "things" and "thing-power" in a way that goes beyond the Cartesian view of the world as divided between thinking, knowing, active subjects and mute, agentless objects (Bennett 2004 and 2010).

Beyond the question of whether the anthropocentric image of power can include the nonhuman, we should also look at the limitations created by its specific elements. Firstly, power is about *domination* and hegemony in the service of national or great power interests, based on the coercive use of material capacities, even if elements of it are understood as normative and discursive, and subject to balancing, contestation, and tests of legitimacy (Morgenthau 1978; Reus-Smit 2004; Clark 2007). Secondly, power is about *influence* – influence that could be subtle and consensual, although the puzzle that is of most interest to scholars seems to be influence that diverts or deters, that persuades an actor to do something they might not otherwise choose to do. Thirdly, power is a *means to an end* and issues from an actor's *intentions*; it is somehow strategic and instrumental in nature (Holsti 1964: 181–182; Morgenthau 1978: 29). And fourthly, power is a *relation* – as Robert Dahl insists – "among people" and not among humans and "animate and inanimate objects." Another interesting criterion of Dahl's is that a power relation requires some direct connection between actors: "there is no 'action at a distance'" (Dahl 1957: 203–204).

In this anthropocentric paradigm, it is almost impossible to see power operating systemically, structurally, anonymously, and accidentally; as being about unintended effects and consequences, many of which we know to be planetary in scale; as aggregating the witting and unwitting actions of numerous actors, institutions, and *things* into larger (and more unpredictable) processes and systems. In such systems (markets, wars, the Internet, ecosystems, oceans), discrete actors or institutions may seek to exercise power with intent and to dominate, but their actions flow into an enormous array of systems subject to complex feedbacks, the emergence of new system-level phenomena, and perverse and magnified effects which resist stasis and escape directed attempts at control. Nonanthropocentric power will resist anthropocentric power in its complexity, its nonintentionality, and its heterogeneity.

## Nonanthropocentric Power in World Politics

Traditionally anthropocentric political theory may insist that power requires a conscious actor with intent, direction, purpose, and strategy, and would accept that while nonhuman things may be active, they are not act*ors*. They thus do not exercise or seek power but merely have *effects*, even if those effects are great. Not only does the Anthropocene challenge how human power is understood because it produces unintended system-level effects; it also necessarily challenges how forms of human sociality can merge with other nonhuman beings. Anthropocentric and state forms of power no longer hold in the Anthropocene – as ironic as that seems, given the revealed scale of human "power" there. Put differently, old notions of human domination and power over a separate realm we called "nature" must be rethought and reversed. This reversal has far-reaching repercussions for human politics and indeed, for the continued survival of life on earth.

Power will have to be understood as complex rather than linear, heterogeneous rather than homogeneous, distributed rather than strategic. Complex systems theory thus profoundly challenges traditional Newtonian models of political and social power, and it is now being extended in a "post-human" direction to take in nonhuman life and the biosphere. "Post-human" here serves as shorthand for understanding the human animal and its societies as existentially bound and vulnerable to the biosphere, and thus entangled in relations with multiple species, landscapes, and elements. As Erika Cudworth and Stephen Hobden argue, such a "complex ecology" approach creates "the potential to analyze intersectionality and multiple power relations beyond the human" (Cudworth and Hobden 2013: 4–9, 24). The Anthropocene brings the largest and most complex social-natural system of all – the earth system – into stark focus.

Against this background, we argue for a model of power that conceptualizes it working across large and complex "thing-systems." There, power and effects are created across vast distances and connect institutions, technologies, substances, ecologies, and communities through the myriad ways that they are caught up in larger processes and systems. In this way, they are connected not only across space but also through time. *Contra* Dahl, there *is* action (and thus power) at a distance. Complex systems can be understood as relational in that there are strongly interdependent actors and processes within them that create change from feedback loops, chaotic behavior, multiple stable states, nonlinear effects, and a non-Gaussian distribution of variables (Ormand 2017; O. R. Young 2017: 236).

In anthropocentric accounts of power, things – resources like oil, coal, food, and uranium – are used to increase a state's capability to influence based on their accumulation and use for war or trade. What happens to our understandings (and experience) of power when these "things" begin to take on influence of their own separate from their immediate human use? Or, put more precisely, how do we formulate a theory of power when the rapacious accumulation and use of natural "resources" (biological, chemical, and mineral) are creating processes that exceed and confound our current system's ability to control them? The accumulation of those items once led to greater power and influence for states in the international order, and now, through the feckless overuse and misunderstanding of natural systems, exerts increasing pressure on human political systems and through processes of species extinction, climate change, and profound ecosystem damage. Yet these "things" do not seek to persuade or offer and grant rewards in the traditional sense. There is no intention expressed in threats of punishment or use of force. Nonhuman actants, energies, and ecologies do have the ability to be powerful in ways that approximate older ideas of power: they can change, effect, destroy, cause insecurity, and induce fear and anxiety, but unlike human uses of power, they do not act with strategic intent.

To add to this complexity, systems also interrelate with other systems. In our above example, complex anthropocentric systems like the global economy would interact with earth systems such as the atmosphere, biosphere, and climate system, creating outputs from multiple systemic inputs. As in all complex systems, the outputs are just as likely to be far away from the average as to settle into a Gaussian distribution (Ball 2017). Although biological systems will not defy physical laws, the strongly interdependent variables create changes that will frustrate prediction and can have unintended consequences in the system or systems involved. The so-called "butterfly effect" is one such example of chaotic change across complex systems.

Complex "thing-systems" embody relations within themselves and with the other systems in which they are nested and enmeshed, creating *assemblages of assemblages* between human and nonhuman actants and processes that extend in scale to the earth system itself and the cosmos. We take the notion of assemblage here from Jane Bennett, who uses the term to develop a theory of "distributed agency" across assemblages, which she defines as "*ad hoc* groupings of diverse elements" and a global "event-space and style of structuration." She explains that "assemblages are not governed by any central head" and their effects "are emergent properties." While components of an assemblage have "a certain vital force," she speaks of "an affectivity proper to the grouping as such: an agency *of* the assemblage" (Bennett 2010: 466–473; also Youatt 2015).

While the planet's biological systems have always been complex and interrelated, our point here is two-fold. Firstly, human resource extraction and fossil fuel use have increasingly affected earth systems through the latter part of the Holocene, forcing a change in human understandings of our effect on geologic time and an ontological shift into global social nature. Secondly, technology and human ability to measure and incorporate complexity into scientific studies have increased throughout the twentieth and twenty-first centuries. Satellite and drone imaging and metagenomic sequencing (Fishel 2017) stand as two examples of novel techniques that allow human researchers to save immense amounts of data and analyze entire communities, rather than single snapshots in time or an individual bacterium grown in a lab. These techniques change our ways to organize and make order out of systems that have always been complex.

To assume a complex thing-systems perspective that incorporates the biosphere requires challenging the place of intentionality in the theory of power on two levels. Firstly, self-conscious human actors cannot so easily exercise social and political power in complex systems – their intent may be frustrated, the change created may be far from the intended outcome, or the intent may be narrowly framed and disregard the cascading and disastrous social, economic, or environmental consequences. Hence, intentionality can lead to grossly irresponsible and illegitimate outcomes unintended by those wielding power. Here, the modernist (Newtonian–Cartesian) *ontology* of power fails its *ontic* context (systemic complexity and interrelation) in both actual and normative terms. There is a failure both to see the real (affected communities and ecologies) and to generate a practice of responsibility towards them. We take up these questions of responsibility below.

Secondly, to restrict power relations to those between actors with self-conscious intent serves to blind us to the fact that nonhuman species, life-forms, and processes – especially when they form into dynamic and complex assemblages of human and nonhuman actants – have profound, beneficial, and sometimes destructive effects that we think it right to understand as forms of power. When bound into such assemblages, nonhuman actants and processes have enormous, wide-ranging, and cascading effects that are changing the nature of life on earth. They can nurture multiple forms of life; they can destroy forms of life; all while undergoing the degradation and change of their own life systems. They are forms of power in themselves because they are wreaking such profound and irreversible change, and because they are producing effects that traverse and transcend all the category divisions (political, economic, cultural, social, technological, and environmental) that theorists have used to restrict power to matters deemed "political." It cannot be denied that such assemblages (forest burning–palm oil–extinction–transboundary pollution assemblages; tsunami–nuclear accident–insecurity assemblages; climate change–hurricane–poverty–failing state assemblages) exert enormous *influence* on social–natural–economic systems, but in ways that are chaotic and complex and reflect no single strategic intent. It may still be possible to see human-exercised power as a means to an end (such as earth system and biodiversity protection, climate change mitigation, social justice, and ecological security), but such efforts create great challenges of coordination and cooperation across myriad actors and spheres, and across societies and ecosystems. Such "eco-system-power" will have to be understood as shared and distributed; and collective efforts to channel it responsibly will not survive a radical normative pluralism in which the very ends of power remain perpetually in dispute – which is currently the case in capitalist economies and global climate change discourse and governance.

The Anthropocene spurs a recognition that things tend to organize themselves. Humans can begin to see – or see once again as non-Western cosmologies are brought back into ecological studies – that even when affected by human activities, nonhuman animals and ecosystems have their own desires, responses, and forms of self-organization. Nonanthropocentric power cannot be understood as a kind of human power over nature, or a power to do things *to* an otherwise inert nature. Humans now have influence without control, agency without power; they create effects that escape their immediate intent, or were not even imagined, which then turn back on them. Power dissipates; influence is difficult to target; and dominance is a chimera. Power, in its nonanthropic sense, crosses the (fictive and modernist) "boundary" between the human and the nonhuman, between society and nature; power inheres in the very processes of social/nature and cannot be disentangled from them.

It may be that practices of environmental sustainability, management, and governance can seek to exercise "control" – or at least influence – in the interests of ecological repair and resilience, but only if they appreciate how power is shared complexly with nonhuman animals, things, and systems. This must include abandoning the hubristic assumption (still all too present in environmental governance) that human interests in resource utilization and extraction can be bargained against ecosystem preservation. Human actors and institutions may seek to exercise or accumulate power with strategic intent, but they immediately find that power can only be exercised in complex relations with others, in assemblages of human and nonhuman, material and ideational. Power, exercised across complex social-ecological systems, is not what we thought.

Bruno Latour writes that the Anthropocene era is "something that has deprived [the Moderns] forever of the fundamental distinction between Nature and Society" (Latour 2013: 10). This unfettering of a divided nature and society leads to more attachments to things, to that which we historically tried in vain to keep separate. Restricting the idea of power to a solely human sociality denies the entangled reality in which we exist. Crucially, accepting such an entangled reality denies that power is domination; we should now value power based on how many restorative and responsible attachments it makes with those within the system, rather than what it provokes or forces into being. This idea of entangled action is a vital step to less exploitative and amoral, and more connected, ontologies of power:

> The theory of action itself is different, since we are now interested in mediators making other mediators do things. "Making do" is not the same thing as "causing" or "doing": there exists at the heart of it a duplication, a dislocation, and a translation that modifies at once the whole argument. It was impossible before to connect an actor to what made it act, without being accused of "dominating," "limiting," or "enslaving" it. This is no longer the case. The more attachments it has, the more it exists. And the more mediators there are the better.
> *(Latour 2007: 217)*

Latour stresses that a whole new system of coordinates will be needed to replace the modern division between nature and culture and proposes rethinking our institutions and diplomacy to this end (Latour 2007: 23). One important implication for world politics is how to create global (diplomatic-political) institutions that will be shaped by and support a just global politics that addresses the ecological crisis, honors our entanglement, and accepts responsibility for the awesome yet less controllable powers of social\nature. Our final section will offer ways to engage in this rethinking of human subjectivity and its connection to the wider nonhuman worlds that exist, and to the practice and institutionalization of world politics.

## Responsibility in the Anthropocene: Exercising Entangled Power

What forms of (global) politics and policy would "thing-systems" power promote and imply? In this final section of the chapter, we make some general comments in this regard; however, we caution that the link between such a theory of power and political practice must be situated and take regard of multiple forms of difference (Schlosberg 1999; Lövbrand et al. 2015: 216). While this theory would have salience in a range of spheres, including economic policy and armed conflict, here we will focus on environmental protection. In particular, implications for politics, policy, and governance must be considered through an account of political and ethical *responsibility*.

We have argued – contrary to the focus in International Relations on human institutions and their domination and control of nature as resource – that nonhuman animals, actants, and processes have powerful and wide-ranging effects that are entangled with human actions, institutions, discourses, and processes in fraught and complex assemblages that crisscross the boundary between the social and the natural, fusing them into unprecedented and mobile combinations. These combinations have increased, intensified, and sped up, and this, in part, has pressed scientists to name an epoch in humanity's (perhaps dubious) honor. In the

"Planet Politics" manifesto, we argue that such a situation must be addressed by a *cosmopolitics* pursued "at multiple scales and locales ... that [would be] simultaneously a practice of governance and of subversion, of regulation and resistance"; one intent on "amplifying marginalized voices and creating new forms of solidarity and governance to confront the dystopian power of big energy, big farming, big finance, and fossil fuel capitalism" (Burke et al. 2016: 507). The question of political responsibility in the Anthropocene is framed by such a cosmopolitics: by an urgent imperative to reverse ecological degradation and find ways to responsibly exercise the collective human power enacted within global social nature.

Who or what exercises such responsibility? Here, even as we argue that nonhuman actants and assemblages exercise power, moral and political responsibility must be taken up by human actors and institutions. While, given what we know about the capacity of animals for caring and attachment even across species lines, it would not be accurate to deny them the capacity for moral agency, we acknowledge that it is humans (so far as we know) that possess the self-reflexive and interrogatory capacity for complex moral reasoning and self-consciousness which we understand to be the conditions for moral agency and, thus, responsibility. After Toni Erskine (2003), we also attribute such moral agency to institutions and, after Iris Marion Young (2011), extend responsibility to collectives of citizens and institutions implicated in problematic processes and injustices. Above all, it is humans who can understand the scope of the Anthropocene and earth system and must manage this dark collective power to destroy.

A theory of life and power as entangled and systemic has two conjoined ethical implications. Firstly, as we argue at length below, governance and responsibility must be thought of in *relational and futural* terms; the theory must honor the radical interdependence of things, societies, and ecosystems, and sustain them through timelines that extend from hundreds to millions of years. Secondly, it must challenge the modern, instrumental vision of nature as mere *resource*, as something that can be alienated and used at the will of humans; it must honor the intrinsic *moral worth of ecosystems and nonhuman life*, and make the preservation of the earth system and ecosystems an overwhelming priority. In short, it forces a strongly *ecocentric* ethics and practice of governance. As writers such as Valerie Plumwood (2002 and 2006), Max Horkheimer (2003), and Donna Haraway (2016) attest, the human domination, exploitation, and destruction of "nature" has been deeply bound up with the domination and abuse of some humans and states by others. When paired with the modernist ontology of human reason based in a radical separation from "an inferiorized and manipulable nature," power politics has created and treated nature as something divorced from the human, understood only through resource extraction for state competition, or to dominate another, with no legal or moral rights (Plumwood 2002: 4; Gupta 2016). Outside the subfield of global environmental politics, these forms of domination and control remain hidden from International Relations due to its anthropocentric ontological boundaries (Burke et al. 2016; compare Nicholson and Jinnah 2016).

In a political ethics of entanglement, we posit three forms of interlinked responsibility: general, specific, and futural. Firstly, we can make a general proposition that, in the deeply entangled array of assemblages that make up global social nature and the earth system, everyone is responsible – with a special focus on the role of capitalism vis-à-vis the subjugation of the state to corporate interests (Klein 2014). Given the generalized spread of fossil fuel and energy consumption, the globalized markets for seafood, meat, wood, palm oil, and agricultural products, the global production of rubbish and plastics, and the global operation of transnational corporations across multiple jurisdictions, all states have a role in enabling multiple forms of ecological degradation and greenhouse gas emissions. They and their citizens have moral responsibilities and democratic powers that go along with such entanglement and reach. This implication in global ecological degradation – whether as capitalists or consumers, government or citizens – is paired with a universal vulnerability of all communities to the degradation of the earth system. As Angela Harris argues via the feminist legal theorist Martha Fineman, "the advent of the Anthropocene era requires heightened awareness of the relationship between humans and the environments in which they live, including a series of positive obligations of the state vis-à-vis both humans and what we think of as 'the environment' or 'nature.'" In other words, human subjectivity must recognize that in each moment of the human course of life "humans exist only in, and because of, complex relations of 'interbeing' with nonhuman and nonliving systems" (Harris 2014: 107 and 115). In short, our governance must come from this place of embodiment, entanglement, and vulnerability. This will include an understanding of the state as a cluster of relationships; conceptualizing humans as ecologically vulnerable makes these relationships visible. Therefore, just as power can only be exercised in relation, responsibility inheres in our relations.

Such relationality affects our ethical relationships with the many other forms of life (and nonlife) on this planet. An ethic of entanglement demands that we respond, reimagine, and receptively approach the world with care in all its complexity. Humans must take responsibility for wrongs to multiple Others, even if we may not be able to communicate with them in a shared world or know precisely what these claims may be (Fishel 2017: 74–75). As Donna Haraway (2016) has recently argued, this reimagining will include new forms of kin-making that exceed previous notions of family and species. For Haraway, this kin-making is a way to "stay with the trouble" created by the Anthropocene.

This dyad of relationship and responsibility has been thought of in an anthropocentric way by a range of thinkers, such as Emmanuel Levinas, Martin Buber, William Connolly, and Judith Butler (Burke 2007). In *Precarious Life*, Butler affirms the value of liberal notions of autonomy but also asks us to consider "the demands that are imposed on us by living in a world of beings that are by definition physically dependent on one another." She goes on to argue that this way of imagining community "affirms relationality not only as a descriptive or historical fact of our formation, but also as an ongoing normative dimension of our social and political lives," one in which "we are compelled to take stock of our interdependence" (Butler 2004: 27). Iris Marion Young insists that social connection generates a general responsibility to ameliorate and reverse "structural injustice," because "all those who dwell within the structures must take responsibility for remedying injustices they cause, though none [may be] specifically reliable for the harm in a legal sense" (I. M. Young 2011: 105). Even as we acknowledge that Young's work was resolutely anthropocentric, it is a useful way of thinking about how large-scale harms, injustices, and insecurities are created though millions of anonymous contributing actions – across complex systems and assemblages of assemblages – and generate a collective responsibility. Such insights must now be extended, like our understandings of power, beyond the social and the human, into an ethics of *worlding* (Barad 2007; Mitchell 2014; Burke et al. 2016: 518–519).

In practical terms, we must also acknowledge that given that multiple actors and activities have simultaneous and distributed effects across complex systems, efforts to manage and reform them must be similarly distributed. A general and distributed responsibility in this sense reflects a structural necessity of the way in which complex social-natural assemblages function. It can be argued that the adoption of the *2030 Agenda for Sustainable Development* and the Sustainable Development Goals by the United Nations General Assembly in 2015 is just such a recognition of a globalized and general responsibility, even if the way that responsibility is subsequently framed and narrowed by the declaration has serious limitations. As we note below, the design and modality of global environmental governance institutions are strongly challenged by globalization and social-ecological complexity (Conca 2016; O. R. Young 2017).

Secondly, such a general responsibility must fall more heavily on specific actors and institutions – corporations, governments, and particular kinds of actors and communities whose activities have the greatest ecological impact and from whom change would create the most benefit. Corporate freedoms to exploit and despoil animal populations and ecosystems must be radically restrained and made subject to much more rigorous tests of sustainability, ecosystem repair, and animal welfare. Governments at every jurisdictional level, and especially national governments, have a responsibility to impose rigorous environmental regulation and responsibilities on business, including robust criminal provisions. At the international level, this should also extend to the adoption of a statute of crimes against biodiversity.

This would not be a "high politics" of defense and security, or even trade, but a new and urgent kind of high politics crossing multiple jurisdictions committed to mitigating human impacts upon sensitive ecologies and the earth system. Nor would it be a "geopolitics" based on the control and exploitation of territory for grand strategic purposes; rather, it would be a *geo*-politics that acknowledges humanity's geological embeddedness in and vulnerability to the earth (Dalby 2017). Nor do we see responsibility in terms of what international environmental agreements such as the United Nations Framework Convention on Climate Change term "common but differentiated responsibilities," which, while aimed at allowing for different stages of development, has in practice led to unseemly bargaining and burden shifting, in which costs and responsibilities are seen as being borne exclusively by human institutions within national jurisdictions (Stevenson 2012). Yet the earth system has no borders, and while international society has failed since the signing of the Kyoto Protocol to meaningfully arrest dangerous climate change, it is species and ecologies that bear ever greater and more irreversible costs, extinction being the most irreversible of all. The failure here is not in attempting to develop a principle of interstate justice, but in the way that the fundamental needs of nonhuman populations and the global ecology have been pushed into the background.

States must avoid seeing global agreements to decarbonize the planet and protect biodiversity as a threat to their sovereignty and eliminate power politics entirely from their approach to global governance. As Joyeeta Gupta argues, in the Anthropocene the "premises of traditional geopolitics" – a hierarchy of a wealthy and powerful core dominating a poor and powerless periphery, and a refusal to accept limits – are no longer viable. Questions of global social and environmental justice must thus be addressed together: If the world is to transition to genuine environmental sustainability, neoliberal globalization must be replaced by "inclusive development" and power politics must yield to "global constitutionalism and the rule of law" (Klein 2014; Gupta 2016: 5929 and 6083). There is something grossly immoral and irresponsible about neoliberal states damaging environmental governance and protection on behalf of sectoral human (primarily corporate) interests, and thus endangering the entangled dependence of their own and all global citizens on the global ecology. States must interiorize a profound understanding of human social entanglement with ecologies and the earth system and make it central to their approach to International Relations; they must become "green states" (Eckersley 2004).

Thirdly, such an exercise of responsibility must address that other crucial element of the Anthropocene – the long temporal extension, from hundreds to billions of years, of ecological effects such as sea level rise, habitat change, and toxic substances such as radioactive waste, which are also the hallmark of complex systems within systems (see also Galaz, Chapter 6). For example, uranium-238, the naturally occurring isotope used to generate fissile material for weapons and reactors, which is also present in nuclear waste, has a half-life of 4.4 billion years. The fossil record stretches ahead in new forms: molecules of carbon dioxide and methane moving through the atmosphere in increasing concentrations; man-made elements such as plastics and plutonium polluting the oceans or awaiting disposal, in long and latent threat. Elsewhere, we have called this "responsibility-in-time": "an extraordinary kind of strategic and moral responsibility" that is "temporally and structurally intertwined ... both for the past and for future generations of humans, animals, plants, forests and fish" (Burke 2016: 73–90). Power exercised across complex social-ecological assemblages must be pursued with the long-term future in mind, for living communities not yet created (Fishel 2015).

## Conclusion

One especially sobering conclusion that can be drawn from our model of thing-system power distributed across complex assemblages is that the moral demands of the Anthropocene are confronted by a challenging – and politically complex – work of *distributed change* that must take in multiple sectors and activities across the gamut of human economic, industrial, agricultural, and domestic life. Such work will include creative and reformed practices of governance at many levels – local, community, city, state, national, regional, and global – but must be committed to involving and representing human and nonhuman communities and creating new and more effective institutional forms, linkages, and powers. It must challenge the reification by which governance has been reduced to elite bargaining in expensive rooms, whether by state diplomats or big nongovernmental organizations in green-washing partnerships with corporations (Dauvergne 2016). Hence, a planetary assemblage politics must equally involve activism, resistance, and subversion: it must use the earth-centered politics evident at Standing Rock to spur more effective, inclusive, and accountable governance pursued through the United Nations. In this way, it is consistent with the "normative" vision of "earth system governance" as Frank Biermann conceives it – a "critical theory focusing on the reform and reorganization of human activity in a way that helps us to navigate the Anthropocene" – and can contribute to that broader collective project of transformation. It would also complicate the predominantly anthropocentric account in earth system governance of governance actors and agency (Biermann 2014: 795 and 808).

It is important for human governance actors to acknowledge, whether they are diplomats or park rangers, the reality that environmental governance occurs in partnership with nonhuman life and agency across complex systems. Much environmental and earth system science understands this; however, what is crucial now is that a strongly *ecocentric ethos* infuses environmental governance at every level, so that the fundamental needs of nonhuman animal populations and ecosystems are put first. A model of thing-systems power strongly suggests that nonhuman animals and ecosystems should increasingly have representation in political assemblies and governance institutions based on innovative models of cross-national and ecosystem-centered deliberative democracy (Burke and Fishel 2016). Thing-systems power challenges us to add the nonhuman into far more deliberatively rich and responsible forms of environmental governance (Dryzek 1995; Dryzek and Stevenson 2014).

A thing-systems perspective also forces us to confront the weakness of existing institutional structures and modes of global environmental governance, which struggle to grapple with complex systems or gain purchase across the globalized production and commodity chains that, argues Ken Conca, "confound regulatory strategies at the international or domestic level" and make the "law-and-development approach" increasingly problematic – a problem compounded by corporate lobbying against environmental regulation and limits in both national and international trade and investment law (Conca 2016; Gupta 2016; Young 2017). Hence, environmental change strategies must confront the dissipation of power away from states to corporations and dismantle the structures that enable it, including the postwar structure of global economic governance divorced from ecological and social justice imperatives.

Our perspective can thus contribute to a rich ongoing debate about the limitations of existent environmental governance and politics; it can add the claims and presence of the nonhuman to proposals for environmental human rights, risk management across uncertainty, and attention to the function of normative and ethical principles in global regimes (Conca 2016: 855; Young 2017: 2685). One crucial need – made ever more political as ultraconservative governments attack environmental science, destroy data banks, and dismantle key regulatory bodies such as the US Environmental Protection Agency – is for increased investment in knowledge and information. Unpredictably changing complex systems require intensive monitoring and research; this is the intelligence system for ecological security.

Even as we applaud the creativity and effort that have gone into the creation of major global environmental treaties and governance bodies, thing-systems power reminds us that mitigating the totality of human ecological impacts in the Anthropocene is only begun by the signing of a treaty – and can be systemically undermined by its design. Hopeful developments like the Paris Agreement on Climate Change and the United Nations General Assembly's adoption of the Sustainable Development Goals expose a profound gap between a long-overdue recognition of the moral challenges of the Anthropocene and a preparedness to change our systems.

The Paris Agreement has near-universal membership of states and has come into force, yet its pledges so far are modest and inadequate. Its preamble, which recognizes "the importance of ensuring the integrity of all ecosystems, including oceans, and the protection of biodiversity, recognized by some cultures as Mother Earth," appears like a lonely plea written in fading ink. Again, *Homo sapiens* is front and center in the document itself, with no mention of the extinction of other living beings (Hance 2016). And the *2030 Agenda for Sustainable Development*, which seems to appreciate the complex interplay of processes that make up social nature and appears as an exciting statement of global consensus around the need to "heal and secure our planet," still assures "respect [for] each country's policy space and leadership" and contains no commitment to reform the governance of the world economy or to control the rapacious and grossly irresponsible behavior of major mining, chemical, agricultural, and fossil fuel corporations. Meanwhile, major global regimes such as the United Nations Convention on the Law of the Sea or the Convention on Biological Diversity grant states far too much freedom to control and exploit the ecosystems within their jurisdictions, which has been devastating for forests and fisheries. Their texts quickly reduce the living complexity of biodiversity into an instrumentalized "resource" for human use. Here, the Hobbesian principle of state sovereignty – which locates power solely within the body and territory of the state and is embedded as such in global governance and law – fails to honor the globally entangled structure of power and life that characterizes our post-Holocene predicament on planet earth.

A responsible global politics of the Anthropocene can only be sustained if our understanding of power acknowledges our systemic and complex entanglement with the nonhuman and the earth system. One crucial pillar of our political theory must shake and transform. A new theory of power, by itself, does not constitute a new politics, but it can clear the way there.

# References

Ball, Philip. 2017. How Life (and Death) Spring from Disorder. *Quanta Magazine*, January 27. Accessed January 29, 2017. https://www.quantamagazine.org/20170126-information-theory-and-the-foundation-of-life/

Barad, Karen. 2007. *Meeting the Universe Halfway*. Durham: Duke University Press.
Barnett, Michael, and Robert Duvall, eds. 2005. *Power in Global Governance*. Cambridge and New York: Cambridge University Press.
Bennett, Jane. 2004. The Force of Things: Steps toward an Ecology of Matter. *Political Theory* 32 (3): 347–372.
Bennett, Jane. 2010. *Vibrant Matter: A Political Ecology of Things*. Durham and London: Duke University Press.
Bially Mattern, Janice. 2008. The Concept of Power and the (Un)Discipline of International Relations. In *The Oxford Handbook of International Relations*, edited by Christian Reus-Smit and Duncan Snidal, 691–698. Oxford and New York: Oxford University Press.
Biermann, Frank. 2014. *Earth System Governance: World Politics in the Anthropocene*. Cambridge, MA and London: The MIT Press.
Biermann, Frank, Michele M. Betsill, Joyeeta Gupta, et al. 2010. Earth System Governance: A Research Framework. *International Environmental Agreements* 10: 277–298.
Bull, Hedley. 1977. *The Anarchical Society*. London: Macmillan.
Burke, Anthony. 2007. *Beyond Security, Ethics and Violence: War against the Other*. London and New York: Routledge.
Burke, Anthony. 2016. Nuclear Time: Temporal Metaphors of the Nuclear Present. *Critical Studies on Security* 4 (1): 73–90.
Burke, Anthony, and Stefanie Fishel. 2016. Politics for the Planet: Why Nature and Wildlife Need Their Own Seats at the UN [United Nations]. *The Conversation*, 1 July.
Burke, Anthony, Stefanie Fishel, Audra Mitchell, Simon Dalby, and Daniel Levine. 2016. Planet Politics: A Manifesto from the End of IR [International Relations]. *Millennium: Journal of International Studies* 44 (3): 499–523.
Butler, Judith. 2004. *Precarious Life: The Powers of Mourning and Violence*. London: Verso.
Clark, Ian. 2007. *International Legitimacy and World Society*. Oxford and New York: Oxford University Press.
Conca, Ken. 2016. The Changing Shape of Global Environmental Politics. In *New Earth Politics*, edited by Simon Nicholson and Sikina Jinnah. Cambridge, MA: The MIT Press.
Cudworth, Erika and Stephen Cobden. 2013. *Posthuman International Relations: Complexity, Ecologism, and Global Politics*. London: Zed Books.
Dahl, Robert. A. 1957. The Concept of Power. *Systems Research and Behavioral Science* 2 (3): 201–215.
Dalby, Simon. 2009. *Security and Environmental Change*. Cambridge: Polity.
Dalby, Simon. 2017. Firepower: Geopolitical Cultures in the Anthropocene. *Geopolitics* Accessed July 17, 2017. https://doi.org/10.1080/14650045.2017.1344835
Dauvergne, Peter. 2016. *Environmentalism of the Rich*. Cambridge, MA: The MIT Press.
Dryzek, John. 1995. Political and Ecological Communication. *Environmental Politics*. 4 (4): 13–30.
Dryzek, John, and Hayley Stevenson. 2014. *Democratising Global Climate Governance*. Cambridge and New York: Cambridge University Press.
Eckersley, Robyn. 2004. *The Green State*. Cambridge, MA: The MIT Press.
Erskine, Toni, ed. 2003. *Can Institutions Have Responsibilities? Collective Moral Agency and International Relations*. Houndmills and New York: Palgrave.
Fishel, Stefanie. 2015. Remembering Nukes: Collective Memories and Countering State History. *Critical Military Studies* 1 (2): 131–144.

Fishel, Stefanie. 2017. *The Microbial State: Global Thriving and the Body Politic*. Minneapolis: University of Minnesota Press.
Gupta, Joyeeta. 2016. Toward Sharing Our Eco-Space. In *New Earth Politics*, edited by Simon Nicholson and Sikina Jinnah. Cambridge, MA: The MIT Press.
Hamilton, Clive. 2017. *Defiant Earth: The Fate of Humans in the Anthropocene*. Cambridge and Malden, MA: Polity and Sydney: Allen and Unwin.
Hance, Jeremy. 2016. What Does the Paris Agreement Mean for the World's Other Eight Million Species? *The Guardian*, January 6.
Haraway, Donna. 2016. *Staying with the Trouble: Making Kin in the Chthulucene*. Durham and London: Duke University Press.
Harris, Angela P. 2014. Vulnerability and Power in the Age of the Anthropocene. *Washington and Lee Journal of Energy, Climate, and the Environment* (6) 1: 98–161.
Holsti, Kal. 1964. The Concept of Power in the Study of International Relations. *Background* 7 (4): 179–194.
Homer-Dixon, Thomas F. 1999. *Environment, Scarcity, and Violence*. Princeton: Princeton University Press.
Horkheimer, Max. 2003. *Eclipse of Reason*. New York: Continuum.
Intergovernmental Panel on Climate Change. 2014. *Climate Change 2014: Synthesis Report. Summary for Policymakers*. Geneva: Intergovernmental Panel on Climate Change.
Klare, Michael T. 2002. *Resource Wars: The New Landscape of Global Conflict*. New York: Henry Holt and Company.
Klein, Naomi. 2014. *This Changes Everything: Capitalism versus the Climate*. New York: Simon and Schuster.
Latour, Bruno. 1993. *We Have Never Been Modern*, trans. Catherine Porter. Cambridge, MA: Harvard University Press.
Latour, Bruno. 2007. *Reassembling the Social: An Introduction to Actor-Network-Theory*. Cambridge, UK: Oxford University Press.
Latour, Bruno. 2013. *An Inquiry into Modes of Existence: An Anthropology of the Moderns*. Cambridge, MA: Harvard University Press.
Lövbrand, Eva, Silke Beck, Jason Chilvers, et al. 2015. Who Speaks for the Future of Earth? How Critical Social Science Can Extend the Conversation on the Anthropocene. *Global Environmental Change* 32: 211–218.
Mitchell, Audra. 2014. Only Human? Towards Worldly Security. *Security Dialogue* 45 (1): 5–21.
Morgenthau, Hans J. 1978. *Politics among Nations: The Struggle for Power and Peace*. New York: Alfred A. Knopf.
Ormand, Carol. 2017. *What Constitutes a Complex System?* Accessed January 29, 2017, http://serc.carleton.edu/NAGTWorkshops/complexsystems/introduction.html
Plumwood, Valerie. 2002. *Environmental Culture: The Ecological Crisis of Reason*. London and New York: Routledge.
Plumwood, Valerie. 2006. Feminism. In *Political Theory and the Ecological Challenge*, edited by Andrew Dobson and Robyn Eckersley. Cambridge, UK: Cambridge University Press.
Reus-Smit, Chris. 2004. *American Power and World Order*. Cambridge: Polity.
Schlosberg, David. 1999. *Environmental Justice and the New Pluralism: The Challenge of Difference for Environmentalism*. Oxford and New York: Oxford University Press.
Nicholson, Simon, and Sikina Jinnah, eds. 2016. *New Earth Politics*. Cambridge, MA: The MIT Press.

Stevenson, Hayley. 2012. *Institutionalizing Unsustainability: The Paradox of Global Climate Governance*. Berkeley and London: University of California Press.
Youatt, Rafi. 2015. *Counting Species: Biodiversity in Global Environmental Politics*. Minneapolis: University of Minnesota Press.
Young, Iris Marion. 2011. *Responsibility for Justice*. Oxford and New York: Oxford University Press.
Young, Oran R. 2017. *Governing Complex Systems: Social Capital for the Anthropocene*. Cambridge, MA: The MIT Press.

# 6

# Time and Politics in the Anthropocene: Too Fast, Too Slow?

VICTOR GALAZ

Time has always been a main topic in sustainability sciences and environmental politics. Ever since the 1972 United Nations Conference on the Human Environment in Stockholm, achieving social, economic, and ecological sustainable development for all – including future generations – has been a key motivation for environmental politics. Such an ambition requires decision-making processes, policies, and institutional mechanisms that are able not only to consider global inequalities and the way human activities modify our environment, but also to overcome short-term interests and consider the governance of planet earth and its natural capital for the long term.

The importance of time for environmental politics and governance is nothing new to all of those working in the field of "green" politics, earth system governance, and related fields in the wider sustainability sciences. Consider, for example, Andrew Dobson's work on green political thought (2000 and 2007) and its explicit discussion about the need to explore models of democracy and citizenship that internalize both international and intergenerational responsibilities. As a contrasting example, but with similar temporal dimensions, Oran Young's highly influential work on institutional dimensions of global environmental change includes several important observations about the need for institutions that are able to navigate change and complexity over time, and with a firm eye on the sustainable stewardship of global environmental commons (Young 2010 and 2011).

Nor is the importance of time new to institutional scholars in general. For example, game theoretical institutional approaches have made impressive advances in understanding the key role time perceptions play in prisoners' dilemma games, where the possibilities for repeated games and long-time horizons drastically improve the possibilities for collaborative solutions (Axelrod 1984). Paul Pierson's seminal work *Politics in Time* (2004) is another example of the role of understanding the temporal dimensions of the emergence and impacts of institutions.

My approach here is slightly different, however. In this chapter, I explore what the proposed Anthropocene epoch implies for the way scholars of environmental institutions and governance understand and analyze the temporal perspectives of institutions and political decision-making. Some of what I argue will sound familiar, as it builds on existing and well-known work in this domain. But some will provide new perspectives by explicitly bringing out assumptions about the temporal dimensions of institutional emergence, change, and effectiveness as they relate to the temporal dynamics of the earth system including its deeply embedded "technosphere." As I show, the temporal assumptions we make as scholars are important, since they shape our analytical frameworks, methods, and data. On a more practical level, they also affect the policy recommendations scholars provide to public debates about global environmental governance (e.g., Biermann et al. 2012).

The chapter is structured in four sections. In the first section, I briefly summarize my understanding of the Anthropocene epoch, and the difference it makes for our understanding of the institutional challenges that we are facing today. The use of "we" here is intentionally inclusive, since I believe these issues cut across divides between North and South, young and old, affluent and deprived. In the second section, I focus on the role of so-called "deep time." Here, I contrast mainstream approaches in the study of global environmental institutions and governance (or "earth system" governance) with the temporal perspective of earth system science, including climate science. The third section focuses on ultra-speed; that is, processes facilitated by algorithms that unfold at temporal scales so fast that they may sometimes overwhelm human cognitive capacities. In the fourth and last section, I summarize the argument. Here, I argue that this broad temporal spectrum of phenomena that unfold at ultra-speed, and in deep time, is an interesting feature of the institutional challenges posed by the Anthropocene that until now has received very limited attention.

## Temporal Dimensions of the Anthropocene

Whether the human enterprise has entered a new geological epoch at all, and in that case, when in the history of planet earth that entry should be pinpointed, has been debated intensively in the last years (e.g., Zalasiewicz 2015; Steffen et al. 2016; Waters et al. 2016). This debate has multiple dimensions. One of them is the complex and implicit political dimensions embedded in the timing of the Anthropocene. As I have argued elsewhere (Galaz 2014 and 2015a), arguments of an "early" Anthropocene (5,000–8,000 years ago) versus placing the start at the beginning of the "Great Acceleration" (1950s and onwards) entail intriguing political dimensions, since they guide the way we perceive the risks and opportunities of entering this unprecedented state of planet earth. In addition, it also begs us to explore the role of human agency and causation at global scales, over very long time periods (see also Castree, Chapter 2). Bluntly put: should the Anthropocene be viewed as a risky anomaly in the history of our planet with potential detrimental impacts on humanity (Steffen et al. 2011)? Or is the Anthropocene simply an extension of human societies' ingenious ability to innovate and engineer ecosystems to our species' benefit (Ellis 2012)? A number of social scientists have taken on the challenge to explore these political dimensions from very different perspectives (e.g., Lövbrand et al. 2009; Galaz 2014; Brondizio et al. 2016; Clark 2017).

My approach in this chapter is much more limited, and focuses on the temporal dimensions of the Anthropocene. Thus, while the concept holds numerous challenging questions for the social sciences in general, my focus is on exploring the institutional challenges posed by the way the earth system behaves. In that endeavor, I integrate insights from resilience and complexity thinking, which I believe to be central to the Anthropocene epoch. As I have discussed in detail earlier (Galaz 2014), this analysis includes recent insights about the risk for nonlinear and "tipping point" behavior in systems, the importance of cross-scale interactions, and the persistent prospect of surprises emerging.

## Institutional Dimensions of "Deep Time"

As many have noted, the notion of the Anthropocene inevitably brings in issues about geological timescales. In contrast to more conventional perceptions of time in institutional analysis (which may extend to a few generations back or forward in time), geological timescales span from hundreds of thousands to millions of years. The *Holocene,* for example, is the latest formal geological epoch, with its start about 12,000 years ago. This epoch was preceded by the *Pleistocene*, with its start about 2.6 million years ago. Some denote this very long temporal perspective on the history of humanity and planet earth as "Big History" (Christian 1991) or "deep time" (Wilkinson 2005).

The fact that the human enterprise now modifies the earth system at such scale, that these geological timescales are even being considered for debate, is in itself a shift from previous debates around sustainable development in the modern environmentalism of the 1970s. As Clark (2017) notes, the "geological strata" are "becoming political in different ways" (Clark 2017: 3) as scientific insights about possible abrupt changes in the earth system are being framed as political problems. In a different contribution, Brondizio and colleagues (2016) explore the different spread of the Anthropocene concept and dominating narratives. Temporal dimensions are also present in this discussion, since the concept raises "important normative questions about how the future should be" (Brondizio et al. 2016: 4) as well as forcing us to understand the roots of environmental change, and the temporal evolution of "societies in a world system" (Brondizio et al. 2016: 5). Insights from the earth system governance research community (e.g., Biermann et al. 2012; Kanie et al. 2012) also raise issues about the need to reform institutions to safeguard a sustainable future.

While time is a key issue in all these contributions, they also seem to overlook that the temporal scales of political decision-making and institutional evolution interplay in complex ways with the temporal behavior of the earth system. Allow me to elaborate on this last point, starting with a modified figure from Clark and colleagues (2016). The figure shows model-simulated temperature anomalies starting 20,000 years ago and projected 10,000 years into the future. One key and well-known argument in the paper is that many temperature anomaly trajectories are possible depending on the carbon dioxide emission pathway the world enters in the next few decades (blue lines with temperature anomalies ranging from 0 to 6 degrees Celsius).

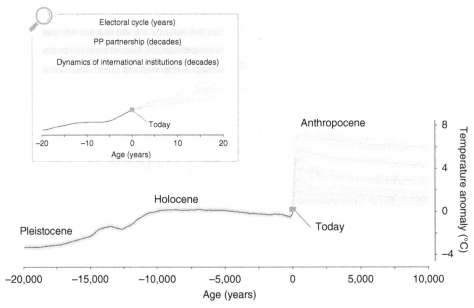

Figure 6.1 Comparing temporal scales – "deep time" versus "political time." The grey and blue lines show the historical and future development of temporal anomalies as a result of climate change. These long-term (or "deep-time") possible trajectories are contrasted with the conventional temporal focus of political scientists and institutional scholars, such as a) electoral cycles, b) studies about public–private (PP) partnerships in, for example, global governance, and c) studies about policy innovations. The figure has been remade from Clark et al. (2016).

## *Three Observations Are Central to My Argument*

One is obvious: that deep time and political time differ considerably. While the former deals with earth system changes that play out over thousands (and sometimes even millions) of years, the latter addresses changes that play out at much shorter timescales (often decades). Clearly, the specifics of political time differ between different subdisciplines. As an example, scholars of political elections or policy studies would generally study phenomena that play out over electoral cycles or shifts in government, ranging from years to decades. In a similar way, scholars of international environmental institutions would normally study the emergence, evolution, and sometimes collapse of regimes over timescales that span decades (e.g., Young 2011 and his synthesis analysis of international environmental regimes). On some occasions, political science scholars with an interest in political history extend their studies to hundreds of years (e.g., Kokkonen and Sundell's (2014) study about the stability of monarchies between the years 1000 and 1800).

The key question now, of course, is whether this temporal discrepancy is a problem we as a research community need to take seriously at all. My answer would be that this indeed is a problem, which brings me to the second observation about the links between political and deep-time scales. In this example, this has to do with the disproportionally large impacts political decisions to be taken within the next decade will have on the behavior of the earth system in deep time.

Clark et al. (2016) provide an excellent example. Their argument is not only that policymakers need to consider longer time perspectives in existing climate projections (from hundreds of years to millennia), but also that political decisions made in the next few years and decades will have profound impacts "not just for this century, but for the next ten millennia and beyond" (Clark et al. 2016: 360). The main reason for this is the behavior of the climate system as a complex system in which changes in initial conditions (in this case, carbon dioxide emissions) do not result in immediate or proportional responses at the system level (say, global temperature anomalies). These time lags are sometimes denoted "committed changes," which occur as global mean temperatures, sea-level rise, and associated ecosystem changes continue to respond "long after the stabilization of radiative forcing" (e.g., Jones et al. 2009: 484). In other words, the existence of feedbacks, connections between subsystems, and nonlinearities in the earth system (Steffen et al. 2004) allows this kind of temporal asymmetry between political and geological timescales.

This, I believe, has important and poorly explored implications for the study of global governance institutions in the Anthropocene epoch. The question for scholars of institutions and politics in the Anthropocene is, therefore, not only to explore the properties of effective, efficient, and legitimate earth system governance (e.g.,

Biermann 2014; Kanie et al. 2012) or the realization of the transformative potential of the Sustainable Development Goals (e.g., Hajer et al. 2015). Nor is the challenge only to explore leverage points for changes in the international system that would address the dynamics of "planetary boundaries" (Biermann et al. 2012; Galaz et al. 2012).

Instead, the challenge is also to analyze the temporal asymmetry between political and geological timescales. Underdal (2010: 389 et seq.) denotes this phenomenon *time inconsistency,* referring to time lags in the climate system, and observes that our empirical understanding of the political decision-making dimensions and challenges to discounting for long-term decision-making is highly limited (Underdal 2010: 389). Unfortunately, however, he does not specify the temporal scales that are of main interest for such an analysis. This is troublesome, since the asymmetry between political and geological timescales may span hundreds, thousands, or even millions of years. While this might sound like an impossible agenda for research, a number of feasible and interesting analytical challenges are possible to identify.

The example of solar geoengineering can help us elaborate this issue in more detail. "Solar geoengineering," or "solar radiation management," refers to the idea that dangerous climate change can be avoided, or at least fended off, by injecting small reflective particles such as sulfate aerosols into the upper atmosphere. These particles would reflect incoming solar radiation before it reaches the surface of the earth, thereby lowering global temperatures immediately after being deployed. This, it is argued, would be both a quicker and a cheaper way to steer away from dangerous climate change, compared with relying on carbon emission reductions alone (e.g., Moreno-Cruz and Keith 2013).

This proposal is, of course, highly contested due to its environmental, and not least political, risks (e.g., Keith et al. 2010; Parson and Keith 2013; Barrett et al. 2014). Numerous scholars have focused on the global governance challenges posed by the potential deployment of solar geoengineering technologies. This governance debate has focused on a number of issues, including the difficulties of getting sovereign states to agree on such deployment at all, the possibilities of unilateral state deployment, the risks of a "Greenfinger" scenario in which a rich private actor undertakes solar geoengineering on his or her own, and the regulation of small-scale experiments (e.g., Victor 2008; Blackstock and Long 2010; Bodansky 2013; Barrett 2014). Interestingly enough, however, few geoengineering governance scholars explore the challenges for institutions and modes of governance to maintain the international collective mobilization associated with such deployment well into the foreseeable future.

This is surprising, considering that such a drastic intervention in the climate system would not only require deployment before numerous climate feedback processes start to kick in that may lead to substantially increased temperature levels (for example, by changes in "tipping elements" in the climate system; see Lenton et al. 2008; Lenton 2011). Such geoengineering intervention also needs, unless complemented with drastic emission reductions, to be kept in place for perpetuity. The reason is known as the "termination effect" (Goes et al. 2011; Jones et al. 2013). This effect entails the rapid "rebound" warming effect that would unfold if solar radiation management techniques were swiftly terminated for reasons such as political instability, a global disaster, or international conflict. Thus, while solar geoengineering may be able to "mask" a global warming effect, the abrupt termination of such an intervention would lead to an immediate return to warmer temperatures. In a worst-case scenario, such a rebound would be so quick as to considerably overwhelm both human and bio-geophysical adaptive capacities.

Put differently, while experimentation and the possible deployment of solar geoengineering require us to think about the development and evolution of institutions over decades (that is, the temporal scale at which we normally study these issues), its effectiveness, due to the slower dynamics of the climate system and a potential termination effect, forces us to take a much longer time perspective (hundreds to thousands of years). The longer solar geoengineering is deployed, the larger and more devastating the rebound effect is likely to be. Thus, the stronger is the incentive to explore these deep-time institutional challenges.

Some of this ground has been covered by legal and ethics scholars. This includes Burns (2011) and his discussion about legal dimensions of intergenerational equity associated with solar geoengineering, and Wong (2014), who elaborates the ethical challenges emerging after a deployment of solar geoengineering or what he calls "post-implementation scenarios." However, there is a tangible gap in this literature related to what could be seen as the deep-time dimensions of earth system governance.[1]

For example, how do we ensure that a possible solar geoengineering deployment agreement is robust against geopolitical tensions hundreds and maybe even thousands of years into the future? Can international regimes be set up in such a way that it makes such termination *less* likely over time, considering that climate risks increase with time? What mechanisms can ensure that unexpected negative effects of solar geoengineering are compensated fairly across space (that is, between regions) and time (that is, between present and future generations)?

Addressing these sorts of "deep-time" questions forces us earth system governance scholars to broaden our empirical and methodological portfolio and move

---

[1] A slightly different stream of literature explores the risks entailed with the possible future evolution of "artificial superintelligence," that is, the rapid and nonlinear evolution of machines with an intelligence that supersedes human intelligence by orders of magnitude. While this emerging field of inquiry does contain a number of intriguing proposals on how to guide the development of such artificial intelligence, these fall beyond the scope of this chapter (Yudkowsky 2008; Bostrom 2014).

beyond conventional analyses of environmental regimes, institutional interactions, and global governance studies, which tend to focus on much shorter timeframes.

Before I conclude this chapter with a few reflections on what such an agenda might look like, I would like to turn our attention to temporal dynamics at the other extreme – ultra-speed.

## Institutional Dimensions of Algorithms and "Ultra-speed"

Geological time scales are critical for our understanding of the institutional and political challenges associated with the Anthropocene. An often-mentioned aspect of these rapid changes is the role of technology. This is not surprising, since technological change – ranging from the extraction of fossil fuels to the emergence of carbon dioxide–intense modes of production, consumption, and transportation – has been fundamental for the rapid growth of the human population as well as the exponential extraction of natural resources often captured under the term "Great Acceleration" (Steffen et al. 2011).

Technological change and advances have also been fundamental for our current scientific understanding of the earth system (e.g., satellite monitoring technologies) as well as an important power, risk, and cost distributer. By the latter, I mean that technologies often distribute risks and costs across time, space, and social groups in ways that sometimes are difficult to predict in advance (Galaz 2014). The most recent example of this is the ardent debate around the social implications of the "gig-economy," including platforms like Uber, and growing concerns around racial bias and worker rights challenges embedded in its business models (Calo and Rosenblat 2017).

Technological advances also influence the temporal aspects of the "systems to be governed" in the Anthropocene. As a simple example, the development of global markets, global trade, and almost frictionless information flows at the international level creates immense opportunities, but also new types of globally networked risks (Helbing 2013). These global connections lay the foundation for crises that spread quickly (minutes, hours, days, months) across the planet, forcing decision-makers to act promptly despite less than perfect information and knowledge. Examples include the 2008–2009 global "food crisis" and emerging infectious disease outbreaks such as Ebola. Effective governance of crisis events such as these requires functioning early warning systems, coordinated multisectoral and multi-national responses, as well as a capacity to avoid blame games and navigate contentious improvement reforms before the next crisis unfolds (Galaz et al. 2010 and 2017).

Here, however, I would like to direct the attention to phenomena that (through algorithms) play out at temporal scales that are considerably faster than one second, but with longer-term implications. Such phenomena, I would argue, are also interesting features of the Anthropocene era if we include its very closely aligned technological dimensions (see, for example, Allenby 2008).

## *Algorithms and the Anthropocene*

What is, then, the relationship between algorithms and governance in the Anthropocene epoch?[2] A quick definition is appropriate at this stage. By algorithms, I mean step-by-step sequences of operations that solve particular computational tasks (for a more elaborate discussion of the term, see MacCormick 2014). The word "computational" is important in this case, since my focus here is on those that run on digital computers of some sort.

Modern-day algorithms may build on very different techniques (e.g., rule systems, decision trees, deep learning, or neural networks), but all have tangible influences in our daily lives (e.g., communicating through Facebook messages, looking for literature or a restaurant through Google searches, sending money to your colleague using your smartphone, or receiving driving directions through an app). Sometimes these algorithms operate smoothly. For example, I have benefited greatly from the Chrome extension Google Scholar when searching for the publication years of the literature added at the end of this chapter. Other times, these algorithms contain biases that have severe implications for people: for example, algorithms that as a result of biased input data discriminate against citizens of color by providing unjustifiably low credit scores, or uses of machine learning that incorrectly assess the likelihood of a person of color committing a future crime (Angwin et al. 2016; O'Neil 2016).

Algorithms are, however, also a fundamental part of the way we perceive, modify, and respond to the natural world around us. That is, they are critical aspects of the formation of the Anthropocene.

One very clear example of this relates to climate models and data. It is probably not surprising that today's advanced climate models are fully dependent on the sophisticated information-processing capacities provided by modern computers. It should be noted, however, that both climate data itself and associated assessments of climate impacts are fully dependent on the use of clever algorithms. As Edwards (1999 and 2013) elaborates in much detail, it is impossible for climate scientists to use raw data (collected through local weather stations or satellites) directly. Instead, data quality needs to be checked, corrupt measurements automatically removed, remaining data converted into common units and formats,

---

[2] The discussion below has benefited tremendously from discussions with participants and coauthors of the "Biosphere Code Manifesto." For details see Galaz (2015b).

missing data interpolated, and data provided in such format and with such granularity as to be at all usable for climate models. In addition, such data also needs to be processed through numerous algorithms (e.g., radiation algorithms, cloud parametrization algorithms, evaporation algorithms, and others) in order to be able to provide details about possible on-the-ground climate impacts. Edwards goes so far as to argue that this data filtering and processing is so important as to render the simplistic separation between models and data highly misleading for the climate sciences (Edwards 1999: 439).

Another example of the close interplay between algorithms and the way social and political actors perceive and respond to environmental change is captured by Ochieng (2017). His analysis of national monitoring, reporting, and verifications systems for schemes on reducing emissions from deforestation and forest degradation around the world elaborate how the algorithms underpinning these systems – which eventually determine carbon mitigation and compensation calculations – have been challenged by social actors with vested interests.

Not all uses of algorithms are contentious, of course. On the contrary, the algorithmic revolution now permeates a number of government and private decision-making processes which, in sum, alter the biosphere. These include network algorithms to support landscape planning for Montreal's greenbelt in Canada,[3] the use of machine-learning methods that underpin species distribution models which feed into conservation decisions (Cantrell et al. 2017), genetic learning algorithms to make fish stock assessments, image-processing algorithms to classify the existence of gold ores, three-dimensional object recognition algorithms to support deep sea mining of rare earth minerals, algorithms used in agriculture to help analyze weather and soil data to maximize production, and many more.[4]

Hence, algorithms operate through actors and hardware at all spatial scales, with tangible influence on the ways we perceive global environmental change (e.g., climate models and data), try to influence the behavior of state and non-state actors (e.g., through the monitoring, reporting, and verification of schemes on reducing emissions from deforestation and forest degradation), and optimize our technologies' capacities to extract or modify natural capital from landscapes and seascapes.

What does all of this have to do with time? My main point is that this development creates another poorly explored time inconsistency – that between the execution of an algorithm (which operates at sub-second timescales) and its possible longer-term consequences (such as conservation or land planning decisions with implications far into the future, or the resulting extraction of a marine

---

[3] See the project "An Ecological Network for our Region" led by Andrew Gonzales at Quebec Center for Biodiversity Science, http://ecologicalnetwork.weebly.com.

[4] These last examples are from the project "The Biosphere Code," published at http://thebiospherecode.com and in Galaz (2015b).

resource). One extreme example of these phenomena is ultrafast financial trade and its associated governance implications.

## *Ultra-speed and Governance*

Speed is of the essence in today's financial markets. The ability to collect and analyze information swiftly and to conduct trade faster than competitors has always been critical for financial actors. The continued exponential increases in computing power and progressively more sophisticated computer algorithms have nevertheless pushed the limitations of financial analysis and trade over the last decade. The development of so-called "algorithmic trade" is making rapid progression globally, involves several types of automated trading strategies with minimal human intervention, and today incorporates an increasing number of asset classes, including financial instruments for commodities like sugar, coffee, oil, and wheat (Galaz et al. 2015; Galaz and Pierre 2017).

Information flows in financial markets are so fast as to substantially outperform human information-processing capacities. In 2011, for example, the firm Fixnetix developed a microchip that can help algorithms execute trades in 740 nanoseconds – 740 billionths of a second (0.000000740 seconds). It takes about 200 milliseconds (or 0.2 seconds) for the eye to blink. During the same time span, a financial algorithm is able to execute about 5,000 trades. This change in financial markets is so dramatic that scholars now refer to it as a new "machine ecology," where changes in the system's behavior are considerably faster than human response time (Johnson et al. 2013).

None of these changes in speed would be interesting if it were not for the fact that the progression of algorithmic trade seems to be creating new types of financial risks. As elaborated in Galaz and Pierre (2017), these include large price swings and market instability triggered by unforeseen feedback loops, errant algorithms, and/or incorrect input data.

The 2010 "Flashcrash" is a good illustration of this. In the course of about 30 minutes, US stock market indices, stock-index futures, options, and exchange-traded funds experienced a sudden price drop of more than 5 percent followed by a rapid rebound. Similarly unexpected and very rapid volatility in prices for oil and gas futures has been observed in the last few years. One of the most extreme examples, however, is from April 2013, when the value of the stock market index S&P500 rapidly dropped by USD 121 billion, followed by a quick recovery. The reason was a hijacked Twitter account of the major news company Associated Press sending out false messages of a terror attack in the White House, thereby triggering immediate automated sales.

Similar but less severe price instabilities can be found for financial instruments for commodities. As elaborated in Galaz and colleagues (2015), recent price volatilities for sugar, cocoa, and coffee have induced heated debates between producer organizations and international stock exchanges.

The progression of these technologies hence carries not only possible benefits (such as reduced transactions costs) but also possible and contested financial risks. The speed at which algorithms operate defies more conventional models of governance, where deliberation, trust, reciprocity, and consent are integral to the pursuit of collective action (e.g., Pierre and Peters 2005).

Thus, the interesting governance challenge is how to respond to phenomena of this type that play out at extremely rapid temporal scales but which may entail larger and more slowly developing system risks.

## *Key Governance Challenges*

A number of approaches are possible as we try to explore the governance dimensions of ultra-speed. Some of these may build on theoretical insights based on the behavior of complex systems (e.g., Helbing 2013). Others can instead be more firmly based on studies of real-world policymaking and recent attempts to steer the influence of algorithms (Galaz and Pierre 2017). I propose that two main issues are critical as we attempt to advance a research agenda that is able to unpack the role of algorithms and associated technologies in the environment and our possibilities to navigate the Anthropocene epoch.

The first issue has to do with *algorithmic and data transparency*. The ability of algorithms to provide decision-making support or information that guides social behavior is contingent on large amounts of data and the specific assumptions embedded in the coding (Pasquale 2015; O'Neil 2016). In financial markets, this has contributed to severe transparency challenges as government agencies struggle to gain overview and monitor illicit activities hidden in massive amounts of data. As a comparison, the amount of data leaked in the "Panama leak" contained 11 million documents, equivalent to 2.6 million megabytes of data. The same amount of trade data is created by the New York Stock Exchange every twenty-six seconds (Galaz and Pierre 2017). Hence, any critical analysis can only be assumed if we, as scholars, have the capacity to grasp such large amounts of data and gain insights into what sometimes are "black box" algorithms protected by intellectual property (Pasquale 2015). Hence, recent calls to advance "algorithmic transparency" or "algorithmic accountability" will not only be of benefit to computer scientists, journalists, and nongovernmental actors exploring the embedded biases and social consequences of the algorithmic revolution (Diakopoulos 2014; Kroll et al. 2017). They will also prove important as earth system governance scholars try to explore the ways by which these shape decision-making related to, and our perceptions of, environmental change.

The second issue has to do with whether governance interventions are possible to *"slow down" systems*. Speed is essential in financial markets, and allows those financial actors with enough resources to capitalize on their speed advantage. As an example, being able to pick up the latest news about unexpectedly large projected increases in profits in a major tech company, and immediately trade on that information, can prove highly profitable. A similar speed advantage can be gained by an actor developing an improved image-processing algorithm to extract additional marine resources in the poorly regulated high seas. However, such speed may create problems for policymakers and agencies, since rapidly evolving crises or surprises (say, a "flash crash") require equally rapid interventions. Slowing down systems allows regulating actors not only to better monitor trading activities, but also to intervene if it is considered necessary. That is why financial regulators around the world attempt to add "speed-bumps" and a number of checks and balances as a means to slow down and partly regain control. This includes the proposal to request that algorithm traders register their formula with regulators before activating it in the market (Galaz and Pierre 2017). The question is: Would such interventions also be needed for additional sectors more closely associated with environmental change, where algorithms also are making quick progression? And what would such governance mechanisms look like?

## Conclusion

Time is, as the saying goes, of the essence. My ambition with this chapter has been to explore the implicit temporal dimensions of the Anthropocene and to elaborate two extremely opposing temporal spectra, both of which are seldom analyzed in earth system governance research: *ultra-speed*, with interactions and phenomena that play out at sub-second scales, and *deep time*, with phenomena that span hundreds to thousands of years.

This selection might seem extreme, especially since much of the literature in our domain, whether we choose to denote it as earth system governance or studies of international environmental institutions, normally spans a few decades. This temporal choice in the conventional literature is logical for at least two reasons: first, because the evolution of international environmental institutions only began to take off in the mid-1940s (Kim 2013); and second, because the emergence, change, and effectiveness of these institutions can only be assessed empirically at this temporal scale (e.g., Young 2010). Many related fields of inquiry in the political sciences embed similar temporal assumptions (summarized in Figure 6.1).

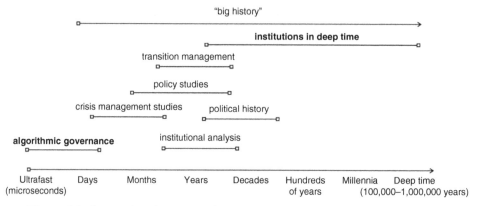

Figure 6.2 Contrasting the temporal assumptions of a selection of disciplines in environmental social sciences and political science.

These assumptions, however, should be questioned as we increasingly understand the operations of the earth system and the way technological change drives novel phenomena. The examples provided in this chapter all illustrate this argument. The facts that decisions to be made in the next few decades will have ramifications for the climate system millennia into the future, that a possible decision to deploy solar geoengineering needs to be underpinned by institutions that are both robust and adaptive in deep time, and that microsecond algorithm-based "decisions" may have larger repercussions and create system risks, all point to intriguing new phenomena closely related to the Anthropocene. Figure 6.2 summarizes this chapter's modest contribution in contrast to other related fields of research in the political sciences.

Relevant literature includes, from top to bottom, big history (e.g., Christian 1991); institutions in deep time (this chapter); transition management (e.g., Loorbach 2010); policy studies (e.g., Marsh and Rhodes 1992); crisis management studies (Boin et al. 2005); political history (e.g., Kokkonen and Sundell 2014); institutional analysis (e.g., Young 2010 and 2011); and algorithmic governance (this chapter).

The difficult question is, of course, how to move such a research agenda ahead. I believe two components to be critical for such an endeavor. First, we need to ask new types of questions. Second, we need to form new creative alliances with research communities that normally are not part of the earth system governance community.

In the case of ultra-speed as an example, we may ask ourselves whether, and in that case how, institutions and governance may guide the development of algorithms that underpin modifications of the biosphere, or that are fundamental for our understanding of environmental change. Questions about agency, adaptiveness, allocation, and effectiveness will be just as critical as before for this new research agenda; however, this time with a very different empirical and temporal focus. Such analysis will require new collaborations with, for example, computer scientists, digital social scientists, and historians of technology to truly be able to decipher the complex interplay between algorithms, institutions, and politics.

The questions related to deep-time challenges are just as intriguing and difficult. For example, is it possible to enhance the capacities of global governance institutions to mobilize political action within known earth system "windows of opportunity" (decades) with implications in "deep time" for the earth system? Can international collective action be maintained over long enough timescales (more than 100 years) despite the fact that responses to these actions will be substantially delayed due to "committed changes" in the earth system? And if solar geoengineering is ever deployed, which governance mechanisms would be able not only to steer away from the possible devastating "termination effects" but also to reduce incentives to defect over deep time? Such explorations will force us to forge new alliances with scholars of "big history," futurologists, and historical ecology.[5] Conventional case study methodologies and the usual databases over international institutions will benefit from being complemented with methods such as agent-based modelling (e.g., Vasconcelos et al. 2013) and a diversity of scenario and visioning approaches (e.g., Vervoort et al. 2010; Bazzanella et al. 2012; Merrie et al. 2014).

The Anthropocene epoch thus not only forces us to consider the profound influence of human activities on planet earth. It also forces us to take a closer look at the intriguing development of, and interactions between, temporal scales. Hopefully, this chapter has managed to inspire some new thinking in this exciting research domain.

## References

Allenby, Brad. 2008. The Anthropocene as Media: Information Systems and the Creation of the Human Earth. *American Behavioral Scientist* 52 (1): 107–140.

Angwin, Julia, Jeff Larson, Surya Mattu, and Lauren Kirchner. 2016. Machine Bias – There's Software Used across the Country to Predict Future Criminals. And It's Biased against Blacks. *ProPublica* (May 23). Accessed April 17, 2017. https://propublica.org/article/machine-bias-risk-assessments-in-criminal-sentencing

Axelrod, Robert. 1984. *The Evolution of Cooperation*. New York, NY: Basic Books.

Barrett, Scott. 2014. Solar Geoengineering's Brave New World: Thoughts on the Governance of an Unprecedented Technology. *Review of Environmental Economics and Policy* 8 (2): 249–269.

---

[5] Those familiar with the international program Integrated History and Future of People on Earth (IHOPE) will recognize some of this thinking.

Barrett, S., T. M. Lenton, A. Millner, et al. 2014. Climate Engineering Reconsidered. *Nature Climate Change* 4 (7): 527.

Bazzanella, Liliana, Luca Caneparo, Franco Corsico, and Giuseppe Roccasalva, eds. 2012. *The Future of Cities and Regions: Simulation, Scenario and Visioning, Governance and Scale*. Dordrecht: Springer Science and Business Media.

Biermann, Frank. 2014. *Earth System Governance: World Politics in the Anthropocene*. Cambridge, MA: MIT Press.

Biermann, Frank, K. Abbott, S. Andresen, et al. 2012. Navigating the Anthropocene: Improving Earth System Governance. *Science* 335 (6074): 1306–1307.

Blackstock, Jason J. and Jane C. S. Long. 2010. The Politics of Geoengineering. *Science* 327 (5965): 527–527.

Bodansky, Daniel. 2013. The Who, What, and Wherefore of Geoengineering Governance. *Climatic Change* 121 (3): 539–551.

Boin, Arjen, Paul Hart, Eric Stern, and Bengt Sundelius. 2005. *The Politics of Crisis Management: Public Leadership under Pressure*. Cambridge, UK: Cambridge University Press.

Bostrom, Nick. 2014. *Superintelligence: Paths, Dangers, Strategies*. Oxford: Oxford University Press.

Brondizio, Eduardo S., Karen O'Brien, Xuemei Bai, et al. 2016. Re-conceptualizing the Anthropocene: A Call for Collaboration. *Global Environmental Change* 39: 318–327.

Burns, William C. G. 2011. Climate Geoengineering: Solar Radiation Management and Its Implications for Intergenerational Equity. *Stanford Journal of Law, Science and Policy* 4 (1): 38–55.

Calo, Ryan, and Alex Rosenblat. 2017. The Taking Economy: Uber, Information, and Power. *Columbia Law Review* 117 (6).

Cantrell, Bradley, Laura J. Martin, and Erle C. Ellis. 2017. Designing Autonomy: Opportunities for New Wildness in the Anthropocene. *Trends in Ecology and Evolution* 32 (3): 156–166.

Christian, David. 1991. The Case for 'Big History'. *Journal of World History* 2 (2): 223–238.

Clark, Nigel. 2017. Politics of Strata. Theory, Culture and Society 34: 10.1177/0263276416667538.

Clark, Peter U., Jeremy D. Shakun, Shaun A. Marcott, et al. 2016. Consequences of Twenty-First-Century Policy for Multi-Millennial Climate and Sea-Level Change. *Nature Climate Change* 6: 360–369.

Diakopoulos, Nicholas. 2015. Algorithmic Accountability: Journalistic Investigation of Computational Power Structures. *Digital Journalism* 3 (3): 398–415.

Dobson, Andrew. 2000. *Green Political Thought*. London: Routledge.

Dobson, Andrew. 2007. Environmental Citizenship: Towards Sustainable Development. *Sustainable Development* 15 (5): 276–285.

Edwards, Paul N. 1999. Global Climate Science, Uncertainty and Politics: Data Laden Models, Model Filtered Data. *Science as Culture* 8 (4): 437–472.

Edwards, Paul N. 2013. *A Vast Machine: Computer Models, Climate Data, and the Politics of Global Warming*. Cambridge, MA: MIT Press.

Ellis, Erle C. 2012. The Planet of No Return: Human Resilience on an Artificial Earth. Breakthrough Journal (Winter). Accessed December 20, 2016. http://thebreakthrough.org/index.php/journal/past-issues/issue-2/the-planet-of-no-return

Galaz, Victor. 2014. *Global Environmental Governance, Technology and Politics: The Anthropocene Gap*. Cheltenham: Edward Elgar.

Galaz, Victor. 2015a. Planetary Boundaries and the Anthropocene. In *Encyclopedia of Global Environmental Governance and Politics*, edited by Philipp H. Pattberg and Fariborz Zelli. Cheltenham: Edward Elgar.

Galaz, Victor. 2015b. A Manifesto for Algorithms in the Environment. *The Guardian*, October 5, 2015. https://www.theguardian.com/science/political-science/2015/oct/05/a-manifesto-for-algorithms-in-the-environment

Galaz, Victor, and Jon Pierre. 2017. Superconnected, Complex and Ultrafast: Governance of Hyperfunctionality in Financial Markets. Complexity, Governance and Networks, in print.

Galaz, V., F. Moberg, E. K. Olsson, et al. 2011. Institutional and Political Leadership Dimensions of Cascading Ecological Crises. *Public Administration* 89 (2): 361–380.

Galaz, Victor, Frank Biermann, Beatrice Crona, et al. 2012. Planetary Boundaries: Exploring the Challenges for Global Environmental Governance. *Current Opinion in Environmental Sustainability* 4 (1): 80–87.

Galaz, Victor, Johan Gars, Fredrik Moberg, et al. 2015. Why Ecologists Should Care about Financial Markets. *Trends in Ecology and Evolution* 30 (10): 571–580.

Galaz, V., J. Tallberg, A. Boin, et al. 2017. Global Governance Dimensions of Globally Networked Risks: The State of the Art in Social Science Research. *Risk, Hazards & Crisis in Public Policy* 8 (1): 4–27.

Goes, Marlos, Nancy Tuana, and Klaus Keller. 2011. The Economics (or Lack Thereof) of Aerosol Geoengineering. *Climatic Change* 109 (3–4): 719–744.

Hajer, Maarten, Måns Nilsson, Kate Raworth, et al. 2015. Beyond Cockpit-ism: Four Insights to Enhance the Transformative Potential of the Sustainable Development Goals. *Sustainability* 7 (2): 1651–1660.

Helbing, Dirk. 2013. Globally Networked Risks and How to Respond. *Nature* 497 (7447): 51–59.

Johnson, Neil F., Guannan Zhao, Eric Hunsader, et al. 2013. Abrupt Rise of New Machine Ecology beyond Human Response Time. *Scientific Reports* 3 (11): 2627.

Jones, Andy, J. M. Haywood, Kari Alterskjær, et al. 2013. The Impact of Abrupt Suspension of Solar Radiation Management (Termination Effect) in Experiment G2 of the Geoengineering Model Intercomparison Project (GeoMIP). *Journal of Geophysical Research Atmospheres* 118 (17): 9743–9752.

Jones, Chris, Jason Lowe, Spencer Liddicoat, and Richard Betts. 2009. Committed Terrestrial Ecosystem Changes due to Climate Change. *Nature Geoscience* 2 (7): 484–487.

Kanie, N., M. M. Betsill, R. Zondervan, F. Biermann, and O. R. Young. 2012. A Charter Moment: Restructuring Governance for Sustainability. *Public Administration and Development* 32 (3): 292–304.

Keith, David W., Edward Parson, and M. Granger Morgan. 2010. Research on Global Sun Block Needed Now. *Nature* 463 (7280): 426–427.

Kim, Rakhyun E. 2013. The Emergent Network Structure of the Multilateral Environmental Agreement System. *Global Environmental Change* 23 (5): 980–991.

Kokkonen, Andrej, and Anders Sundell. 2014. Delivering Stability: Primogeniture and Autocratic Survival in European Monarchies 1000–1800. *American Political Science Review* 108 (2): 438–453.

Kroll, Joshua A., Joanna Huey, Solon Barocas, et al. 2017. Accountable Algorithms. *University of Pennsylvania Law Review* 165: 633–705.

Lenton, Timothy M. 2011. Early Warning of Climate Tipping Points. *Nature Climate Change* 1 (4): 201–209.

Lenton, T. M., H. Held, E. Kriegler, et al. 2008. Tipping Elements in the Earth's Climate System. *Proceedings of the National Academy of Sciences* 105 (6): 1786–1793.

Loorbach, Derk. 2010. Transition Management for Sustainable Development: A Prescriptive, Complexity-Based Governance Framework. *Governance* 23 (1): 161–183.

Lövbrand, Eva, Johannes Stripple, and Bo Wiman. 2009. Earth System Governmentality: Reflections on Science in the Anthropocene. *Global Environmental Change* 19 (1): 7–13.

MacCormick, John. 2014. *9 Algorithms that Changed the Future: The Ingenious Ideas that Drive Today's Computers*. Princeton: Princeton University Press.

Marsh, David, and Roderick A. W Rhodes. 1992. *Policy Networks in British Government*. Oxford: Clarendon Press.

Merrie, Andrew, Daniel C. Dunn, Marc Metian, et al. 2014. An Ocean of Surprises: Trends in Human Use, Unexpected Dynamics and Governance Challenges in Areas beyond National Jurisdiction. *Global Environmental Change* 27: 19–31.

Moreno-Cruz, Juan B., and David W. Keith. 2013. Climate Policy under Uncertainty: A Case for Solar Geoengineering. *Climatic Change* 121 (3): 431–444.

Ochieng, Robert M. 2017. *The Role of Forests in Climate Change Mitigation: A Discursive Institutional Analysis of REDD+ MRV*. PhD Thesis, Wageningen University and Research, the Netherlands.

O'Neil, Cathy. 2016. *Weapons of Math Destruction: How Big Data Increases Inequality and Threatens Democracy*. New York: Crown Publishing Group.

Parson, Edward A., and David W. Keith. 2013. End the Deadlock on Governance of Geoengineering Research. *Science* 339 (6125): 1278–1279.

Pasquale, Frank. 2015. *The Black Box Society: The Secret Algorithms that Control Money and Information*. Cambridge, MA: Harvard University Press.

Pierre, Jon, B., and Guy Peters. 2005. *Governing Complex Societies: Trajectories and Scenarios*. Basingstoke: Palgrave Macmillan.

Pierson, Paul. 2004. *Politics in Time: History, Institutions, and Social Analysis*. Princeton, NJ: Princeton University Press.

Steffen, Will, Angelina Sanderson, Peter D. Tyson, Jill Jager, Pamala A. Matson, Berrien Moore III, Frank Oldfield, Katherine Richardson, Hans J. Schellnhuber, Billie L. Turner II, and Robert J. Wasson, eds. 2004. *Global Change and the Earth System: A Planet under Pressure*. Berlin: Springer.

Steffen, Will, Åsa Persson, Lisa Deutsch, et al. 2011. The Anthropocene: From Global Change to Planetary Stewardship. *Ambio* 40 (7): 739–361.

Steffen, Will, Reinhold Leinfelder, Jan Zalasiewicz, et al. 2016. Stratigraphic and Earth System Approaches to Defining the Anthropocene. *Earth's Future* 4 (8): 324–345.

Underdal, Arild. 2010. Complexity and Challenges of Long-Term Environmental Governance. *Global Environmental Change* 20 (3): 386–393.

Vasconcelos, Víctor V., Francisco C. Santos, and Jorge M. Pacheco. 2013. A Bottom-Up Institutional Approach to Cooperative Governance of Risky Commons. *Nature Climate Change* 3 (9): 797–801.

Vervoort, Joost M., Kasper Kok, Ron van Lammeren, and Tom Veldkamp. 2010. Stepping into Futures: Exploring the Potential of Interactive Media for Participatory Scenarios on Social-Ecological Systems. *Futures* 42 (6): 604–616.

Victor, David G. 2008. On the Regulation of Geoengineering. *Oxford Review of Economic Policy* 24 (2): 322–336.

Waters, Colin N., Jan Zalasiewicz, Colin Summerhayes, et al. 2016. The Anthropocene Is Functionally and Stratigraphically Distinct from the Holocene. *Science* 351 (6269): 137–148.

Wilkinson, Bruce H. 2005. Humans as Geologic Agents: A Deep-Time Perspective. *Geology* 33 (3): 161–164.
Wong, Pak-Hang. 2014. Maintenance Required: The Ethics of Geoengineering and Post-Implementation Scenarios. *Ethics, Policy and Environment* 17 (2): 186–191.
Young, Oran R. 2010. *Institutional Dynamics: Emergent Patterns in International Environmental Governance*. Cambridge, MA: MIT Press.
Young, Oran R. 2011. Effectiveness of International Environmental Regimes: Existing knowledge, Cutting-Edge Themes, and Research Strategies. *Proceedings of the National Academy of Sciences* 108 (50): 19853–19860.
Yudkowsky, Eliezer. 2008. Artificial Intelligence as a Positive and Negative Factor in Global Risk. In *Global Catastrophic Risks*, edited by Nick Bostrom and Milan M. Cirkovic, 308–345. Oxford: Oxford University Press.
Zalasiewicz, Jan. 2015. Epochs: Disputed Start Dates for Anthropocene. *Nature* 520 (7548): 436–436.

# 7

# Democracy in the Anthropocene: A New Scale

AYŞEM MERT

The Anthropocene poses a challenge to contemporary imaginaries of democracy. The scale of ecological crises today is increasingly recognized as planetary (e.g., Steffen et al. 2007; Biermann et al. 2009; Rockström et al. 2009), whereas there is no stable political system in place to address these challenges at the corresponding scale of governance. The severity of environmental problems and the lack of an immediate body to tackle these challenges may trigger technocratic and eco-fascistic tendencies, particularly in the absence of a democratic imaginary to address social necessities in the face of impending catastrophes. Furthermore, the existing governing structures as we enter the Anthropocene are results of Holocene experiences. They have to respond to unprecedented circumstances and a relatively unstable and unpredictable physical environment. However, the practices they have institutionalized into their operations emerged in the steady conditions of the Holocene, where decision-making could take a long time (see Galaz, Chapter 6). If they are to protect citizens and the public good, prepare for potential calamities, and help re/build resilient communities, these structures, institutions, and practices will have to change drastically. It is not certain whether democratic practices and institutions will be a part of the Anthropocene governance architecture, and if so, which ones.

Inversely, it is certain that *some* practices of contemporary governance will be retained and some others reinterpreted as they settle into the logics of our planetary future (Biermann 2014). The political experiences of contemporary societies will necessarily influence and sediment into the logics of the future governance models, and democracy has been the most formative structure of the preceding era for many societies. In this sense, the Anthropocene is also an opportunity to rethink and reconstruct novel democratic imaginaries and correct the failures of the existing systems. This is critical for any discussion of democracy in the Anthropocene, considering the level of disillusionment voters have conveyed in the liberal democratic societies for the last several years. Acknowledging this political context,

Jedediah Purdy (2015: 257) notes that in the past decade citizens' capacity "to rework their own common lives has been hollowed out in overt and explicit ways, and eroded by a decline in political imagination." He argues against "calling for more democracy when democracy seems a formula for failure," which would further alienate and frustrate the citizens (Purdy 2015: 267). Instead, he suggests taking *the Anthropocene question* as a challenge to the present democratic imaginary, in the sense that the democracy that can address the question of what kind of world to make together cannot be more of the same.

Another way the Anthropocene challenges contemporary liberal democratic imaginary is related to the overwhelming hegemony of the Western ideals, practices, and institutions of democracy since the end of the Cold War. While parts of the world do not share these values, institutions of nominal democracy have spread across the world since the 1990s, and these norms formed the basic principles of global governance architecture in both the United Nations system and the Bretton Woods institutions. Global environmental problems have captured worldwide political attention at the so-called "end of history," in an era where liberal democracy has supposedly triumphed over alternatives. As Simon Niemeyer (2014: 16) notes, "the failure to anticipate and address the anthropocenic challenge is, then, viewed as a failure of democracy."[1] These observations raise questions regarding the conditions for democracy in the Anthropocene, which I aim to investigate in this chapter: What specific challenges does the Anthropocene pose for contemporary democratic imaginaries? What kind of a democracy could anticipate, mitigate, and adapt to Anthropocenic transformations? What kind of a democratic imaginary would be possible in the Anthropocene? If we understand the Anthropocene as a new scale, what kind of democracy could address its tensions?

## Two Frames of the Anthropocene

The Anthropocene is a multilayered narrative, still in the making (Lidskog and Waterton 2018). As this volume shows, it has various dimensions and connects to fundamental cosmological and political concepts. In its encounter with each concept, there are ongoing debates and contestations about how to reconstruct these relations. In contrast, some argue that the Anthropocene is problematic or dangerous in its most general premise, and propose alternative frames

---

[1] Niemeyer (2014: 16–17) aptly questions this conclusion, since the liberal paternalism that characterizes most modern democracies precludes a deeper transformation towards deliberative democracy. It is equally necessary to question the misleading equivalence established between democracy and capitalism. Francis Fukuyama's (1989: 3) argument was not so much about democratization as, rather, the triumph of Western liberalism as the only viable political system that ensures prosperity. While it is beyond the purview of this chapter, it is important to note this difference, and that its critique is made in democratic theory even though it is largely uncited in global environmental governance literature.

(Swyngedouw 2015; Moore 2017; Swyngedouw and Ernstson 2018). In order to examine its encounter with democracy, it is necessary to sketch two important frames of the Anthropocene which do not completely preclude the relevance or usefulness of the term. In what follows, I sketch two prevalent frames of the Anthropocene, and call these *positivist* and *deconstructivist* framings. Their juxtaposition reveals how the concept has captured the imaginations of scientists and society at large, but also summarizes how each frame depicts solutions to environmental crises and decision-making in the Anthropocene. While many frames of the Anthropocene have emerged lately, these two represent the main propositions of most other frames. Furthermore, the hegemonic contestation between these two frames proves most relevant to the debates on democracy.

## *The Positivist Framing of the Anthropocene*

When the initial debates on the Anthropocene started in the early 2000s, it was not obvious that the term would be so divisive or so central to the study of environmental politics. As Noel Castree (Chapter 2) investigates in detail, it has taken over a decade of scientific contestations for the term to emerge in earth system science and geology. Despite the overwhelming interest in the Anthropocene from various scientific disciplines, the term is far from signifying a common meaning in the epistemic community. Even if the term gets official approval from scientific agencies, it appears that contestations among researchers will continue regarding when the Anthropocene has started, what its markers are, and how science should respond to it (also see Wissenburg 2016).

Despite disagreements and controversies, the epistemic debates have been formative in framing the concept of the Anthropocene, particularly with the subsequent involvement of the eco-modernist, rationalist, and post-positivist traditions in the social sciences (also see Fremaux and Barry, Chapter 9). I will call this dominant frame, which encompasses a range of scientific conceptions of the Anthropocene, *the positivist framing of the Anthropocene*. It regards the Anthropocene as a new geological epoch characterized by the unprecedented impact of a single species on planetary ecosystems. It focuses on the human capacity to transform and destroy the planet, and frames the ecological crisis as the result of historically aggregated industrial and economic activities of all humans. The changes in the bio-geochemical cycles threaten most, if not all, life-forms on the planet. This threat to "life" has components that are traditionally regarded as "natural" (such as floods, tornadoes, droughts, or hurricanes), but societies experience its effects deeply in their social, economic, and cultural practices and institutions as well.

The positivist framing constructs the Anthropocene and the ecological crisis in a particular way, and proposes potential solutions that span the spectrum of modernistic imaginaries. Some argue for stakeholder involvement in making short-term decisions coupled with the input from social scientists on the desirability and plausibility of these decisions in the long term (Berkhout 2014; Knight 2015; Bai et al. 2016). This would allow certain democratic practices (such as stakeholderism and limited public participation) to be central to decision-making in the Anthropocene.

Others, alternatively called climate interventionists or "planet-hackers," argue for large-scale human interventions to address climate change (Kintisch 2010). Proponents rarely discuss how decisions should be made regarding the research on and the application of geoengineering, although there are at least two public–private or private–private initiatives that aim to produce guidelines.[2] In the absence of projects that can be readily applied, the politics of geoengineering concerns the financing of research projects that involve potentially severe environmental risks and major uncertainties. With the emergence of the Anthropocene narrative in this positivist framing, geoengineering solutions have become increasingly normalized. In two articles on the use of stratospheric sulfate aerosols, Paul Crutzen (2006; Rasch et al. 2008) argued that geoengineering could solve "policy dilemmas" in climate governance. Other scientists and opinion leaders also argued for various technologies that could potentially fix the climate without necessarily transforming economic and political structures in societies. Large university programs have been established to work on geoengineering, particularly in the UK and the USA. In sum, it has become possible to petition for public funding of these ambitious and risky projects (Anshelm and Hansson 2014: 135), and compete with low-risk adaptation and mitigation policies.[3]

A third stance is that the Anthropocene requires human societies to choose one of the following strategies: Either greenhouse gas emissions will be severely reduced through socioeconomic transformations, or high-technology solutions will be investigated and employed to achieve an end-of-pipe solution. Remaining indecisive between these two strategies, however, would have catastrophic effects (Karlsson 2013). All these visions share the belief that techno-science can provide effective solutions to the planetary crisis. They all imagine futures in which experts take on authoritative roles in decision-making and risk management. The narratives

---

[2] The Academic Working Group on International Governance of Solar Climate Engineering of the Carnegie Council is in dialogue with the United Nations. The Solar Radiation Management Governance Initiative of the Royal Society collaborates with the Environmental Defense Fund and The World Academy of Sciences.
[3] For instance, in a controversial promotional video, the Solar Geoengineering Research Program of Harvard University states that it is too expensive and slow to switch to clean energy production. A redirection of 1 percent of climate mitigation funds to geoengineering research, it is argued, could help invent a solar shield for the earth for USD 10 billion per year. https://geoengineering.environment.harvard.edu/

employed in each case try to balance the need for democracy with the need for efficient decision-making. Despite these common features, there is no consensus on the best course of action in the face of climate change, and these contestations continue on the platforms where science and policy interface (Wissenburg 2016).

## *The Deconstructivist Framing of the Anthropocene*

Outside the scientific debate, the Anthropocene captured the popular imagination in an unforeseen fashion.[4] As soon as it was coined, the term gained widespread use in popular culture, the art world, and the media. Other than the myriad of visual art exhibitions and films that have been produced in the last fifteen years, magazines such as *Time, Scientific American, New Scientist,* and *Grist* covered "the Anthropocene story" multiple times, mentioning the scientific controversies only sparingly. Their focus was often the new paradigm humanity was in, most famously represented by the cover of *The Economist* (2011) with the headline "Welcome to the Anthropocene."

This popular rendering of the term is not divorced but, rather, derived from the earlier scientific debates. Many of them often reify the role of the human species as a whole and its planetwide transformative power. Nonetheless, popular representations give more space to the alternative interpretations and narratives of the Anthropocene and focus often on its underlying dilemmas and contradictions. The popular scientific magazines cite a myriad of environmental problems that will immediately influence life in the Anthropocene. Other publications and websites discuss the impossibility of maintaining coherent social structures such as a capitalist world economy, global industrial production, and institutions such as traditional family structures and large-scale political organizations. Particularly in the art world, the ontological implications and dilemmas of the Anthropocene are performed, (re)constructed (Logie 2017), and discussed with explicit reference to philosophy, for instance of Peter Sloterdijk (Davis 2016), Deleuze and Guattari (Jazvac 2015; Davis 2016), and Martin Heidegger (Jazvac 2015), among others. Be it in popular science media or artistic representation, I call these narratives that aim to show its underlying logics, problems, and dilemmas *the deconstructivist framing of the Anthropocene*.

One focus of the deconstructivist framing is the ontological novelty that the concept represents, introducing a continuum of coexisting rationales and bringing an end to dichotomies such as nature/culture, human/nonhuman, rational/irrational,

---

[4] Alexandra Nikoleris and colleagues (Chapter 4) show that numerous fictional narratives have already existed which imagined futures on similar premises to that of the Anthropocene. Their study constructs *the Anthropocene imagination* based on these narratives. This is related to but somewhat different from the popular/scientific narratives that presently employ the term, and actively seeks to give meaning to the Anthropocene by co-constructing it and revealing its internal predicaments.

agency/structure, being/becoming. While the positivist framing of the Anthropocene is criticized for overlooking them (Lövbrand et al. 2015), the emergent narratives frame the subject in the context of qualitative questions of meaning, value, responsibility, and purpose. In this respect, the deconstructivist framing of the Anthropocene is in immediate dialogue with the long-standing debates in the humanities and the social sciences.

Subdisciplines of the social sciences and the humanities have been deconstructing such dichotomies since the 1960s. Learning from the critical, constructivist, and post-structuralist traditions, these interpretations also take the Anthropocene as a novel imaginary with diverse trajectories. Most notably, some of the leading scholars of environmental social science have extended the conversation on the Anthropocene by cultivating "multiple interpretations of the Anthropocene [so that] the social sciences can help to extend the realm of the possible for environmental politics" (Lövbrand et al. 2015: 211). Others see this as nature having morphed into human environment (Arias-Maldonado, Chapter 3) or as a reciprocal transformation wherein "the earth's future being is being transformed through a living process of inter-being" (Graham and Roelvink 2010: 322). The Anthropocene is sometimes welcomed as an opportunity to engage with questions on ethics and politics in a time of rapid biophysical change (Rose et al. 2012: 1) and to rethink modernist ontologies to end the separation between nature and human (Latour 2015).

In all its diversity, the deconstructivist framing of the Anthropocene proposes a number of organizing principles to decision-making rather than models. For some, deliberation is central to democratic decision-making, whereby institutional and ecological reflexivity should guide institutional governance (Niemeyer 2014; Dryzek and Pickering 2017). Others focus on epistemic pluralism that underpins "a knowledge politics comprising multiple forms of human and non-human expertise" (Lorimer 2012). Pluralism can also refer to the inclusion of nonhumans as important participants in governance, whereby nature regains some agency as an *actant*. Real-life examples of such pluralism are the Pachamama laws in South America and the recently recognized legal personas of the Whanganui and Ganges rivers. These proposals are based (among others) on Bruno Latour's (1993) earlier ideas such as the "parliament of things" as well as Donna Haraway's (2003) call to leave the nature/culture dualism behind and understand politics as embedded in naturecultures. Before discussing the potential of these principles for democracy in the Anthropocene, the next section examines the ontological conditions and dynamics of the Anthropocene under which democracy will be reimagined.

## Three Ontologies of the Anthropocene

While the positivist framing of the Anthropocene is currently more dominant as a discourse, critical scholars also engage with the Anthropocene scholarship. One of the most prominent works of this kind, seeking to understand the concept "as a socially and culturally bounded object with many possible meanings and political trajectories," was written by Eva Lövbrand and colleagues (2015: 212). In their critique of the positivist framing, the authors argued that three claims underpinned the proposed advent of the Anthropocene, which they called the post-natural, the post-social, and the post-political ontology of the Anthropocene. Each of these claims has implications for an inquiry into democracy in the Anthropocene; therefore, I briefly summarize their critique and discuss the democratic implications of each claim.

### *The Post-social Ontology of the Anthropocene*

*The post-social ontology of the Anthropocene* perceives humans as a species that operates as a subsystem among other complex but interconnected bio-geochemical systems of the earth (Lövbrand et al. 2015: 213–214). A multiplicity of cultures and social relations is subsumed under the abstract conception of a single humankind. Therefore, not only are the causes of anthropogenic change narrated from the point of view of a singular human history, but more importantly, the solutions to the impending change are also overgeneralized and similarly restricted. This is problematic, since the adaptive capacities and historical responsibilities of societies are unequal as a direct result of these relations of domination. Ahistorical narrations of how the pressures on the planet's ecosystems and cycles have accumulated conceal injustices of the past. Historical roots of injustice in colonialism and industrial development are thus obscured, as well as its current causes in the oppressive and violent practices that reproduce socioeconomic inequalities (also see Baskin, Chapter 8). In other words, the post-social ontological position is an intervention that semantically unlinks environmental change from social categories and the historical inequalities therein. These include, but are not limited to, nationality, age, class, race, gender, power, and capital. On the one hand, as Linda Wallbott (2016) notes, the immediate meaning of the Anthropocene as a geological concept already blurs the specific normativity that puts Western industrial activities as the main reference point in framing earth's history. On the other, differences in responsibilities for environmental change (causes) and differences in experiences of it (results) are absent, and arguably muted in the positivist frame. *The post-social ontology of the Anthropocene* therefore raises questions about the political feasibility of complex democratic solutions that take into account equity and justice, based on plural accounts of history.

Another challenge the post-social claim poses to democratic governance concerns not the past but the present behavior of individuals. Globalization and the widespread use of communications technologies have resulted in a confluence of behavioral options: They prescribe a dominant strategy, which results in masses of people hearing the same news, responding by buying and selling stocks, currencies, or houses simultaneously, and consuming or abstaining from the same products all at once, at times resulting in economic or ecological crises. When crises are caused by the decisions of an anonymous mass, it becomes impossible to hold individuals personally accountable in their functions as citizens, shareholders, or consumers. Carbon emissions increase when every household requires a car, or when we consume industrial meat products, but no one would consider it illegal and few would consider it unethical to own a car or eat steak. The argument that our individual actions are too ambiguously linked to environmental degradation, despite the discernibility of their cumulative effect, is not new. Researchers from various ideological and scientific backgrounds have studied this as an economic problem caused by rational behavior (Hardin 1968), environmental displacement and distancing caused by globalization (Christoff and Eckersley 2013), or global inequality and prioritization of the environmental concerns of the affluent (Dauvergne 2016). The novelty of the Anthropocene narratives is that harmful production and consumption habits are no longer just shared with other individuals or communities. They are also shared with past generations, as narratives such as planetary boundaries or the hockey-stick graphs on pollution and carbon emissions represent. Since holding previous generations responsible for the unintended consequences of their actions is impossible, the concepts of agency and liability are even further diffused in the Anthropocene. In our responsibility towards next generations, we are burdened by the decisions and behaviors of our ancestors. This unsettles some of the familiar (although contested) concepts in governance, such as common but differentiated responsibilities.

This diffusion also challenges the current democratic imaginaries at the level of individual agency. The democratic agency of the individual in her numerous identities (as voter, citizen, consumer, shareholder, and so on) has not been sufficiently theorized or exercised to respond to this challenge. We are deemed at once very powerful (so much so that our actions threaten all life on the planet) and lacking the agency to correct the system in a meaningful or decisive way. What is not clear in this picture is that the individual is only powerful in her function as an economic agent, whereas the agency required to meaningfully contribute to positive change is that of the citizen, in the realm of the political. A *democratic* imaginary of the Anthropocene requires the empowerment of the democratic citizen among the various identities each individual develops. It also requires a better understanding of how individuals and groups find ways of fostering solidarity with distant peoples and places. Politically, this can be understood as the formation of equivalential chains between different political demands (Laclau and Mouffe 1985; Glynos and Howarth 2007). While emerging as local demands, eco-political movements have been global and transnational in their outreach for this reason. Nevertheless, there are also philosophical and spiritual dimensions to such identification, which subsumes not only other humans but also nonhuman beings. Historically, these dimensions have been the concern of many eco-philosophers, such as Arne Næss (*deep ecology*), Aldo Leopold (*land ethics*), and Val Plumwood (*shadow places*). On the other hand, the intergenerational ethics and politics evoked by the Anthropocene require further consideration of these philosophical traditions.

## *The Post-political Ontology of the Anthropocene*

The second ontological claim that underpins the proposed advent of the Anthropocene focuses on "post-politics of environmental urgency," wherein ecological collapse is imminent and it is too late to innovate new institutions or governance mechanisms (Lövbrand et al. 2015). *The post-political ontology of the Anthropocene* assumes that humanity's unprecedented social and economic development since the Second World War has put ecological systems at such unprecedented levels of risk that in order to avoid planetwide ecological collapse, human intervention and biochemical input into the ecosystems must be significantly reduced (Steffen et al. 2007; Rockström et al. 2009). Paradoxically, such a fundamental social transformation is expected to take place within the already existing institutional structure, although these institutions were ineffectual in preventing the ecological crisis, if not responsible for it.

While the post-political ontology is a part of the Anthropocene narrative (see also Swyngedouw and Ernstson 2018), it is by no means novel. Efforts to depoliticize, economize, technocratize, and securitize environmental politics have been an ongoing part of the liberal and neoliberal agendas for several decades. Each one of these techniques aims to circumvent the emerging ideological contestation by representing the political conflict in other terms (economic, technical, military, and so forth). In the post-political ontology of the Anthropocene, another type of hegemonic struggle replaces politics: contestations over techno-managerial solutions (Swyngedouw 2013).

To depoliticize the ecological crises and potential ways of addressing it would have ramifications for the democratic imaginary. When the logic of policymaking is techno-managerial, even stakeholder participation would mean that stakeholders would select one of the highly technical alternatives presented by experts. These participants would need to have sufficient expertise to comprehend the technical details of each option, or the funds to afford to hire experts to represent their interests. In the best cases, the policy options would have to be mediated by the experts and translated to the citizens. The result would not be a system that encourages citizen participation or pluralism.

Imagining democracy under post-social or post-political ontologies of the Anthropocene also precludes the possibility of epistemic pluralism. While knowledge of those who benefit(ed) disproportionately from relationships of domination is regarded as universal, underrepresented sources and forms of knowledge of the less industrialized, modernized, or Westernized are marginalized. As a result, techno-scientific solutions appear as the best, if not the only, way to address the challenges of the Anthropocene. Proponents of epistemic pluralism argue that efficiency concerns should make the decision-making procedures more democratic, since inclusive and diverse processes produce better outcomes than exclusive and homogeneous ones (Stevenson 2016: 410). According to this view, political institutions should maximize the ways and capacities for participation of various objective and subjective knowledge-holders. The manifestation of this principle may be a radical democracy (e.g., following Chantal Mouffe's agonistic pluralism) as well as a deliberative model (in line with the work of John Dryzek).

If efficiency demands epistemic diversity, and the post-political ontology of the Anthropocene emphasizes the urgency of the problem, it becomes necessary to ask whether the solutions techno-science offers (however limited and uncertain) could be integrated into democratic governance processes. I would like to entertain two possible examples. Let us imagine, first, that carbon storage and sequestration, nuclear fission, ocean fertilization, and space mirrors are proposed as alternative ways to tackle climate change in the future. Within the United Nations system, decision-making mechanisms can be arranged to invest in and promote one of these projects, to be decided by nation-states and funded through public–private cooperation. Such a decision taken by intergovernmental processes would be regarded as democratically legitimate in today's international politics. In this scenario, the democratic deliberation of the options would depend on the states involving their citizens and civil society in their votes. Relatively more democratic states could to some extent encourage and promote public deliberation in others. On the other hand, the number of options would have to be very limited, and decisions would reflect concerns over the efficiency of addressing the perceived problem and its dominant framing. When faced with controversy, and in the absence of intergovernmental consensus, the relatively more democratic regimes would refrain from costly investments and their potential implications for their short-term election success. In other words, the result would be the political inertia of not choosing either of the potential solutions to the ecological crisis, of which Rasmus Karlsson (2013) forewarns.

To use a more utopian example, let us imagine devising a global referendum to select one of the options above, in which registered residents of all existing municipalities worldwide can vote. This arrangement could circumvent the problems regarding the participation of residents and citizens, and potentially encourage open and inclusive public debates at the subnational level. It could be regarded as more democratic than nation-state democracies, which are limited to parliamentary representation, or than global governance processes, where democracy is associated with accountability, transparency, and self-reporting. To use Simon Niemeyer's (2014) terminology, *the most basic democratic requirement* in this scenario would then be to deliberate these options and their implications into the future. However, even if the referendum increases deliberation and consultation among citizens, none of these technologies effectively addresses climate change, or is presently available, or is predictable in terms of unintended consequences. The translation of each option into layman's terms would once again require experts to interpret the policy options, relegating the deliberative quality of the process. My point is that a nominal democracy, whereby the appearance of participation is ensured, can easily obscure the deeper challenge of the democratic *production* of actual solutions to fundamentally political questions.

Another implication of the post-political ontology of the Anthropocene has been the resurfacing of eco-authoritarian arguments. It has been noted that climate change is a super-wicked policy problem, characterized by four features: "time is running out; those who cause the problem also seek to provide a solution; the central authority needed to address it is weak or non-existent; and, partly as a result, policy responses discount the future irrationally" (Levin et al. 2012). However, the argument that climate change is unlike any other pollution problem and requires exceptional political processes is called "climate exceptionalism" (Nagle 2010). Proponents argue that democracy takes too long and does not always reach the best result for the public good; therefore, we cannot wait for the public to deliberate or even nation-states to negotiate a global climate policy. Some argue for putting democracy on hold for a while, whereas others do not advocate authoritarian solutions, but only emphasize that democratic institutions are not up to the task, and the short-term limits of rule do not allow for the much-needed decisive action (Ball 2006: 133). This tendency of the post-political ontology to produce antidemocratic arguments is not new; it follows directly from the neo-Malthusian eco-authoritarianism debates of the 1970s (Niemeyer 2014: 20). Since the 1970s, the two main premises of antidemocratic environmental arguments have been severity and complexity: The first refers to the fact that environmental crises are urgent, deep, and protracted (thus requiring undemocratic solutions), whereas the second emphasizes their complexity (hence the need for technocratic rule).

Empirical studies on the examples of China and the Soviet Union find that authoritarian systems have failed to match the (rather poor) record of liberal democracies in addressing ecological crises (Gilley 2012; Shahar 2015). Furthermore, antidemocratic eco-authoritarian arguments do not clearly state at what scale, to what degree, and until when democracy should be put on hold. If the Anthropocene represents a radical and irreversible transformation, a return to the normal, steady-state, Holocene conditions cannot be expected. In other words, there is no "for a while" when it comes to climate change (Stevenson and Dryzek 2014: 4). Furthermore, there is no democracy to put on hold in the international system; and any authority needs democratic legitimation, particularly if the goal is global environmental regulation (Stevenson and Dryzek 2014: 4–6). They also note that democratic states have better environmental performance and that reflexive public opinion often demands stronger, not weaker, climate action.

In sum, the post-political "solution" to climate change is not supported by empirical evidence, at state level or at large. Purdy (2015: 258–259) concludes, therefore, that there is no empirical support for resurgent fantasies of green authoritarianism, when the actual challenge is the lack of a political vision to counter the demand for more consumption. However, democratic societies can still choose to put democracy on hold, particularly in times of trauma. This is the other, subtler, and arguably more dangerous antidemocratic threat in the Anthropocene, which has so far not been debated in literature. It will be articulated more forcefully after major calamities devastate communities, economies, and a number of states at once, such as Hurricane Irma of 2017. In times of severe dislocations, when the previous order in society is no longer within the realm of the possible and no alternative has so far emerged, citizens prioritize establishing an(y) order, regardless of its content: "When structural dislocation goes deep down to the very bottom of the social, the need for order expands indefinitely" (Torfing 1999: 151).

Ernesto Laclau (1996: 62 and 2005: 88) recognizes this element in Hobbes' *Leviathan*, written in the aftermath of the English Civil War, in which the sovereign is given almost complete authority over others to protect the peace and prevent discord in the commonwealth. Hobbes does not discuss the content of the order to come: for him, the order of any sovereign is better than radical disorder. Climate change in the Anthropocene signifies increasingly unstable and extreme weather conditions that will make parts of the world unsafe to live in or uninhabitable altogether. Currently, many societies and communities are experiencing dislocation momentarily or permanently. Nonetheless, what most of humanity has experienced thus far as a result of the ecological crises is not radical disorder. This is likely to happen in the future, when weather conditions become even more extreme and unpredictable, continuously. Imagine, for instance, that instead of three hurricanes roiling the Atlantic (a first in 2017), seventeen do. Aid cannot be gathered or delivered, and this is no longer newsworthy. A case where order itself becomes impossible represents much more than the "contingency found in all empirical reality: it is the very definition of the state of nature" (Laclau 1990: 70).

In other words, the survival of democratic institutions that emerged in the Holocene is going to depend on their capacity to ensure basic security and order, and on co-constructing the discourses that justify the transformations required to do so. Institutions and societies that can survive under swiftly changing circumstances are characterized by institutional and ecological reflexivity (Wynne 1993; Mol 1996). Institutional reflexivity is the capacity of organizations to critically analyze the results of their past choices and (if necessary) reform themselves. One of the main problems with global governance institutions today is their lack of institutional reflexivity (Voss et al. 2006), with only a few exceptions (Beck et al. 2014). Furthermore, it is argued that societies would have to couple institutional reflexivity with ecological reflexivity in the Anthropocene (Schlosberg 2007 and 2012). Ecological reflexivity means that once a policy is in place, there are monitoring processes that pay attention to the way ecosystems respond to it. As these processes evaluate and reflect upon these responses, previous policy decisions are continuously reconsidered, at times cancelled, and possibly improved.

It is critical for the institutions of the Anthropocene to produce evaluation and monitoring mechanisms that are inbuilt in their decision-making process, that allow them to change course and adapt to new information about their performance. However, there is also a tension between institutional reflexivity and taking responsibility for failed or suboptimal policies. Continuous institutional reflexivity requires a careful consideration of how accountability and success are defined for political agents, be they individuals or institutions. In today's representative democracies, political agents are afraid of losing legitimacy if they change the course or terms of a policy. Often, they employ a self-celebratory rhetoric regardless of actual results. Otherwise, they avoid political decisions that are unpopular in the short term. These issues, many of which are direct results of the representative democratic model, need to be resolved before radical disorder becomes the organizing principle of life for most societies.

### *The Post-natural Ontology of the Anthropocene*

The third and final premise Lövbrand and colleagues (2015: 213) posit is *the post-natural ontology of the Anthropocene*, which refers to the end of nature as a pure, singular, and stable category: "In the Anthropocene, nature is domesticated, technologized and capitalized to the extent that it can no longer be considered natural." The positivist framing of the Anthropocene engages with post-nature in a celebratory fashion: "It's no longer us against 'Nature'. Instead, it's we who decide what nature is and what it will be" (Crutzen and Schwägerl 2011: 3). This position is both continuous and novel. It follows from the well-established intellectual tradition that understands man as the main and legitimate agent that transforms nature to civilization; man dominates nature and turns it into value. The philosophical origins of the thought are present in Plato (Form and Ideas) and Aristotle (hylomorphism), the monotheistic concept of the Great Chain of Being, and the Cartesian substance dualism. The novelty is not so much in the celebration of this role but, rather, in the recognition that the dualities between nature/culture and mind/body are dissolving – and that this observation is finding a place in a positivist narrative.

The eco-modernists who employ the dominant framing of the Anthropocene celebrate the human agency and decision-making power on the future of the planet. They suggest a techno-scientific stewardship model that is more responsible in the way it rules over nature (Steffen et al. 2007; Breakthrough Institute 2017; Ellis et al. 2017) without engaging critically with politics of technology or the free market. As a result, the positivist framing is criticized both by nature conservationists for having given up on Nature (Wilson 2016) and by neo-Marxists (Swyngedouw 2013; Moore 2017) for not paying attention to the role of capitalism. As discussed above, issues that are central to the theory *and* practice of democracy are often overlooked in the positivist paradigm, particularly the concepts of justice and equity, processes of growth-oriented economic planning, and the potential agencies of the vulnerable, the underrepresented, and the nonhuman.

What is more interesting regarding the post-natural ontology of the Anthropocene is the diversity, depth, and complexity of the alternative deconstructivist framing, since this could be a significant source for reconstructing democracy in the Anthropocene. Social constructivists and post-/Marxists have debated the necessity of an anti-essentialist conception of nature since the early 1990s. Various philosophers have reflected on the death of nature (Merchant 1998), post-nature (Curry 2008), and after nature (Strathern 1992; Escobar 1999). These terms refer not only to destruction of ecosystems but also to the difficulty of understanding and representing nature in an age of such unprecedented intervention in nature.

It is important to recognize the difference in the level of reflexivity between the post-natural ontologies of positivist and deconstructivist frames. In the positivist framing, the Anthropocene both challenges and reproduces the Enlightenment, both problematizes the human influence on the planet and mediates the very mentality that caused the ecological crisis (Lövbrand et al. 2015). The deconstructivist frame describes a conceptual transformation emerging with the Anthropocene, wherein it is impossible to imagine an unmediated nature. It problematizes the way nature is narrated in rationalist, eco-modernist, and positivist accounts of the Anthropocene as an object to be quantified and even more precisely managed through science. It does not, however, suggest that humans have agency in or power over the exact direction or content of the socio-ecological changes taking place. To construct a democratic imaginary wherein political agency is possible for citizens, institutions, and civil society, as well as the nonhuman environment and future generations, the Anthropocene has to be reconstructed not only as an epoch but also as a new scale.

## The Anthropocene as a New Scale for Democracy

In International Relations, people are assumed to be represented by their respective governments, and the relations between states are considered an anarchy. Most International Relations textbooks prior to 1989 do not even contain the word "democracy" (Archibugi and Held 2011: 433). A recurrent academic debate about democracy beyond the nation-state subsumes the observation that state-centered democratic concepts are not applicable to non-electoral, non-territorial modes of governance, particularly the global and hybrid mechanisms around which global environmental governance architecture is built (Bäckstrand 2012: 170). In response to the increasingly hybrid, polycentric, and transnational nature of the global system, scholars reinterpret democratic concepts for global and transnational governance institutions (Nanz and Steffek 2004; Scholte 2011), particularly in environmental governance (Bäckstrand 2006; Dingwerth 2007).

Currently, the debates about democratizing global governance institutions focus on stakeholder participation, accountability, and transparency (largely organized around the principle of voluntariness). Policy practitioners and governance researchers often assume that representation is impossible at a global scale, and encourage these as second-order democratizing principles and criteria. However, it is often found that nation-level criteria as nonbinding ground rules fail to address the democratic deficit at the global level, where there is no *shadow of hierarchy* (Mert 2009). Furthermore, Karin Bäckstrand (2010) notes that the intense academic and corporate interest in accountability and transparency indicates that some of these measures have been institutionalized into the dominant system of rules. They have ended up legitimizing and maintaining existing power imbalances, rather than democratizing these institutions. This is also true for participation measures in global and transnational environmental governance. The power imbalances between North and South are often nominally concealed by including a like-minded Southern actor without much say over the decisions. It is more difficult to ensure the inclusion and participation of the more vulnerable groups, less represented demands, and the rights of nonnational minorities. Others have problematized the content of democratization measures. Most transparency measures are geared towards disclosing information without any behavioral change on the side of the governance institutions and the corporations, whereas accountability at the global level means accountability to a limited number of actors, often experts and the international development elite (Negri and Hardt 2004).

In other words, governance and International Relations scholarship generally assumes that states have a high threshold of democracy, while at larger scales "the threshold of acceptability should not be as high as a well-ordered society" (Keohane 2011: 100). Scholars tend to apply nation-level democratic principles to the international level, mainly because states are the main agents in present international society. However, this nation-level bias structures and limits the democratic imaginary. For instance, in a recent debate, Robert Keohane (2016: 938) notes that "no global government could harness the emotional support of nationalism." He continues to argue that the necessary infrastructure for democracy is absent at the global level; therefore, the best possibility is maintaining some key features of democracy, such as accountability of elites to publics, widespread participation, protection of minority rights, and deliberation within civil society. Paradoxically, his aim is to warn against a hypocritical nominal democratization that is void of substance.

The dominance of state-level democratic imaginary focuses International Relations debates on the possibilities of democratic representation when the whole world population constitutes the *demos*. Many scholars of International Relations regard this as a problem: "While [political theorists] want to democratize global institutions such as the UN [United Nations] or the WTO [World Trade Organization], there is not yet a people or *demos* on the global level to undertake this task. [They try] to speak *for* the people by constructing a theory *without* the people" (Näsström 2010). This is, however, a misleading argument for three reasons. First, as Robert Dahl (1989: 3) observes, advocates of democracy have always presupposed that "a people" already exists, as a fact, a creation of history, even when the accuracy of this argument is dubious. Secondly, there have been numerous examples of extraordinarily diverse and large populations organizing around democratic regimes, such as the USA, Brazil, and India. Thirdly, from a normative viewpoint, defining *demos* always concerns bias and exclusion. If there is any way of describing "a people" without bias and exclusion, this would include all of the planet's population, which the Anthropocene makes possible. Although the habitual questions and solutions of democratic theory are less pertinent at the global level due to blurry definitions of *demos,* territoriality, and representation, a loosely connected, albeit largely unorganized, *demos* already exists for the purposes of a discourse on the democratization of *planetary* governance. This *demos* takes action, too: Masses of people make demands regarding multilateral agreements at environmental summits, or at global trade and finance meetings; they gather to protest the structures that allow the financial elites to govern the world's largest economies; and they take action virtually in global social networks every day. If we distance ourselves from the disabling assumption that a global *demos* does not exist, it becomes possible to ask a critical question: How can the issues that concern all (that is, all of humanity and the nonhuman environment) be governed in a more democratic fashion?

There is no inherent reason for democracy in the Anthropocene to be based on nation-state principles. In its historical development as a regime, democracy has been fundamentally transformed when it has been applied to a new political scale. During the American and French Revolutions, the principles of an ancient, small-scale regime were reinterpreted and significantly transformed to suit the needs of larger nation-states with an extensive *demos*. Most importantly, representation, which was previously a monarchic tradition, was introduced as a democratic procedure. For Aristotle, elections belonged to the logic of oligarchy; for Montesquieu and Rousseau, to that of aristocracy. Elections began to serve the purpose of deciding "who gets the office," generating representative councils, and ensuring accountability. Today, every democratic nation-state employs representation in its practice of democratic rule. This was the first scalar revolution in the history of democracy.

In the Anthropocene, democracy requires to be reinterpreted once again. A second scalar revolution is to fundamentally transform the practice and conception of democracy for the planet. The Anthropocene threatens and potentially invigorates the practice of democratic governance at once; it forces us to think innovatively about democracy, to deconstruct certain traditions and learn from peripheral and marginalized knowledge-bases and the nonhuman environment. The conclusions summarize the findings and examine the necessary changes for a democratic imaginary in the Anthropocene.

## Conclusion

Using the three ontologies of the Anthropocene as a lens to examine democracy and the conditions under which it will be practiced in the Anthropocene has provided the following observations.

Institutions and societies that can be adaptable under swiftly changing circumstances will be institutionally and ecologically reflexive. This means critically analyzing the results of past choices and policies from the viewpoint of socio-ecological change and reforming them accordingly. On the one hand, this requires deliberation beyond which technological solutions might fix the ecological problem, and an ongoing public debate. Democratic governance institutions in the Anthropocene will have to incorporate procedures that cyclically examine the results of their policies on socio-ecological systems and make improvements and changes in policy. On the other hand, accountability and success in politics must be redefined, replacing the image of an individual politician who persuades all stakeholders of her plan, with that of a community, which commits to a policy that is constantly monitored and redrafted.

In terms of agency, democracy in the Anthropocene requires the empowerment of the democratic citizen. As opposed to various other identities (e.g., the consumer, the shareholder, or the entrepreneur), when their identity as a democratic citizen becomes central to the lives of people, a democratic imaginary for the Anthropocene can emerge.

In a post-natural democracy, scientific practice in the Anthropocene also has to take on some democratic qualities. Managerial and techno-scientific solutions can jeopardize the democratic quality of the debate if promoted as the main, or the only, solutions that can address the ecological crises. Epistemological pluralism must be a building block for science in the new epoch. Theorizing a post-natural democracy makes it possible to discuss the various futures of the planet with previously marginal communities who have different knowledge-making traditions and ways of relating to nature (Hulme 2010). Scientific as well as political institutions should maximize the ways and capacities for participation of various objective and subjective knowledge-holders so that communities can adapt to and mitigate the ecological crises in a multiplicity of ways.

The challenge for the activists and the scientists who aim to address climate change is to refrain from climate exceptionalism. It is true that climate change is different from most of the pollution problems that modern societies have tackled until now. This was also the case with every new environmental issue, such as ozone depletion, transboundary air pollution, and acid rain, when they emerged in the political horizon as policy areas. It is the case with many contemporary environmental problems today for which there is no immediate solution, such as biodiversity loss or global marine pollution. However, as Baber and Bartlett (2016: 167), remind us, "there is nothing so unique about the issues of environmental governance that puts them out of the reach of democratic deliberation." Narrating climate change as a policy area that requires a different set of rules evokes antidemocratic impulses that have been around since the 1970s.

Finally, the greatest challenge to democracy will come from the way citizens respond to the continuous dislocations resulting from the uncertain socio-ecological conditions of the Anthropocene. The extreme conditions and the uncertainties of political, economic, meteorological, and institutional futures will bring with them feelings of deep uncertainty and insecurity. The survival of democratic institutions that emerged in the Holocene will depend on how they provide citizens with basic security while also providing them with narratives around which transformations that are required can be debated and agreed upon.

## References

Anshelm, Jonas, and Anders Hansson. 2014. Battling Promethean Dreams and Trojan horses: Revealing the Critical Discourses of Geoengineering. *Energy Research and Social Science* 2: 135–144.

Archibugi, Daniele, and David Held. 2011. Cosmopolitan Democracy: Paths and Agents. *Ethics and International Affairs* 25 (4): 433–461.

Baber, Walter F., and Robert V. Bartlett. 2016. Democratic Accountability in the Anthropocene. In *Environmental Politics and Governance in the Anthropocene: Institutions and Legitimacy in a Complex World*, edited by Philipp Pattberg and Fariborz Zelli, 167–182. Cheltenham: Edward Elgar.

Bäckstrand, Karin. 2006. Democratizing Global Environmental Governance? Stakeholder Democracy after the World Summit on Sustainable Development. *European Journal of International Relations* 12(4): 467–498.

Bäckstrand, Karin. 2010. From Rhetoric to Practice: The Legitimacy of Global Public-Private Partnerships for Sustainable Development. In *Democracy and Public-Private Partnerships in Global Governance*, edited by Magdalena Bexell and Ulrika Mörth, 145–166. London: Palgrave Macmillan.

Bäckstrand, Karin. 2012. Are Partnerships for Sustainable Development Democratic and Legitimate? In *Public-Private Partnerships for Sustainable Development: Emergence, Influence and Legitimacy*, edited by Philipp Pattberg, Frank Biermann, Sander Chan, and Ayşem Mert, 165–181. Cheltenham: Edward Elgar.

Bai, Xuemei, Sander van der Leeuw, Karen O'Brien, et al. 2016. Plausible and Desirable Futures in the Anthropocene: A New Research Agenda. *Global Environmental Change* 39: 351–362.

Ball, Terence. 2006. Democracy. In *Political Theory and the Ecological Challenge*, edited by Andrew Dobson and Robyn Eckersley, 131–147. Cambridge: Cambridge University Press.

Beck, Silke, Maud Borie, Jason Chilvers, et al. 2014. Towards a Reflexive Turn in the Governance of Global Environmental Expertise. The Cases of the IPCC and the IPBES. *GAIA. Ecological Perspectives for Science and Society* 23(2): 80–87.

Berkhout, Frans. 2014. Anthropocene Futures. *The Anthropocene Review* 1 (2): 154–159.

Biermann, Frank. 2014. *Earth System Governance: World Politics in the Anthropocene*. Cambridge, MA: MIT Press.

Biermann, Frank, Michele M. Betsill, Joyeeta Gupta, et al. 2009. Earth System Governance: People, Places and the Planet. Science and Implementation Plan of the Earth System Governance Project. *IHDP Report* 20. Accessed June 25, 2018. http://www.earthsystemgovernance.org/wp-content/uploads/2010/03/Biermann-et-al.-2009-Earth-System-Governance-People-Places-and-the-Planet.-Science-and-Implementation-Plan-of-the-Earth-System-Gove.pdf

Breakthrough Institute. 2017. *Breakthrough Dialogue 2017: Democracy in the Anthropocene*, Accessed April 24, 2018. https://thebreakthrough.org/index.php/dialogue/breakthrough-dialogue-2017-announced-democracy-in-the-anthropocene

Christoff, Peter, and Robyn Eckersley. 2013. *Globalization and the Environment*. Lanham, MD: Rowman and Littlefield Publishers.

Crutzen, Paul J. 2006. Albedo Enhancement by Stratospheric Sulfur Injections: A Contribution to Resolve a Policy Dilemma? *Climatic Change* 77(3): 211–220.
Crutzen, Paul J., and Christian Schwägerl. 2011. *Living in the Anthropocene: Toward a New Global Ethos*. New Haven, CT: Yale School of Forestry and Environmental Studies, Yale University.
Curry, Patrick. 2008. Nature Post-Nature. *New Formations* 64: 51.
Dahl, Robert Alan. 1989. *Democracy and Its Critics*. New Haven, CT: Yale University Press.
Dauvergne, Peter. 2016. *Environmentalism of the Rich*. Cambridge, MA: MIT Press.
Davis, Heather. 2016. Molecular Intimacy. In *Climates: Architecture and the Planetary Imaginary*, edited by James Graham, Caitlin Blanchfield, Alissa Anderson, Jordan H. Carver, and Jacob Moore, 205–211. Baden: Lars Müller Publishers.
Dingwerth, Klaus. 2007. *The New Transnationalism: Transnational Governance and Democratic Legitimacy*. Basingstoke: Palgrave Macmillan.
Dryzek, John S., and Jonathan Pickering. 2017. Deliberation as a Catalyst for Reflexive Environmental Governance. *Ecological Economics* 131: 353–360.
Ellis, Erle C., Bradley Cantrell, and Laura J. Martin. 2017. Transparency and Control of Autonomous Wildness: A Reply to Galaz and Mouazen. *Trends in Ecology and Evolution* 32(9): 630.
Escobar, Arturo. 1999. After Nature: Steps to an Antiessentialist Political Ecology. *Current Anthropology* 40(1): 1–30.
Fukuyama, Francis. 1989. The End of History? *The National Interest* 16: 3–18.
Gilley, Bruce. 2012. Authoritarian Environmentalism and China's Response to Climate Change. *Environmental Politics* 21(2): 287–307.
Glynos, Jason, and David Howarth. 2007. *Logics of Critical Explanation in Social and Political Theory*. Abingdon: Routledge.
Graham, J. K., and Gerda Roelvink. 2010. An Economic Ethics for the Anthropocene. *Antipode* 41(1): 320–346.
Haraway, Donna. 2003. *The Companion Species Manifesto: Dogs, People, and Significant Otherness*. Vol. 1. Chicago: Prickly Paradigm Press.
Hardin, Garrett. 1968. The Tragedy of the Commons. *Science* 13(162): 1243–1248.
Hardt, Michael, and Antonio Negri. 2004. *Multitude: War and Democracy in the Age of Empire*. London: Penguin.
Hulme, Mike. 2010. Problems with Making and Governing Global Kinds of Knowledge. *Global Environmental Change* 20(4): 558–564.
Jazvac, Kelly. 2015. *Interview with Ben Valentine: One Artist's Quest to Turn Beach Plastic into Art*. Accessed May 4, 2018. https://hyperallergic.com/231979/one-artists-quest-to-turn-beach-plastic-into-art/
Karlsson, Rasmus. 2013. Ambivalence, Irony, and Democracy in the Anthropocene. *Futures* 46: 1–9.
Keohane, Robert O. 2011. Global Governance and Legitimacy. *Review of International Political Economy* 18(1): 99–109.
Keohane, Robert O. 2016. Nominal Democracy?: A Rejoinder to Gráinne de Búrca and Jonathan Kuyper and John Dryzek. *International Journal of Constitutional Law* 14(4): 938–940.
Kintisch, Eli. 2010. *Hack the Planet: Science's Best Hope – or Worst Nightmare – for Averting Climate Catastrophe*. New York: Wiley.
Knight, Jasper. 2015. Anthropocene Futures: People, Resources and Sustainability. *The Anthropocene Review* 2(2): 152–158.

Laclau, Ernesto. 1990. *New Reflections on the Revolution of Our Time*. Abingdon: Routledge.
Laclau, Ernesto. 1996. *Emancipation(s)*. London: Verso.
Laclau, Ernesto. 2005. *On Populist Reason*. London: Verso.
Laclau, Ernesto, and Mouffe Chantal. 1985. *Hegemony and Socialist Strategy: Towards a Radical Democratic Politics*. London: Verso.
Latour, Bruno. 1993. *We Have Never Been Modern*. Cambridge, MA: Harvard University Press.
Latour, Bruno. 2015. Telling Friends from Foes in the Time of the Anthropocene. In *The Anthropocene and the Global Environmental Crisis: Rethinking Modernity in a New Epoch*, edited by Clive Hamilton, Christophe Bonneuil, and François Gemenne, 145–155. Abingdon: Routledge.
Levin, Kelly, Benjamin Cashore, Steven Bernstein, and Graeme Auld. 2012. Overcoming the Tragedy of Super Wicked Problems: Constraining Our Future Selves to Ameliorate Global Climate Change. *Policy Sciences* 45(2): 123–152.
Lidskog, Rolf, and Claire Waterton. 2018. The Anthropocene: A Narrative in the Making. In *Environment and Society*, edited by Magnus Boström and Debra J. Davidson, 25–46. Basingstoke: Palgrave Macmillan.
Logie, Sinan. 2017. *Fluid Structures. Anthropocene Sections*. Accessed January 22, 2018. http://sinan-logie.blogspot.com.
Lorimer, Jamie. 2012. Multinatural Geographies for the Anthropocene. *Progress in Human Geography* 36(5): 593–612.
Lövbrand, Eva, Silke Beck, Jason Chilvers, et al. 2015. Who Speaks for the Future of Earth? How Critical Social Science Can Extend the Conversation on the Anthropocene. *Global Environmental Change* 32: 211–218.
Merchant, Carolyn. 1998. The Death of Nature. *Organization and Environment* 11(2): 198.
Mert, Ayşem. 2009. Partnerships for Sustainable Development as Discursive Practice: Shifts in Discourses of Environment and Democracy. *Forest Policy and Economics* 11(5): 326–339.
Mol, Arthur P. J. 1996. Ecological Modernisation and Institutional Reflexivity: Environmental Reform in the Late Modern Age. *Environmental Politics* 5(2): 302–323.
Moore, Jason W. 2017. The Capitalocene, Part I: On the Nature and Origins of Our Ecological Crisis. *The Journal of Peasant Studies* 44(3): 594–630.
Nagle, John Copeland. 2010. Climate Exceptionalism. *Environmental Law* 40: 53–88.
Nanz, Patrizia, and Jens Steffek. 2004. Global Governance, Participation and the Public Sphere. *Government and Opposition* 39(2): 314–335.
Näsström, Sofia. 2010. Democracy Counts: Problems of Equality in Transnational Democracy. In *Transnational Actors in Global Governance*, edited by Christer Jönsson and Jonas Tallberg, 197–217. Basingstoke: Palgrave Macmillan.
Niemeyer, Simon. 2014. A Defence of (Deliberative) Democracy in the Anthropocene. *Ethical Perspectives* 21(1): 15–45.
Purdy, Jedediah. 2015. *After Nature: A Politics for the Anthropocene*. Cambridge, MA: Harvard University Press.
Rasch, Philip J., Paul J. Crutzen, and Danielle B. Coleman. 2008. Exploring the Geoengineering of Climate Using Stratospheric Sulfate Aerosols: The Role of Particle Size. *Geophysical Research Letters* 35(2): L02809.
Rockström, Johan, Will Steffen, Kevin Noone, et al. 2009. Planetary Boundaries: Exploring the Safe Operating Space for Humanity. *Ecology and Society* 14(2): 32.

Rose, Deborah Bird, Thom van Dooren, Matthew Chrulew, et al. 2012. Thinking through the Environment: Unsettling the Humanities. *Environmental Humanities* 1(1):1–5.

Schlosberg, David. 2007. *Defining Environmental Justice*. Oxford, UK: Oxford University Press.

Schlosberg, David. 2012. Justice, Ecological Integrity, and Climate Change. In *Ethical Adaptation to Climate Change: Human Virtues of the Future*, edited by Allen Thompson and Jeremy Bendik-Keymer, 165–183. Cambridge, MA: MIT Press.

Scholte, Jan Aart, ed. 2011. *Building Global Democracy? Civil Society and Accountable Global Governance*. Cambridge: Cambridge University Press.

Shahar, Dan Coby. 2015. Rejecting Eco-Authoritarianism, Again. *Environmental Values* 24(3): 345–366.

Steffen, Will, Paul J. Crutzen, and John R. McNeill. 2007. The Anthropocene: Are Humans Now Overwhelming the Great Forces of Nature. *AMBIO: A Journal of the Human Environment* 36(8): 614–621.

Stevenson, Hayley. 2016. The Wisdom of the Many in Global Governance: An Epistemic-Democratic Defense of Diversity and Inclusion. *International Studies Quarterly* 60(3): 400–412.

Stevenson, Hayley and John S. Dryzek. 2014. *Democratizing Global Climate Governance*. Cambridge: Cambridge University Press.

Strathern, Marilyn. 1992. *After Nature: English Kinship in the Late Twentieth Century*. Cambridge: Cambridge University Press.

Swyngedouw, Erik. 2013. The Non-Political Politics of Climate Change. *ACME: An International Journal for Critical Geographies* 12(1): 1–8.

Swyngedouw, Erik. 2015. Depoliticized Environments and the Promises of the Anthropocene. In *International Handbook of Political Ecology*, edited by Erik Swyngedouw and R. Bryant, 131–146. London: Edward Elgar.

Swyngedouw, Erik and Henrik Ernstson. 2018. Interrupting the Anthropo-ObScene: ImmunoBiopolitics and Depoliticizing More-than-Human Ontologies in the Anthropocene. Theory, Culture and Society. Accessed June 20, 2018. https://doi.org/10.1177/0263276418757314

*The Economist*. 2011. The Geology of the Planet: Welcome to the Anthropocene. 26th May. Accessed September 22, 2018. https://www.economist.com/leaders/2011/05/26/welcome-to-the-anthropocene (Accessed September 22, 2018)

Torfing, Jacob. 1999. *New Theories of Discourse*. Oxford: Blackwell Publishers.

Voss, Jan-Peter, Dierk Bauknecht, and René Kemp, eds. 2006. *Reflexive Governance for Sustainable Development*. Cheltenham: Edward Elgar.

Wallbott, Linda. 2016. The Practices of Lobbying for Rights in the Anthropocene Era: Local Communities, Indigenous Peoples and International Climate Negotiations. In *Environmental Politics and Governance in the Anthropocene: Institutions and Legitimacy in a Complex World*, edited by Philipp Pattberg and Fariborz Zelli, 213–230. Cheltenham: Edward Elgar.

Wilson, Edward O. 2016. *Half-Earth: Our Planet's Fight for Life*. New York, NY: W.W. Norton and Company.

Wissenburg, Marcel L. J. 2016. The Anthropocene and the Body Ecologic. In *Environmental Politics and Governance in the Anthropocene. Institutions and Legitimacy in a Complex World*, edited by Philipp Pattberg and Fariborz Zelli, 15–30. Cheltenham: Edward Elgar.

Wynne, Brian. 1993. Public Uptake of Science: A Case for Institutional Reflexivity. *Public Understanding of Science* 2(4): 321–337.

# 8

# Global Justice and the Anthropocene: Reproducing a Development Story

JEREMY BASKIN

On the face of it, the narrative of the Anthropocene poses a major challenge to standard accounts of global justice being achieved through "development." The magnitude of human disruption and alteration of the planet's landscapes, ecologies, and climates, and the bio-geophysical limits which are revealed, sit uneasily with notions of the "rest" following the development path of the "West." And yet, key proponents of the concept – the "Anthropocenists," as Bonneuil and Fressoz (2016) label them – have been reluctant to draw this conclusion.

In this chapter, I explore this paradox by bringing the ideas of the Anthropocene and of global justice into conversation. A standard account might assume the facticity of the Anthropocene and then ask how existing normative accounts of global justice might need to be adapted. Instead, I cast a critical eye on both concepts and suggest that a particular, and troubling, developmentalist account of justice is already implicit in how the concept of the Anthropocene is frequently understood. I ask what conceptions of global justice travel with the idea of the Anthropocene and, relatedly, what imaginaries of democracy and development accompany it. More specifically, I ask what the Anthropocene concept means for the institutionalized belief – for example, expressed in the Millennium Development Goals and their current successor, the Sustainable Development Goals – that poverty and inequality can and will be overcome through some combination of democracy, growth, and development. I argue that, in its mainstream version, the Anthropocene concept is still largely embedded in a Eurocentric development story. This diminishes and compromises its analytical value, and dulls the politically radical potential of its attention to planetary limits.

In engaging with the Anthropocene, I work in the tradition of what Arias-Maldonado calls "the counter-Anthropocene": "a demand for nuances, whereas the Anthropocene might just involve a political oversimplification of very complex socionatural realities" (2015: 90; see also Arias-Maldonado, Chapter 3). I begin by clarifying briefly what I mean by both the "Anthropocene" and "global justice."

Secondly, I analyze some of the most authoritative and canonical scientific texts on the Anthropocene concept. I examine how these accounts understand "the human" of the Anthropocene, drawing out their implicit accounts of justice, and explore how they incorporate the multiple social systems, values, and relations of power which must accompany any repositioning of humans as central geological agents. Thirdly, I unpack the commonalities between cosmopolitan notions of global justice and the Anthropocene idea, particularly in relation to the work that "development" does for both. I also explore in what ways each concept destabilizes the other. Finally, I suggest that the Anthropocene idea might have much to learn from post-development notions of human well-being.

My focus is on discussing these concepts as ideas while recognizing that they are ideas that do "work" in the world, ideas that arise from material concerns and that have material effects. I treat the Anthropocene as akin to a claim, even a paradigm, rather than as an established scientific concept.[1] My close attention to the scientific accounts of the Anthropocene is because the scientific standing of the concept is widely presumed and, indeed, lends it authority, often in ways which may discourage scrutiny of the normative work and political assumptions that it contains.

## Clarifying the Terms

The term "global justice" is used in a variety of ways, most commonly in response to the persistence of vast poverty and the reality of growing inequality in the world, both within and between nations. The rise in the share of wealth and income of the top 1 percent and 0.1 percent is well documented (Piketty 2014). Less commonly noted are declining incomes among the bottom 40 percent (Organisation for Economic Co-operation and Development 2015), or that, since 1960, the income gap between the global North and South has roughly tripled in size (Hickel 2016). Standard institutional accounts report a sharp decline in extreme poverty: from "nearly half of the population in the developing world" living on less than USD 1.25 a day in 1990 to only 14 percent in 2015 (United Nations 2015). But such claims have credibly been accused of using increasingly narrow definitions of poverty, and thereby massively undercounting those who cannot meet basic needs (Hickel 2016). Indeed, as Pogge and Sengupta have argued, more reasonable poverty lines may even show a rise in the number of people living in poverty over

---

[1] Although it relies on certain well-established facts about the condition of the planet, the Anthropocene is *not* currently recognized as a scientific concept or a geological epoch. Further, there is little immediate prospect of it being ratified by the International Commission on Stratigraphy, the relevant scientific entity in such matters. Leading knowledge-brokers within that epistemic community appear highly skeptical that it meets the requirements for recognition as a new geological period (Finney 2014; Walker et al. 2015).

the past twenty-five years (2015). Today, almost 60 percent of the world's population live on less than USD 5 a day (Hickel 2016).

Global justice is posited as a desirable and ethically defensible horizon of what humanity could and should aim for when considering such realities. Global justice comes in many variants. These include varieties of "cosmopolitanism," which commonly acknowledge the equal moral worth and global stature of each individual, but differ over the extent of the obligation to rectify harms that this normatively imposes on more privileged individuals and nations (Brock 2009; Risse 2012). Individualism, universality, and generality are key underpinning principles of this approach (Pogge 1992). Others, such as the World Social Forum, use the term "global justice movement" to encapsulate the common goals of many disparate organizations and social movements which are resistant to globalization, environmental degradation, and the imposition of neoliberal economic agendas (Sen et al. 2003; Della Porta et al. 2015). This grouping typically uses the term in a more descriptive, collective and localized, and less "universal" sense than cosmopolitan theorists. Indeed, as Brock notes, they sometimes regard the liberal discourse associated with cosmopolitan global justice as "nothing more than global capitalism's useful handmaiden" (2009: 10). Here, I touch on the use of the concept "global justice" as a term of art in cosmopolitan political theory, and I also reflect on the more colloquial "global justice movement" usages. But I mainly use the term as shorthand for the idea that the deep inequality and extensive poverty which exist globally are unjust and must be confronted.

Similarly, there is no single, commonly accepted definition of the Anthropocene (see Biermann and Lövbrand, Chapter 1). Proponents of the concept typically combine the *observational* (describing the magnitude of human influence) with a *temporal claim* (this is a new epoch) with an *explanation* (how this situation came to pass) and with a *prescription* (what should be done). The Anthropocene concept is both novel and ambitious. Central to it is the argument that one needs to "think together" human activities and the more-than-human world. If the workings of the earth system are to be accurately understood, then human activities (the anthroposphere) should be incorporated in much the same way as the atmosphere or cryosphere already are. In other words, they are linked or "coupled" spheres. Humans, as a species, are thereby made central to a revised understanding of the workings of the earth as a system. So, too, is the idea that the boundaries between humans and "nature" are dissolving or being reconstituted.

The Anthropocene concept I am discussing here is the claim that the human impact on the earth as a bio-geophysical system has become so marked that a new geological epoch has commenced, in which humanity is now the dominant earth-shaping force; that this epoch commenced around 1950, although its roots are in the industrial revolution in Europe;[2] that this imposes a duty on humanity to consciously and responsibly manage or govern the earth;[3] and that this challenges established understandings of the relationship between the "natural" and the "social."

It is impossible to bring the anthropogenic in without also bringing in the multiple social systems, values, and relations of power which accompany and help constitute the human. The combination of observation, temporal claim, explanation, and prescription which constitute the Anthropocene idea makes it obvious that the concept is fundamentally political. Perhaps surprisingly, then, as I show in the next section, mainstream scientific accounts of the Anthropocene rarely mention explicitly one of the most notable features of the contemporary human world: the persistence of vast poverty and the growth of inequality both within and between nations. And yet, as I will show too, despite their apparent absence, assumptions about development and justice pervade the Anthropocene concept.

## What Account of Justice Is Contained in the Anthropocene Idea?

What explicit, and implicit, account of justice, then, can be found in the Anthropocene concept? I address this question by examining four key texts. These texts all emanate largely from the scientific community, and the earth system sciences in particular. They claim scientific authority, and are aimed at elaborating the Anthropocene concept (see Castree, Chapter 2, for an account of how these texts are located within the Anthropocene canon). They are the closest to an "official" account as it is possible to be. The four texts examined here are: (a) the

---

[2] Those seeking to have the Anthropocene officially recognized as a new geological epoch appear to have settled on a date of around 1950 and linked it to the so-called "Great Acceleration" (Zalasiewicz et al. 2015; but see also Bonneuil and Fressoz 2016: 53–54). This is the thrust of an article coauthored by most members of the Anthropocene Working Group of the International Commission on Stratigraphy, including Paul Crutzen and all the authors I will shortly discuss. They propose a mid-twentieth-century starting boundary point for the Anthropocene. In doing so, they reject arguments linking the commencement of the proposed epoch to the rise of agriculture (Ruddiman 2005) or to the industrial revolution (which some of the same authors had previously proposed). Although they recognize that the post-1950 period has antecedents, their proposal is concerned with finding when the measurable anthropogenic effects exceeded a threshold. The authors also recommended a specific date and even a precise second when the epoch could be said to have commenced: when the first nuclear device was exploded on July 16, 1945 at 5:29:21 (± 2 secs) Mountain War Time.

[3] This duty to be good stewards and planetary managers typically comes in two variants. In the Anthropocene's humbler *Aidosean* version, as I have called it elsewhere in reference to the Greek goddess of shame, modesty, and humility (Baskin 2015), this entails consciously and carefully managing the world back to a "safe operating space," ecologically speaking (see, for example, Steffen et al. 2011b: 747). In more *Promethean* versions, it is argued that "we" humans need to embrace our dominance and manage our way forward by engineering a new and "better Anthropocene" (see, for example, Ellis 2011). In both versions, expectations for new technologies are central. So, too, is the suggestion that since "we" are shaping the earth, we need to consciously manage or govern it.

foundational articles by Paul Crutzen (2002 and 2006a; Crutzen and Stoermer 2000);[4] (b) an article presented to the Swedish Academy of Sciences by Will Steffen, Paul Crutzen, and John McNeill (2007); (c) a later article by these same authors plus Jacques Grinevald (Steffen et al. 2011a) explicitly discussing conceptual and historical questions; and (d) a short video "Welcome to the Anthropocene" scripted by the International Geosphere-Biosphere Programme and screened at the opening of the 2012 United Nations Conference on Sustainable Development (International Geosphere-Biosphere Programme 2012).

In reading these texts, I have been concerned to ask what explanations they offer for the anthropogenically shaped world they describe. In particular, I ask in what ways they acknowledge inequality and injustice in the world and describe the social institutions that shape these effects. I also explore what prescriptions they imagine: what implicit or explicit management or governance of the Anthropocene they envisage to address such problems. One is not, of course, expecting a detailed or nuanced account, but only clues as to how these issues are imagined.

## *Crutzen's Early Accounts*

In the foundational Anthropocene text by Crutzen and Stoermer (2000), published in the newsletter of the International Geosphere-Biosphere Programme and in two largely identical pieces by Crutzen (2002 and 2006a), there is repeated listing of the symptoms of anthropogenic influence. There is little mention, however, of what might be driving the Anthropocene. The closest to an account of why the Anthropocene came about is a reference to the epoch commencing with the invention of the steam engine. Other technologies, such as the Haber–Bosch process, are repeatedly cited. In the later piece there is the suggestion (but no more) that population explosion is a driver (2006a: 14), and fossil fuel use and deforestation are mentioned in general terms but again, mainly as symptoms of already being in the Anthropocene. Neither inequality nor injustice is mentioned, apart from a sentence in the "Geology of Mankind" article which notes that "[s]o far, these effects have largely been caused by only 25 percent of the world population" (Crutzen 2002: 23), although how this percentage is derived is not specified. If the Anthropocene is an injunction to "think together" the social and the natural, then, it is perhaps surprising that the preponderant feature of the contemporary social order is neglected.

When it comes to imagining what should be done, Crutzen argues that:

Hopefully, in the future, the "anthropocene" will not only be characterised by continued human plundering of Earth's resources and dumping of excessive amounts of waste

---

[4] Strictly speaking, these are three different articles. I treat them as one, since their content is largely identical.

products in the environment, but also by vastly improved technology and management, wise use of Earth's resources, control of human and domestic animal population, and overall careful manipulation and restoration of the natural environment.

*(Crutzen 2006a: 17)*

With the single exception mentioned, "mankind" is treated throughout as a homogeneous unit when thinking about the causes of the Anthropocene. But when solutions are imagined, Crutzen treats experts as a separate category. It is up to scientists and engineers, he argues, "to guide mankind towards global, sustainable, environmental management" (Crutzen and Stoermer 2000: n.p.), possibly including large-scale geoengineering projects "to 'optimize' climate" (Crutzen 2002: 23).[5]

In these early accounts of the Anthropocene, technology is understood both as the explanation for the Anthropocene's emergence and as the central mechanism for responding to this new epoch. There is no suggestion that the anthropogenic impacts described might have had differential effects, or might have been avoidable if other political and economic trajectories had been chosen. In effect, the development trajectory that brought about the Anthropocene is naturalized even as it goes largely unexamined.

## *Adding the "Great Acceleration"*

A more sophisticated account was produced by Paul Crutzen together with leading earth system scientist Will Steffen and environmental historian John R. McNeill for the Royal Swedish Academy of Sciences (Steffen et al. 2007). This elaborated account gives additional insight into the implicit and explicit assumptions of key Anthropocene proponents. It reprises and adds to the evidence and observations of major anthropogenic impacts on the bio-geophysical world while also giving a more fulsome account of how the Anthropocene epoch came about, as well as normative suggestions as to what should be done.

Its account of history is largely a progress narrative, with even an attempt at optimism. Technological changes – from the control of fire, to the domestication of animals and the emergence of agriculture, to the expansion in the use of fossil fuels – are emphasized. Europe is seen as the driver of "the onset of industrialization" in "the footsteps of the Enlightenment" (Steffen et al. 2007: 616). The massive global expansion since the late 1800s is largely linked to enterprise and innovation, such as the Haber–Bosch process for fixing nitrogen. The silences in this account are revealing. This expansion is not linked to colonial conquest and imperial dispossession, or to the global imposition of Western cultures of

---

[5] The year before, Crutzen had published an influential article calling for a lifting of the taboo on solar geoengineering (Crutzen 2006b). I analyze the geoengineering turn in detail elsewhere (Baskin 2017).

modernity and extraction, nor to the shattering of indigenous institutions of production and social organization. Rather, "the remarkable explosion of the human enterprise from the mid-twentieth century" and "a new regime of international institutions after 1945 ... helped create conditions for resumed economic growth" (2007: 617–618). The Anthropocene, in short, is presented here as part of the standard Western development story of "progress" rather than as a story of "subjugation" or active "underdevelopment" of the many by the few. It is the post-1945 world from the perspective of "the global North."

Even the examples of "signs of hope" that are presented in the article reveal these underlying assumptions. One, "a trend of dematerialization in several advanced economies" (Steffen et al. 2007: 619), is grounded in an implicit *telos* wherein progress entails the Rest following the West. Another, the 1960s rise of what the article calls "modern environmentalism" (2007: 618), clearly has in mind Western environmentalism as the beacon rather than, say, the traditions more resistant to extraction, sometimes called the "environmentalism of the poor" (Guha and Martinez-Alier 1997; Nixon 2011). The article concludes by stating that there are three possible ways the declining natural environment might be dealt with. The first they term "business-as-usual," by which they appear to mean continuing the current economic trajectory largely unchanged, and which they counsel against. A second is "geo-engineering," which they are uncomfortable with, but fear that "global [climate] changes ... may force societies to consider" (2007: 619). They favor a third way, mitigation, "to take the human pressure off of the Earth System by vastly improved technology and management, wise use of earth's resources, control of human and domestic animal population, and overall careful use and restoration of the natural environment" (2007: 619). Both the second and third options they present are in the tradition of what is sometimes called "eco-modernism" (see Fremaux and Barry, Chapter 9).

In short, the Steffen, Crutzen, and McNeill interpretation (2007) imagines techno-science as largely determinant of the social order, as both cause and solution. It is strongly Eurocentric (more accurately North Atlantic-centric) in its account of how "humanity" arrived at its current condition. And it appears to universalize and naturalize a particular model of development. Justice questions and inequality go unexplored. The bio-geophysical limits of the earth system are to be resolved not through extracting and producing less, but through better management and "cleaner" and more eco-efficient technologies.

### *Probing More Deeply*

A more probing presentation of the Anthropocene idea, one which takes some of the above limitations into account, can be found in an article by Steffen et al.

(2011a) subtitled "conceptual and historical perspectives." The differences can perhaps be attributed to the addition of a fourth coauthor, Grinevald, a historian of science, to the three coauthors of the article just analyzed.[6] The article mainly rehearses the evidence and arguments found in the previous article discussed (Steffen et al. 2007). But it also contains traces of a more critical analysis. It suggests, for example, as a partial explanation of the output expansion in the post-1945 period: "More and more public goods were converted into commodities and placed into the market economy, and the growth imperative rapidly became a core societal value that drove both the socio-economic and the political spheres" (2011a: 850).[7] It also acknowledges the differential contribution by countries to the emissions causing the climate problem, and notes that "equity issues are often magnified in the Anthropocene" (2011a: 856). It states, too, that "[t]he belief systems and assumptions that underpin neo-classical economic thinking ... are directly challenged by the concept of the Anthropocene" (2011a: 862). This account is, of course, disruptive of mainstream developmentalist discourse in both its "more growth" and "green growth" versions, a discourse which sees the quest to produce more as the primary solution to, rather than a central cause of, global injustice. However, the extracts cited here are relatively isolated in the text and not always integrated with the argument as a whole.

### *Explicit Attachment to Institutional Developmentalism*

One detects a sharp retreat from this more radical interpretation (Steffen et al. 2011a) in the fourth of the core documents I examine. "Welcome to the Anthropocene" is a short, professionally produced, video intended for wide distribution (Welcome to the Anthropocene 2012). It was prepared by a number of scientific institutions and collaborative research programs and scripted by the International Geosphere-Biosphere Programme, and has an associated website. It was clearly intended as a popular explication of the Anthropocene concept while still claiming scientific credibility. It was screened at the opening of the 2012 United Nations Conference on Sustainable Development, thereby adding institutional authority to the account (http://anthropocene.info).

Some key extracts from the script also largely summarize it. It opens with: "this is the story of how one species changed a planet." Starting in England, "several brilliant inventions occurred ... they ignited the industrial revolution." "New artificial fertilizers meant we could feed more people." Since 1945, "globalization, marketing,

---

[6] Jacques Grinevald is a retired historian of science who has studied Vernadsky, an early "inventor" of the "Biosphere" idea, and has an interest in ecological economics and the idea of degrowth (décroissance).
[7] Strictly speaking, these trends are more associated with the post-1980 period of globalization and economic liberalization, the so-called Washington Consensus, rather than with the post-1945 period as a whole.

tourism and huge investments helped fuel enormous growth ... In a single lifetime the well-being of millions has improved beyond measure ... never have so many had so much." The video does then note in passing that "one billion are malnourished," its only reference to poverty. Inequality is not mentioned at all, a point I shall return to shortly. A succession of facts about environmental pressures are then presented: "we have grown into a phenomenal global force." The narrator then informs us: "We have entered the Anthropocene, a new geological epoch dominated by humanity." But "relentless pressure" on the planet "risks unprecedented destabilization." The video concludes: "But our creativity, energy and industry offer hope. We have shaped our past, we are shaping our present, we can shape our future. We are the first generation to realize this new responsibility. We must find a safe operating space for humanity for the sake of future generations. Welcome to the Anthropocene" (Welcome to the Anthropocene 2012).

The most visually striking aspect of the video is that no human appears in it at all. We see a satellite image of the earth, and the viewer soars out of Europe and then circumnavigates the earth from outer space, while the satellite image is overlaid by graphs and lines in continual motion. These contain no actual data but only upwardly trending graphs suggestive of data and of a connected and electrified world. Visually, the video rehearses the globalized "view from nowhere," which has been widely interpreted in analyses of the "blue marble" imagery of the 1970s. It can be understood as an outgrowth of contemporary Northern environmentalism and the associated power and knowledge hierarchies which pervade it (Litfin 1997; Jasanoff 2004; Agrawal 2005). This is an Anthropocene in which humanity is central but humans and human societies are absent. It is a surveilled and abstracted humanity. When data is presented as global averages, the data becomes separated from situated and grounded knowledge, and is thereby both abstracted and deprived of meaning (Jasanoff 2010). The symptoms of anthropogenic impact presented have no apparent cause. The Anthropocene is held to be novel, and we are described as the first generation to realize we have new responsibilities. But nothing new is proposed.

The single mention of poverty and the silence regarding inequality are also revealing of the implicit account of development that is being embraced. Poverty, when considered in isolation, can be understood as an unfortunate circumstance which can be progressively addressed. Poverty, in this narrative, reflects a lack of something, an absence which needs filling, and even this lack is commonly narrowed to a lack of income, such as in the pervasive "one dollar a day" discourse. By contrast, emphasizing inequality is more likely to promote the understanding that poverty is a created condition, that it is not only about income, and that it may be related to socioeconomic structures of power.

The understanding of the Anthropocene and the implicit account of development in the video "Welcome to the Anthropocene" (2012) are, in combination, depoliticizing moves, ones in which knowledge is abstracted from relations of power. And yet, through being located in the 2012 United Nations Conference on Sustainable Development, the video has political effects and provides a supportive narrative for the institutionalized discourse of sustainable development – the idea that "development" needs only to be made "greener," not itself questioned as a possible driver of environmental devastation, let alone productive of increasing inequality. Indeed, the effect of the video is to link the Anthropocene diagnosis with the Sustainable Development Goals solutions that the conference initiated.[8] In this example, the Anthropocene comes closest to being simply an ideology propagating the latest "green growth" face of contemporary globalization and development (International Bank for Reconstruction and Development 2012) (see also Fremaux and Barry, Chapter 9).

## Some Common Threads

One can make a number of observations after a close reading of these four authoritative accounts.

First, throughout these core texts there is little attention to politics. The human is brought in, but without the social and power relations which constitute actual humans and their societies. Not surprisingly, therefore, considerations of global in/justice (a relational question) in the Anthropocene are largely ignored. Relatedly, there is a tendency to regard the Anthropocene as an epoch inaugurated by particular technologies such as steam power or nuclear weapons. If it is technically driven, then, again unsurprisingly, technical solutions are the first port of call for the problems of the epoch. Visible throughout is a tendency both to universalize particular humans as "the human" of the Anthropocene and to naturalize the currently dominant socioeconomic order of "market globalism" (Steger 2009). These tendencies are accompanied by an implicit embrace of standard developmentalist assumptions and discourses adopted by influential global institutions such as the World Bank and the International Monetary Fund. But this superficially

---

[8] The Sustainable Development Goals, adopted by the United Nations General Assembly in September 2015, are an attempt to set a global development agenda which balances "people, planet and profit." It includes goals such as a reduction in the number of people living on less than USD 1.25 a day or having insufficient food: poverty-focused targets which are largely a continuation of the Millennium Development Goals. Its innovation is both to make the Sustainable Development Goals applicable to all nations, rich and poor, and to combine poverty-alleviation objectives with environmental goals and market-friendly perspectives. Its environmental-related goals include ensuring greater water availability, less contaminated water, and reduced use of toxic chemicals. These typically emphasize the need to manage resources for human good (that is, instrumentally and anthropocentrically), rather than seeing any intrinsic value in the more-than-human world and its protection. The Sustainable Development Goals also include the promotion of more global free trade and the World Trade Organization, as well as "sustain[ed] per capita economic growth in accordance with national circumstances and, in particular, at least 7 per cent gross domestic product growth per annum in the least developed countries" (United Nations 2015: clause 8.1).

apolitical treatment is, in fact, deeply political. Taken together, the "official" Anthropocene (to the extent there is one) currently being institutionalized encapsulates the mind-set of the global North.

Secondly, there is a gradual adoption of a mid-twentieth-century starting point for the Anthropocene. This places the temporal claim in the very recent period; indeed, within living memory. This is made explicit in a later paper by Jan Zalasiewicz and twenty-five coauthors (including all the above authors), most members of the Anthropocene Working Group, and other influential proponents for geological recognition of the Anthropocene (Zalasiewicz et al. 2015). The authors acknowledge that humans became increasingly "influen[tial] on the Earth System thousands of years ago," but they argue that this was regional and "diachronous," or happening at different times. Human influence became more pronounced with "the onset of the Industrial Revolution," but only from the mid-twentieth century did it become large enough and "both global and near synchronous" to be regarded as a geological force (Zalasiewicz et al. 2015: 201). Indeed, they understand the synchronicity to be a function of "the phenomenon of globalization, or, the emplacement of a strongly globally interlinked technosphere" (Zalasiewicz et al. 2015: 200).

Thirdly, the texts typically evade the fact that the drivers of inequality and the drivers of the Anthropocene are largely the same. What if it is the same system that has coproduced the devastating natural effects and the inequality and social disruption which are features of the contemporary world? Those who have argued that the epoch is better named the "Capitalocene" (see, for example, Moore 2016) largely have this analytical blind spot in mind. Only the third text analyzed here (Steffen et al. 2011a) makes some gestures in this direction. If the Anthropocene as an idea is indeed an invitation to "think together" what "modernity" has previously treated as separate spheres, the natural and the social, then this coproduced world surely needs to be considered in its entangled totality. Only then do questions of global justice become central and unavoidable components in understanding the drivers of, and necessary responses to, the Anthropocene. It is perhaps revealing that it is mainly bio-geophysical indicators that are cited as markers of the Anthropocene, not social indicators or power relations.

Fourthly, the preferred responses to the Anthropocene are typically both technicist and managerialist. Occasionally, it is argued that the objective is to return the earth to Holocene-like conditions: the only "safe operating space" we know (Steffen et al. 2011b; Welcome to the Anthropocene 2012). Anthropocene proponents of a more Promethean bent argue the need to embrace our new God-like status and build a good post-nature world: "the first responsibility of a conquering army is always to govern" (Lynas 2011: 13). But in both instances, the effect of these interventions would appear to be twofold: firstly, and explicitly, to manage and reduce the anthropogenic pressures being placed on the physical earth and its more-than-human inhabitants; secondly, and implicitly, to do so without challenging the mainstream progress and development narratives originating in the global North.

Finally, one is left with a sense that the Anthropocene being outlined is both radical and conservative.[9] It is radical in its rethinking of the workings of the earth system to include the anthropogenic, and in its understanding of the human and the more-than-human as linked systems. But it is distinctly conservative in its interpretation of the social implications of this insight and in its account of the epoch's origins. Rather than urging a rethinking of the model of progress and development which brought the earth to this condition, the texts analyzed offer little but "de-linking" and the dream of sustainable development. De-linking growth and development from their negative environmental impacts, rather than rethinking development, is the predominant imaginary in the accounts of the Anthropocene considered here. The unpersuasive explanation of the Anthropocene's genesis and the managerialist/technicist solutions imagined each reinforce the other. And both are shaped by the extremely short temporal horizon that is believed to define this novel epoch, a period in which imagining alternatives has been severely truncated by the same processes of modernization driving the epochal shift (Scott 2004).

## The Anthropocene and Development as Justice

In the accounts of the Anthropocene analyzed here, there is a clear attraction to the sustainable development paradigm and to eco-modernism. Sustainable development may be understood as marking a break with earlier purely growth-centric approaches to development. But it is more plausible to see continuities, to understand sustainable development as an effort to "green" the existing growth paradigm rather than replace it (see Fremaux and Barry, Chapter 9). Indeed, a line of continuity can be drawn between the racist and colonial "civilizing mission" approaches pre-1945 and the developmentalist approaches post-1945. The latter come in various incarnations, including Rostowian growth through industrialization (and its Soviet counterpart), "trickle-down" growth, "inclusive growth," "green growth," and "sustainable inclusive growth" (Rist 1997; Vitalis 2015). On this reading, sustainable development is the latest iteration of the development narrative.

Many cosmopolitan accounts of global justice also lean towards such narratives, seeing development (and human rights) as central to addressing inequality and poverty in the world. Pogge and Sengupta (2015), for example, hold to this core

---

[9] I use the term "radical" in the positive and literal sense of getting to the root of an issue.

belief even while critical of key elements of the Sustainable Development Goals. The proponents of the Anthropocene considered here do not have an explicit account of global justice and of how inequality and poverty might be tackled. To the extent that they have an implicit account of global justice, it would appear to be towards cosmopolitan versions of justice, or at least to converge around the importance of "development" in addressing inequality and poverty.

To skeptics of the Anthropocene concept itself, this convergence is not surprising. Arguably, in the universal claims and generalized account of the human found in both the Anthropocene accounts considered here and cosmopolitan accounts of global justice, there is an imperial quality. And in the reimagining of nature in the Anthropocene concept, there is often a colonial quality too: most obviously in the crude claim that in the Anthropocene, as Crutzen and Schwägerl have put it, "nature is us" (2011).

But it is puzzling that many of the proponents of the Anthropocene concept, such as those considered in detail here, attach themselves to the standard development narrative as the route to achieving justice. And it is puzzling for two reasons. Firstly, the standard approaches to development and justice are deeply anthropocentric. In the case of cosmopolitan accounts of justice, they are unapologetically so and are heavily focused both on the human and on the obligations of each human to the other. It is beyond the scope of this chapter to explore this anomaly in any depth. Suffice it to say that it entails a retreat from the Anthropocene concept's most generative insight: the need to "think together" the social and the natural. Surely, from an Anthropocene perspective, justice needs to be thought about in relation to the linked social-natural entanglement which makes up the earth and the world? This implies thinking about justice for other species and for the more-than-human, for "nature," too, in ways which engage with, but perhaps go beyond, existing thinking on environmental justice (Schlosberg 2013; see also Burke and Fishel, Chapter 5).

The second reason is that an attachment to mainstream development narratives seems inconsistent with many of the observational insights about the state of the earth that are central to the Anthropocene concept. Development, following Rist, can be understood as "a set of practices requiring the transformation and destruction of the natural environment and of social relations with the aim of increasing the production of commodities, goods and services" (1997: 13). As a concept, "development" became prominent, arguably was invented, in the aftermath of the Second World War, concurrently with when the Anthropocene is said to have begun (Rist 1997; Escobar 2011; Pahuja 2011). It is the standard answer given to how global justice might be pursued. In mainstream accounts, simplifying somewhat, development comes in two forms. For some, economic growth of developing countries (and improved governance) is the central answer: only the production of more will get rid of the poor. For others, some improved version of development and growth is needed (inclusive growth, green growth, capability growth, sustainable development, and so on): one which creates fewer negative social and environmental externalities and which is less focused on growth alone. The International Monetary Fund's Poverty Reduction Strategy is an example of the former, and the World Bank's Inclusive Green Growth strategy (International Bank for Reconstruction and Development 2012) an example of the latter.

On the face of it, it seems hard to reconcile either of these prescriptions about what should be done to achieve global justice with the observations about the earth that are made by the Anthropocene concept's proponents. The evidence of human impacts on the more-than-human world – growing emissions, toxicity above levels which can be absorbed, rising extinction rates, and so on – is compelling. This evidence would seem to support two interrelated arguments: first, that there needs to be a reduction in the human footprint: that *contraction* is critical; second, that technology must be mobilized to manage the effects of the human impacts already underway through *containment and control*. I emphasize for discursive purposes the separation of these logics, although they are, in practice, often entwined. In more Promethean accounts of the Anthropocene, the latter is emphasized; in more Aidosean accounts, the former. In all accounts, some combination of both is proffered.

We can place alongside this the logic of developmentalist discourses. These rest on some notion of justice resulting in *convergence*, that global inequalities need to be tackled and overcome, and that a greater degree of equality of living conditions and life chances for every person, both within and between nations, is required. Growth is at the heart of all the standard accounts – even when they differ as to whether this is best achieved through "trickle-down growth," "export-led growth," "inclusive growth," or even "inclusive green growth." The dominant institutional accounts typically avoid the idea of contraction altogether. The combination of "contract and converge" has animated much discussion around climate justice (Baskin 2009), and it would seem to be an obvious way to integrate concerns about global justice with the idea of the Anthropocene. And yet, this approach is avoided in the Anthropocene literature we have discussed. This is either because the Anthropocene concept itself is anthropocentric at heart, and premised on an eco-modernist ideal, or because the concept's key proponents are embedded in the standard multilateral institutional assumptions about development. To the extent that the need for contraction is acknowledged, it is contraction of impact achieved through technology, or "de-linking"/"de-coupling," that is imagined.

There is some, albeit limited, acknowledgement that the drivers of injustice/inequality and of human dominance of earth systems may be connected. More typically, however, the bland statement is made that "business-as-usual" is untenable and a version of eco-modernism or "green development" is embraced, one which stresses uncoupling or de-linking growth from its negative environmental impacts. It is at the heart of the "mitigation" option favored by Steffen and colleagues (2007) and the de-linking growth from negative impacts narrative that pervades the "Welcome to the Anthropocene" video. Dauvergne (2016) has called such approaches "environmentalism of the rich."

De-linking is not as such objectionable, but its potential for making a major difference should not be overstated. Not only does de-linking have a poor record when it comes to reining in absolute environmental impacts, but it also leaves in place the systemic drivers that have brought the world to this condition. It is politically unthreatening to the elites whose practices of production and consumption are the key drivers of the Anthropocene. And it offers little by way of solutions to injustice and inequality. Indeed, it allows evasion of these problems and may plausibly be seen as likely to exacerbate inequality, as one throwaway line in the third text analyzed acknowledges (Steffen et al. 2011a: 856). The embrace of development (only greener) in turn reinforces the "containment and control" logic of the Anthropocene and reduces the significance of its "contract" logic.

Attaching the Anthropocene to green development narratives, as all the texts analyzed do (most transparently the "Welcome to the Anthropocene" video), is to attach it to a discourse that is likely to exacerbate global injustice and not be very "green." In practice, and out of desperation if de-linking fails to rein in anthropogenic impacts, one can anticipate the turn towards increasingly Promethean proposals as to what should be done to manage living in the Anthropocene. Solar geoengineering, which some of those discussed here have raised, albeit uncomfortably, is the most extreme example of this. The pursuit of technologies of hubris such as these, as Szerszynski and Galarraga have noted, is hard to reconcile with democracy (2013). As Baxi has suggested, such practices may involve simply creating "new geographies of injustice" (2016).

There are other approaches to development that are largely invisible in Anthropocene discourses, but which would seem to sit more comfortably with the Anthropocene concept. Here, one can think of the global justice movement traditions mentioned at the beginning of this chapter, and associated transition discourses from the global North and South which emphasize the pluriversal rather than universal nature of their arguments and propositions. These include "de-growth" thinking (see, for example, Jackson 2009; Latouche 2009). There is also what has been termed "post-development" and "alternatives to development" (see, for example, Esteva et al. 2013; Gibson-Graham et al. 2013; Hage 2015), as well as ideas of *Buen Vivir* (see, for example, Acosta 2010), among others (for an overview see Escobar 2015).

There are those who emphasize that poverty and inequality are not natural conditions: they have been enhanced through colonization and empire, and inequality has been entrenched through processes one can shorthand as "globalization." Further, the accompanying projects of extraction, industrialization, and waste disposal (including in the Soviet bloc) have led to the condition of planetary overload which the Anthropocene so aptly summarizes. Inequality and planetary overload have been produced in tandem. "Transition discourses," as Escobar labels them, "take as their point of departure the notion that the contemporary ecological and social crises are inseparable from the model of social life that has become dominant over the past few centuries" (2015: 452).

Adopting this line of argument, "development" as traditionally understood in the "West" is part of the problem rather than the solution. Rather, alternatives to development thinking and even "de-growth" are needed: for convergence towards a more equal world, there will need to be contraction of some sort (see Fremaux and Barry, Chapter 9). In these accounts, justice and a decent life for people can only be achieved through recognition of the bio-geophysical boundaries of the world, respect for the agency, independence, and interests of the more-than-human world, a rejection of some of the linear progress narrative and instrumental reason, and acknowledgement of the interdependence of the human and the "natural" worlds. There is a need for a fundamental rethinking of many of the key tenets of modernity. It is apparent that there is a notable lack of engagement by leading proponents of the Anthropocene concept with such accounts.

## Conclusion

When it comes to global justice, the mainstream Anthropocene narrative has attached itself to a narrative of "de-linking" rather than one of "rethinking" along the lines suggested above. Leading Anthropocenists, as I have shown, *are* suggesting a radical rethinking of the society–nature relationship and the place of humans on earth and in shaping the world. But they appear unable to embrace the radical social and political implications of this position and the rethinking of existing patterns of extraction, production, distribution, and consumption (and their associated institutions), which would seem to be required. Instead, they have embraced a mainstream development narrative which largely consists of "business-as-usual" but greener, and retained an attachment to the very economic and global institutions which are associated with the contemporary predicament.

The effect is to constrain the emergence of radical new imaginaries, at least in the Aidosean tradition, of what it will mean to live in the Anthropocene.[10] The effect is to marginalize notions of resistance and preclude the thought that "another world is possible." Instead a naturalized, depoliticized, and demobilizing account is offered:

---

[10] Radical imaginaries are, of course, emerging in the Promethean tradition of Anthropocene thinking (see, for example, Ellis 2012; Ecomodernist Manifesto 2015).

"another world is happening and manageable." One symptom of the constrained imaginary that remains is the absence within the standard Anthropocene narrative of a compelling account of global (in)justice. We are offered a notion of the human that combines geopower and geodestiny, as Bonneuil and Fressoz (2016: 90–93) put it. But it is a vision long on risk management but short on justice. Lövbrand et al. (2015) have suggested that the Anthropocene concept invites us to think critically about ontology and about the post-natural, the post-political, and the post-social. Perhaps it is time to think about post-development too.

## References

Acosta, Alberto. 2010. El Buen Vivir en el Camino del Post-Desarrollo: Una Lectura Desde la Constitución de Montecristi. Quito: Fundación Friedrich Ebert. Accessed June 19, 2018. www.fuhem.es/media/cdv/file/biblioteca/Analisis/Buen_vivir/Buen_vivir_posdesarrollo_A._Acosta.pdf

Agrawal, Arun. 2005. *Environmentality: Technologies of Government and the Making of Subjects*. Durham, NC: Duke University Press.

Arias-Maldonado, Manuel. 2015. *Environment and Society: Socionatural Relations in the Anthropocene*. Springer Briefs in Political Science series. New York: Springer.

Baskin, Jeremy. 2009. The Impossible Necessity of Climate Justice? *Melbourne Journal of International Law* 10: 424–437.

Baskin, Jeremy. 2015. Paradigm Dressed as Epoch: The Ideology of the Anthropocene. *Environmental Values* 24: 9–29.

Baskin, Jeremy. 2017. *Geoengineering, the Anthropocene and the End of Nature*. Unpublished PhD thesis, University of Melbourne, Australia.

Baxi, Upendra. 2016. Some Newly Emergent Geographies of Injustice: Boundaries and Borders in International Law. *Indiana Journal of Global Legal Studies* 23 (1): 15–37.

Bonneuil, Christophe, and Jean-Baptiste Fressoz. 2016. *The Shock of the Anthropocene*. London: Verso.

Brock, Gillian. 2009. *Global Justice: A Cosmopolitan Account*. Oxford Scholarship Online. Oxford: Oxford University Press.

Crutzen, Paul J. 2002. Geology of Mankind. *Nature* 415 (January): 23.

Crutzen, Paul J. 2006a. The "Anthropocene." In *Earth System Science in the Anthropocene*, edited by Eckhart Ehlers and Thomas Krafft, 13–18. Berlin: Springer.

Crutzen, Paul J. 2006b. Albedo Enhancement by Stratospheric Sulfur Injections: A Contribution to Resolve a Policy Dilemma? *Climatic Change* 77: 211–219.

Crutzen, Paul J. and Christian Schwägerl. 2011. Living in the Anthropocene: Toward a New Global Ethos. Yale Environment *360*: 2–3. https://e360.yale.edu/features/living_in_the_anthropocene_toward_a_new_global_ethos.

Crutzen, Paul J., and Eugene F. Stoermer. 2000. The Anthropocene. *Global Change Newsletter* 41: 17–18.

Dauvergne, Peter. 2016. *Environmentalism of the Rich*. Cambridge, MA: MIT Press.

Della Porta, Donnatella, ed. 2016. *Global Justice Movement. Cross-National and Transnational Perspectives*. Abingdon, Oxon: Routledge.

Ecomodernist Manifesto. 2015. Accessed June 19, 2018. http://www.ecomodernism.org/

Ellis, Erle C. 2011. A World of Our Making. *New Scientist* 210 (2816): 26–27.

Ellis, Erle C. 2012. Planet of No Return: Human Resilience on an Artificial Earth. *The Breakthrough Journal 2*. Accessed June 19, 2018. http://thebreakthrough.org/index.php/journal/past-issues/issue-2/the-planet-of-no-return

Escobar, Arturo. 2011. *Encountering Development: The Making and Unmaking of the Third World*. Princeton: Princeton University Press.

Escobar, Arturo. 2015. Degrowth, Postdevelopment, and Transitions: A Preliminary Conversation. *Sustainability Science* 10: 451–462.

Esteva, Gustavo, Salvatore Babones, and Philipp Babcicky. 2013. *The Future of Development: A Radical Manifesto*. Bristol: Policy Press.

Finney, Stan C. 2014. The "Anthropocene" as a Ratified Unit in the ICS International Chronostratigraphic Chart: Fundamental Issues That Must Be Addressed by the Task Group. In *A Stratigraphical Basis for the Anthropocene*, edited by Colin N. Waters, Jan A. Zalasiewicz, Mark Williams, Michael A. Ellis, and Andrea M. Snelling, 23–28. London: Geological Society (Special Publications 395).

Gibson-Graham, J. K., Jenny Cameron, and Stephen Healy. 2013. *Take Back the Economy: An Ethical Guide for Transforming Our Communities*. Minneapolis: University of Minnesota Press.

Guha, Ramachandra, and Joan Martinez-Alier. 1997. *Varieties of Environmentalism: Essays North and South*. London: Earthscan Publications.

Hage, Ghassan. 2015. *Alter-Politics*. Melbourne: Melbourne University Press.

Hickel, Jason. 2016. The True Extent of Global Poverty and Hunger: Questioning the Good News Narrative of the Millennium Development Goals. *Third World Quarterly* 37 (5): 749–767.

International Bank for Reconstruction and Development. 2012. *Inclusive Green Growth*. Washington, DC: International Bank for Reconstruction and Development.

International Geosphere-Biosphere Programme. 2012. Welcome to the Anthropocene (short film). http://www.anthropocene.info/short-films.php.

Jackson, Tim. 2009. *Prosperity without Growth: Economics for a Finite Planet*. London: Earthscan Publications.

Jasanoff, Sheila. 2004. Heaven and Earth: The Politics of Environmental Images. In *Earthly Politics: Local and Global in Environmental Governance*, edited by Sheila Jasanoff and Marybeth Long Martello, 31–52. Cambridge, MA: MIT Press.

Jasanoff, Sheila. 2010. A New Climate for Society. *Theory, Culture and Society* 27 (2–3): 233–253.

Latouche, Serge. 2009. *Farewell to Growth*. Cambridge, UK: Polity Press. (Translated from French.)

Litfin, Karen. 1997. The Gendered Eye in the Sky: A Feminist Perspective on Earth Observation Satellites. *Frontiers* 18 (2): 26–47.

Lovbrand, Eva, Silke Beck, Jason Chilvers, et al. 2015. Who Speaks for the Future of Earth? How Critical Social Scientists Can Extend the Conversation of the Anthropocene. *Global Environmental Change* 32: 211–218.

Lynas, Mark. 2011. *The God Species: How the Planet Can Survive the Age of Humans*. London: HarperCollins.

Moore, Jason W., ed. 2016. *Anthropocene or Capitalocene? Nature, History, and the Crisis of Capitalism*. Oakland, CA: PM Press.

Nixon, Rob. 2011. *Slow Violence and the Environmentalism of the Poor*. Cambridge, MA: Harvard University Press.

Organisation for Economic Co-operation and Development. 2015. *In It Together: Why Less Inequality Benefits All*. Paris: Organisation for Economic Co-operation and Development Publishing.

Pahuja, Sundhya. 2011. *Decolonising International Law: Development, Economic Growth, and the Politics of Universality*. Cambridge, UK: Cambridge University Press.

Piketty, Thomas. 2014. *Capital in the Twenty-First Century*. Cambridge, MA: Harvard University Press.

Pogge, Thomas. 1992. Cosmopolitanism and Sovereignty. *Ethics* 103 (1): 48–75.

Pogge, Thomas, and Mitu Sengupta. 2015. The Sustainable Development Goals (SDGs) as Drafted: Nice Idea, Poor Execution. *Washington International Law Journal* 24 (3): 571–587.

Risse, Mathias. 2012. Global Justice. In *The Oxford Handbook of Political Philosophy*, edited by David Estlund. Oxford, UK: Oxford University Press.

Rist, Gilbert. 1997. *The History of Development: From Western Origins to Global Faith*. London: Zed Books.

Ruddiman, William F. 2005. *Plows, Plagues and Petroleum*. New Jersey: Princeton University Press.

Schlosberg, David. 2013. Theorising Environmental Justice: The Expanding Sphere of a Discourse. *Environmental Politics* 22 (1): 37–55.

Scott, David. 2004. *Conscripts of Modernity: The Tragedy of Colonial Enlightenment*. Durham: Duke University Press.

Sen, Jai, Anita Anand, Arturo Escobar, and Peter Waterman. 2003. *World Social Forum: Challenging Empires*. New Delhi: Viveka Foundation.

Steffen, Will, Paul J. Crutzen, and John R. McNeill. 2007. The Anthropocene: Are Humans Now Overwhelming the Great Forces of Nature? *Ambio* 36 (8): 614–621.

Steffen, Will, Jacques Grinevald, Paul J. Crutzen, and John R. McNeill. 2011a. The Anthropocene: Conceptual and Historical Perspectives. *Philosophical Transactions of the Royal Society A* 369: 842–867.

Steffen, Will, Åsa Persson, Lisa Deutsch, et al. 2011b. The Anthropocene: From Global Change to Planetary Stewardship. *Ambio* 40: 739–761.

Steger, Manfred B. 2009. *Globalisms: The Great Ideological Struggle of the Twenty-first Century* (3rd edition). Plymouth, UK: Rowman and Littlefield.

Szerszynski, Bronislaw, and Maialen Galarraga. 2013. Geoengineering Knowledge: Interdisciplinarity and the Shaping of Climate Engineering Research. *Environment and Planning A* 45(12): 2817–2824.

United Nations. 2015. *The Millennium Development Goals Report*. New York: United Nations.

Vitalis, Robert. 2015. *White World Order, Black Power Politics: The Birth of American International Relations*. Ithaca, NY: Cornell University Press.

Walker, Mike, Phil Gibbard, and John Lowe. 2015. Comment on "When Did the Anthropocene Begin? A Mid-twentieth century Boundary is Stratigraphically Optimal". *Quaternary International* 383: 204–207.

Welcome to the Anthropocene. 2012. Accessed June 19, 2018. https://vimeo.com/39048998

Zalasiewicz, Jan, Colin N. Waters, Mark Williams, et al. 2015. When Did the Anthropocene Begin? A Mid-Twentieth Century Boundary Level Is Stratigraphically Optimal. *Quaternary International* 383: 196–203.

# Part III

## The Practices of Political Study in the Anthropocene

# 9

# The "Good Anthropocene" and Green Political Theory: Rethinking Environmentalism, Resisting Eco-modernism

ANNE FREMAUX AND JOHN BARRY

Although geologists have not officially agreed that we have left the Holocene, the "Anthropocene" has already been widely adopted as the new *signifier* of the current geological epoch (Castree, Chapter 2). The Anthropocene concept poses significant challenges to the way we understand both green politics and human/nature relationships. Indeed, by placing emphasis on the power of the *Anthropos*, the concept has generated new narratives of mastery and technological optimism in an era characterized by environmental and social uncertainties (Lidskog and Waterton 2016). In Anthropocene debates, we find the promotion of techno-hybrid ontologies by neo-materialists (Barad 2007; Bennett 2010; Braidotti 2013), techno-optimistic talk of a "good Anthropocene" from "eco-modernists" (Ellis 2011a; Arias-Maldonado 2015),[1] and eco-managerial aspirations of earth system stewardship and governance (Barry 2016a). The emergence of the idea of the Anthropocene has also, in Chakrabarty's words, spelled "the collapse of the age-old humanist distinction between natural history and human history" (2009: 201), and led some to posit, and welcome, a world made up of human–nature hybrids, entanglements, and assemblages (see Arias-Maldonado, Chapter 3). Luke (1997) uses the neologism "urbanatura" to describe our current situation, denoting new "technonatural formations" as opposed to "old nature." But the much-heralded "end of nature" does not come without problems and contradictions.

In this chapter, we argue that it is possible to acknowledge the increasing intertwinement of nature and society around us – and inside us – without abandoning the analytic (and ethically significant) distinction between human societies and nature's "non-identity" (otherness). While orthodox scientists aim at reducing

---

[1] Eco-modernists, also called "eco-pragmatists" or "neo-environmentalists," advocate the decoupling from nature (in order to save it) and celebrate the "end of nature" as well as "the death of (romantic) environmentalism." They advocate more technology, and especially a "'neoliberal conservation' guided by economic rationality and human-centred managerialism" (Asafu-Adjaye et al. 2015). Ecomodernism is associated with prominent environmental figures such as Ted Nordhaus, Michael Shellenberger, and Steward Brand (2009) but also the physicist David Keith (2013) and filmmaker Robert Stone, who coauthored the *Ecomodernist Manifesto* (2015).

nature to a passive entity suitable for human manipulation, eco-modernists consider nature as a techno-malleable hybrid entity already overcome by culture and technology (what Curry (2003) calls "cultural resourcism"). In both cases, the nonhuman world is a *tabula rasa*, whether mere inert matter, dynamic but meaningless chaos, or already technologically mediated imbroglio "upon which human beings struggle to write, read and erase each other's social, cultural and political concerns" (Curry 2003: 340). Especially, as we argue in this chapter, postmodern affirmative "identity thinking" which proclaims "nature is dead" is an attempt to reduce the other to the self, the object to its representation, the making to the knowing. Following Nigel Clark in *Inhuman Nature* (2011), we contend that too much "hybridity" and "social nature" is too arrogantly anthropocentric (with the stress on the *arrogance*, not necessarily the anthropocentrism). It is also, on the surface, insufficiently political, but the rejection or disavowal of democratic politics only shows the political commitment to the capitalist status quo (willingly, as in the case of eco-modernism, or unwittingly, in the case of earth system science).

Against the unapologetically anthropocentric world picture offered by the "good Anthropocene" and the further capitalist exploitation of the earth it promotes (Crist 2013), we argue that the repeated failures of ecological modernization and environmental managerialism should be an opportunity to rethink our place on the planet and to accept the fragility and vulnerability of the human species in the face of complex and unpredictable natural phenomena. In short, what needs to be developed is not a new form of human self-assured hubris but our capacities for gratitude, humility, respect, and restraint, all of which are central normative features of green political and moral theorizing (Barry 1999; 2007). The great challenge that lies ahead of us is not the further humanization of the planet but, rather, the further humanization of humanity. What needs to be managed and controlled is not the earth itself and its various biophysical entities and processes. Rather, and here exhibiting long-established green political ideas, *what is in need of management is humanity's relationship with the earth*. This clear focus on human self-governance brings green politics (and ethics) "back in," thus countering the depoliticized and depoliticizing arguments of "the good Anthropocene."

## Most-modern and Postmodern Narratives in the Anthropocene

From the earth system science perspective, our planet is going through a huge change. Leaving behind thousands of years of exceptional stability in climate temperature range and sea levels that characterized the Holocene (and in which human civilization evolved), we are now entering a new era of uncertainty and significant transformations (see Castree, Chapter 2). In brief, humanity is leaving the "safe operating space" of the stable, accommodating environment offered by the Holocene (Rockström et al. 2009; Steffen et al. 2015), "the only state of the Earth System that we know for sure can support contemporary society" (Steffen et al. 2011: 739). Thus, the advent of the Anthropocene can be viewed as an event, a turning or tipping point of no return that, because of its radical novelty, signifies something that has never happened before. This event leaves us somewhat bereft of relevant analogues, historical equivalents, symbols, narratives, or metaphors. It overwhelms our cognitive and creative capacities and our representations of the world. The Anthropocene is not simply a "world historical" event, but a "world changing" event.

Indeed, the Anthropocene represents a radical break, a point of no return, a dangerous upheaval that calls for the rethinking of our paradigms of thought and action. As Lidskog and Waterton (2016: 395) put it, "the Anthropocene has become more than a concept; it has become a set of compelling narratives." The scientific narrative mostly held by earth system scientists offers a "science-driven vision of Earth stewardship" (Lövbrand et al. 2009). This narrative, as Bonneuil shows (2015), is very often naturalist: the human species is seen as socially and historically "unified" and issues of class, gender, race, and geographical position are all erased, as an undifferentiated "humanity" faces the "planet." It celebrates scientists, considered as the new shepherds of humanity for having developed a global environmental consciousness and for planning to "save the planet" thanks to more science and green geo-technologies. If this story line admits the agency of nature (its "complexity" and "indeterminacy"), it still remains caught in the traditional reductionist theme of the technological mastery of nature and the dualistic separation between superior human rational minds and inferior nonhuman passive matter. We find here optimistic eco-modernists such as Ellis (2013a), Shellenberger and Nordhaus (2011), and Lynas (2011), who celebrate the "age of human" as the achievement of the cornucopian dream to create and recreate the planet according to our wishes. The *bios*, here, is seen as something "artefactual" and "technical" which can be manipulated, managed, and crafted to our ends. In this sense, geoengineering advocates and transhumanists in favor of human enhancement belong to the same Promethean narrative that we term a "humanist most-modern narrative" (Figure 9.1).

This narrative is intertwined with "the posthumanist most-modern [post-nature] narrative" promoted by a very "heterogeneous network of post-modern, eco-constructivist philosophers, natural scientists and pro-industry, techno-utopian think-tanks" (Bonneuil 2015: 23–24). In this theoretical patchwork, we find neo-materialists who "neutrally" contend that nature is now a hybrid techno-nature, proponents of the post-humanist cyborg scenario (Haraway 1991), so-called "postmodern" thinkers such as Bruno Latour, who urges us to love our techno-nature creatures and to dismiss the precautionary principle as "a legal epistemological monster" (Latour 2011: 23), as well as eco-modernists such as Arias-Maldonado who use the post-nature narrative as a way to achieve the "modernization" of nature (and the depoliticization of socio-ecological processes). We call this narrative the "post-humanist most-modern narrative" insofar as, while ostensibly upholding a decentered and post-modern perspective (humans being themselves hybrid realities), it remains caught in the very modern Promethean conceit that nature can be controlled, made, and remade at human will. It urges the production/reproduction of nature through technological artefacts, using, for doing so, the naturalist argument that nature and society have, de facto, always been intertwined. These common features make these two narratives belong to the "most-modern"[2] rather than "postmodern" story line. We must acknowledge that the form taken by the mastery of nature narrative is new, subtle, and insidious. This post-nature narrative seeks to overcome the fake distinctions inherent in the modern project, such as the one between nature and culture, but eventually, it overcomes the dualist ontology only to offer a techno-nature monism that reduces nature to a scientific and technological by-product of society. This artificial holism opposes the naturalist holism defended by Spinoza and deep ecology (and deserves the same critiques relative to affirmative or undifferentiated thinking[3]) or the relational ontology offered by some postmodern thinkers[4] who bring to the forefront human dependency on natural processes, reclaiming, by doing so, a sense of organic connectedness with nature (what we have called the "*post-humanist postmodern narrative*"). Indeed, beside the most-modern narrative, which expresses the arrogance of humanism in the Anthropocene, other positions exist, which call for more modesty and the re-embedding of humans in nature (Gibson et al. 2015). In brief, genuine postmodern positions acknowledge humans' belonging to the world; humans' fundamental vulnerability and ignorance in the face of complexity (what postnormal science calls the "unknown unknowns"; Ravetz 2006). These postmodern positions encompass: 1) the "post-humanist narratives" (the lower-left quadrant of Figure 1) that particularly focus on the philosophical representation of the problem, in particular anthropocentric approaches that seek to organize the world around exclusive human interests; and 2) the "humanist postmodern narrative" (the lower-right quadrant of Figure 1) that works on the political and ethical reappraisal of modernity, the realization of its emancipatory ideals while keeping

---

[2] *Most-modernity* is associated, here, with the destructive techno-stance towards nature which aims at replacing or reproducing the natural capital by technological means.

[3] Such a conception of totality dissolves the rich differentiation and determination of empirical content into what Hegel described, talking of Hölderlin's and Schelling's conception of absolute, as a "night in which all cows are black" (2005: 94).

[4] Radical postmodernists such as Smith (2001; 2011), Alaimo (1994; 2010), Mathews (1996; 2003), and Gibson et al. (2015) seek to develop ontologies/ethics that decenter the figure of the autonomous and self-sufficient human in favor of a humbler positioning in the world.

epistemologically and ethically (but not ontologically) the human subject in the center. Weak anthropocentrism,[5] for instance, suggests that one can be human-centered without being focused only on human self-interest. Barry calls this argument "reflexive anthropocentrism," a concept flexible enough "to accommodate the normative thrust of the ecocentric concern with protecting the interests of the non-human world" (Barry 1999: 39). An anthropocentrism without the arrogance, as it were.

Humanist and post-humanist postmodern positions deal, in various ways, with the legitimate ethical anxieties raised by the Anthropocene. They form a coalition which brings together such different thinkers as authentic postmodern theorists (radical ecologists, ecofeminists, etc.) and neo-humanist, neo/eco-Marxists who consider the Anthropocene (and the disappearance of nature) as both unjust and unsustainable, linked to the domination of the North and oriented towards the sustainability of a capitalist "world-system" within the earth system (Bonneuil 2015: 28). According to this postmodern story line, which gathers post-humanist and reflexive humanist positions,[6] the concept of the Anthropocene not only involves the geological and ecological fate of our planet but also calls into question the possibility for us, for other species, and for further generations to survive, or more precisely, to survive in *decent and humane conditions*. If the Western part of the world[7] has technically transformed the planet, becoming the first global human force of transformation, never has humanity appeared so badly equipped, politically and ethically, to direct the world in this age of uncertain and irreversible changes. What is at stake, therefore, is our ability to make decisions concerning processes that go far beyond what humans can imagine and conceptualize: "And here lies the real challenge to democracy … We have never thought how to govern the irreversible" (Hamilton et al. 2015: 10).

---

[5] The concept of "weak anthropocentrism" can originally be found in Norton (1984). Other developments of this notion can be found in Norton (1991), Hayward (1997), and Barry (1999).

[6] Actually, reflexive humanists are sometimes called "neomoderns." "Neomodern" is a term which gathers theorists (philosophers, political and social scientists, etc.) who contend that modernity has failed by deviating from its initial emancipating project and that the construction of a neohumanism freed from modern dross of domination such as ethnocentrism, (strong) anthropocentrism, paternalism, and colonialism would have a chance to give birth to a better world. Neomodernism is especially associated with the works of Agnes Heller. It follows Habermas' critiques of postmodernism. Most green theorists who contend a weak form of anthropocentrism can also be called "neomoderns."

[7] Debates are taking place to identify the "Anthropos," the generic human being of the Anthropocene, and, more particularly, to criticize the grand post-social and post-historical narrative that has made "humankind" responsible for the geological changes we are facing; that is, an abstract and undifferentiated "humanity" taken as a whole. See on this issue Bonneuil and Fressoz (2016: 65 sq.) and Crist (2013). The vocabulary of the Anthropocene and its supposed neutral components are indeed misleading. As Lövbrand et al. note, the vocabulary of the Anthropocene is depoliticized and devoid of social content: "[t]here are no actors, interests or social categories acknowledged within this humanity, neither any evidence of social injustice or asymmetry" (2014: 7).

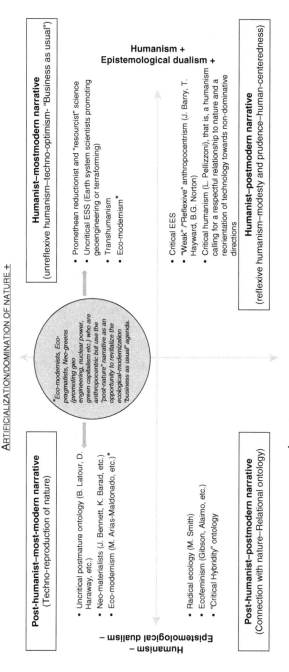

Figure 9.1 A postmodernist-most-modernist mapping of the ecological field.

## The Death of Nature in the Anthropocene: Long Live Neoliberal Nature!

One cannot stress enough the extent to which ideas and representations, no matter how relative, partial, or reductive, mold our perceptions of the world and impact on reality. So it is with the idea of "the death of nature."[8] As Vetlesen asserts, "[w]e could not have engaged in the activities that now threaten to spell the end of nature (nature as we used to know it) were it not the fact that for at least four centuries we have regarded and treated (nonhuman) nature as dead" (2015: 129). Indeed, the more nature has been considered as dead matter devoid of spiritual, human, and moral values – becoming merely a collection of means as opposed to a sphere of meaning (Barry 1999) – the more it has been abused, exploited, artificially manipulated, instrumentally dominated, and eventually destroyed. The radical configuration and (technical) success of the mechanistic and instrumental worldview inherited from the sixteenth and seventeenth centuries have entailed the exploitation of the natural world for human purposes and the moral acceptance of an imperialist domination over what was considered as pure "mechanical" processes. From then on, humans have considered themselves as separate from the natural world: no longer as *a part of* it but as *apart from* it. This dominating-instrumentalizing attitude towards nature was in many respects an imperative to create "heaven on earth" (Barry 2017). Now, in the Anthropocene and in the face of having unintentionally created "hell on earth," the same instrumentalizing logic is not questioned or problematized, but rather, strengthened and empowered in order to solve the problems it has created. Just as Achilles possessed a spear that could heal the wounds it inflicted, so we have a modern mythic mind-set that technology, science, and the capitalist free market can heal, guided by earth system science and governance, our wounded planet.

At the same time as the Anthropocene is announced, geoengineering and large-scale technological systems are indeed promoted, sometimes even very optimistically, in spite of the dangers and uncertainties they carry with them. As Wood, one of the cheerleaders for geoengineering, proclaims, "we've engineered every other environment we live in – why not the planet?" (in Hamilton et al. 2015: 9). This vision, although not unanimously shared by all earth scientists, still offers interesting windows of opportunity to politicians who would like to *revitalize* the economy through large-scale technological innovations and/or to simultaneously *devitalize* democracy by giving more power to experts while ensuring the

---

[8] The "end of nature" means that the whole earth has been literally (and not metaphorically) socially constructed. According to the (most/hyper)-modern conception, nature is conceived as an ontological exterior reality that humans have managed progressively to conquer until its quasi-final disappearance. The epistemological separateness of nature from humans (nature–culture distinction) leads to its empirical destruction ("death of nature"). The so-called "postmodern" post-natural ontology, supposed to overcome the dualism between nature and culture, between facts and values (everything is nature *and* culture at the same time), has actually taken as a starting point the modern regime of truth according to which nature, as an autonomous entity, is dead.

continuation of centralized controls. Such a situation raises the danger of technocratic and scientific "benign authoritarianism" within reactions to and (ab)uses of the Anthropocene, which echoes earlier 1970s antidemocratic/political ecological voices such as eco-authoritarians like Heilbroner, Ophuls, and Hardin (Barry 1999). In the face of urgent and large-scale unprecedented challenges, democratic decision-making can be bypassed and replaced with the rule of experts and scientists, who, along with the technologies they control and create, become the rescuers of humanity and of a humanized, radically altered earth.[9]

The – quasi-religious – modern faith in the power of technology to achieve "progress" is today taken up by those who either uncritically promote the Anthropocene or more normatively call for a "good Anthropocene." According to eco-modernists, for instance, carbon-free technologies such as nuclear power or other technological fixes of energy supply must be pushed forwards to provide cheap, clean, and abundant energy to high-tech societies, in order to go on "bio-fuelling the hummer" (Barry 2012: 23). Ecological modernization is in some aspects the precursor of eco-modernism. It brought market and monetary instruments such as eco-taxes, corporate environmental management, green consumption and production (eco-labeling), valuation of ecological goods and services, environmental insurances, green niche markets, and so forth – in order to make sustainability an attractive object of profit, that is, to reconcile the imperatives of ecological sustainability and capitalism/economic growth (Barry 2012); and thus, ecological modernization can be seen as an early iteration of "green capitalism" (Barry 2005), a position taken up anew by contemporary eco-modernists, where the objective is to sustain capitalism and the capitalist-industrial domination of the planet.

Eco-modernists have found in the post-natural ontology of the Anthropocene a new rationale for their objective (that is, more technology, more business, more economic growth, etc.). By embracing the hybridist constructivist metaphysics according to which nature and technology have always been mixed or were always meant to be mixed, they can present the technological domination of nature as a "natural" fact that works for the very preservation of nature itself (understood as "techno-nature"). In this way, nothing "natural" in nature can ever be found or preserved. In such a technophilic and ontologically human-centered vision, applied science occupies a prominent place:

> It is through technological development that our relationship with nature can become *healthier* and *cleaner*, as well as, of course, *sustainable*. ... It is plain to see that *a refined dominion of nature is but another name for sustainability*. ... *[S]ustainability is domination*.
>
> (Arias-Maldonado 2012: 70–71; emphasis added)

---

[9] On the incompatibility between democracy and geoengineering, see, for instance, Szerszynski et al. (2013).

As the author notes himself, this view is surely "anthropocentrical *arrogance*" in the eyes of some (old-fashioned) environmentalists and green political theorists. But in times of "Post-natural Sustainability," "a bit of Prometheanism seems hard to avoid" (Arias-Maldonado 2012: 70).[10] Here, post-structuralist constructivists can (albeit unintentionally) provide support for this "good Anthropocene" in which the putative "humanization of the world" becomes in effect the "capitalization of the world." What this view really offers is, indeed, a discourse on sustainability with opportunities for capitalist investment needs. It will never grant any protection of nature as it incidentally claims, for one simple reason: in such a view, nature does not exist anymore. Eco-modernism thus requires a complete reorientation of green political theory and the jettisoning of its "romantic," "naïve," and outdated (as well as "regressive" and "reactionary") view of nature as "other," as well as associated normative and political claims and ideas. According to eco-modernists, we have now entered a "post-nature" era, which needs, in turn, "post-environmentalist," "pragmatist," and "non-romantic" green thinkers.

The novelty and "originality" of eco-modernism compared with the former tenets of ecological modernization is the alliance it promotes between green capitalism and postmodern discourses on the "end of nature." By blurring the boundary between the social and the natural, post-natural discourses take "nature" away from public and political discourses. The new postmodernist discourses try to wipe out, by doing so, the ancient self-evidence of a self-existing nature existing outside of us that we would need to "protect" and "preserve" in order to survive. Eco-modernism works itself like a self-fulfilling prophecy. The more nature is destroyed or threatened, the more humans become dependent upon technology to survive. In brief, the *theoretical* discourses on the "end of nature" and the related Promethean sense that we do not *need* nature (in that we can hybridize or technologically replace it) lead to its *real* material destruction. This kind of reasoning is trapped into affirmative thinking (only technology exists), contradictions, and straw-person positions (nature is pristine or is not), and into a cultural holism that lacks nuance (everything is technological). Here we find the direct link between eco-modernism and a so-called "postmodernism" which actually contains more "most-modern" than postmodern substance.

Indeed, under the pretext of overcoming the false dichotomies of modernity, "postmodern"[11] and post-humanist thinkers, such as Bruno Latour and Donna Haraway have tried to show how much nature and culture are entangled; how

---

[10] Here we are tempted to remark that just as one cannot be a "little bit pregnant," it may also be the case that suppress one cannot be a "little bit Promethean."

[11] This word is intentionally put between quotation marks in order to express our doubts. Indeed, the anti-naturalism and the role that is given to technologies by this form of "postmodernism" are actually very modern ("most-modern"): they remain completely situated in the prejudices of modernity (blind faith in technology, domination of nature narrative, dualism insofar as nature is seen as pristine or as not existing at all, and so forth).

much our world is actually made up of imbroglios, assemblages, and hybrid entities. For them, everything is interconnected; everything is linked and attached: "the nonhuman world," says Haraway, "is dialogic ... a co-productive participant in human social relationships" (quoted in Soulé and Lease 1995: 3). The world is made up of "naturecultures" and hybrids. Post-nature techno-thinkers have refashioned nature as a flexible hybrid, a relational reality that can be easily deconstructed and reconstructed by market forces. Post-nature ontologists overcame the failures of the Enlightenment (dualisms) to better embrace the capitalist point of view of a nature considered as a "flexible hybrid amenable to further market and technological deconstruction-reconstruction" (Bonneuil 2015: 26). This post-nature metaphysics, and the (post-)politics it is associated with, is the opposite of a theory of emancipation. As Adorno, Horkheimer, and Marcuse argued, the objectification of the world through technology, science, and rational forms of organization ends up transforming humans themselves into objects of exploitation and reification, subjecting humans to these very instruments and logics of alienation (Horkheimer and Adorno 2002[1947]; Marcuse 1969).

Today, the *progressive* transformation of nature into "techno-nature" places humanity under the power of technical apparatuses as well as under the threat of their undemocratic and unintended outcomes, such as pollutants, climate change, or ecological "sacrifice zones" (hybrid "monsters").[12] Our survival becomes more and more dependent on capitalistic or public willingness to invest in the production/reproduction of natural mechanisms. This process can be described in terms of the "neoliberalization of nature." That is, everything can be produced and reproduced; natural products become "commodities-in-the-making," and nature itself is nothing more than an internal differentiation of society and economic production processes. This capitalist approach to the "commodified" (and marketizable) biophysical world under neoliberal rules receives, thanks to post-nature theorists, a new momentum. Indeed, to say that there are no grounds anymore for an ontological divide between the natural and the artificial, that life transmutes into technology and vice versa, means nothing less than nature can be reframed as an internal differentiation of "capitalist resource flows." Nature, understood as an exterior reality, does not exist anymore, and the crucial ecological idea of "natural limits" is dismissed and "transcended."[13] The absence of thick characterization of what "nature" and "society" are facilitates the absorption of nature by capitalist-

---

[12] As Smith shows, the *production* of nature is different from the *control* of nature (Smith 2006).
[13] As Cafaro (2014: 138–139) rightly says, preserving nature "involves setting limits to the degree of human influence that is acceptable ... This in turn, limits the degree to which real conservationists can accept the dominant trends of the Anthropocene. Rather than embrace the Anthropocene, conservationists should act to rein its excesses ... a central part of our agenda should involve creating a truly sustainable economy: one that recognizes limits to growth."

techno processes and opens the path to post-/transhumanist projects. This "most-modern" narrative intensifies and accelerates the process launched by capitalist modernity. Because nature is now considered as completely integrated into social mechanisms, it can be stripped, in its meaning, of all kind of alterity, of specific agency, and, as a consequence, it can become materially even more supervised, managed, and manipulated. Eco-modernists (or post-environmentalists) are therefore not "postmodern" but, rather, "hypermodern" or "*most*-modern," in Spretnak's term (1997: 36). They do not aim at correcting the mistakes of capitalist modernization but, rather, at deepening and extending them. Their position is therefore very different from genuine postmodern positions or post-dualist narratives which understand the need for human decentering in order to open up the path to "a plurality of non-scientific framings, knowledges and cosmologies" (Lövbrand et al. 2014: 6).

When "destruction" becomes "transformation," when "human capital" and "natural capital" become interchangeable/substitutable (as opposed to "complementary"), it is the sign that a process of epistemic and ontological *derealization* is at work. But more than that: it is also a sign of the renunciation of politics and democratic choices in the making of possible socio-ecological futures. In this regard, eco-modernism represents an emasculation of collective agency, a rejection of politics, political struggle, political mobilization, resistance, and critique of the status quo. It is a persistent call to abandon politics and switch instead to management and engineering. In short, it hardly challenges, but rather aligns with, dominant relations of power, and works for the intensive appropriation, commodification, and financialization of the biophysical world (what we have called the "neoliberalization of nature").

The concept of the Anthropocene came, for eco-modernists, at precisely the right time to provide some added urgency and legitimacy to their program. This latter can be quickly summarized in the call for more technology, more capitalism, more technological innovation, more expertise, less politics, less contestation, more top-down governance,[14] and less nature (embodying the return to a period preceding the development of green political theory). The eco-modernist narrative of the Anthropocene and its impetus to artificialize/commodify the planet further gives a new justification for those attempts to "green business as usual." This is why we need to be particularly cautious with the Janus-faced character of the Anthropocene, a concept that can be understood as a scientific narrative of potential collapse (Steffen et al. 2007; Rockström et al. 2009); as an alarm siren calling for

---

[14] Swyngedouw (2013) defines environmental post-politics as a sociopolitical order where struggles and contestations are replaced by techno-managerial planning. When disagreement is allowed, it is with respect to the choice of technologies that should be used, to managerial adjustments, and to the urgency and timing of their implementation (Lövbrand et al. 2014: 9).

the *decentering* of humankind (Clark 2014); as a call for more prudence, more modesty, more inclusive freedom, more respect for the natural world; for our pulling back, slowing, and scaling down; for restraint and membership rather than ownership and domination (Burke and Fishel, Chapter 5); that is, as a call for humanity to become better members of the planetary community as opposed to expert managers of it.[15] But, as can be seen in its eco-modernist interpretation, the concept of the Anthropocene can also be used as a denial of planetary boundaries, as an opportunity for *most-moderns* to advance their hubristic and Promethean claims and pursue the techno-colonization and commodification of the world. Eco-modernism vindicates a greater degree of socio-natural engineering and experimentation with the planet against moral positions such as restraint and caution; it chooses geoengineering and technical (hazardous) innovations against post-growth alternatives; it chooses management and scientific governance against democracy and privileges the agency of Western affluent countries over the people in the global South.

## The "Non-identity" of Nature or the Return of the Repressed

It is certainly true to say that nature and culture have always been interrelated, but this interrelationship is too often used as a pretext to absorb nonhuman beings into the dynamics of technology and the globalized economy and to deny the otherness (non-identity) of nature. Here we take a dialectical approach, according to which nature is identical (a product of human action) as well as non-identical (a process which escapes human power and knowledge). And we take this dialectical view of nature, including the non-identity of nature, as a foundational ethical and ontological principle of green political theorizing. The technological colonization of the earth carried out by natural sciences and neoliberal economics, as well as the constructivist discourses elaborated by social sciences that announce the "end of nature," typify two forms of anthropocentric hubris, two forms of idealism that fail to recognize the value of nature's agency. Nature, indeed, is never simply a social product. Neither is it a simple raw material that passively awaits human inventiveness and ingenuity. It is a complex system that can react in surprising and unpredictable ways to human intervention and disturbance.

The Anthropocene represents a convergence of different anthropogenic theories (modern and "postmodern" but all "*most-modern*"), which celebrate the end of nature: whether it has been destroyed or just assimilated, nature, according to those

---

[15] As Lövbrand et al. say, for critical environmental scholars, the Anthropocene "is a concept that emphasizes humanity's material dependence, embodiment and fragility, and hereby invites us to rethink long-held assumptions about the autonomous, self-sufficient human subject that begins and ends with itself" (Lövbrand et al. 2015: 4).

narratives, does not exist anymore. With this disappearance is also celebrated the end of the old "romantic" environmentalism that relied on an obsolete idea of nature conceived as independent of us, this exteriority assigning material (and therefore moral) limits to our actions.[16] The concept of the Anthropocene means nothing less than that, the phenomenon of anthropization being so extended, policies of environmental conservation are old-fashioned. Our impact on the world, it is argued, is so pervasive that the traditional environmental ideals of preservation (which aimed at preserving, restoring, and valuing natural environments) are just sentimental, outdated, and obstructive pipe dreams, alongside the human virtues of humility and restraint that accompanied those ideals. If nature does not exist and has, maybe, never existed, why bother protecting it? An article in *The New York Times* written by environmental professionals (including the chief scientist for Nature Conservancy) entitled "Hope in the Age of Man" (Marris et al. 2011) illustrates this worrisome moral and metaphysical perspective. It argues that viewing our time as "the age of man" is "well-deserved, given humanity's enormous alteration of earth" and concludes that because "this is the Earth we have created," we should, therefore, "manage it with love and intelligence. ... We can design ecosystems ... to new glories" (!).

However, the idea of the control of nature fails in the face of the non-identity of nature, in front of what Neyrat calls "the inconstructible part of the Earth" (2016) or what Adorno (1973) defined as "the non-mediated" (what is not reducible to concepts). As O'Connor explains, there is "an irreducible, nonidentical moment" in our experience of reality (quoted in Cook 2011: 37). There is actually a "surplus" in nature that can never be summarized in a final synthesis. This surplus is displayed in our experience in the form of ecological tragedies and risks: this is what we can name "the return of nature in the Anthropocene." To ignore nature's non-identity, or, in other words, to pursue the domination and appropriation project while ignoring its dramatic impacts, leads to the "return of nature" within human history in the form of biological dysfunctionalities and environmental catastrophes in the same way as the non-respect of bodily needs and signals leads to the development of major health problems.

Thus, we hold that there is still a role and, indeed, need for green political thinking and action which urges a (pre)cautionary approach to human–nature relations (especially in relation to our metabolic or material interactions), which advocates respect (if not reverence) for the nonhuman world, and links that to "speaking truth to power." This means challenging, resisting, and opposing prevailing views of the "good" life and dominant powerful social,

---

[16] We do not mean here the old and obsolete forms of naturalism that took nature as a normative guide (nature as the model of morality for stoics, for instance) but the fact that the material limitations of nature need to be taken into account; for instance, the moral obligations towards next generations (intergenerational justice).

political, and economic forces, and actively encouraging and participating (in) democratic contestation and debate around alternative visions of the good society. What is needed is a conceptualization of green political thinking that does not abandon utopian-radical impulses, principles, and policies for the sake of a Faustian neoliberal pragmatism clustered around "ecomodernizing business as usual." In this way, there is still a need for a green political theory that resists the shifting of the terms of debate "beyond politics" to science, engineering, and technology. In brief, there is still a need for a green political theory that promotes an unapologetic (radical) political perspective; one that focuses on non-technological issues such as global and social injustices, gender, and class inequality; one that struggles for a better, sustainable social order beyond capitalism, in the face of so called "pragmatic realist" eco-modernists who dismiss this green political project as at best "dreamy" and utopian, and at worst a product of the "guilty middle class" from the global North who are denying the fruits and material benefits of the technological manipulation of the planet to the global South (Symons and Karlsson 2015; Barry 2016a).

The lesson to be learned is that nature can never be totally subsumed under social practices and that its own logic (its own meaning) must be respected in order to avoid negative and tragic feedback loops or consequences. If the concept of the Anthropocene is to be kept, this is therefore as a call for more prudence or as a way to confer a great freedom on humans: that is, the freedom to change the current path and to avoid leading earth and humanity to ruin. To repeat a point made earlier: *what needs to be managed is not the earth, but rather, humanity's relationship to the earth.* What is needed, indeed, is a reflexive form of "societal relationships with nature" (Görg 2003a; 2003b; 2005) that would respect natural idiosyncrasies or nature's "non-identity" and attempt to identify and rectify distorted, exploitative, and unjust human social, political, and economic relations. The concept of "nature's non-identity" borrowed from Adorno (1973) defines what, in nature, is ungraspable and unknowable by concepts and therefore escapes the process of domination. Adorno, as Hailwood notes, criticizes the fact that instrumental reason has attempted (and still attempts) to override non-identity; that is, to "reduce everything to the graspable" (Hailwood 2015: 132). Capitalist modernity has been unable to respect nature's non-identity, while "most-modern thinkers" totally deny the existence or significance of this non-identity. Acknowledging and respecting the non-identity of nature is perhaps one of the most important positive ontological and normative implications of the Anthropocene for the social and political sciences. Thus, we can see that it is only by denying or neglecting the non-identity of nature that one could (falsely in our view) construct a (mythic) vision of the "good Anthropocene" as eco-modernists have done.

While eco-constructivist approaches defend that nature and society are totally intertwined, the critical theory tradition (inspired by the Frankfurt School) emphasizes the fact that a distinction can be made between nature and culture, without going back to a former dualism of the two. On the one hand, nature is a social construction: nature is constructed discursively through language and, empirically, through human practices. But on the other hand, nature produces society (dialectic interdependence of nature and society) and also remains a principle of production on its own which displays processes that societies cannot control, know, or manage. The dialectic perspective criticizes the subsumption of nature under the purposes of society; that is to say, the technical and symbolic project of appropriation (which reaches its climax in the concept of the Anthropocene). This project dismisses the natural rootedness of societies, exposing societies to the risks entailed by the "omission" of the natural processes that *also* inform them. An adequate concept of society should therefore acknowledge the autonomous, complex, and rich agency of nature, and its indifference to us, or, in other words, "release the non-identical ... disclose the multiplicity of different things" (Adorno 1973: 6). Otherwise, the relentless project of commodification and objectification of the world will go on rebounding (1) in the destruction of natural processes on which we depend for our own living (social processes being always already materially embedded); (2) in more uncontrollable reactions from nature that translate into forms of destructive ecological risks like global warming, acidification of oceans, viral microorganisms, radioactivity, and so forth; and (3) in the continuation of unjust and exploitative human social relations and their institutionalization, justified in part in the name of those exploitative human-natural processes. This is, of course, to say nothing new – the critique of the "good Anthropocene" here is but a footnote to the diagnosis outlined in Horkheimer and Adorno's *Dialectic of Enlightenment*. Whereas green political theory sees their analysis as a warning, those eco-modernists and others calling for a "good Anthropocene" seem to take it as a guide or operating manual.

## Conclusion

In the end, the (eco-)modernist project of control leads to its opposite: less rather than more control, and *rather fewer people (elites) in more control*. This is the reason why thinkers like Latour or Ellis need to sell uncertainty and monstrosity as positive elements within the (new) package of progress and (hyper)modernity in the Anthropocene. In case sceptics or cautious old green complainers/campaigners ask (like *The Lorax*?) "why," the answer is quite simple: "it's development, stupid!" (Latour 2007). However, the *ineliminable non-identity of nature* (which is not amenable to technological manipulation) is essential to accept in describing the properties of nature that are at odds with human knowledge and human constructions and which "pop up" materially in the forms of dangers and ecological disasters (the hypermodern version of "the revolt of nature" or the "return of the repressed").

Human societies are anchored in biophysical conditions, and the more they ignore those fundamental dependencies, the more they will be reminded of them through "natural" disasters and ecological catastrophes. The option which is then given to us is not anymore to master nature, but rather, *to master our relationships with nature* (Barry 1999), focusing not only on the way we socially construct our natural environment but also on the way our societies are materially mediated through their physical conditions. It means, therefore, to have a particular interest in the way natural agency reacts to both our intentions/aims and our social practices. This is the only way to experience nature's non-identity. It also means reflecting on our practices, changing our political economy, and revaluing what needs to be valued. The aim can no longer be to gain greater control of our material environment (which rebounds in the form of less control, as we have seen) but to evaluate which kinds of social relationships and practices are able to respect the non-identity, agency, and intrinsic value of nature while meeting humanity's own socially determined (and ideally, politically and democratically determined) needs. Respect for nature, acknowledgement of its non-identity, must be rendered compatible with meeting human needs and aspirations, including desires for the "good life" and associated conceptualizations of the "good society." For reasons outlined earlier, this is a political process, made all the more political in that such self-management of human–nature relations is never settled, always provisional and dynamic, and therefore requires constant negotiation and renegotiation.

Recognizing nature's non-identity, that is, its specific agency and material objective reality, might encourage a precautionary approach. This may entail self-imposed limitations on some of our behaviors, and caution and modesty in the form of the acknowledgement of our "non-knowledge" and of the "powerlessness of our power": Nature's non-identity remains beyond what we can know and expresses itself only through experience. To respect the otherness of nature and accept our own limitations should not be viewed as "sacrifice" or negative in terms of human aspirations. To do so would be to fall into the trap laid by eco-modernists and their critique of "romantic-utopian" green politics. Rather, and again to emphasize one of the main arguments of this chapter, what green political theory needs to do is be explicit about the normative value-bases of its position, and the centrality of politics in general and democratic politics in particular in addressing the problems and opportunities presented by the Anthropocene.

Politically, and in the context of a liberal post-democracy, the Anthropocene should be considered as a democratic invitation for people to seize control of their political destiny (not to, God-like, seize the "tiller of creation" and/or "manage the planet"). Indeed, contrary to the prevailing view that tends to transform climate change and other environmental issues into technical issues that could be answered by scientists and "fixed" by technologies, the shift to the Anthropocene should be an invitation for us to rethink politics in a more democratic way, taking into account the necessity to limit ourselves, to repair what is repairable, or to withdraw as much as possible where it is necessary for sustainability and/or ethical reasons. It also forces us to envisage, debate, and disagree about sustainable, just, and democratic ways to act, so that good lives do not have to cost the earth or be at the cost of human exploitation. Such a conception of politics needs to replace the individualistic ethos of liberal democracies by a concern for the common good, and to replace the current nihilist "destruction of nature as usual" scenario by new philosophical and political narratives, which call for the respect of the ecological communities we all belong to.

Green politics in the "turbulent times" of the Anthropocene may have much to learn from other political traditions that also developed within unsettled and unsettling times, and are also attentive to the resilience and flexibility needed to navigate turbulent times, such as the civic republican transition (Barry 2012; 2016a; Cannavò 2016, Fremaux 2019 forthcoming). This is part of what we mean by "green political theorizing in the Anthropocene," being guided while doing so by seeking democratic control and governance over human–human relations as part and parcel of seeking democratic control and governance not over nature, but over our complex, provisional, metabolic, and nonmaterial relationship to it. Another Anthropocene is possible.

## References

Adorno, Theodor W. 1973. *Negative Dialectics*. New York: Continuum.
Alaimo, Stacy. 1994. Cyborg and Ecofeminist Interventions: Challenges for an Environmental Feminism. *Feminist Studies* 20(1): 133–152.
Alaimo, Stacy. 2010. *Bodily Natures: Science, Environment, and the Material Self*. Bloomington: Indiana University Press.
Arias-Maldonado, Manuel. 2012. *Real Green*. Farnham, UK: Ashgate.
Arias-Maldonado, Manuel. 2015. *Environment and Society: Socionatural Relations in the Anthropocene*. Cham: Springer.
Asafu-Adjaye, John, Linus Blomqvist, Stewart Brand, et al. 2015. *An Ecomodernist Manifesto*. Oakland, CA: Breakthrough Institute. http://www.ecomodernism.org/
Barad, Karen. 2007. *Meeting the Universe Halfway*. Durham, NC: Duke University Press.
Barry, John. 1999. *Rethinking Green Politics: Nature, Virtue and Progress*. London: Sage.
Barry, John. 2005. Ecological Modernization. In *Debating the Earth: The Environmental Politics Reader*, edited by John Dryzek and David Schlosberg, 303–322. Oxford: Oxford University Press.
Barry, John. 2007. *Environment and Social Theory*. London: Routledge.

Barry, John. 2012. *The Politics of Actually Existing Unsustainability: Human Flourishing in a Climate-changed, Carbon Constrained World*. Oxford: Oxford University Press.
Barry, John. 2016a. Bio-fuelling the Hummer? Transdisciplinary Thoughts on Techno-Optimism and Innovation in the Transition from Unsustainability. In *Transdisciplinary Perspectives on Transitions to Sustainability*, edited by Edmond Byrne, Gerard Mullally, and Colin Sage, 106–124. London: Routledge.
Barry, John. 2016b. Citizenship and (Un)sustainability: A Green Republican Perspective. In *The Oxford Handbook of Environmental Ethics*, edited by Stephen M. Gardiner and Allen Thompson, 304–320. Oxford: Oxford University Press.
Barry, John. 2017. *What's the Story of Economic Growth: Understanding our Most Powerful Story as Myth, Ideology, Meme and Religion*. Unpublished manuscript.
Bennett, Jane. 2010. *Vibrant Matter: A Political Ecology of Things*. Durham, NC: Duke University Press.
Bonneuil, Christophe. 2015. The Geological Turn. Narratives of the Anthropocene. In *The Anthropocene and the Global Environmental Crisis. Rethinking Modernity in a New Epoch*, edited by Clive Hamilton, Christophe Bonneuil, and François Gemenne, 17–31. London: Routledge.
Bonneuil, Christophe, and Jean-Baptiste Fressoz. 2016. *The Shock of the Anthropocene*. London, New York: Verso.
Braidotti, Rosi. 2013. *The Posthuman*. Cambridge: Polity.
Cafaro, Philip. 2014. Expanding Parks, Reducing Human Numbers, and Preserving all the Wild Nature We Can: A Superior Alternative to Embracing the Anthropocene Era. In *Keeping the Wild: Against the Domestication of Earth*, edited by George Wuerthner, Eileen Crist, and Tom Butler, 137–145. San Francisco, CA: Island Press.
Cannavò, Peter. 2016. Environmental Political Theory and Republicanism. In *The Oxford Handbook of Environmental Political Theory*, edited by Teena Gabrielson, Cheryl Hall, John M. Meyer, and David Schlosberg. 72–88. Oxford: Oxford University Press.
Chakrabarty, Dipesh. 2009. The Climate of History: Four Theses. *Critical Inquiry* 35 (Winter): 197–222.
Clark, Nigel. 2011. *Inhuman Nature: Sociable Life on a Dynamic Planet*. London: Sage.
Clark, Nigel. 2014. Geopolitics and the Disaster of the Anthropocene. *The Sociological Review* 62 (S1): 19–37.
Cook, Deborah. 2011. *Adorno on Nature*. Durham, UK: Acumen.
Crist, Eileen. 2013. On the Poverty of our Nomenclature. *Environmental Humanities* 3: 129–147.
Curry, Patrick. 2003. Re-Thinking Nature: Towards an Eco-Pluralism. *Environmental Values* 12(3): 337–360.
Ellis, Erle C. 2011a. Anthropogenic Transformation of the Terrestrial Biosphere. *Philosophical Transactions of the Royal Society A* 369(1938): 1010–1035.
Ellis, Erle C. 2011b. Neither Good nor Bad. *New York Times*, May 23.
Ellis, Erle C. 2012. The Planet of No Return. Human Resilience on an Artificial Earth. *Breakthrough Journal* (Winter).
Ellis, Erle C. 2013. Using the Planet. *Global Change* 81: 32–35.
Fremaux, Anne. 2019 (forthcoming). *After The Anthropocene: Green Republicanism in a Post-Capitalist World*. New York: Palgrave.
Gibson, Katherine, Deborah R. Rose, and Ruth Fincher, eds. 2015. *Manifesto for Living in the Anthropocene*. New York: Punctum Books.
Giddens, Anthony. 1994. *Beyond Left and Right*. Cambridge: Polity.

Görg, Christoph. 2003a: Gesellschaftstheorie und Naturverhältnisse. Von den Grenzen der Regulationstheorie. In *Fit für den Postfordismus? Theoretisch-Politische Perspektiven des Regulationsansatzes*, edited by Ulrich Brand and Werner Raza, 175–194. Münster: Westfälisches Dampfboot.

Görg, Christoph. 2003b. Nichtidentität und Kritik. Zum Problem der Gestaltung der gesellschaftlichen Naturverhältnisse. In *Kritische Theorie der Technik und der Natur*, edited by Gernot Böhme and Alexandra Manzei, 113–134. Paderborn: Wilhelm Fink Verlag.

Görg, Christoph. 2005. Jenseits von Naturalismus und Naturbeherrschung. Naturverhältnisse in der Kritischen Theorie. In *Alle reden vom Wetter. Wir nicht. Beiträge zur Förderung der Kritischen Vernunft*, edited by Asta der FH Münster. Münster: Westfälisches Dampfboot.

Hailwood, Simon. 2015. *Alienation and Nature in Environmental Philosophy*. Cambridge, UK: Cambridge University Press.

Hamilton, Clive, Christophe Bonneuil, and François Gemenne, eds. 2015. *The Anthropocene and the Global Environmental Crisis: Rethinking Modernity in a New Epoch*. Abingdon, Oxon: Routledge.

Haraway, Donna. 1991. *Simians, Cyborgs and Women: The Reinvention of Nature*. New York: Routledge.

Hayward, Tim. 1997. Anthropocentrism: A Misunderstood Problem. *Environmental Values* 6: 49–63.

Hegel, G.W.F. 2005. *Hegel's Preface to the Phenomenology of Spirit*. Princeton: Princeton University Press.

Horkheimer, Max, and Theodor W. Adorno. 2002 [1947]. *Dialectic of Enlightenment: Philosophical Fragments*. Stanford, CA: Stanford University Press.

Latour, Bruno. 2007. "It's Development, Stupid!" or: How to Modernize Modernization (Unpublished manuscript). Accessed June 20, 2018. http://www.bruno-latour.fr/sites/default/files/107-NORDHAUS&SHELLENBERGER.pdf

Latour, Bruno. 2011. Love Your Monsters. In *Love Your Monsters: Postenvironmentalism and the Anthropocene*, edited by Michael Schellenberger and Ted Nordhaus, 17–25. San Francisco: Breakthrough Institute.

Lidskog, Rolf, and Claire Waterton. 2016. Anthropocene. A Cautious Welcome from Environmental Sociology. *Environmental Sociology* 2 (4): 395–406.

Lövbrand, Eva, Johannes Stripple, and Bo Wiman. 2009. Earth System Governmentality: Reflections on Science in the Anthropocene. *Global Environmental Change* 19 (1): 7–13.

Lövbrand, Eva, Silke Beck, Jason Chilvers, et al. 2014. Taking the (Human) Sciences Seriously: Realizing the Critical Potential of the Anthropocene. Paper presented at the EPCR General Conference. Glasgow, September 6.

Lövbrand, Eva, Silke Beck, Jason Chilvers, et al. 2015. Who Speaks for the Future of Earth? How Critical Social Science Can Extend the Conversation on the Anthropocene. *Global Environmental Change* 32: 211–218.

Luke, Timothy W. 1997. At the End of Nature: Cyborgs, "Humachines", and Environments in Postmodernity. *Environment and Planning A* 29 (8): 1367–1380.

Lynas, Mark. 2011. *The God Species*. London: Fourth Estate.

Marcuse, Herbert. 1969. *An Essay on Liberation*. Victoria, Australia: Penguin Press.

Marris, Emma, Peter Kareiva, Joseph Mascaro, et al. 2011. Hope in the Age of Man. *New York Times*, December 7.

Mathews, F. 1996. Community and the Ecological Self. In *Ecology and Democracy*, edited by F. Mathews, 66–100. London and Portland, OR: Frank Kass.

Mathews, F. 2003. *For Love of Matter: A Contemporary Panpsychism*. Albany, NY: Suny Press.
Neyrat, Frederic. 2016. *La Part Inconstructible de la Terre – Critique du Géo-constructivisme* (Kindle edition). Paris: Seuil.
Norton, Bryan G. 1984. Environmental Ethics and Weak Anthropocentrism. *Environmental Ethics* 6 (2): 131–148.
Norton, Bryan G. 1991. *Toward Unity among Environmentalists*. New York: Oxford University Press.
Ravetz, Jerome R. 2006. Post-normal Science and the Complexity of Transitions Towards Sustainability. *Ecological Complexity* 3 (4): 275–284.
Rockström, Johan, Will Steffen, Kevin Noone, et al. 2009. Planetary Boundaries: Exploring the Safe Operating Space for Humanity. *Ecology and Society* 14 (2): 32.
Smith, Mick. 2001. *An Ethics of Place: Radical Ecology, Postmodernity, and Social Theory*. Albany, NY: State University of New York Press.
Smith, Mick. 2011. *Against Ecological Sovereignty: Ethics, Biopolitics, and Saving the Natural World*. Minneapolis, MN: The University of Minnesota Press.
Smith, Neil. 2006. Nature as Accumulation Strategy. In *Coming to Terms with Nature: Socialist Register 2007*, edited by Leo Panitch and Colin Leys, 16–36. Monmouth: The Merlin Press.
Soulé, Michael, and Gary Lease, eds. 1995. *Reinventing Nature? Responses to Postmodern Deconstruction*. San Francisco: Island Press.
Spretnak, Charlene. 1997. *The Resurgence of the Real: Body, Nature, and Place in a Hypermodern World*. New York, NY: Addison-Wesley.
Steffen, Will, Paul J. Crutzen, and John R. McNeill. 2007. The Anthropocene: Are Humans Now Overwhelming the Great Forces of Nature? *Ambio* 36 (8): 614–621.
Steffen, Will, Åsa Persson, Lisa Deutsch, et al. 2011. The Anthropocene: From Global Change to Planetary Stewardship. *Ambio* 40 (7): 739–761.
Steffen, Will, Katherine Richardson, Johan Rockström, et al. 2015. Planetary Boundaries: Guiding Human Development on a Changing Planet. *Science* 347 (6223).
Swyngedouw, Erik. 2013. The Non-Political Politics of Climate Change. *Acme* 12 (1): 1–8.
Symons, Jonathan, and Rasmus Karlsson. 2015. Green Political Theory in a Climate Changed World: Between Innovation and Restraint. *Environmental Politics* 24: 2, 173–192.
Szerszynski, Bronislaw, Matthew Kearnes, Phil Macnaghten, et al. 2013. Why Solar Radiation Management Geoengineering and Democracy Won't Mix. *Environment and Planning A* 45 (12): 2809–2816.
Vetlesen, Arne J. 2015. *The Denial of Nature: Environmental Philosophy in the Era of Global Capitalism*. London: Routledge.

# 10

# Coproducing Knowledge and Politics of the Anthropocene: The Case of the Future Earth Program

SILKE BECK

The term "Anthropocene" is used nowadays as a conceptual frame to understand the evolving human–environment relationship and to (re)focus efforts for finding solutions to human-induced environmental problems. The latter task is generally referred to by the umbrella term of "transformations towards sustainability." Work in this area has led to the recognition that the old forms of knowledge production are no longer tenable and that new forms and, indeed, a new social contract for science are needed, whereby scientific freedom is exchanged for the promise or expectation of socially beneficial impacts (Latour 2015; Castree 2016). This chapter takes stock of the debate about novel forms of knowledge production that are designed to respond to the challenges of the Anthropocene. It focuses on the global research platform "Future Earth: Research for Global Sustainability." This is a ten-year initiative to advance global sustainability science and to provide an international research agenda for addressing the challenges raised by the Anthropocene. Future Earth has even co-launched the first magazine to provide a forum for debate about global sustainability, *Anthropocene: Innovation in a Human Age*. This magazine forum seeks to link global research with concrete examples of encounters with the Anthropocene (Future Earth 2016).

Several social scientists have been actively involved in setting up Future Earth. The International Social Science Council has advocated knowledge coproduction as a central feature of Future Earth's mission (Hackmann et al. 2014). The emergence of Future Earth can thus be seen as a test case for examining how social scientists have been engaged and can engage with processes of knowledge coproduction in the Anthropocene context. More generally, the concept of coproduction of scientific knowledge has gained prominence in many contexts over the past few decades. There is much conceptual confusion around the issue, however, due to the many distinct meanings of coproduction. Within (social) science, at least two approaches exist: one can be characterized as *practical–procedural* because it uses coproduction as a strategic instrument to achieve particular goals; the other, which treats coproduction as an analytic concept to explore the dynamics and context of knowledge production, can be called *social–philosophical*. However, this distinction, along with alternative categorizations, remains contested. This chapter explores whether and in what ways both meanings of coproduction can be linked. Based on an analytical understanding of the challenges and pitfalls of practical–procedural processes of coproduction in Future Earth, I will reflect on how Future Earth can offer a platform for green political scholars to engage with the Anthropocene in constructive and legitimate ways.

This chapter is divided into three sections. The first discusses the way in which Future Earth has introduced the principle of coproduction as a strategic instrument to enhance the usefulness and impact of global environmental change research. It also describes how the *practical–procedural* form of coproduction adopted by Future Earth is received by different scientific communities. In the second section, I use the analytical understanding of coproduction in a *social–philosophical sense* (Jasanoff 2004) to explain why the novel forms of knowledge promoted by Future Earth have become a site of contestation and what the implications are for the continued study of the Anthropocene. The third section demonstrates that Future Earth – often criticized from various sides for its monolithic instrumentalism – also offers opportunities for green political scholars to discover novel forms of knowledge production as a means of engaging with the Anthropocene. The concluding section considers the lessons learned from the Future Earth experience. It explores whether coproduction in the practical–procedural sense is indeed a helpful and practicable approach or whether the challenges posed by the Anthropocene require the invention of entirely new terminologies, practices, and ethics. I conclude that Future Earth offers a global platform for nested processes of experimentation aimed at exploring the Anthropocene, linking local or national activities to global research programs on transformations towards sustainability.

## The Future Earth Research Platform

### *The Turn towards Solution-oriented Global Environmental Research*

The emergence of Future Earth can be read as a response to thirty years of global change research. Its foundations are the many decades of international research on global environmental change conducted in projects sponsored by the World Climate Research Programme, the biodiversity research program DIVERSITAS, the International Geosphere-Biosphere Programme, and the International Human Dimensions Programme on Global Environmental Change. To allow a more integrated study of the earth system, these major global research programs were incorporated in 2001 into the Earth System Science Partnership under the auspices of the International Council for Science. In late 2012, this Earth System Science Partnership closed down, and these global change programs transitioned into a more institutionalized program for integrated earth system research, known as Future Earth. Over twenty projects, ranging from the Global Carbon Project to the Earth System Governance Project, have joined Future Earth since then. Future Earth also offers one of the platforms in which the concept of the Anthropocene has been further developed (for an overview, see Jerneck et al. 2011). Although there was strong support for the integrative ambitions of the Earth System Science Partnership among the participating research networks, Ignacuik et al. (2012) note that the partnership failed to foster any fundamental transformation of established research practices. In response to the 2012 United Nations Conference on Sustainable Development in Rio de Janeiro, Future Earth began to shift from the goal of understanding the causes and impacts of global environmental change to providing solutions to address them. This turn was triggered by a recognition that while global research programs have provided considerable understanding, they have not delivered comprehensive solutions (for an overview, see International Social Science Council and United Nations Educational, Scientific and Cultural Organization 2013; Leemans 2016). To put the solution-oriented turn into practice, coproduction was made a core objective of the new research initiative as well as a principle for the design of the initiative itself (Leemans 2016: 107).

In this context, Future Earth adopted coproduction as a strategic instrument to make the findings of earth system science "usable" and "actionable" and thus "to intensify the impact of research" as a means of achieving sustainable development more quickly (Future Earth 2014).

Research will often be most useful, and the results most readily accepted by users, if priorities are shaped with the active involvement of potential users of research results and if the research is carried out in the context of a bi-directional flow of information between scientists and users. An effective response to global environmental change will be aided by the co-creation of new knowledge with a broad range of stakeholders through participatory practices.

*(International Council for Science 2010: 6)*

In order to catalyze new research and to mobilize a community of researchers and practitioners around exploring solutions, Future Earth has set up a "Knowledge-Action Network" on Transformations. This network is closely involved in international processes such as the United Nations Sustainable Development Goals, the United Nations Framework Convention on Climate Change, and the Convention on Biological Diversity. The transformation towards sustainability has become a core research agenda of Future Earth. It has been set up to restructure the broad field of sustainability science by placing the social sciences and humanities at the heart of interdisciplinary research. This represents a step change in terms of scale and scope for research programming on this topic. Here, coproduction of knowledge is considered to be critical to the process of societal transformation.

The debate about coproduction has some common ground with the contentious discussions taking place around sustainability science, "mode-2" knowledge production, and transdisciplinarity (on the evolution of sustainability science and its core issues and research strategies, see Kates et al. 2001; Jerneck et al. 2011). Future Earth has adopted the concept of coproduction as developed in the context of sustainability science (for an overview, see Clark et al. 2016). This *practical–procedural* approach starts from what its advocates call a "utilitarian" perspective (Prokopy et al. 2016). This utilitarian approach is guided by the assumption that coproduction is the strategic instrument best suited to produce usable and actionable outcomes. Instruments of coproduction can be purposefully designed and implemented to facilitate science policy interactions in the service of sustainable transformations (Dilling and Lemos 2011). To sum up, the strategy of Future Earth is based on knowledge coproduction in a practical–procedural sense, with the aim of becoming more effective "in producing knowledge that is truly useful – and used – for achieving sustainability goals" (Clark et al. 2016: 62).

## *Impacts and Implications of Future Earth's Coproduction of Knowledge*

In the previous section, I indicated how the solution-oriented turn in global environmental research has led to a novel emphasis on the coproduction of knowledge. Coproduction is thus one of the emerging research themes in Future Earth generally and in the Knowledge-Action Network on Transformations in particular. This section seeks to explain why coproduction in this context has turned into a subject of contentious debate in various scientific communities at the national and international level.

**Transformative mission.** As mentioned earlier, concepts and practices of coproduction are neither new nor unique. The term "transdisciplinary research," for instance, emerged in the 1980s, mainly in connection with sustainability and climate research (German Council of Science and Humanities 2015). Concepts of transdisciplinary research have since been refined, however, within the context of transformations towards sustainability. In its flagship report *World in Transition: A Social Contract for Sustainability*, the German Advisory Council on Global Change pioneered a broader notion of the term when referring to the concept of transformative research:

Transformative research supports transformation processes in practical terms through the development of solutions and technical as well as social innovations, including economic and social diffusion processes and the possibility of their acceleration, and demands, at least in part, a systemic perspective and inter- and cross-disciplinary methods, including stakeholder participation.

*(German Advisory Council on Global Change 2011: 322)*

The transformative mission is also promoted by advocates of *Sustainability Science*. Clark et al. note: "Many researchers we know would be willing to focus more of their work on sustainability problems if they believed that doing so would actually help, in the framing of Amartya Sen, to 'inform agitation' on the front lines of action for sustainable development" (Clark et al. 2016: 62). Susi Moser, speaking for the Sustainability Science community and promoting this concept within Future Earth, claims that emerging scholarship in codesign could itself be transformative – in relation to both knowledge production and the value science has for society. She acknowledges that knowledge coproduction "places science in the midst of transformative changes underway" (Moser 2016: 107).

This transformative mission adopted by global environmental change research in support of transformations towards sustainability, however, has also sparked much controversy and resistance from representatives of the mainstream scientific communities.

**Scientific resistance.** First, the solution-oriented turn of global environmental research has been perceived as a major challenge to traditional basic research. One prominent example is the reaction from Peter Strohschneider, president of the German Research Foundation. In his view, the solution-oriented turn of global environmental change research represents a major shift, a reorientation from autonomous, curiosity-driven basic research to a "practical tool to work out scientific solutions" (Strohschneider 2016). For Strohschneider, the solution-oriented turn leads to a thorough-going normative shift in the frame of reference governing the research system, namely, towards the single overarching normative goal of sustainability: the practical handling of concrete problems is privileged over curiosity-driven research. This turn, he claims, invites a new form of "environmental instrumentalism" where "all" research is reduced to the scheme of problem and solution ("solutionism") (Strohschneider 2014). As a result, science is simply transformed into a means to achieve a goal predefined by society. This complete shift of the public research system, he says, is a threat to the autonomy of universities, and the freedom of science. For Strohschneider, this instrumentalism indicates a loss of autonomy on the part of science: it is no longer setting its own goals and research agenda in a bottom-up manner (2014). According to Rik Leemans, however, it was precisely the involvement of relatively autonomous scientific organizations that was one of the main strengths of the original international environmental change programs such as the International Human Dimensions Programme, and yet this has been "ignored" during the establishment of Future Earth (2016: 109).

Strohschneider seems to assume that transformative research requires a fundamental transformation of the entire research system and that it thus challenges the division of labor between basic and applied science and a plural, differentiated scientific system (2014). His intervention has resulted in a lively debate in Germany over the direction of Future Earth and whether novel forms of knowledge production will replace traditional academic basic research and thus bring about a major transformation of the science–society contract. As a response to this emerging controversy, the German Council of Science and Humanities (2015) has issued a position paper on novel forms of knowledge production as a topic for science policy.

**Push for unification.** Secondly, parts of the scientific community criticize both the perceived *instrumentalism* of solution-oriented research and the quest for a *unified account* of global environmental problems and univocal decision support. Scientific integration was a key rationale for setting up global environmental change research and, somewhat later, earth system research. A step in this direction was taken when the Earth System Science Partnership was established (Steffen et al. 2004: 32). The basic premise of this bridging of research traditions, explain Ignacuik et al. (2012), is that no single discipline can respond effectively to the increasing human-induced transformations of the earth system. If we are to fully understand why and how the earth's environment is changing and to promote adequate policy responses, we need to conduct holistic appraisals of the Anthropocene. This idea has also been taken up by Mark Stafford-Smith, chair of the Future Earth Science Committee, who asserts, with colleagues, that "achieving a sustainable world will require research to build the consensus ... for effective action at national and global scales. There is no other viable way forward" (Stafford-Smith et al. 2012: 6). In this quest for coordinated and solution-oriented global environmental research, many have called for a deeper involvement of the social sciences. Scholars across the social sciences are being asked to align their work with global change research agendas and thus to participate and commit themselves more fully "to actions that reduce the known risks to Earth's support system" (Stafford-Smith et al. 2012: 5). The quest for a unified account of the Anthropocene and for univocal decision support, however, has also prompted several controversies. According to Strohschneider (2014), such forms of orchestration tend to underestimate the complexity of the challenges of transformation and the importance of surprising scholarly insights; they reduce, he insists, the potentially endless range of questions and issues that researchers may legitimately deal with. This form of compulsion to produce facts also undermines scientific creativity and effectively prohibits the exercise of systematic doubt as part of the process of science. As a result, political goals are taken for granted and thus exempted from scientific appraisal.

## Understanding Coproduction in a Social–Philosophical Sense

Strohschneider's critique resonates with key voices in the social sciences who have responded to the emerging debate on the Anthropocene. Andy Stirling, for instance, claims that concepts such as "earth system" lead to "monolithic instrumentalism" (2015). I thus look now at how social scientists have engaged with the issue of coproduction in the context of Future Earth. Melissa Leach (2014) and Sheila Jasanoff (2014), both leading social scientists, have been invited by Future Earth to explain their understanding of coproduction. Their answers – and subsequent positioning – indicate that, even while sharing standpoints informed by Science and Technology Studies, different modes of participation in Future Earth are possible for social scientists in general. Melissa Leach, for example, participates actively as a member and cochair of Future Earth's *Science Committee*; she thus represents a form of formally *invited* participation. Sheila Jasanoff (2004) and Mike Hulme (2015), by contrast, deliberately decided not to participate directly in Future Earth. Jasanoff distinguishes explicitly between "co-production as an analytic approach and co-production as a strategic instrument in the hands of knowledgeable social actors" (2004: 281). Jasanoff and Hulme both focus exclusively on an analytic understanding of coproduction and are highly critical of solution-oriented interventions and practical involvement. Scholars such as Jasanoff and Hulme thus represent an alternative form of engagement, in the sense that they view knowledge production as a topic of scientific research rather than developing it as a strategic instrument for practical engagement. By placing themselves at a distance from practical engagement, they are better able, they say, to develop an analytic understanding of coproduction and to define the research agenda independently of any predetermined terms and agendas developed by Future Earth. This, in turn, enables them to adopt a fundamentally critical position and alternative framings in a bottom-up manner (Hulme 2015). In the next section, I discuss how such an *analytic* understanding of coproduction (Jasanoff 2004) can help to explain some of the implications and impacts of Future Earth's practical–procedural efforts to put coproduction into practice as a strategic instrument.

### *Framing Effects*

The analytic concept of coproduction is based on the assumption that there are intrinsic links between ways of representing and knowing a phenomenon, on the one hand, and ways of acting upon it so as to transform it, on the other (Jasanoff 2004). Applied to the coproduction of knowledge in Future Earth, Leach explains that the design of a scientific enquiry is also the "design of a particular view of society" (2014). In this analytic understanding, scientific representations deliver both a *description* of the Anthropocene and a set of tacit *prescriptions* for how transformations towards sustainability should be managed in response. In this way, the definition of a problem – such as the advent of the Anthropocene along with its causes and impacts – and the search for appropriate ways to respond are reiterative and mutually reinforcing. Thus, processes of knowledge coproduction in Future Earth provide relevant fora for designing transformations towards sustainability as responses to the Anthropocene. Accordingly, the provision of solutions in response to the challenges posed by the Anthropocene functions as a kind of regulatory science whereby political choices are anticipated and assessed. The development of solutions is not simply about assessing scientific facts about the causes of global environmental change and predicting future trajectories. Instead, it is an emerging politics of anticipation, whereby science is asked not just to act as a Cassandra, warning of future catastrophes, but to furnish policymakers with regulatory science to anticipate and measure the performance of policies in the future. In this sense, the provision of solutions is a political intervention that may define future options for action and future choices by predetermining the often irreversible path of developments (Beck and Mahony 2017).

Such an analytic understanding of coproduction helps to explain why, as a strategic instrument used by Future Earth, knowledge coproduction involves bringing in numerous, sometimes contradictory goals with regard to transformations towards sustainability. The challenges of the Anthropocene affect a range of stakeholders with differing social backgrounds, heterogeneous bodies of knowledge, and heterogeneous normative ideas. One of the challenges of coproducing knowledge in Future Earth is to grapple with different interpretations of the core concept of transformations towards sustainability – an area of contested and politicized perspectives and priorities on what should be sustained for whom (Leach 2014). International research platforms such as Future Earth have played only a partial (yet significant) role in informing the formulation of policy objectives under the United Nations Framework Convention on Climate Change or the Sustainable Development Goals that are now being fed back into scientific research agendas. In this way, Future Earth may act as a filter for identifying which scientific findings should be collected and investigated further – a process named "problem closure" (Hajer 1995: 62). Future Earth's choices regarding this agenda for solution-oriented research will probably influence (and will inevitably be influenced by) the choices of individual research communities. Its performative character – its definitional power to set the stage for global environmental research in response to the Anthropocene – offers a particular explanation of why knowledge coproduction so often prompts controversies and contestation. Coproduction processes within Future Earth may serve to redefine the division of authority between state and non-state actors by identifying the causes of the Anthropocene, assessing its regional impacts, and thus detecting potential winners and losers, while attributing historical and future responsibilities for solving the problems. They often also have an impact upon more fundamental values, such as development and justice (Jasanoff 2004; Beck et al. 2016).

Scholars such as Jasanoff and Hulme use the analytic concept of coproduction to explain the emergence of particular framings and their political effects and implications. The narrow and monolithic framing of global environmental problems, Hulme explains, is shaping the types of policies and institutions that can be imagined in response. Climate change, one of the prominent precursors of the Anthropocene, has been framed as a global problem that needs to be solved through global collective action (Hulme 2015). As a result, the spectrum of options available to respond to global warming has been reduced to one single silver bullet solution. The range of policy choices that are compatible with the current range of scientific findings is narrowed down to improving climate projections and creating new economic policy instruments, thus neglecting a range of policy alternatives. They are policies that invite techno-managerial planning and expert administration at the expense of democratic debate and contestation (Lövbrand et al. 2015). As an example, it is often claimed that there are no alternatives to emergency measures such as geoengineering when it comes to combating global warming (Stirling 2015).

This unease with the monolithic framing of the Anthropocene is not the sole reserve of scholars in science and technologies studies but, rather, resonates more broadly with the experience of many other social science scholars. The major problem they identify in a global framing of environmental concerns is that it does not do justice to the diversity of local and regional contexts and may result in the marginalization of local views (Brondizio et al. 2016). More specifically, it may contribute towards constraining the autonomy of organizations to take actions that match local needs. All these scholars highlight the fact that the challenges raised by the Anthropocene are not universal but, rather, emerge within different sociocultural settings, have different context-specific implications, and will therefore most likely generate different social responses (Liverman 2009; O'Brien and Barnett 2013). Following the narrow framing of climate change, the notion of an Anthropos (or "humanity") as a global, unified "geological force" threatens to mask the diversity and differences in actual conditions and in impacts upon humankind.

The analytic concept of coproduction helps in recognizing these implicit and often unintended framing effects of practical–procedural efforts to use coproduction as a strategic instrument. Much of the focus of the latter is on ways of enhancing the relevance and usefulness of knowledge, which is often assumed to have an (almost automatic) impact on policy (Leach 2014). As a consequence, knowledge coproduction in Future Earth may be restricted to procedural questions, such as what mechanisms and procedures can improve the effectiveness and salience of their outcome. What this tends to ignore, however, is the political context and implications of these very mechanisms and procedures. An analytic understanding of coproduction seeks to explain why optimistic ideas that more and better coproduction will automatically achieve better outcomes may thus fail, and paradoxically, lead to their opposite. Leach (2014) cautions: "We've seen many efforts to generate what's seen as participation, say to bring indigenous people into climate change debating fora, or to try to generate participatory stakeholder discussions at the national or international level. Very often that's tokenistic and involves asking people to represent others in a way that's not always legitimate." In an analytical perspective, useful knowledge may not just be a neutral input into policy that offers policymakers useful information; rather, it may turn out to be a set of performative and reiterative practices which change the context in which such knowledge is applied (Jasanoff 2004). Given their performative dimension, coproduction processes do not (almost automatically) have an impact on policy; instead, they may have unpredictable dynamics and contingent outcomes.

The development of scenario methodologies in the Intergovernmental Panel on Climate Change, for example, illustrates the political role of pathways in climate policymaking. New "representative concentration pathways" were not meant to be predictions of particular social and technical futures but, rather, heuristics to inform the independent evaluation of different climate policy options. The representative concentration pathway 2.6, in particular, was a product of coproduction between scientists and EU policymakers, the latter being keen on pathways which showed the technical feasibility of keeping the rise in global mean temperatures below 2 degrees Celsius. The pathway held huge political significance in the run-up to the Paris talks, as it showed that the target of 2 degrees Celsius was still feasible. The pathway therefore quickly became a fact that mattered. The Paris Agreement to hold global temperature rise to "well below two degrees Celsius" was informed by this buttressed sense of technical feasibility, creating a slippery slope from a "possible" pathway to a political reality – the pathway informed and justified political aspirations to a certain end (the target of a maximum of 2 degrees' rise in global mean temperature) while also becoming a policy option in terms of both ends and means, thereby bringing new things – such as bioenergy with carbon capture and storage – firmly into political debate. In this way, the representative concentration pathway 2.6 was performative: pathways and scenarios do not just represent possible futures, but also help to bring certain futures into being (Beck and Mahony 2017).

Scholars of science and technology studies highlight the contingent nature of knowledge production, which challenges the idea that coproduction processes can be directed in a predetermined way. Since the outcomes and impacts of knowledge production are open-ended, unpredictable, and uncertain, they are not fully manageable. At the same time, new, unpredictable knowledge can create the transformative breakthroughs that change society's ways of thinking and acting (Strohschneider 2014). Given the political and performative nature of knowledge coproduction, an analytical understanding of coproduction seeks to identify the feedback loops between knowledge making and politics (Jasanoff 2014).

## *Agency and Power*

The political impact and implications of knowledge coproduction also raise questions about the kinds of authority and agency asserted in it and, consequently, about the accountability, representativeness, and legitimacy of experts who claim to speak for the future of the earth (Lövbrand et al. 2015; Turnhout et al. 2016). Meta-assessments reveal that practical–procedural efforts to make coproduction work tend to underestimate the extent to which knowledge and power can be unequally available and differentially composed. They also tend to ignore the unequal power relations involved in defining problems and identifying appropriate research strategies, while also neglecting the explanatory power incorporated within more disciplinary approaches (Klenk and Meehan 2015). The analytical concept of coproduction, by contrast, draws attention to the power and agency reproduced by knowledge production: how, Leach asks, for example, can "one indigenous person speak for the diversity of all indigenous people?" (2014).

The analytical concept of coproduction is guided by a normative vision of "democratizing politics" (Jasanoff 2014). In such a normative view, the participation of nonexperts is not simply a matter of bringing stakeholders to a common table for instrumental reasons. It is based instead on the democratic instinct that coproduction also may involve giving stakeholders a voice, empowering them to have a say in decisions that affect their own lives. The underlying idea is, as Jasanoff explains, that all of these "stakeholders sitting around the table are bringing in perspectives that are not shared by the others. Then you get a good product that can only come about if everybody has brought their insight into it" (Jasanoff 2014).

To sum up: such an analytical understanding of coproduction seeks to draw attention to questions of political representation and to account for its political and normative implications in a systematic way. Applied to the composition of and modes of representation in Future Earth, initial empirical findings suggest that there is currently an asymmetrical mode of coproduction at work. Much like its predecessors – the International Geosphere-Biosphere Programme, the International Human Dimensions Programme, and the World Climate Research Programme – Future Earth was established in a top-down manner by an alliance of science councils, funding agencies, and United Nations organizations (Lahsen 2016; Leemans 2016; van der Hel 2016). A small group of high-level natural scientists representing the international research programs and user organizations (e.g., funders and sponsors) have defined the goals and governance structure of Future Earth. As one participant notes, although novel groups such as early-career professionals were invited by Future Earth to participate in agenda-setting processes, their proposals have been marginalized (see Lahsen 2016).

Even if instrumental features may have dominated in the initial stages of its development, Future Earth has made systematic efforts to broaden the disciplinary, geopolitical, and societal participation in its committees (van der Hel 2016). Instrumental modes of coproduction may serve to establish narrow and monolithic framings (through mainstreaming and standardization) but they may also mobilize resistance, such as by the basic science communities at the national level, and thus have necessarily contingent effects. Power imbalances, biased representation, and the lack of access and capacity are persistent challenges to international research platforms (see Blicharska et al. 2017). These persistent problems highlight the importance of openly addressing questions of inclusion and representation, rather than defending the ideal of neutral, aggregated, and thus more balanced expertise. "Enabling multiple voices to be heard is the critical challenge" for coproduction in Future Earth, says Melissa Leach (2014). The active participation of social scientists may result in issues of representation being included in both the research agenda of global funding initiatives and the practical–procedural decision processes. Mainstreaming processes engaged in by invited participants may be supported by the critical appraisal of scholars who prefer to stay outside. This may then turn such issues into a matter of basic science research. Issues of justice and the participation of different groups in different governance arrangements, for instance, have been taken up as a topic on the research agenda of the research call in the area of transformations towards sustainability (Belmont Forum 2017).

## The Reflexive Turn

Science journalist Andy Revkin compares the Anthropocene ("both the word and the unfolding age") to a variously interpretable Rorschach image (2016). Much in the same way, it is possible to identify in Future Earth's efforts to experiment with knowledge coproduction both monolithic and instrumental features as well as opportunities for green political scholars to engage usefully with the Anthropocene. The present chapter so far has shown that the emergence of novel forms of knowledge production has served as a site of self-reflection for different scientific communities, enabling them to position themselves in relation to novel challenges such as those posed by the Anthropocene. In response to the emergence

Figure 10.1 The knowledge arena: sustainability science as a collective learning process.

of Future Earth, the German Research Foundation, for example, has started to consider the potential input of basic bottom-up research to support decision-making for transformations towards sustainability (German Council of Science and Humanities 2015). The same goes for various other social science communities (see Lövbrand et al. 2015; Brondizio et al. 2016; Castree 2016).

This section explores whether an analytical understanding of coproduction can productively inform coproduction as a strategic instrument and can help render Future Earth's efforts more responsive, responsible, and democratically accountable. How can this analytical understanding be used to reconfigure practical forms of coproduction in more profoundly reflexive ways (in the sense of institutional reflexivity) despite the fact that these studies remain marginal to scholarship and global knowledge production in the realm of global environmental change?

As Figure 10.1 indicates, there are attempts inside Future Earth to reconceptualize knowledge coproduction as a reiterative learning process rather than treating it as a linear, one-way transfer from science to policymaking (see Cornell et al. 2013).

Similarly to concepts of adaptive governance (Berkhout 2012), invited social scientists such as the former interim executive director of Future Earth, Frans Berkhout, also call for an incremental approach that enables sufficient flexibility to be responsive and to adjust in a transparent way in order to better capture the changing landscape (Berkhout 2014). Knowledge production must, so the argument goes, remain capable of being revised in the light of the uncertainties, long periods of time, continuously growing knowledge, and changing evaluations that are involved.

The political significance of solution-oriented research has led a number of scholars to call for deeper reflexivity among both scientists reflecting on and scientific institutions practically engaged with coproduction (Strohschneider 2014; Castree 2016; Moser 2016: 107). A number of factors serve to underline the need for institutional reflexivity (Chilvers and Kearnes 2016). As this chapter has shown, the role of global environmental research is radically changing with the turn towards solutions. This trend will be further reinforced by the growing demand for scientific support for evaluating the Sustainable Development Goals and tracking progress towards their achievement. Solution-oriented research constitutes an important part of the governance of transformations towards sustainability itself, effectively filling the role of a powerful non-state actor. At the same time, these trends are open-ended and may have unintended effects. They are prompting a new round of debate about the remit and role of coproduction. The turn towards solutions constitutes a major challenge to conventional ideals of scientific neutrality and autonomy. New questions are therefore being asked about the roles and responsibilities of experts and expert organizations in the Anthropocene. As demonstrated by this chapter, the discussions on coproduction not only reignite an older debate about scientific autonomy and the societal boundaries of research but also offer new opportunities for novel forms of experimentation.

The solution-oriented turn and the growing significance of novel forms of knowledge production have also been accompanied by a growing demand for their evaluation (Leemans 2016; Moser 2016; see also Alcamo 2017). Although the issue of responsibility on the part of global environmental research in support of transformations towards sustainability has recently been raised in scientific discourse (see Wapner, Chapter 11), a systematic framework to guide such deliberations that can be applied in a self-reflective manner across disciplines is lacking as yet. Evaluating the manner in which research is conducted is seen as a key mechanism for leveraging transformation in response to the Anthropocene. Moser (2016), for instance, claims that an evaluation framework with specific indicators and metrics is needed to account for the actual impact of coproduction in Future Earth and to show its success. Other scholars hold that a consistent procedure for impact evaluation is required to improve both the methods and procedures of knowledge production and to allow the sponsors and stakeholders to obtain feedback for improving their performance and accountability (Leeman 2016; Alcamo 2017). Initial efforts to evaluate experiences of coproduction within Future Earth indicate that while there is a growing demand for metrics and tools to evaluate their impact, there are currently no widely accepted and coherent metrics, criteria, and indicators for judging overall the quality of procedures and for comparing the performance of knowledge production. Neither is there a uniform answer or a "one-size-fits-all" metric that might apply to all cases (Moser 2016). The definition of "political impact" varies significantly across policy fields, cultural contexts, and political levels (Moser 2016; van der Hel 2016). This experience resonates with an analytical understanding of coproduction that underlines the political and thus contested dimension of knowledge production. While scholars working within Future Earth continue to call for the establishment of a central, comprehensive monitoring system and the efficient application of standardized rules and procedures (see Alcamo 2017), other scholars are calling for a thorough discussion of broader notions of political relevance beyond economic criteria, based on an analytical rather than instrumental understanding of coproduction (Felt et al. 2013). This discussion has so far also entailed shifting attention from the *how* to the *why* of knowledge coproduction in Future Earth, to the broader significance and political implications of these activities. In the analytical understanding of coproduction, the main challenge is not to measure its impact or demonstrate its success (Moser 2016; Alcamo 2017) but rather, to evaluate its performance – its political impacts and implications – in a systematic way. The crucial question is therefore not *how much* coproduction is desirable but *what kind*; *who* should participate in it; and *to what purpose* (Stilgoe et al. 2013).

Given the ideal of neutral science, there is a reluctance by many scientists contributing to Future Earth to explicitly define the normative or desirable ends of knowledge coproduction. As a result, the principles guiding it – both within Future Earth and beyond – often remain vague in terms of their rationale and purpose. Given the political significance of research in support of transformations towards sustainability, solution-oriented research itself merits full and thorough consideration as to its responsibility in terms of societal goals and values. With its focus on contributing to transformations towards sustainability, Future Earth explicitly subscribes to the moral and political norms of justice, as stated, for instance, in the Brundtland conceptualization of sustainable development and, more recently and in greater detail, in the Sustainable Development Goals (United Nations 2015). Coproduction processes inside Future Earth can offer a site for "opening a conversation around fundamental issues underlying global change and pathways to sustainability" (Brondizio et al. 2016). Recognizing this "political" nature of coproduction requires the scientists and stakeholders involved to be modest and reflective about their own positions (Leach 2014). It also suggests the need for renewed attention to be paid to avowedly normative questions about whose visions are being accorded legitimacy at the expense of what other ways of envisioning engagement (Lövbrand et al. 2015). What alternative options and voices have been excluded? Are those who insist on legitimacy the right ones to be speaking of it?

With regard to Future Earth's desire to achieve societal and economic impacts by means of solution-oriented research, the analytical understanding of coproduction insists that there is a need to unpack participants' motivations for engaging in the coproduction of knowledge and for asserting that it is conducted for substantive and normative reasons rather than being an instrumental approach suited to expediting the process of achieving predefined policy goals such as transformations towards sustainability.

Rather than clinging to the optimistic idea that more coproduction will automatically achieve a greater impact and better outcomes, it is necessary to acknowledge that there will always be diverse views about inclusivity and appropriate representation (Chilvers and Kearnes 2016). Constructive engagement also demands active and deliberative forms of reflexivity by diverse actors and institutions. Whether or not the governance structure of Future Earth as it currently stands is fit for purpose to address challenges such as ensuring that the full diversity and plurality of views have a voice from the outset is as yet unresolved, says Leach (2014). Case studies on the emergence of Future Earth have revealed the impact of conflicting trends, including the emphasis on novel forms of knowledge production, on the one hand, and established funding policies and structures that act to constrain them, on the other (Felt et al. 2016; Lahsen 2016; van der Hel 2016). The key challenges to its modus operandi also relate to the institutional changes needed to encourage the coproduction of knowledge as well as the development of processes and norms for dealing with the new problems thrown up by a commitment to coproduction.

## Conclusion

The Anthropocene forces us to engage in a renewed examination of concepts of knowledge production. Future Earth is an example of knowledge production designed to respond to the challenges of the Anthropocene. This chapter has shown how and in what ways it offers an important platform for developing a research agenda to address the challenges raised by the advent of this newly designated era. What are the lessons to be drawn from Future Earth for green political scholars? How can and should they engage with international platforms such as Future Earth?

The findings of this chapter suggest that there is currently no universally valid and legitimate mode of coproduction in response to the Anthropocene. This normative and institutional void invites green political scholars to rethink the meaning of coproduction while also offering diverse entry points into scholarly engagement with the Anthropocene. It raises questions such as: what are the most effective and legitimate sites for intervening in debates about the Anthropocene? Does Future Earth, in its attempts to coproduce solution-oriented research, provide an appropriate format for engaging with the Anthropocene?

Given the performative nature of Future Earth in terms of setting the research agenda for global research and gaining the attention of policy communities, green political scholars can accept the invitation to "jump into the Future Earth cockpit and wrestle the controls from the geoscientists or even seek to place a moderating hand on the steering wheel" (Hulme 2015). They can try to influence processes of agenda setting – such as transformations towards sustainability – and to push more reflexive forms of knowledge production within Future Earth (*mainstreaming*). At the same time, there are also legitimate reasons for hesitating to accept this invitation and instead opting for other forms of engagement with the Anthropocene, outside the institutional arrangements of Future Earth. Advocates of engagement outside the main programs highlight the constraints and side effects of joining such programs, such as the imperative of scientific integration and mainstreaming within global research platforms. In their view, the quest for a unified account and a set of rules for projecting and anticipating political solutions does not constitute a robust and equitable response to the challenges raised by the Anthropocene. The pitfalls of such an approach are manifested, among other things, in its narrow reference to "the problem" (singular) to be confronted, which thus serves to place constraints on the imagination with regard to solutions (Hulme 2015; Lövbrand et al. 2015). As an alternative, they encourage experimentation with new forms and formats by bringing in largely neglected sources of knowledge and voices (see also Beck et al. 2016).

As an alternative to the Future Earth approach, bottom-up forms of nested engagement may offer the opportunity to address the Anthropocene in a relatively "autonomous" way: rather than taking for granted the terms being offered by global platforms such as Future Earth, such nonaffiliated modes of inquiry could help to define a research agenda on their own terms in a bottom-up way. Following this line of argument, the German Council of Science and Humanities (2015) recommends forms of basic research – on the conditions and potential of different forms of participation – as an important contribution science can offer in support of transformations towards sustainability.

Alternative forms of engagement also offer an opportunity to challenge the instrumental mode of developing solutions for transformations towards sustainability and to explore alternative ways of engaging with the Anthropocene. A more important and also politically more powerful role for green political scholars may lie in cultivating multiple, divergent, and conflicting epistemic frameworks and eco-political possibilities that are distributed across different scientific disciplines and localities (Lövbrand et al. 2015). Such forms of alternative engagement may enable critical engagement with dominant as well as new ways of seeing, knowing, and acting upon nature, and may also offer scope for local activists to exercise initiative and autonomy by taking action that matches local needs.

There are also political reasons for favoring distributed but nested forms of engagement. Even if research platforms such as Future Earth are the powerful agents of change in global governance (Hulme 2015), there are also multiple sites where transformations towards sustainability are taking place. Distributed forms of engagement can also contribute a more precise understanding of where changes are happening on the ground. Transformations towards sustainability will start in many different places: with social movements, in diverse new cultural settings, through new technologies, and by means of political struggle. They are embodied and lived out in communities, neighborhoods, and networks. The social contextualization of the Anthropocene debate may increase social and policy relevance (Brondizio et al. 2016). Distributed forms of engagement appear to be more sensitive to the social and ecological circumstances and coping strategies of particular communities in response to the Anthropocene. This ideal of polycentric governance and epistemic subsidiarity already resonates with the decentralized structure of "knowledge-action networks" within Future Earth (van der Hel 2016). By studying these forms of epistemic subsidiarity (Beck et al. 2016), scholars of science and technology studies can contribute not only to making sense of public controversies, but also to bridging "the gap between co-production as an analytic approach and co-production as a strategic instrument in the hands of knowledgeable social actors" (Jasanoff 2004: 281). This is an acknowledgement that appreciation of the complexities does not reside exclusively within science and technology studies, and it is a call for scholars of science and technology studies to build connections with new, like-minded actors in new places in order to diversify the field's empirical reach, and to enhance its "real world" impact.

Such distributed forms of engagement correspond with flexible, responsive, bottom-up approaches to politics and to a model of democracy as a set of complex networks of interlinked spaces in which deliberations occur (Miller 2009: 145). Each of these spaces exhibits norms and practices that correspond to multiple aspects of knowledge production: who participates, under what conditions, how participation is governed, how policy ideas are framed, evidentiary rules and standards, openness and transparency, and processes of review and certification. Such forms of alternative engagement may serve to facilitate coordination and cooperation even among people and organizations that are in many respects far apart. The Anthropocene as a narrative can serve to link these local initiatives to global agendas such as the Sustainable Development Goals. If insider and outsider forms of engagement are linked in a constructive or complementary way and are dovetailed with each other, distributed engagement with the Anthropocene can offer an independent form of evaluation in order to boost not only public accountability and the legitimacy of Future Earth's coproduction processes but also its responsiveness and its own institutional reflexivity. However, the means of achieving a more deliberative and questioning mode of understanding the Anthropocene and potential solutions in more contextual and self-aware ways remains an important topic for exploration.

## References

Alcamo, Joseph. 2017. Evaluating the Impacts of Global Environmental Assessments. *Environmental Science and Policy* 77: 268–272.

Beck, Silke, and Martin Mahony. 2017. The IPCC [Intergovernmental Panel on Climate Change] and the Politics of Anticipation. *Nature Climate Change* 7 (5): 311–313.

Beck, Silke, Tim Forsyth, Pia M. Kohler, Myanna Lahsen, and Martin Mahony. 2016. The Making of Global Environmental Science and Politics. In *The Handbook of Science and Technology Studies* (4th edition), edited by Ulrike Felt, Rayvon Fouché, Clark A. Miller, and Laurel Smith-Doerr, chapter 36. Cambridge, MA: MIT Press.

Belmont Forum. 2017. Transformations to Sustainability. Accessed April 5, 2017. http://www.belmontforum.org/news/the-transformations-2-sustainability-call-is-open-today/

Berkhout, Frans. 2012. Adaptation to Climate Change by Organizations. *Wiley Interdisciplinary Reviews: Climate Change* 3 (1): 91–106.

Berkhout, Frans. 2014. What Does Coordination Achieve. Accessed January 29, 2017. http://www.futureearth.org/blog/2014-may-30/what-does-coordination-achieve

Blicharska, Malgorzata, Richard J. Smithers, Magdalena Kuchler, et al. 2017. Steps to Overcome the North-South Divide in Research Relevant to Climate Change Policy and Practice. *Nature Climate Change* 7 (1): 21–27.

Brondizio, Eduardo S., Karen O'Brien, Xuemei Bai, et al. 2016. Re-conceptualizing the Anthropocene: A Call for Collaboration. *Global Environmental Change* 39: 318–327.

Castree, Noel. 2016. Geography and the New Social Contract for Global Change Research. *Transactions of the Institute of British Geographers* 41 (3): 328–347.

Chilvers, Jason, and Matthew Kearnes, eds. 2016. *Remaking Participation: Science, Environment and Emergent Publics*. London: Routledge.

Clark, William C., Lorrae van Kerkhoff, Louis Lebel, and Gilberto C. Gallopin. 2016. Crafting Usable Knowledge for Sustainable Development. *Proceedings of the National Academy of Sciences* 113 (17): 4570–4578.

Cornell, Sarah, Frans Berkhout, Willemijn Tuinstra, et al. 2013. Opening up Knowledge Systems for Better Responses to Global Environmental Change. *Environmental Science and Policy* 28: 60–70.

Dilling, Lisa, and Maria Carmen Lemos. 2011. Creating Usable Science: Opportunities and Constraints for Climate Knowledge Use and their Implications for Science Policy. *Global Environmental Change* 21 (2): 680–689.

Felt, Ulrike, Daniel Barben, A. Irwin, et al. 2013. Science in Society: Caring for Our Futures in Turbulent Times. Science Policy Briefing 50 for the European Science Foundation.

Felt, Ulrike, Judith Igelsböck, Andrea Schikowitz, and Thomas Völker. 2016. Transdisciplinary Sustainability Research in Practice: Between Imaginaries of Collective Experimentation and Entrenched Academic Value Orders. *Science, Technology and Human Values* 41 (4): 732–761.

Future Earth. 2014. *Impact*. Accessed January 29, 2017. http://futureearth.org/impact

Future Earth. 2016. Future Earth Launches New Magazine for the Anthropocene. Accessed May 10, 2017. http://futureearth.org/news/future-earth-launches-new-magazine-anthropocene

German Advisory Council on Global Change. 2011. World in Transition. A Social Contract for Sustainability. Accessed May 5, 2017. http://www.wbgu.de/en/flagship-reports/fr-2011-a-social-contract/

German Council of Science and Humanities. 2015. Grand Societal Challenges as a Topic for Science Policy. Positionspapier. https://www.wissenschaftsrat.de/download/archiv/4594-15_engl.pdf.

Hackmann, Heide, Susanne C. Moser, and Asunción Lera St. Clair. 2014. The Social Heart of Global Environmental Change. *Nature Climate Change* 4 (8): 653–655.

Hajer, Maarten. 1995. *The Politics of Environmental Discourse: Ecological Modernization and the Policy Process*. Oxford: Oxford University Press.

Hulme, Mike. 2015. Changing What Exactly, and From Where? A Response to Castree. *Dialogues in Human Geography* 5 (3): 322–326.

Ignacuik, Ada, Martin Rice, Janos Bogardi, Josep G. Canadell, Shobhakar Dhakal, John Ingram, Rik Leemans, and Mark Rosenberg. 2012. Responding to Complex Societal Challenges: A Decade of Earth System Science Partnership (ESSP) Interdisciplinary Research. *Current Opinion on Environmental Sustainability* 4: 147–158.

International Council for Science. 2010. *Grand Challenges in Global Sustainability Research: A Systems Approach to Research Priorities for the Decade*. Prepublication Version. Paris: International Council for Science.

International Social Science Council and United Nations Educational, Scientific and Cultural Organization. 2013. *World Social Science Report: Changing Global Environments*. Paris: OECD Publishing and UNESCO Publishing.

Jasanoff, Sheila, ed. 2004. *States of Knowledge: The Co-Production of Science and Social Order*. London: Routledge.

Jasanoff, Sheila. 2014. *To Be Inclusive, You Need More Voices*. Accessed May 10, 2016. http://www.futureearth.org/blog/2014-jul-23/be-inclusive-you-need-more-voices-qa-sheila-jasanoff

Jerneck, Anne, Lennart Olsson, Barry Ness, et al. 2011. Structuring Sustainability Science. *Sustainability Science* 6 (1): 69–82.

Kates, Robert W., William C. Clark, Robert Corell, et al. 2001. Sustainability Science. *Science* 292 (5517): 641–642.

Klenk, Nicole L., and Katie Meehan. 2015. Climate Change and Transdisciplinary Science: Problematizing the Integration Imperative. *Environmental Science and Policy* 54: 160–167.

Lahsen, Myanna. 2016. Toward a Sustainable Future Earth: Challenges for a Research Agenda. *Science, Technology and Human Values* 41 (5): 876–898.

Latour, Bruno. 2015. Telling Friends from Foes in the Time of the Anthropocene. In *The Anthropocene and the Global Environment Crisis: Rethinking Modernity in a New Epoch*, edited by Clive Hamilton, Christophe Bonneuil, and François Gemenne, 145–155. London: Routledge.

Leach, Melissa. 2014. *Co-Design for Relevance and Usefulness*. Accessed May 10, 2016. http://www.futureearth.org/blog/2014-jul-23/co-design-relevance-and-usefulness-qa-melissa-leach

Leemans, Rik. 2016. The Lessons Learned from Shifting from Global-Change Research Programmes to Transdisciplinary Sustainability Science. *Current Opinion in Environmental Sustainability* 19: 103–110.

Liverman, Diana M. 2009. Conventions of Climate Change: Constructions of Danger and the Dispossession of the Atmosphere. *Journal of Historical Geography* 35 (2): 279–296.

Lövbrand, Eva, Silke Beck, Jason Chilvers, et al. 2015. Who Speaks for the Future of Earth? How Critical Social Science Can Extend the Conversation on the Anthropocene. *Global Environmental Change* 32: 211–218.

Miller, Clark. 2009. Epistemic Constitutionalism in International Governance: The Case of Climate Change. In *Foreign Policy Challenges in the 21st Century*, edited by Michael Heazle, Martin Griffiths, and Tom Conley, 141–163. Cheltenham: Edward Elgar.

Moser, Susanne C. 2016. Can Science on Transformation Transform Science? Lessons from Co-Design. *Current Opinion in Environmental Sustainability* 20: 106–115.

O'Brien, Karen, and John Barnett. 2013. Global Environmental Change and Human Security. *Annual Review of Environment and Resources* 38: 373–391.

Prokopy, Linda S., J. Stuart Carlton, Tonya Haigh, et al. 2016. Useful to Usable: Developing Usable Climate Science for Agriculture. *Climate Risk Management* 15: 1–7.

Revkin, Andrew. 2016. *An Anthropocene Journey*. Accessed May 10, 2017. http://anthropocenemagazine.org/anthropocenejourney/

Stafford-Smith, Mark, Owen Gaffney, Lidia Brito, Elinor Ostrom, and Sybil Seitzinger. 2012. Interconnected Risks and Solutions for a Planet under Pressure – Overview and Introduction. *Current Opinion in Environmental Sustainability* 4: 3–6.

Steffen, William L., Angelina Sanderson, Peter D. Tyson, et al. 2004. Global Change and the Earth System: A Planet under Pressure. Executive Summary Stockholm, International Geosphere-Biosphere Programme.

Stilgoe, Jack, Richard Owen, and Phil Macnaghten. 2013. Developing a Framework for Responsible Innovation. *Research Policy* 42 (9): 1568–1580.

Stirling, Andrew. 2015. *Time to Rei(g)n Back the Anthropocene?* Accessed January 29, 2017. http://steps-centre.org/2015/blog/time-to-reign-back-the-anthropocene

Strohschneider, Peter. 2014. Zur Politik der Transformativen Wissenschaft. In *Die Verfassung des Politischen. Festschrift für Hans Vorländer*, edited by André Brodocz, Dietrich Herrmann, Rainer Schmidt, Daniel Schulz, and Julia Schulze, 175–194. Berlin: Wessel.

Strohschneider, Peter. 2016. Foreword – The Contribution of Science in Implementing the SDGs [Sustainable Development Goals]. Accessed May 5, 2017. http://www.dkn-future-earth.org/aktuelles/news/deutschland/new-dkn-future-earth-report-out-now-the-contribution-of-science-in-implementing-the-sdgs.html

Turnhout, Esther, Art Dewulf, and Mike Hulme. 2016. What Does Policy-Relevant Global Environmental Knowledge Do? The Cases of Climate and Biodiversity. *Current Opinion in Environmental Sustainability* 18: 65–72.

United Nations. 2015. *Transforming Our World: The 2030 Agenda for Sustainable Development*. Outcome Document for the UN Summit to Adopt the Post-2015 Development Agenda: Draft for Adoption. New York. https://sustainabledevelopment.un.org/content/documents/21252030%20Agenda%20for%20Sustainable%20Development%20web.pdf

van der Hel, Sandra. 2016. New Science for Global Sustainability? The Institutionalisation of Knowledge Co-production in Future Earth. *Environmental Science and Policy* 61: 165–175.

# 11

# The Ethics of Political Research in the Anthropocene

PAUL WAPNER

What happens when scholars study a radically changing world? What do researchers do when fundamentally new facts present themselves, facts that shatter previous disciplinary assumptions? Although a conceptual innovation, the Anthropocene captures a fundamentally new reality. It points to humanity's ubiquitous presence on earth. It indicates that, after living for millennia by influencing only pockets of the planet, humanity's impact has become coextensive with the earth itself. Can the study of politics simply carry on in light of this novel condition? Can the discipline continue in its traditional ways as it tries to explain the political world in the Anthropocene?

In 1948, Albert Einstein sent a letter to the Peace Congress of Intellectuals in Wrocław, Poland. Writing after the end of the Second World War, Einstein argued that the advent of nuclear weapons represented an unprecedented historical break. Nuclear weapons granted "mankind [sic] the means for his [sic] own mass destruction" (Einstein 1995: 140). They gave humans power over life and death on a scale unimaginable to previous generations and with implications for all future generations. For Einstein, crossing this threshold could not go unnoticed. It demanded new obligations for states and the international community, and, as his letter makes clear, new responsibilities for intellectuals. Nuclear weapons were "not comparable to anything in the past. It is impossible, therefore, to apply methods and measures which at an earlier age might have been sufficient" (Einstein 1995: 148). The Anthropocene confronts scholars with a similar challenge. Although the Anthropocene does not represent, in and of itself, mass destruction, the dangers it includes force scholars to reassess their disciplinary practices. At a minimum, it calls on them to recontextualize the questions they ask and adopt a sensitivity towards what is at stake. As I will show, this involves conceptual, epistemological, and ethical expansion. It requires researchers to extend their foci horizontally to further reaches of time and space, and vertically deeper into the lives of those who are most vulnerable to the perils associated with the Anthropocene.

The chapter advances such expansion. It does so by making two main points. First, it argues that the Anthropocene is not ethically neutral but rife with injustices that demand scholarly attention (see Baskin, Chapter 8). The Anthropocene is unfolding in ways that exacerbate unfair treatment of the most vulnerable. Although the Anthropocene represents the Age of Humans, it more accurately should be termed the Age of *Some* Humans. Not everyone has their hands on the reins of planetary, ecosystem power. Far from it. A quick study of the social dynamics of climate change – arguably the most dramatic expression and current driver of the Anthropocene – reveals that the patterns of carbon extraction, processing, and emissions greatly amplify social injustices (see Baskin, Chapter 8). Recognizing and understanding the dynamics involved is essential for carrying on relevant political research in the Anthropocene.

Second, the chapter suggests guideposts for carrying out relevant Anthropocene scholarship in light of attending injustices. It calls on researchers to question two academic orthodoxies that have long influenced the discipline of political studies but which work against an appreciation of the ethical dimensions of the Anthropocene: namely, the veneration of value-neutrality and the exclusive focus on the human sphere in political analysis. The chapter makes the case for relaxing strict standards of value-neutrality and explains how this can, paradoxically, discipline inquiry in the Anthropocene. It makes clear, in other words, the scholarly benefit of normative political studies. Further, the chapter also explains how the more-than-human dimension of life does not disappear or even diminish in the Anthropocene but remains an abiding presence and has an, often unseen, political influence. The chapter calls for researchers to expand their scholarly gaze beyond the state, civil society, the economy, and similar social parameters to include the nonhuman in their inquiries and thus be able to capture the broader terrain of Anthropocene politics. Taken together, these two recommendations aim to fold ethical considerations into contemporary political scholarship.

The chapter ends by noting that the Anthropocene demands that we, as researchers, not only "revolutionize our thinking," as Einstein (1995: 150) recommended, but also "revolutionize our feelings." Although merely a geological designation, the Anthropocene calls on scholars of politics to deepen their sympathies and work on behalf of the most vulnerable.

## The Injustice of Climate Change

In *The End of Nature*, Bill McKibben (1989) set the popular stage for the Anthropocene. McKibben showed how the scale and intensity of human intervention into the earth's water, soil, air, and biological functions signal not simply a crossing of the divide between humans and nature but humanity's wholesale colonizing of the nonhuman world. For McKibben, this was long in the coming. Increasing human population matched with wealth, technological power, and insatiable consumption have been driving people to dig deeper into and across the earth to extract resources and dump wastes. While one could see this in deforestation, water contamination, and loss of biological diversity, it was climate change that McKibben announced as the death knell of nature. As he put it, "We have changed the atmosphere and thus we are changing the weather. By changing the weather, we make every spot on earth man-made and artificial" (McKibben 1989: 58). Climate change, in other words, indicates humanity's comprehensive takeover of the natural world. It reveals that humanity is not simply one among many species but the dominant one. By placing its signature everywhere, humanity robs nature of its ontological independence and becomes the central pulse and default driver of the planet's ecological fate. One can no longer wake up in the morning and comment on what a beautiful day the earth has given us; one must acknowledge what a beautiful day humanity has partially manufactured, and how humanity will partly manufacture all days going forward. As the most dramatic instance of the end of nature, climate change provides the conceptual entryway into the Anthropocene.

Focusing on climate change reveals the moral dimensions of the Anthropocene. Throughout the entire process of carbon excavation, processing, and emissions, some people benefit while many others suffer. This is because the carbon economy is a gigantic shell game wherein the benefits of burning carbon accrue in certain areas and to certain people while the costs impose themselves elsewhere. At the heart of the enterprise is a type of moral blindness. Many simply do not wish to see that the carbon economy lives off the practice of displacement – the shifting of burden and pain to those least likely to complain or have the political resources to resist.

Consider the extraction of fossil fuels. This does not happen through some process that magically lifts oil, gas, and coal deposits to the earth's surface but involves much drilling, pulverizing, exploding, and otherwise debasing land and water with significant consequences to surrounding communities. For instance, those living near coalmines – especially where miners blow off the tops of mountains to expose coal deposits – endure defaced landscapes, polluted streams, increased flooding, and unsafe coal slurry impoundments (Bozzo 2012). Similarly, those living near oil installations live with explosions from seismic surveys; air, water, and soil contamination from drilling fluids and refinery effluents; blowouts; and the defilement of surrounding land as it is used for industry infrastructure (Dabbs 1996). This is also the case with those living around hydraulic fracturing facilities. The depletion and contamination of drinking water, the rumble of earth-moving vehicles, and persistent anthropogenic earthquakes are among the hazards that local communities must endure (United States Environmental Protection Agency 2016). Meanwhile, on the other side of town, as it were, are those who get to enjoy the benefits produced by such hardship. They live off, but spatially far from, what have been called "sacrifice zones" (Lerner 2012). At work is not simply the dynamics of economic markets but the moral choice to ignore or depreciate the lives of those living on the frontlines of extraction (Maniates and Meyer 2010). It involves the privileged displacing the afflictions of fossil fuel extraction to those who are too marginalized to care or resist.

Displacement also takes place when fossil fuels are burned. Yes, carbon emissions circulate throughout the atmosphere and pay no attention to zip codes, county or state lines, or even nation-state boundaries. They accumulate in the blanket of greenhouse gases that surrounds the planet and thus do not discriminate. However, once they have lodged into the layer of gases, the effects are anything but fair. Widespread research has shown that the poor disproportionately suffer from climate change. The poor occupy the most fragile lands; they live in the most insecure structures; they lack access to resources to respond to intensified storms, and are the last to receive aid (Parenti 2011; Wapner 2016). Moreover, they have made the lowest contribution to climate change. Countries like Nepal and Bangladesh, for instance, get almost all their energy from hydroelectric power and a small amount from biomass. Yet, due to a combination of topography and poverty, they are among the most vulnerable to climate disruption (VeRisk Maplecroft 2010; Szabo et al. 2016). To be sure, the wealthy do not target the poor with the consequences of climate change, but the result is still the same. Able to avoid climate hardship, the privileged live essentially off the backs of the most vulnerable or, put more accurately, export the dangers associated with climate change.

Displacement involves not only exploiting those living "downstream," as it were – those who must live today with the burdens of extraction, processing, and so forth. It also includes robbing future generations. Consider the temporal dimension of fossil fuel extraction. Life becomes fossilized over geological time. Oil, gas, and coal represent thousands, if not millions, of years of decay. Thus, for all intents and purposes, they should be considered finite. And yet, current generations are using them at breakneck speeds that not only outpace replenishment but promise scarcity to future generations. If humanity keeps digging fossil fuels out of the ground, at some point, there will be little to none left for future generations. This may seem like a nonissue, since, having burned so much fossil fuel, the planet will have already experienced or will have set into motion the conditions for catastrophic climate change. However, it points to a broader pattern at the heart of the carbon economy – namely, a moral indifference to future generations. Using oil, gas, and coal with abandon today robs those coming after us of carbon options.

It refuses to live with the reality of finite reserves and simply displaces the burden of living without fossil fuels to future generations. It represents the exportation across time of carbon burdens (Galaz, Chapter 6). This takes on a moral character to the degree that, like current generations who live downstream, future generations have no political or economic voice, and thus they are the most apt to be ignored or exploited.

The carbon economy likewise displaces burdens across time when it comes to emissions. The world is already feeling the effects of climate change in the form of intensified storms, fiercer and more frequent wildfires, rising sea levels, melting glaciers, and punishing heatwaves. As mentioned, these may visit everyone, but they take a disproportional toll on the poor and politically weak. However, it is well known that current climate realities pale in comparison to future projections. The international community has agreed that once temperatures increase over 2 degrees Celsius, the world will face runaway climate change as positive feedback loops such as melting permafrost and the over-acidity of the oceans come into force. The Intergovernmental Panel on Climate Change estimates that, at current and even reduced levels of fossil fuel consumption, the world will likely cross the 2-degree threshold sometime before the end of the century (Intergovernmental Panel on Climate Change 2013). One might ask how those of us living today can continue burning fossil fuels, cutting down trees, grazing cattle, and otherwise emitting greenhouse gases knowing that the direst effects will come in the future. On some level, the only reasonable answer is that we simply do not care enough about those coming after us. By using fossil fuels or contributing to the buildup of greenhouse gases today, we are essentially choosing to export the costs across time – to those whom present generations never see, and certainly do not hear from.

There is a final category of beings who silently suffer the consequences of climate change, namely, other species. Mining, processing, transporting, and burning fossil fuels involve all kinds of violence perpetrated on the more-than-human world. We rarely hear about this, because, of course, plants and animals have no voice in our world. We only learn about their suffering when humans speak up on their behalf. Sadly, this is all too rare. Consider, for instance, drilling facilities, which are the beginning of the extractivist process. Their use and release of effluents are known to contaminate aquatic environments with lethal and sub-lethal effects. Marine life is especially sensitive to various concentrations of toxic substances used to extract oil (Wake 2005). On land, extraction of fossil fuels can involve deforestation – and thus the loss of habitat – because areas are cleared to locate, excavate, and transport deposits. Moreover, runoffs from petroleum processing and petrochemical plants often contaminate nearby soil and streams, and pollute the air (Ingelson and Nwapi 2014). The same happens with regard to coalmining, hydraulic fracking, and conventional natural gas installations. This takes its toll on various plants, birds, and other local creatures. Plants and animals have essentially no role in the buildup of carbon dioxide and other greenhouse gases. Yet, they stand at the frontline of climate hardship.

Other species suffer also from the emissions side. As should be obvious, increasing temperatures, changes in precipitation, rising sea levels, more acidic oceans, wildfires, and all the rest affect not simply humans but other animals, plants, and microorganisms. In fact, when it comes to on-the-ground effects of climate change, plants, animals, and so forth suffer arguably more than humans, since most of them lack the ability to flee disasters. Animals are trapped in particular habitats by the buildup of human settlements and infrastructure. They cannot simply migrate across cities, highways, and other large-scale human edifices. As many have noted, humans have created islands of habitat for the nonhuman world that not only are too small to maintain certain animal populations in the absence of climate change but are certainly too hemmed in to allow escape as temperatures rise, wildfires break out, and waters flood (Quammen 1997). Habitat fragmentation creates, essentially, "prisons" for animals in a climate age. The problem is even more dire for plants. Plants can migrate across land. In fact, the boreal forests of North America were largely formed by trees and other species moving north following the last ice age. But we know that plants can move only so fast, and most analyses report that their speed is less than required to escape the pressures of climate change (Quammen 1997). Moreover, plants have the same challenge as animals in moving across large-scale human structures. They too are essentially trapped in their degrading habitat.

Those living downstream, in the future, and of a different species share one thing in common. They each lack political standing and thus are most easily exploited. One could say that this is not a moral issue but simply one of representation. But this would ignore the knowledge that many have of the consequences of their carbon actions as well as moral judgements that are implicitly being made. To be sure, very few are deliberately choosing to injure the most vulnerable. However, this does not relieve them of moral responsibility. When others suffer as a consequence of one's actions, moral duties emerge.

Climate change underpins the Anthropocene. It is the primary expression of humanity's impact on the earth. Scholars differ about the origins of the Anthropocene, but almost every account includes the buildup of anthropogenic greenhouse gases as a marker distinguishing the present era from the Holocene (Walters et al. 2016). To the degree that the dynamics of climate change involve structural patterns of injustice, one must understand the Anthropocene through morally sensitive lenses. Seen as such, it appears that *how* the Anthropocene is unfolding is as important as the fact of the Anthropocene itself. As mentioned, this is not precisely the Age of Humans but the Age of *Some* Humans. Recognizing this calls upon scholars to sensitize themselves to questions of justice and enlarge their sympathies for those on the receiving end of climate change.

## Moral Sensitivity in Political Research

Caring about others involves not simply developing a more compassionate sensibility but adopting a fiercer, more focused research agenda. That the Anthropocene is deepening social injustice should send shudders down everyone's back. Part of a researcher's obligation in the Anthropocene is translating such concern into engaged scholarship. This involves questioning orthodoxies that have long animated the study of politics and finding the moral fiber to move beyond them in the service of a more humane Anthropocene.

One central tenet of political research is value-neutrality. For decades, social scientists have been trained to set their political commitments aside so as not to blind themselves to false observations. The job of the political analyst is to see the world in the way it *is*, not as they wish it *should* be. In politics, this is particularly challenging because many come to research subscribing to worldviews – such as Realism, Liberalism, or Marxism – that overlay events with implicit assumptions. This can lead to starry-eyed utopianism or corrosive cynicism in terms of speculating about political possibility, and such predispositions can often sneak into one's research. One of the hallmarks of modernity, which produced the social sciences as disciplines, is the commitment to objectivity revealed through reason rather than faith or other nonrational epistemological capacities. As a result, social scientists (and all researchers) have been repeatedly warned against letting emotions, principled commitments, and philosophical orientations contaminate reason. Cold reason, not warm fuzzy affections, produces objective knowledge, and thus, researchers must endeavor to keep values out of their work.

Over the past few decades, especially with the advent of postmodern political studies, many scholars have recognized the poverty, or at least false promise, of objectivity, and the limitations of reason as the sole form of inquiry. Many now understand that it is impossible to rid oneself of value commitments. (Indeed, it is difficult even to notice the precise ways such commitments interfere in one's scholarship.) Postmodern insights suggest that every researcher is animated by interests, and that the "will to truth" itself is a guise for advancing one's agenda (Foucault 2014). Notwithstanding this understanding, much social science – and a fair amount of scholarship on global environmental politics – proceeds as if inquiry could still be free from value commitments. This is not to discount the value of utilizing empirical evidence within political research in the Anthropocene. While value-neutral studies continue to add to our understanding of the discipline, most researchers give an epistemological wink to postmodern criticisms and then continue as if merely being aware of the critiques gives license to do proper social scientific work. Put differently, social inquiry still pines for the imprimatur of "objective science" to be worthy. And this, as most of us have long been told, appears fundamentally at odds with values, principles, and commitments.

The injustices that sit at the core of Anthropocene shake up the aspiration for value-free research. They expose the raw character of our times, and thus, should pull at the heartstrings of researchers. In doing so, they do not so much cloud one's vision as provide significance and direction for research. This does not mean that scholars should abandon reason or engage simply in screeds against injustice. On the contrary, it calls on researchers to double down their efforts to understand the political world with all available means, including reason. This is necessary because, if one wants to change conditions, one needs an accurate reading of them. It *does* mean, however, that researchers should not hide or otherwise minimize their normative commitments. Such concerns actually discipline one's research; they provide strictures for pursuing knowledge of what is most valuable. The Anthropocene raises the moral stakes of political research and thus provides, arguably for the first time, the momentum to move more fully beyond the orthodoxy of value-neutrality and embrace normative political scholarship. For decades, normative work has been viewed as mere commentary or, at best second-rate research compared with so-called rigorous, exacting, rationalistic knowledge production. Living in the Anthropocene requires abandoning this prejudice and seeing the compatibility between normative and scientific work. Normative commitment is not the enemy but a necessary component of rationalist scholarship. In this sense, the Anthropocene simply provides new energy and justification for normatively oriented work.

Practicing normative research opens up an additional tool for scholars; namely, their critical capacity for interpreting political life. In his study *Representations of the Intellectual*, Edward Said constantly reminds readers of the Gramscian insight that intellectual work takes place under ideational hegemony. Research is never free floating or somehow outside socioeconomic, political conditions. However, Said recognizes that, with deep, persistent work, scholars can occasionally get out from underneath conventional strictures and, in so doing, take up the responsibility of speaking "truth to power" (Said 1996). This includes unmasking perpetrated falsehoods and, at a deeper level of intellectual excavation, making connections that are often denied and citing alternative courses of action that could have been taken. It involves, in other words, assuming a critical perspective and expressing the moral implications of doing so. For Said, the intellectual is neither a "pacifier nor a consensus-builder, but someone whose whole being is staked on a critical sense, a sense of being unwilling to accept easy formulas or ready-made clichés, or the smooth, ever-so-accommodating confirmations of what the powerful or conventional have to say, and what they do" (Said 1996: 23). Said, however, goes even further. He makes clear that taking up the responsibility of critical insight requires being sensitive to and assuming the obligation to work on behalf of the most vulnerable. He recognizes the structural violence that courses through society – much like the exploitation that accompanies carbon economies – and believes that scholars must name these and align themselves with their victims. As he puts it, "There is no question in my mind that the intellectual belongs on the same side with the weak and unrepresented" (Said 1996: 23). For Said and others, responsible scholarship is not simply about filling in knowledge gaps, knocking down "strawmen," or otherwise engaging in purely academic pursuits. Ideas matter; inquiry has consequences; research must advance the plight of the underprivileged. Anything less than this is an implicit exercise in shoring up hegemonic structures themselves.

A second orthodoxy of political studies, and one that has special significance to environmental affairs, involves the so-called "unit of analysis" question. For decades, Political Science, International Relations, and related disciplines focused almost exclusively on the state as the main actor in public affairs. Domestically, the government holds dramatic power over collective life, and internationally, the state serves as the primary agent of world events. Scholars have traditionally taken this to mean that all relevant political activity centers on the state, and therefore, research should concentrate primarily on state affairs. Since at least the 1990s, the state-centric model has been qualified as scholars recognized the importance of nongovernmental entities in domestic and global life. Activist groups, research institutes, corporations, artists, cultural trend-setters, and other actors in civil society significantly influence the way people think about and act in relation to public issues (Rosenau 1990). They have targeted and manipulated mechanisms of power strewn throughout societies, and their efforts rival state action in shaping widespread thought and behavior (Keck and Sikkink 1998; Betsill and Corell 2007). Moreover, researchers have also shifted foci away from individual agents to structural factors in trying to understand world affairs. They have come to see states and other actors as embedded in various cultural and material regimes that animate and instrumentalize individual actors, and this trend has also softened the state-centric model of politics.

The Anthropocene adds another crucial yet neglected unit of analysis; namely, the more-than-human world. In addition to state and non-state actors and structural forces, the Anthropocene calls on researchers to include other species and ecological factors in their work. This may seem counterintuitive. After all, as humanity's presence has grown coexistent with the earth itself, it may seem that the nonhuman world has grown less rather than more significant. Indeed, the whole idea of the Anthropocene is to underline the importance of human influence, and thus, it would seem inappropriate for researchers to target inquiry beyond the human realm. However, this would ignore the wider biopolitical context of the Anthropocene. Humanity may be the primary force shaping evolution, atmospheric conditions, and terrestrial ecosystems, but it does not do so in a vacuum. It is still part of, dependent upon, and integrated into the natural world, and no amount of self-reference in terms of the Anthropocene can erase this (see Nikoleris, Stripple, and Tenngart, Chapter 4). Humans cannot exist for a moment without the ecological conditions that support life and cannot act into the world without intermingling with other creatures and geophysical conditions, and this becomes a matter of politics. Indeed, humans do not act *on* the earth; they act with it (see Burke and Fishel, Chapter 5). They both alter the earth's chemistry, biology, and geology, and are altered by them. So, while humans have placed their signature everywhere, this does not mean that everything is human. Likewise, while people have delved deeply into and have modified the biological functioning of given plants and animals, and have forever scarred landscapes, this does not mean that the more-than-human world lacks an inimitable presence or agency. The most genetically modified organism is still not human; the most carbon-saturated sky is not wholly under human regulation. There is something other than humans out there, and this remains even in the midst of the Age of Humans.

When McKibben announced the end of nature, he did not claim that plants, animals, microorganisms, and minerals no longer exist (see Fremaux and Barry, Chapter 9). Rather, he argued that the *idea* of nature had disappeared. People could no longer believe in a separate sphere devoid of human influence. Such independence evaporated with the onslaught of human encroachment and eventual colonization of nature through anthropogenic climate change. As McKibben puts it, "We have deprived nature of its independence, and that is fatal to its meaning. Nature's independence *is* its meaning; without it there is nothing but us" (McKibben 1989: 58). It is important to note that, by saying "there is nothing but us," McKibben is not dismissing the complex panoply of other creatures and nonhuman processes. In fact, he has devoted much of his life to protecting other-than-human beings. Rather, he is claiming that they no longer exist on their own. Humans are now, forever, a part of them. Our characters and fates are bounded together. Humans and ecological elements no longer grow and develop in parallel fashion but coevolve. The world and earth constitute a hybridity wherein one can no longer draw a boundary dividing the human and nonhuman domains.

The insight of hybridity stems from a broader understanding – increasingly confirmed by biology, physics, chemistry, and geology – that no organism exists or develops an essential character on its own, including humans. All beings are part of and co-constituted by wider ecological interdependencies. People may have imagined humans as the exceptional species and twisted this into the social preference for individualism, yet it is increasingly clear that individuality is, at best, a myth. All creatures, including humans, interact with and are partly formed in relation to a broader field of life and the elements. In the context of the Anthropocene, this means that, despite humans being enamored with humanity's geologic influence, there is still something beyond humans that plays a constitutive and, as will be shown, political role. There is still otherness out there. Appreciating this provides important research trajectories.

In a series of books and articles, cultural critic Donna Haraway explores what she calls companion species. Focusing initially on dogs but later on a whole host of other creatures, Haraway points out how people and other beings are bonded in "significant otherness" (Haraway 2003; 2007). That is, species rely on and mutually constitute each other. They signify not separate realms but integrated wholes. They exist in sympoietic relationship (Haraway 2016). Many other thinkers – natural and social scientists as well as humanities scholars – deepen Haraway's views by seeing agency and even subjectivity in other beings, and explain the ways in which these articulate with and help shape human experience (Bennett 2010; Weber 2016). Indeed, there is an emerging industry of studies delineating the agential character of trees, grasses, fish, and even seemingly inanimate objects like rocks, streams, and mountains (Abram 2011; Kohn 2013; Grusin 2015). Crucially, these studies propose literal, not metaphorical, agency and even "intelligence." And, they emphasize the concept of "interbeing" ("this is, because that is") (Hanh 1997) and explain how humans do not simply act on nature but are also instrumentalized by it. For instance, Michael Pollan writes about how tulips, apples, and potatoes are not simply crops forever at the mercy of human intention but are partially manipulators of human activity. They organize human enterprise for their own benefit (Pollan 2002). Likewise, he writes approvingly of the literature on plant intelligence which sees plants in general as possessing a type of awareness or motivation that endows them with an ability to "choose" and explains implications for human life (Pollan 2013). Weber similarly writes of creatures' innate sense of desire and their inseparable relationships with other beings, and how humans are similarly implicated in this mélange (Weber 2016).

Studies such as these caution the self-referential character and even hubris embedded in the Anthropocene, and open up new research possibilities. They invite scholars to develop tools for including the nonhuman dimension of the Anthropocene in political analysis – to develop ways of studying genuine hybridity. A number of thinkers have started down such a path. They build on decades of ethical scholarship arguing for the intrinsic value of the more-than-human world – biocentrism and ecocentrism – and on theoretical work associated with biopolitics – the effort to conjoin biology and power and recognize practices that discipline living bodies (Foucault 2003). Recent scholarship is also connected to efforts to expand the category of "the political," which has long been associated exclusively with humans (Latour 2004). At the heart of such efforts is the attempt to read power into all relationships and use categories of political analysis to understand the assemblage of life (Burke and Fishel, Chapter 5). This includes noticing how other creatures are affected by human politics *and* generative of human politics.

Rafi Youatt, for instance, explains how categories such as sovereignty, community, and security – which often sit at the core of International Relations – cannot be understood separately from the consideration of other creatures. These tenets of political thought and practice are produced, as Youatt puts it, "interspecifically" (Youatt 2016). They emerge as a mélange of species interactions. One cannot fully understand them if one only studies human affairs (Burke et al. 2016). Likewise, Livingston and Puar criticize the "singularity of humanness" in political studies and reveal the complicated character of biosocial life and its political effects. They describe historical instances wherein political events emerge out of "cohabitative interspecies encounters," wherein it is difficult to delineate human versus nonhuman agency (Livingston and Puar 2011). Neel Ahuja provides a specific instance of this in explaining how insects have been used to torture prisoners and how the interplay structures practices of security (Ahuja 2011). Work along these lines draws connections between cultural and ecological inquiry – often linking critical race theory, postcolonial studies, and the so-called "animal turn" – to reveal the mutually constituted character of cultural and biological life.

From a different angle, ethicists are now moving beyond endowing animals with negative rights – the freedom from harm and exploitation – to positive ones, in the sense of granting levels of citizenship and representation to nonhuman animals (Donaldson and Kymlicka 2013). They do so to acknowledge the political significance of other creatures. To be sure, this work is inchoate, suggestive rather than authoritative, and hard to translate into systematic research agendas. However, it represents an important scholarly qualification to the anthropocentric politics of old and the enticingly anthropocentric politics of late – in the Anthropocene. It is difficult to know where such study will lead, but recognizing it and struggling to include the more-than-human in one's research seems important in the Anthropocene. Such a perspective assumes ethical significance in that, while the Anthropocene has the potential to seduce researchers into thinking that humans are the only significant political agent, making room for the more-than-human is a moral act. It is the scholarly equivalent to humility – a virtue that appears increasingly quaint, or at least embattled, in the Anthropocene.

## Conclusion

The Anthropocene represents not simply conceptual innovation but ethical responsibility for researchers of politics. This is because the Age of Humans has not catapulted us beyond social injustices but, rather, engraved them more deeply and more expansively throughout the world. Fossil fuel economies run on injustice. The entire ensemble of excavation, processing, and emissions benefits some and immiserates many others (Klein 2015). By displacing environmental harm across space (to the vulnerable living downstream), across time (to the politically marginal of future generations), and across species (to the silenced world of the more-than-humans), people maintain a carbon economy on the backs of the weak, poor, and powerless. Many tend not to notice, as the slow violence gets masked in the dizzying dynamics of market exchange, economic opportunity, and the seeming right of people to pursue their own livelihoods. Moreover, it is often lost on observers, in that "carbon casualties" (Goode 2016) – whether people or nonhuman creatures – lack a political voice, and thus, their hardships go unheeded and often even unrecorded. In light of this, political researchers face the challenge of expanding their sympathies and translating this into meaningful scholarship.

Earlier, I suggested that this involves two kinds of adjustment. The first entails recognizing the moral imperative to embrace normative work and the importance of adopting a critical scholarly stance. In the shadow of the Anthropocene, value-neutrality appears as a luxury. It represents an intellectual posture for a world undisturbed by moral injury. This may have been relevant in the past when injustices racked only pockets of the world and animated merely sectors of activity. The Anthropocene, however, indicates that injustice is now global in the most literal sense. Extending human presence to the far corners of the earth, and doing so in ways that reward the already rich and powerful and punish the poor and voiceless, has created the specter of both grinding injustice and planetary fragility. If there ever was a time for researchers to embrace their values and let them direct research, the time is now. This does not mean jettisoning methodological rigor, turning scholarship into moral exhortation, or relaxing the standards of honest inquiry. It simply entails infusing one's scholarly aims with ethical momentum and deploying tools of research in the service of understanding and building a more humane Anthropocene. Political scholarship was never completely free from normative sensibilities, but always looked down on them as impediments to quality work. The Anthropocene calls for looking up at them. It encourages researchers to use normative commitments to direct, guide, and discipline scholarship.

Of course, it should go without saying that normative commitment is no guarantee of ethical practice. One can subscribe to any number of standards of value. Indeed, many endorse normative principles that are at odds with caring about the least fortunate or environmental considerations, and thus, the call for embracing normative scholarship may sound like merely wishful thinking. But just because there are different principles at work does not mean that they have no place in public life and, by extension, political scholarship. Explicitly stating one's normative commitments lays one's values on the line, thus exposing them to critique and emulation. More importantly, it awakens one to the purpose of one's scholarship, and this seems particularly relevant in the Anthropocene.

The second adjustment involves expanding the object of analysis. Since its inception, the study of politics has almost wholly ignored the nonhuman world. In its modern formation, it focused domestically on governments and internationally on states. Scholars saw governmental institutions as holding a monopoly of power. Over time, the discipline opened up its gaze to include non-state entities and structural factors, and thus began a process of recognizing the almost ubiquitous, circulatory character of power. Researchers did not, however, extend their eyes beyond the social world. They especially left out the more-than-human dimension of life that includes other animals, plants, microbes, minerals, and general ecological features of earth. The Anthropocene might seem like the least likely age to consider the political consequence of the other-than-human dimension, since it underlines the dominance of human planetary influence. However, as I have tried to show, humanity's commanding geological presence has ironically awakened various scholars to the indispensable power of the nonhuman world. It has opened their eyes not only to ecological interdependencies and the co-constitution of human and nonhuman life, but to the politics of collective existence. If politics means anything, it involves the way power shapes a common destiny. The Anthropocene represents the age of humans and nature conjoining forces and moving towards a coevolutionary future. Despite putting primacy on humans, it involves the entire assemblage of living and nonliving things. Scholars studying politics in the Anthropocene would do well to recognize this.

In 1948, Einstein called on intellectuals to revolutionize their thinking. In the second decade of the twenty-first century, the Anthropocene calls for another revolution. This time, it involves not only a cognitive one, wherein people come to understand new and expansive dangers, but also an ethical one, premised on the deepening and globalizing of social injustice. The Anthropocene calls on political scholars to awaken to this ethical dimension and undertake research that is historically, conceptually, epistemologically, and, most important, morally worthy of the age.

# References

Abram, David. 2011. *Becoming Animal: An Earthly Cosmology*. New York, NY: Vintage Press.
Ahuja, Neel. 2011. Abu Zubayda and the Caterpillar. *Social Text* 29 (1): 127–149.
Bennett, Jane. 2010. *Vibrant Matter: A Political Ecology of Things*. Durham: Duke University Press.
Betsill, Michele M. and Elizabeth Corell, eds. 2007. *NGO Diplomacy: The Influence of Nongovernmental Organizations in International Environmental Negotiations*. Cambridge, MA: MIT Press.
Bozzo, Laura. 2012. Beyond Mountaintop Removal: Pathways for Change in Appalachian Coalfields. *Duke Forum for Law and Social Change* 4 (1): 115–140.
Burke, Anthony, Stefanie Fishel, Audra Mitchell, Simon Dalby, and David J. Levine. 2016. Planet Politics: A Manifesto for the End of IR [International Relations]. *Millennium: Journal of International Studies* 44 (3): 499–523.
Dabbs, W. Corbett. 1996. Oil Production and Environmental Damage. Trade and Environment Database 1996.
Donaldson, Sue, and Will Kymlicka. 2013. *Zoopolis: A Political Theory of Animal Rights*. Oxford: Oxford University Press.
Einstein, Albert. 1995. *Ideas and Opinions*. New York, NY: Broadway Books.
Foucault, Michel. 2003. "Society Must Be Defended": Lectures at the Collège de France, 1975–1976. New York, NY: Picador.
Foucault, Michel. 2014. *Lectures on the Will to Know: Lectures at the College of France and Oedipal Knowledge*. New York, NY: Picador.
Goode, Erica. 2016. A Wrenching Choice for Alaska Towns in the Path of Climate Change. *New York Times*. 29 November.
Grusin, Richard. 2015. *The Nonhuman Turn*. Minneapolis: University of Minnesota Press.
Hanh, Thich Nhat. 1997. *Interbeing: Fourteen Guidelines for Engaging Buddhism*. Berkeley, CA: Parallax Press.
Haraway, Donna. 2003. *The Companion Species Manifesto: Dogs, People, and Significant Otherness*. Chicago, IL: Prickly Paradigm.
Haraway, Donna. 2007. *When Species Meet (Posthumanities)*. Minneapolis, MN: University of Minnesota Press.
Haraway, Donna. 2016. *Staying with the Trouble: Making Kin in the Chthulucene*. Durham, NC: Duke University Press.
Ingelson, Allan, and Chilenye Nwapi. 2014. Environmental Impact Assessment Process for Oil, Gas and Mining Projects in Nigeria: A Critical Analysis. *Law, Environment and Development Journal* 10 (1): 35–56.
Intergovernmental Panel on Climate Change. 2013. Summary for Policymakers. In *Climate Change 2013: The Physical Science Basis*. Contribution of Working Group I to the Fifth Assessment Report of the Intergovernmental Panel on Climate Change. Cambridge, MA: Cambridge University Press.
Keck, Margaret E., and Kathryn Sikkink. 1998. *Activists beyond Borders: Advocacy Networks in International Politics*. Ithaca, NY: Cornell University Press.
Klein, Naomi. 2015. *This Changes Everything: Capitalism vs. the Climate*. New York, NY: Simon and Schuster.
Kohn, Eduardo. 2013. *How Forests Think: Toward an Anthropology beyond the Human*. Berkeley, CA: University of California Press.
Latour, Bruno. 2004. *Politics of Nature: How to Bring the Sciences into Democracy*. Cambridge, MA: Harvard University Press.

Lerner, Steve. 2012. *Sacrifice Zones: The Frontlines of Toxic Chemical Exposure in the United States*. Cambridge, MA: MIT Press.
Livingston, Julie, and Jasbir Puar. 2011. Interspecies. *Social Text* 29 (1): 3–14.
Maniates, Michael, and John Meyer, eds. 2010. *The Environmental Politics of Sacrifice*. Cambridge, MA: MIT Press.
McKibben, Bill. 1989. *The End of Nature*. New York, NY: Random House.
Parenti, Christian. 2011. *Tropic of Chaos: Climate Change and the New Geography of Violence*. New York, NY: Nation Books.
Pollan, Michael. 2002. *Botany of Desire: A Plant's Eye View of the World*. New York, NY: Random House.
Pollan, Michael. 2013. The Intelligent Plant. *New Yorker*, December 23 and 30.
Quammen, David. 1997. *The Song of the Dodo: Island Biogeography in an Age of Extinction*. New York, NY: Scribner.
Rosenau, James. 1990. *Turbulence in World Politics: A Theory of Change and Continuity*. Princeton, NJ: Princeton University Press.
Said, Edward. 1996. *Representations of the Intellectual: The 1993 Reith Lectures*. New York, NY: Vintage.
Szabo, Sylvia, Eduardo Brondizio, Fabrice G. Renaud, et al. 2016. Population Dynamics, Delta Vulnerability and Environmental Change: Comparison of the Mekong, Ganges Brahmaputra and Amazon Delta Regions. *Sustainability Science* 11 (4): 539–554.
United States Environmental Protection Agency. 2016. *Hydraulic Fracturing for Oil and Gas: Impacts from the Hydraulic Fracturing Water Cycle on Drinking Water Resources in the United States (Final Report)*. Doc. no. EPA/600/R-16/236 F. Washington, DC: United States Environmental Protection Agency.
VeRisk Maplecroft. 2010. Risk Calculators and Dashboard. Accessed June 20, 2018. http://maplecroft.com/about/news/ccvi.html
Wake, Helen. 2005. Oil Refineries: A Review of their Ecological Impacts on the Aquatic Environment. *Estuarine, Coastal and Shelf Science* 62 (1–2): 131–140.
Walters, Colin, Jan Zalasiewicz, Colin Summerhayes, et al. 2016. The Anthropocene Is Functionally and Stratigraphically Distinct from the Holocene. *Science* 351 (6269): aad2622.
Wapner, Paul. 2016. Climate of the Poor: Suffering and the Moral Imperative of Radical Resilience. In *Reimagining Climate Change*, edited by Paul Wapner and Hilal Elver, 131–149. London: Routledge.
Weber, Andreas. 2016. *Biology of Wonder: Aliveness, Feeling and the Metamorphosis of Science*. Gabriola Island: New Society Publishers.
Youatt, Rafi. 2016. Interspecies. In *The Oxford Handbook of Environmental Political Theory*, edited by Teena Gabrielson, Cheryl Hall, John M. Meyer, and David Schlosberg, 220–239. Oxford: Oxford University Press.

# 12

# Epilogue: Continuity and Change in the Anthropocene

JAMES MEADOWCROFT

The essays in this volume offer a variety of perspectives on the arrival of the Anthropocene and the implications for green political thought. They trace the origin of the concept in recent scientific argument, consider associated reflection in the social sciences, humanities, and popular culture, and explore political dimensions related to democracy, power and justice, international politics and development, the coproduction of knowledge about global environmental problems and solutions, and the ethics of political enquiry. The discussion ranges widely, engaging with issues of ontology, epistemology, ethics, natural science, culture, history, economics, and politics, demonstrating the extent to which the idea of the Anthropocene has already captured the imagination of critical thinkers, and constitutes a fertile vein for reflection about political and environmental futures. It reveals the sharpness of the controversies, and the significance of the stakes, as different perspectives clash over what the Anthropocene may come to represent.

This short postscript provides some brief concluding reflections. Clearly, it is impossible in a few pages to do justice to the rich tapestry of arguments presented by the contributors. Instead, it draws out some common themes and raises issues for consideration, while occasionally offering a counterpoint to approaches offered earlier in the volume. The discussion is divided into three sections. It starts by considering the place of the Anthropocene within the conceptual lexicon of contemporary environmental argument. It then engages with the theme of change and continuity in the Anthropocene, before concluding with some thoughts on the future of green political theory. References to the earlier chapters are threaded throughout.

## The Anthropocene as a Political Concept

The idea of the Anthropocene was first articulated clearly in the context of scientific debate by practicing global change researchers (Crutzen and Stoermer 2000;

Crutzen 2002). Yet, as Noel Castree (Chapter 2) shows, the scientists who formulated the idea were well aware of the broader societal context and potential political reverberations. The Anthropocene is not the first environmental concept born in such a way: in the mid-1980s, conservation biologists concerned about the lack of attention accorded to the loss of species and habitats formulated the idea of biodiversity (Haila 2017), which rapidly permeated scientific discourse and high-level policy argument, and was soon enshrined in the 1992 Convention on Biological Diversity.

While scientific argument continues to swirl around the Anthropocene – particularly over the date of its onset and whether it should be accorded formal stratigraphic status – it has already been taken up in wider societal discourse (Castree 2014). What, then, are the characteristics of the Anthropocene as a *political* concept? And how does it relate to other concepts that have come to frame environmental argument and policy over the half century since the emergence of modern environmental governance?

Four elements appear particularly salient when considering the Anthropocene as a political idea.

First, *it establishes a temporal break*, defining a historical epoch that marks a qualitative change from all that has gone before. Temporal concepts are invoked in political argument not just to establish chronology (that one thing happened after another), or periodicity (that patterns recur), but above all to signal disjuncture – changes in circumstance that require significant adjustments to political thought and action. The prefixes "pre" and "post" often indicate such watersheds: for instance, "post 9/11" captures the shift in the US and international context in the wake of the 2001 terrorist attacks. It can be used as an analytical device to assess political dynamics, but also as a tool to mobilize practical political action. In the environmental sphere, the phrase "post-Fukushima" points to the altered conditions for public discussion of nuclear power following the reactor accident in Japan.

But the shift associated with the Anthropocene is of a very different order. It is defined not by a political event or intellectual trend but by a physical change at the planetary scale. It marks the moment when humans have become a "geological force." The Anthropocene draws together social and geological time, suggesting that the shorter timescales associated with politics and social evolution have become relevant for understanding change to the biosphere, even as the longer timescales of geologic time are necessary to understand just what human beings have done to the planet. The move is in a sense "totalizing": the break has consequences not just for one specific element of political or social life, but for the overall human experience. The Anthropocene envelops everything, and little on earth is immune to its pull.

Second, the Anthropocene highlights *the scale of our impact on the biosphere, simultaneously emphasizing human power and human powerlessness*. Humans have dramatically altered ecosystems, shifted the operation of global biophysical processes, and left recognizable signatures in the geologic record (Waters et al. 2016). The transformation of the earth has been effected over millennia, with the most dramatic changes arising since the industrial revolution, particularly with the massive expansion in human numbers and technological reach since the mid-twentieth century. The harnessing of the biosphere to human ends (Smil 2013) and our growing ability to manipulate nature at ever smaller and larger scales testify to the collective power of our species. Yet, the global environmental impacts that have propelled us into the Anthropocene have been largely unintended. And they have set in train processes that we cannot control. Some are irreversible, and others might be partially undone only with tremendous effort over millennia.

Climate change is the linchpin that holds together *the political narrative* of the Anthropocene. The combustion of fossil fuels has transformed the atmosphere and oceans, altering conditions for all life. And while it demonstrates the power of humans to influence earth history, our inability to orchestrate an effective collective response (despite overwhelming scientific evidence of the damage being done) and the risks associated with forcing the climate past critical "tipping points" reveal the weaknesses of our civilization. Today, we cannot manage *either* the social development trajectory *or* the biophysical processes our actions have set in motion. Thus, the themes of human mastery and impotence intermingle in the Anthropocene.

Third, the concept of the Anthropocene *embodies an implicit threat*. Increasingly, humans live in a world they have remade. Yet there is plenty to concern us with this remaking. The Anthropocene represents movement away from the Holocene baseline, with its relatively benign climatic conditions, which allowed the flourishing of human civilization (Rockström et al. 2009). The massive environmental transformations at all scales, witnessed particularly over the past half century, and driven by population, technological prowess, and resource use, represent a growing threat to lives and livelihoods and to the future of human societies. The Anthropocene represents a voyage into the unknown, a single unplanned and large-scale "experiment" with the planetary systems that support human life. Major impacts are already discernible, with the degradation of ecosystems, acidification of the oceans, unprecedented rates of species loss, alteration of the nitrogen cycle, and so on. The poorest countries and marginalized societal groups are the most vulnerable to these changes. And, of course, the threat is not just to our own species but also to others with whom we share the planet.

Finally, the Anthropocene demands *an urgent political response*. Passing into the Anthropocene requires a shift in worldview, a new understanding of the way humans are interacting with the biosphere, but also an appreciation of the need to change course if society is to avoid disaster and our descendants are to flourish in the changed planetary circumstances we have unconsciously brought into being (consider Anthony Burke and Stephanie Fishel, Chapter 5). And here politics is critical: providing a mechanism to collectively and deliberately reorder social affairs in light of the new circumstances. It can allow societies to address the urgent issue of climate change and to define human development pathways that veer away from the most dangerous planetary disruption. And yet, if action is paramount, the nature of this political response cannot be read directly from the idea of the Anthropocene. Problems such as climate change must be addressed. But addressed how? What is to be transformed and what is to be preserved from the current development trajectory? Do we need more growth, green growth, or degrowth (Fournier 2008; Victor 2008; Van den Bergh 2010)? The emergence of global government or more responsive local institutions? Enhanced contributions from experts or greater citizen participation? Better technologies or less reliance on techno-fixes? As the essays in this collection have demonstrated, the concept of the Anthropocene provides a focus for critical reflection and a terrain for struggle about alternative futures.

How does the Anthropocene relate to other concepts commonly invoked in environmental argument? The conceptual field of environmental policy is complex and has evolved continuously since the late 1960s, when the domain first emerged as a distinct policy sphere. It includes a variety of "critical organizing concepts," including overarching "meta concepts" that structure the whole field (the environment, sustainable development), specific "problem or issue concepts" (such as climate change, acid rain, ozone depletion), and "meso-level analytical or management concepts" (the precautionary principle, adaptive management or resilience) (Meadowcroft and Fiorino 2017). The Anthropocene is clearly a "meta concept" – intended to provide a high-level and all-encompassing frame. But it is an idea that is only now beginning to penetrate the political sphere and has yet to achieve substantial institutional embedding in the environmental policy domain. In this context, "political sphere" includes political practice and argument (as distinct, say, from specialized scientific, philosophical, or legal spheres), while "institutional embedding" refers to integration of a concept into the routines and mandates of bodies explicitly concerned with governance and policy (Meadowcroft and Fiorino 2017).

Yet, a comparison with the two established environmental policy meta concepts – "the environment" and "sustainable development" (or "sustainability") – is helpful. "Environment" has a long history of usage in English to denote "that which surrounds," and it became prominent with the organism/environment pairing in scientific discourse (Pearce 2010). But it was only in the 1960s that *"the* environment" acquired its distinctive modern usage to denote the surroundings, especially the natural surroundings (air, water, land, ecosystems) on which societies depend, but which were increasingly threatened by human activities (Meadowcroft 2017). This threatened "environment" served as a focus for public concern and emerged as a new domain of state activity involving specialized administrative structures (ministries, agencies), legislation (national clean air and water acts), dedicated budgets and personnel, and knowledge development centered on "environmental protection" (Duit et al. 2015). Argument over the environment, and just what governments should be doing to protect it, became an irreducible element of political life (Meadowcroft 2012a). There is little doubt that the concept's success has been related to its interpretive flexibility (referring to the natural but also the "man-made" environment, with an anthropocentric bias but also an opening to the noninstrumental value of other species); its well-established everyday usage (as surroundings) and its scientific credentials (environmental science); as well as its scalability (we can talk of local, regional, national, and global environments).

Sustainable development shot to international attention with the 1987 report of the World Commission on Environment and Development, the first major international study to place climate change at the core of its concerns (WCED 1987). It was endorsed by world leaders at the United Nations Conference on Environment and Development ("Rio Earth Summit") in 1992 and has over time permeated national and international political discourse, most recently being legitimized with the United Nations "Sustainable Development Goals" for 2030. Sustainable development is an explicitly normative concept referring to a development trajectory that embodies human progress while respecting environmental limits. It has been associated with the promotion of human welfare, inter- and intragenerational justice, protection of global life support systems, and participation in environment and development decision-making (Langhelle 1999). Sustainable development gained traction by recasting the existing development discourse and linking environmental issues with the social and economic needs of poorer countries.

All three concepts reflect concern with what human progress (particularly the rapid growth of industrial civilization in the second half of the twentieth century) has done to the natural world. The environment points to the contexts within which people live and to the damage done to humans and ecosystems. Sustainable development engages with the development process and the risks of undermining the environmental foundations of continued development. And the Anthropocene represents an age in which the transformations effected by humans are already critical. Each of the concepts is explicitly anthropocentric: *the* environment is our human environment; sustainable development is about human progress; while the Anthropocene is the age when the human influence on the whole earth has become decisive. Each concept has a defined focus, but remains open to multiple interpretations and debate about its real implications. The concepts that emerged later provoke adjustments to the earlier ideas: thus, sustainable development insists that environment and development need not be in contradiction, and that environmental issues can only be managed successfully by reorienting development. The Anthropocene raises the question of the "naturalness" of the environment to be protected, and the meaning of the "development" project when the planet has been pushed away from the Holocene norm. Some have suggested that the arrival of the Anthropocene reveals the inadequacy of the environment or sustainable development to gain significant purchase on the human predicament: to talk today of the "natural environment" is profoundly misleading, while the obsession with "development" is what got us to this impasse. And yet, there are also many ways to reconcile these three concepts to build visions of the political future.

Like other concepts invoked in politics, the Anthropocene embodies unresolved tensions. It has gained ground in high-level discussion of the threat to the biosphere, particularly attracting the attention of geologists, geographers, philosophers, cultural critics, and green thinkers. But an explicit contribution in the policy sphere remains to be established. It most clearly transmits a sense of *urgency*: that it is past time political leaders took decisive action on problems such as climate change. But other implications of humans as a "geological force" seem more difficult to translate into the routines of politics and policy. While some worry that the damaging potential of "climate change" remains abstract for most citizens, the implication of a new epoch remains yet more opaque. Experience with the environmental policy domain suggests that as concepts move closer to the mainstream, their more uncomfortable dimensions tend to be occluded. Whether this will prove to be the case with the idea of the Anthropocene remains to be seen.

## Change and Continuity

Arguments about the Anthropocene are closely bound up with understandings of change and continuity – in geological processes and the biosphere, economic and social institutions and practices, patterns of thought and political perspectives. Just what has changed with the onset of the Anthropocene? How has it changed? And why does it matter? These questions recur throughout this volume. Noel Castree considers the assessment of the state change in the earth system associated with the start of the Anthropocene; Arias-Maldonado examines insights on materiality and hybridization derived from the new materialism; Victor Galaz explores the emerging implications of deep time and ultra-speed processes for contemporary life; Ayşem Mert deals with evolving challenges to democracy; Silke Beck considers the novel emphasis on the coproduction of knowledge; while Burke and Fishel move beyond traditional conceptualizations of power to offer an approach suited to the complexity of the new epoch. But in discussing change, the authors inevitably engage also with continuity, with physical processes, institutional patterns, social practices, understandings, and normative values that straddle or transcend the Anthropocene break. After all, the new epoch was brought about by developments that became operative well before its genesis: that is, the activities that modified the stratigraphic sequence, shifted the state of the earth system, and/or altered understandings of the human influence on the planet. And many established patterns of socio-ecological interaction (to say nothing of biophysical phenomena and socio-cultural evolution) continue in the new epoch.

Here, I consider briefly two issues related to this theme of change and continuity: the timing of the Anthropocene and the end of nature.

The appropriate start date (and markers) for the Anthropocene and the determination of its formal stratigraphic status remain issues of debate within the scientific community (Steffen et al. 2016). Although there is substantial support for a mid-twentieth-century onset (which coincides with the beginning of the "Great Acceleration" and nuclear testing), others have proposed an "early Anthropocene" that followed the Neolithic agricultural revolution, or a mid-second-millennium onset related to European contact with the Americas and the Columbian Exchange, or the beginning of the nineteenth century (linked to the industrial revolution) (Waters et al. 2016). There are tensions here about what is being signaled: early human global impacts, the unleashing of the causal driver of subsequent change, or a state shift in the earth system (a deviation from the Holocene baseline). As Castree points out, arguments for these varying options have sometimes provoked sharp exchange. They have become entangled with disciplinary preoccupations and claims about a paradigm shift towards earth system science. Some analysts, for example, have argued that promoting a pre-mid-twentieth-century start date for the Anthropocene could "deflate" the concept, minimize the gravity of the current predicament, and "rob the new geological epoch of its power" (Hamilton and Grinevald 2015).

However, from an explicitly political perspective, it is unclear that arguments over the Anthropocene start date are as significant as some participants assume. Whatever convention scientists ultimately adopt, the critical political point is to appreciate *both* the magnitude of the changes to the earth system now occurring (and their attendant risks) *and* the historical processes through which societies have come to exert such a profound influence on the planet. Indeed, an essential feature of the scientific advance of the past few decades – to which climate and earth sciences, anthropology, and environmental history have all contributed – has been an enhanced appreciation of the extent to which human development has been linked *to an ever more extensive* modification of the biosphere, and of *how far back* this extends. Humans have been transforming local and regional ecosystems for many millennia. And while impacts that are truly global, and that are altering the parameters of earth system processes, are more recent, *the development trajectory that has produced them has very deep roots.* Understanding the political, economic, and social institutions that enabled the expansion of technology, population, consumption, and resource use is critical to attempts to modify them. In other words, it is not just the "newness" or "danger" of the Anthropocene that should preoccupy us, but also the extent to which it is the result of deeply embedded societal processes.

In addition to the timing of the Anthropocene as a geological epoch, there is also the issue of the timing of the *discovery* of the Anthropocene. This can be seen as a product of knowledge generated by the global change research agenda in the decade(s) since 1990. But it can also be understood as part of the broader concern with the scale, severity, and risks of the human impact on global ecosystems that achieved expression with the environmental consciousness of the 1960s and the pledge to alter the global development trajectory embodied in the formal endorsement of sustainable development at the Rio Earth Summit in 1992. No doubt, Hamilton and Grinevald (2015) are correct to caution against scouring earlier scientific literature to find Anthropocene "precursors" and reading back into the work of earlier thinkers concepts they could not have possessed. And yet, as Nikoleris, Stripple, and Tenngart show in their fascinating chapter on popular culture, "the idea of an Anthropocene is not new. Such a world was imagined when few believed that humans could have such an extensive impact" (Chapter 4). So while the causal scientific understandings that underpin the modern concept of "the Anthropocene" were not yet present, ideas of "*an* Anthropocene" (my emphasis) in which humans had dramatically altered the biosphere (perhaps with catastrophic consequences), sometimes exerting powers over the earth or deliberately reengineering human minds and bodies in ways which real-world science cannot yet match, have long been explored in the imagination. Again, there is both continuity and discontinuity in the Anthropocene.

What, then, of the "end of nature"? The suggestion is that with passage into the Anthropocene, nature (at least "planetary nature") has ceased to exist in any meaningful way. Paul Wapner has noted that there are two dimensions to this argument. Empirically, the claim is that the human impact is now so substantial that no part of the earth remains untouched (Wapner 2014). And since nature stands in contrast to society, civilization, human industry, and culture, the spreading human influence has literally dissolved nature. Indeed, by altering the climate, we have added a synthetic dimension to every element of the biosphere (McKibben 1989). The second strand of argument emphasizes the conceptual constitution of nature and the nature/society dichotomy. Concepts constitute the worlds human beings actually inhabit, and ideas of nature vary dramatically across cultures. Thus, the concept of nature as an independent entity – "out there" – is untenable. Both arguments suggest that nature as an autonomous realm that can ground normative claims and requires protection has ended; hence the talk of a "post natural nature" or a "post-nature environmentalism."

As Arias-Maldonado notes, such arguments are not new (Chapter 2), and they connect to longer-standing debates in philosophy, the physical and human sciences, and the humanities concerning the character of the material world, human experience, and the connections between humans and their environment. But they have been absorbed into discussion of the Anthropocene, and it is worth pausing to consider whether the definition of a new geological epoch really *requires* us to jettison "nature."

The first argument takes nature as a material reality, which has (at least at the planetary level) been irrevocably tainted by the impact of humanity. Of course, this tainting only dissolves "nature" if one is working with *the particular conception of nature* that sees the absence of *any* human trace as critical to its identity. Otherwise, nature could perfectly well continue although some (or even many) of its elements had been altered by human activity. The second argument emphasizes the cultural construction of nature, which robs nature of its independence from humanity, and so also its essential (natural) character. But, precisely because concepts are complex, culturally constructed, and mutable, there is nothing to prevent other understandings from coming to the fore – conceptualizations that are sufficiently subtle to entertain a nature that has been differentially influenced at different scales in different ways by human action.

In fact, there is evidence that such conceptualizations have long been embedded in our culture. People take a walk in the countryside and express satisfaction with "getting out into nature." Or they sit in their gardens admiring the natural beauty of a flower or the sunset. Now, it is possible to argue that these people are simply mistaken – they have failed to recognize that nature is no more. The countryside may be a landscape transformed by agricultural activities extending back centuries; the flowers a result of ingenious plant breeding; the sunset enhanced by urban air pollution or particles wafted into the atmosphere by forest clearances. But it is also possible that the ways nature is being used in societal discourse already embody more subtle understandings, which allow nature and the human influence to mingle: appreciation that the farmed landscape also embodies nature; that breeders work with material provided by natural selection; that we change an atmosphere that is a product of nonhuman geological and biological processes.

Moreover, as Castree has shown, arguments about "nature" may be used in a variety of ways, which are seldom clearly distinguished. Elsewhere, I have shown that multiple notions of "limits" are in a similar way entangled in environmental discourse (Meadowcroft 2012b). One of the consequences of this plurality of meanings is that when the concepts are employed, a rich variety of resonances is generated. Indeed, much of the rhetorical force of declaring "the end of nature" is derived from the broader associations of "nature" (as essence, motive power, or physical reality) that go well beyond the image (of independence or purity) which is ostensibly being invoked. There is also an elision of scale that assumes that what happens at one physical scale is pertinent in the same way at radically smaller or larger scales: thus, the human "taint" is perceived to penetrate all the way up and down.

Like other dualisms, the nature/society and nature/human oppositions are both helpful and unhelpful. Humans are both distinct from nature and also natural beings. Their minds and bodies increasingly inhabit a synthetic world even as they remain constituted by natural entities and processes. Their creations are artificial and yet obey natural laws. Humans have *always* lived in complex interdependence with their environment, and those elements with which they have been in most direct contact have been continuously modified by human activity. And yet, nature has been (and remains) present everywhere, even if, as the idea of the Anthropocene tells us, the scale of the human impact has qualitatively changed.

## Thinking Green in the Anthropocene

The encounters presented in this book provide promising avenues for developing critical political thinking in a context where the Anthropocene has taken hold. The authors display varied perspectives and preoccupations, but many messages find support across the contributions: for example, Noel Castree's injunction about adopting "a reflexive attitude towards Anthropocene science" and exploiting the full range of tools and insights from the social sciences and humanities to interrogate the implications of this new epoch (Chapter 2); Jeremy Baskin's preoccupation with inequities embedded in the current international system and his worry that the version of the Anthropocene "currently being institutionalized encapsulates the mind-set of the global North" (Chapter 8); Paul Wapner's focus on integrating ethical commitments into scholarship in this troubled time, and on expanding the preoccupations of political studies beyond the conventional to include the coevolutionary development of humans and the biosphere (Chapter 11); and Fremaux and Barry's emphasis on an established maxim of green political theory that "what is in need of management" is not so much the planet as "humanity's relationship with the earth" (Chapter 9).

There is broad agreement among the scholars that the collective humanity of Anthropocene discourse should be decomposed to reflect societal structures, institutional configurations, and power relations. There is a shared concern with the "depoliticization" of Anthropocene debates and the implicit assumption that technical solutions can be applied without attention to differences of interest and identity, historical circumstance, and the aspirations of diverse communities. There is common rejection of any "triumphalist" impulse that might celebrate the Anthropocene as proof of human technological mastery or social-evolutionary achievement. But even those most concerned with the severity of the ecological and political crises that accompany the Anthropocene, and most skeptical of the potential of existing institutional frameworks to meet these challenges, reject any sense of fatalism or the suggestion that the game is already lost. If the initial horizons of the Anthropocene look bleak, there are also intimations of hope. The future remains open, and political acts and struggles will play a decisive role in determining what is to come. As Simon Dalby recently put it so aptly, "the Anthropocene is neither good nor bad, but is going to be shaped by a politics that is necessary and probably will be rather ugly ..." (2016: 48).

Yet, while the turn towards the Anthropocene requires a refocusing of environmental scholarship and a renewal of green political thinking, there are reasons to be cautious with claims that "this changes everything" or that there is nothing to be learned from the Holocene for the politics of the future. "Everything" is a great deal. And it was during the Holocene that human civilization expanded, and politics (including political institutions, interactions, and ideas) evolved as features of complex societies. Focusing exclusively on the magnitude of the rupture with the past is a useful device to disarm opponents – whatever they thought they knew can now be called into question – but it is not a strategy without risk. It may collide with everyday experience, where some things are changing rapidly, yet other features of the environment, society, and the institutional order appear relatively stable. It can rhetorically telescope time – compressing into this moment changes that will in fact be spread over decades or centuries, and experienced in different social contexts by different generations. It collides with normative beliefs that there is much about contemporary societies that we may legitimately hesitate to jettison. And, it may actually hamper the reflexivity about historical experience required to orient successful social adjustment.

A great virtue of emerging critical discourses of the Anthropocene is the emphasis placed on the intimate connection between the past, present, and future of the biosphere and the technological and social evolution of human communities. They encourage reflection on the big picture: on the character of societal and scientific advance; the advantages and flaws of different modes of social life and economic organization; the nature of the cleavages which split human societies; the ecological impacts of our production and consumption activities; the values of species, ecosystems, and the earth; and appropriate modalities of politics and governance (Lövbrand et al. 2015).

In coming decades, the possibilities for further rapid scientific and technological advance are immense, including in areas such as nanotechnology, biotechnology, artificial intelligence and robotics, neuroscience, virtual reality, the introduction of novel materials, and space science. This will vastly increase the human capacity to manipulate nature and ecosystems, alter physical and social space, further extend the human lifespan, and deliberately manipulate the human genome: for good and ill. These developments will occur in a world where "old" political issues such as great power rivalry, ethnic and religious conflict, economic exploitation and inequity, and poverty and political injustice remain rife, and where the continuing impacts of technologies that are already widely diffused, increased material consumption, and population growth will continue to press on local and regional environments, even as truly global problems such as climate change begin to bite.

The deep connection between human and environmental futures was already implicit in the concept of sustainable development – the idea that one cannot define an optimistic future for human societies without taking both environment and social equity seriously, and that there is no way to deal successfully with environmental problems other than by altering societal development trajectories. Even if one rejects the Western discourse of "development" as hopelessly co-opted or corrupted, this basic truth remains: the future of the biosphere and of humanity is entangled, and defining a more progressive human future cannot be done without also establishing new relationships with the biosphere. For some, the concept of the Anthropocene with its ambitious reach can lend urgency to this effort. But there are also critics who worry that it is too easily associated with unreflective, techno-optimist discourses of manipulation and control. Consider, for example, Andrew Stirling's impassioned critique (2014) or Fremaux and Barry, Chapter 9.

Critical social science and green political thought have much to contribute to helping societies work through these large-scale questions. Yet, in contemplating a path forward, it seems essential that green thinking also engages more explicitly with problems that connect directly with the life-experiences of communities and political actors and not just with philosophical investigation, social critique, and theory building. Imaginaries are essential to inspire action; philosophic groundings can anchor practical arguments; and structured analytics are necessary to unpack co-causation and open up avenues of reform. But there is also a need for direct engagement with real policy choices and dilemmas, with the very messy business of actually existing politics. As the authors of one recent piece on the "good Anthropocene" put it, "thinking radically yet realistically about the future ... is difficult," with the choice often being "developing less radical or more implausible and vague" alternatives (Bennett et al. 2016). To bridge this gap, green thinking needs to be more directly connected to sites of practical struggle, projects for reform, transition experiments, and so on.

In a parallel vein, many social thinkers are struggling to elucidate the concrete implications of the Anthropocene, to bring it down from the grand intellectual heights to tease out specific implications for global, regional, and local governance, to focus discussion on particular problems, and to define particular priorities for action (Biermann et al. 2016; Olsson et al. 2017). Only by making such connections can the potential of the Anthropocene as a grand framing device fully penetrate into the worlds of politics and policy.

Another thing that emerges from this collection is the extent to which green political thought and the environmental movement more generally have always been plural enterprises. There are many varieties of ethical argument that can be mobilized to justify concern with the preservation of species and ecosystems, or the protection of the environment. Multiple theoretical traditions can be harnessed to a green chariot. Environmentalists have never understood nature, or appraised its significance, in simply one way. Utilitarian, aesthetic, spiritual, and intrinsic value arguments have always comingled in describing the significance of landscapes, mountains, rivers, clean air, species, ecosystems, and so on. Moreover, environmental groups adopt radically different ideational stances, campaign priorities, modalities of organization, funding, and intervention techniques. This pluralism should be understood as a fundamental strength, which reflects a capacity to link into the wider diversity of social values and political perspectives. Indeed, attempts to reconstruct green thinking on a single pillar (for example, around a unitary green theory of "value") have sometimes contributed more to arid argument and brittle theory than to building robust movements for social change.

So, as the editors of this volume have argued, whatever green thinking looks like in the future, it need not be afraid of pluralist, multifaceted, and diverse currents. Nor should it be hesitant to display humility. After all, it is common for environmental thinkers to criticize the hubris of ambitious human attempts to reengineer ecosystems, to imagine that technologies can solve any difficulty, or that complex ecological processes can be understood by reductionist approaches. So, perhaps we should also exercise caution with claims that we have understood the preferable patterns and significance of socio-biosphere interactions. After all, the Anthropocene that we actually encounter will be multiple, mutable, and stretching into an uncertain future.

## References

Bennett, Elena, Martin Solan, Reinette Biggs, et al. 2016. Bright Spots: Seeds of a Good Anthropocene. *Frontiers in Ecology and the Environment* 14(8): 441–448.

Biermann, Frank, Xuemei Bai, Ninad Bondre, et al. 2016. Down to Earth: Contextualizing the Anthropocene. *Global Environmental Change* 39: 341–350.

Castree, Noel. 2014. The Anthropocene and the Environmental Humanities: Extending the Conversation. *Environmental Humanities* 5: 233–260.

Crutzen, Paul. 2002. Geology of Mankind – the Anthropocene. *Nature* 415: 23.

Crutzen, Paul, and Eugene Stoermer. 2000. The "Anthropocene." *Global Change Newsletter* 41: 17–18.

Dalby, Simon. 2016. Framing the Anthropocene: The Good the Bad and the Ugly. *The Anthropocene Review* 3 (1): 31–51.

Duit, Andreas, Peter Feint, and James Meadowcroft. 2016. Greening Leviathan: The Rise of the Environmental State? *Environmental Politics* 25 (1): 1–23.

Fournier, Valérie. 2008. Escaping from the Economy: The Politics of Degrowth. *International Journal of Sociology and Social Policy* 28 (11/12): 528–545.

Haila, Yrjo. 2017. Biodiversity: Increasing the Political Clout of Nature Conservation. In *Conceptual Innovation in Environmental Policy*, edited by James Meadowcroft and Daniel J. Fiorino, 207–232. Cambridge, MA: MIT Press.

Hamilton, Clive, and Jacques Grinevald. 2015. Was the Anthropocene Anticipated? *The Anthropocene Review* 2(1): 59–72.

Langhelle, Olus. 1999. Sustainable Development: Exploring the Ethics of Our Common Future. *International Political Science Review* 20(2): 129–149.

Lövbrand, Eva, Silke Beck, Jason Chilvers, et al. 2015. Who Speaks for the Earth? How Critical Social Science Can Extend the Conversation on the Anthropocene. *Global Environmental Change* 32: 211–218.

McKibben, Bill. 1989. *The End of Nature*. New York, NY: Random House.

Meadowcroft, James. 2012a. Greening the State. In *Comparative Environmental Politics*, edited by Paul F. Steinberg and Stacy VanDeveer. Cambridge, MA: MIT Press.

Meadowcroft, James. 2012b. Pushing the Boundaries: Governance for Sustainable Development and a Politics of Limits. In *Governance, Democracy and Sustainable Development: Moving beyond the Impasse*, edited by James Meadowcroft, Oluf Langhelle, and Audun Rudd. Cheltenham: Edward Elgar.

Meadowcroft, James. 2017. The Birth of the Environment and the Evolution of Environmental Governance. In *Conceptual Innovation in Environmental Policy*, edited by James Meadowcroft and Daniel Fiorino, 53–76. Cambridge MA: MIT Press.

Meadowcroft, James, and Daniel J. Fiorino, eds. 2017. *Conceptual Innovation in Environmental Policy*. Cambridge, MA: MIT Press.

Olsson, Per, Michele-Lee Moore, Frances R. Westley, and Daniel McCarthy. 2017. The Concept of the Anthropocene as a Game-Changer: A New Context for Social Innovation and Transformations to Sustainability *Ecology and Society* 22(2): 31.

Pearce, Trevor. 2010. From "Circumstances" to "Environment": Herbert Spencer and the Origins of the Idea of Organism-Environment Interaction. *Studies in History and Philosophy of Biological and Biomedical Sciences* 41: 241–252.

Rockström, Johan, Will Steffen, Kevin Noone, et al. 2009. A Safe Operating Space for Humanity. *Nature* 461: 472–475.

Smil, Vaclav. 2013. *Harvesting the Biosphere: What We Have Taken from Nature*. Cambridge, MA: MIT Press.

Steffen, Will, Reinhold Leinfelder, Jan Zalasiewicz, et al. 2016. Stratigraphic and Earth System Approaches to Defining the Anthropocene. *Earth's Future* 4: 324–345.

Stirling, Andrew. 2014. Emancipating Transformations: From Controlling "the Transition" to Culturing Plural Radical Progress. In *The Politics of Green Transformations*, edited by Ian Scoones, Melissa Leach, and Peter Newell, 54–67. London and New York, NY: Routledge.

Van den Bergh, Jeroen C.J.M. 2010. Environment versus Growth – A Criticism of "Degrowth" and a Plea for "A-Growth." *Ecological Economics* 40(5): 881–890.

Victor, Peter A. 2008. *Managing without Growth: Slower by Design, Not Disaster.* Cheltenham: Edward Elgar.

Wapner, Paul. 2014. The Changing Nature of Nature: Environmental Politics in the Anthropocene. *Global Environmental Politics* 14 (4): 36–54.

Waters, Colin, Jan Zalasiewicz, Colin Summerhayes, et al. 2016. The Anthropocene Is Functionally and Stratigraphically Distinct from the Holocene. *Science* 351 (6269): aad2622.

World Commission on Environment and Development (WCED) 1987. *Our Common Future.* Oxford: Oxford University Press.

# Index

Actant, 55
Actants, 54, 55, 56, 95, 96, 98, 99, 133
Adorno, Theodor W., 180, 183, 184, 185
Agency, 37, 52, 53, 55, 56, 62, 63, 64, 81, 89, 95, 111, 135, 201–202
  Moral, 99
  Nonhuman, 8, 16, 133, 185, 186, 222
  Political, 142, 145
Algorith, 116–120
Algorithm, 10
Anthropocene, 1–3, 5–6, 10–11
  Age, 3, 4, 5, 9, 16, 29
  Bad, 76
  Challenge, 8–9
  Good, 13, 171, 178
  Uncertain, 78
  Working Group, 30, 33
Anthropocentric, 53, 60, 89, 90–94, 95, 101, 162, 172, 223, 232
Anthropocentrism, 175
Anthropos, 2, 41, 91, 171, 199

Barad, Karen, 54
Bennett, Jane, 54, 61, 95
Bially Mattern, Janice, 92
Biopower, 130, 222
Bonneuil, Christophe, 43, 80, 150, 166, 173
Buen Vivir, 164

Capitalism, 78, 178
Capitalocene, 78, 160
Carbon, 17, 73, 135
  Casualties, 224
  Economy, 214–217
Cartesian, 54, 96
  Dualism, 6, 141
  View, 93
Chakrabarty, Dipesh, 41, 79, 171
Clark, Nigel, 13, 41, 111, 172
Climate
  Engineering, 9, 114

Fiction, 6, 70–73
Governance, 102, 105, 131, 200
Justice, 9, 163, 213–218
Science, 12, 44, 117, 192, 195
Suffering, 15
System, 1, 95, 113, 114
Complexity, 10, 64, 87, 94, 95, 174, 208
Connoly, William, 53, 56, 101
Coole, Diane, 52, 56
Coproduction, 14, 191–192, 193, 194–208
Cosmopolitan, 18, 152, 161
Cosmopolitics, 99
Crutzen, Paul, 1, 5, 11, 18, 27, 28, 29, 33, 35, 42, 73, 131, 154–156
Cudworth, Erika, 57, 94

Dahl, Robert, 93, 143
Dalby, Simon, 238
Decarbonize, 102
Deep time, 111–116, 121, 123
Degrowth, 12, 165
Deliberation, 133, 137, 144
Democracy, 10–11, 79, 128–146, 175
  Post-natural, 145
Democratic. *See* democracy
  Institutions, 128, 138, 140, 145
  Legitimacy, 9, 10, 137, 139
  Procedures, 11, 135
Developing countries, 9, 151, 162
Development, 11–12, 102, 150, 158, 161–166, 234
  Green, 163, 164
Discourse, 17, 134, 164, 179, 238
  Environmental, 237
Dobson, Andrew, 109

Earth system, 1, 31–40
  Governance, 88, 103, 121–123
  Governance project, 193
  Management, 42
  Stewardship, 171

Earth system science, 4–5, 29, 33–34, 234
   Partnership, 28, 31, 192, 196
Eckersley, Robyn, 78, 79
Eco-
   centrism, 42, 99, 104, 175, 222
   colonial, 18
   constructivist, 173, 185
   criticism, 7, 41
   managerialism, 3, 17, 171
   modernist, 141
   modernists, 90, 130, 141, 161, 171–175, 178, 184, 186
Ecological, 101, 103, 186, 225
   Crisis, 80, 88, 91, 130, 136
   Modernization, 19, 172, 178
   Processes, 6, 174, 221, 240
   Systems, 4, 136
Edwards, Paul, 117
Ellis, Erle C., 58, 61, 173, 185
Encounter, 3, 17, 223
End of nature, 6, 35, 61, 64, 140, 171, 179, 182, 214, 221, 234, 235, 237
Enlightenment, 4, 5, 38, 141, 155, 180
Entanglement, 51, 54, 57, 58, 63, 90, 100–105
Environment, 2, 4, 32, 68, 78, 100
Environmental
   Governance, 101, 104
   Harm, 11, 224
   Politics, 2, 68, 136
   Scholarship, 204, 238
   Science, 12, 195
Environmental scholarship, 18
Environmentalism, 3, 13–14, 19, 52, 183
   Post-nature, 236
Epistemology, 12, 38, 64
Epoch, 30, 37–40, 229
Epochal change, 4, 33
Equity, 157
Escobar, Arturo, 141
Ethical commitments, 18, 237
Ethics, 12–19, 212–225
   Environmental, 19

Fossil fuels, 214, 215–217
Frankfurt School, 185
Fressoz, Jean-Baptiste, 43, 80, 150, 166
Future Earth, 14, 191–208

Geoengineering, 114–116, 131, 177
Geological
   Agent, 17
   Force, 7, 50, 73–78, 160
   Timescale, 30, 111, 116
Geology, 4
   of mankind, 1, 5, 17

   Social, 2, 5
Geopolitics, 102
Global
   Environmental governance, 104, 142
   Justice movement, 152, 164
Global warming, 185, 199
Globalization, 13, 102, 135
Governance
   Challenges, 114, 120–121
   Environmental. *See* environmental governance
   Global, 10, 11, 102, 129
Great Acceleration, 11, 32, 110, 155
Green political theory, 179, 184, 185, 186, 237
Green political thinking, 2, 13, 46, 183, 238
Gupta, Joyeeta, 102

Hamilton, Clive, 35, 36, 50, 235
Haraway, Donna, 57, 99, 100, 133, 180, 222
Harris, Angela, 100
Historic responsibility, 9
Hobbes, 139
Hobden, Stephen, 57, 94
Holocene, 1, 5, 30, 173
Holsti, Kal, 93
Hulme, Mike, 197, 199
Human
   Impact, 30, 50, 163, 235
   -induced, 30
Humility, 4, 18, 90, 183, 223, 240
Hybrid, 6, 8, 38, 56–64, 180, 221

Imagination, 67, 78
In environmental
   governance, 142
Industrial revolution, 157, 160
Inequality, 151, 152, 158, 160, 163, 164
Interdependency, 18
Intergovernmental Panel on Climate Change (IPCC), 200, 216
International Geosphere-Biosphere Programme (IGBP), 4, 28, 29, 154, 157, 192
International Human Dimensions Programme on Global Environmental Change, 192
International Social Science Council (ISSC), 191, 193

Jasanoff, Sheila, 197, 199, 201
Justice, 101, 153, 161, 213–225
   Global, 151, 161, 165

Keohane, Robert, 143
Kingsolver, Barbara, 71
Kyoto Protocol, 102

Laclau, 139
Latour, Bruno, 45, 53, 57, 59, 91, 97, 173, 185
Leach, Melissa, 197, 200, 202, 206

Leviathan, 139
Lewis, Simon, 35
Literary fiction, 3, 6
Lloyd, Saci, 72, 78
Luke, Timothy, 171
Lynas, Mark, 173

Marcuse, Herbert, 180
Marion Young, Iris, 99, 101
Maslin, Mark, 35
McEwan, Ian, 71
McKibben, Bill, 35, 68
McNeill, John, 154, 155, 156
Modern environmentalism
  modern, 111
Modernity, 160, 179, 184, 185
Moore, Jason, 41, 43
Moral, 214, 216, 224
  Responsibility, 99, 100, 103
  Sensitivity, 218
More-than-human, 16, 152, 161, 220, 223
Morgenthau, Hans, 91

Narrative, 68, 73, 165, 173
Nature, 3, 4, 6, 35, 37, 50–64, 91, 177, 182, 236
  -culture, 180
  Humanized, 186
  Planetary, 26
  Post-natural, 140–142, 236
  Socio-nature, 13
  Techno-nature, 13, 173
Nature-culture, 6
Neoliberal, 102, 136
  Nature, 180
New materialism, 52, 55, 56, 233
Nonhuman
  Agency. *See* agency
  Agents, 8, 11
Northern environmentalism
  Northern, 158

Ontology, 52, 54, 62, 134, 136, 140

Paris Agreement, 105, 200
Philosophy, 5, 132
Pielke, Roger, 46
Planetary, 2
  Boundaries, 32
  History, 18
  Life-support system, 3
  Machinery, 4
Plumwood, Valerie, 60, 99
Political, 43, 68, 87, 234
  Assumptions, 94
  Concepts, 46, 228

Ecology, 6
Time, 113
Politics, 187, 231
  Environmental. *See* environmental politics
  Geo-. *See* geopolitics
  Planet-, 99
  Scientized, 27
Poor, 156, 215, 224
Post-
  modern, 173
  natural, 40, 63, 134, 140
  political, 46, 136
  social, 134
Power, 8, 87–105, 223
  Human, 64, 75
Progress, 155, 178, 185, 232
Promethean, 12, 163, 173

Reflexive, 46, 144, 175, 202
Responsibility, 9, 56, 78, 96, 98–103
  Ethical, 98, 224
  Historical. *See* historical responsibility
Revitalize, 14, 177
Robinson, Kim Stanley, 72, 74, 78
Rockström, Johan, 32

Safe operating space, 33, 78, 158, 173
Said, Edward, 219
Scale, 11, 41, 111, 121, 142, 230, 237
Science, 26, 41, 43
  Anthropocene, 27, 37
  Of integration, 4
  Sustainability, 194
Social, 208
  Constructivism, 5
  Geology. *See* geology:social
Sokal,
  Alan, 45
Solar radiation management, 12, 114
Spaceship, 80
Steffen, Will, 12, 28, 32, 39, 156
Stoermer, Eugene, 1, 154
Stratigraphy, 31, 32, 33
Sub-commission on Quaternary
  Stratigraphy, 1, 31
Sustainable
  Development, 13, 161, 232
  Development Goals, 101, 150
  Growth, 14, 161

Technology, 75, 76, 116, 155
*The Economist*, 67, 132
Thing-system, 88, 95
  power, 92, 98, 103
Time, 9, 109–111
  Deep, 9 *See* deep time

Tipping point, 33
Transformation, 16, 180, 181, 194, 198, 208
Transparency, 120, 142

Ultra-speed, 10, 116
United Nations, 137, 193
United Nations Conference on Sustainable Development, 11, 159
Urgency, 17, 233

Utopia, 138, 184

Vibrant matter, 61

Wapner, Paul, xii, 15, 18, 212, 235
Western Environmentalism, 156
World Climate Research Programme, 28

Zalasiewicz, Jan, 3, 30, 160

CPSIA information can be obtained
at www.ICGtesting.com
Printed in the USA
LVHW102006200519
618494LV00012B/255/P